Hindenburg, Reichspresident, on his eighty-fifth birthday

HINDENBURG

AND

The Saga of the German Republic

●

A man may go whithersoever he pleases, he
may undertake whatever his heart prompts,
but he will invariably turn back into the road
Nature has prepared for him.

—Goethe

Decus hoc aevi, te consule, inibit.

—VERGIL, *Eclogues* iv, 11.

Hindenburg

by
Emil Ludwig

TRANSLATED BY
EDEN AND CEDAR-PAUL

THE JOHN C. WINSTON COMPANY

CHICAGO　　　PHILADELPHIA　　　TORONTO

Hindenburg 2

FOREWORD

THE MOMENT when, by rearmament, the most typically militarist nation in the world is compelling the rest of Europe to arm to the teeth once more, seems appropriate for an account of the most famous German soldier of an epoch which has just drawn to a close. His example might teach us all into what devious paths and conflicts the German will to militarist domination drives an efficient soldier, when, alike in war and peace, important political decisions are intrusted to him. Perhaps non-German readers may be enabled to grasp how little change there has been in Germany under the new form of state; for all that has happened is that the eagerness to attack has become even more savage than that which prevailed during the years 1912 and 1913, to which the present era corresponds. The story of Hindenburg, whose experiences were passive rather than active, will be a symbolic sketch of the German character, and will disclose why the republic has so speedily perished with the full approval of the German people.

It is as a fourth contribution to my study of the psychology of the Germans, that I pen this portrait of Hindenburg. My aim has been to show how an army officer was carried far beyond the limits of his potentialities, not by ambition, but by a "legend" which had accreted round his name; and how, in the most natural way, when he was a very old man, he returned to the principles which only in semblance he had for a brief time abandoned: how a Junker and field marshal and president was driven into dictatorship, first by his environment, and then by longstanding authoritarian instincts, until, most tragically at last, he surrendered power to a group of gangsters, to die profoundly embittered. From the twilit world of mediocrity, he was, a patriarchal elder, dragged forth into the limelight; and what has to be described here is the belated development which an unusually obdurate character may undergo when forced into an inappropriate rôle.

My subordinate aim has been to give a concrete sketch of the German republic—though I have made no such attempt as regards the "Third Realm." In the German Republic, Hindenburg played a notable part; but from the establishment of the Third Realm to the day of his death he remained in the background. Besides, I do not regard myself as competent to deal with the pretensions of the leaders of the Third Realm.

The harmony of proportion I have always aimed at in my biographical studies was impossible in this unique instance—that of a man whose life history did not properly begin until he was sixty-seven years of age, so that half a century of his career demands less space than the ensuing four years. Furthermore, the almost complete lack of private documents complicates the task of Hindenburg's biographer; and even as regards the epoch of his presidency, few official papers are available. I have had little resource beyond personal observation, on the one hand; and, on the other, information privately received from Hindenburg's collaborators and adversaries, whose names I am not free to disclose. I have made use of the excellent books of Rosenberg and Conrad Heiden. By the time all the sources have been unsealed, no one will any longer want to read a book on Hindenburg.

In those days people will only tell one another tales about the old German giant who, after many adventures, was appointed watchman on a dam. One day, in a moment of mental confusion, he opened the sluices to inundate the surrounding country; and there came a flood which destroyed all that had been dear to him, in whose waters he himself at last perished.

Moscia, February, 1935

CONTENTS

LIST OF ILLUSTRATIONS

CHRONOLOGICAL TABLE

1640–1688   Frederick William (the Great Elector), Elector of Brandenburg and Duke of East Prussia.

1688–1701   Frederick III, his son, elector and duke.

1701   Brandenburg-Prussia is made a kingdom, with Frederick III as king under the title, Frederick I.

1713–1740   Frederick William I king of Brandenburg-Prussia.

1740–1786   Frederick II (the Great) king of Brandenburg-Prussia.

1740–1745   Silesian Wars with Austria secure Silesia.

1756–1763   Seven Years' War with Sweden, Russia, Bohemia, Austria, Saxony, France.

1740–1780   Maria Theresa, Queen of Hungary and Archduchess of Austria.

1772, 1793, 1795   Partitions of Poland among Russia, Prussia, and Austria.

1778–1779   War of Bavarian Succession, to prevent Austria from seizing Bavaria.

1785   Formation by Frederick the Great of Fürstenbund, a league of the North German states.

1786–1797   Frederick William II king of Brandenburg-Prussia.

1789   The French Revolution overthrows absolutism in France.

1797–1840   Frederick William III king of Brandenburg-Prussia.

1801   War between Austria and France.

1805   Napoleon defeats Austria and Russia at the battle of Austerlitz.

1806   Holy Roman Empire dissolved by Napoleon.

1806–1807   Napoleon defeats Prussia.

1812   Napoleon's disastrous campaign against Russia.

1813   German states in War of Liberation defeat Napoleon at Battle of Leipzig.

1815   Napoleon finally defeated at Waterloo; Congress of Vienna.

1834   Establishment of the Zollverein or Customs Union.

1840–1861   Frederick William IV king of Brandenburg-Prussia.

1848   Revolution in France overthrows the monarchy.

1862   Bismarck becomes Prime Minister of Prussia.

1864   Prussia and Austria seize Schleswig-Holstein.

1866   Prussia defeats Austria, forms North German Federation.

1870–1871   Franco-Prussian War.

1871–1888   William I, king of Brandenburg-Prussia since 1861, reigns also as William I, German Emperor.

1888   Frederick III king of Brandenburg-Prussia and German Emperor for 99 days.

1888–1918 William II king of Brandenburg-Prussia and German Emperor until the revolution.
1890 Bismarck dismissed as chancellor.
1914, June 28 Assassination of Francis Ferdinand, heir to the throne of Austria, at Sarajevo, Bosnia.
July 28 Austria declares war on Serbia.
Aug. 1 Germany declares war on Russia.
Aug. 2 Luxemburg and Belgium invaded by Germany.
Aug. 3 France declares war on Germany.
Aug. 4 Great Britain declares war on Germany.
Aug. 26 Germans defeat Russians at Battle of Tannenberg.
Sept. 10 Germans pass through Belgium to the Marne.
1915 Germans defeat Russians at Masurian Lakes.
May 5 *Lusitania* sunk by German submarine.
May 25 Italy declares war on Austria.
1916 Germans attack on Western Front, at Verdun.
Aug. 2 Sir Roger Casement executed for treason.
1917 Somme attack continued by Allies, with some success; Germans retreat to "Hindenburg line."
Feb. 1 Germans announce ruthless submarine warfare.
Mar. 11 Russian Revolution.
Apr. 6 United States declares war on Germany.
June 26 First American troops land in France.
1918 Renewed campaigns of Germans in Russia; Allies successful in Italian sector, in Macedonia, Bulgaria, Palestine, Mesopotamia.
Jan. 8 President Wilson announces the aims of the United States in entering the war in the "Fourteen Points."
Mar. 21 Germans begin their last great drive on the Western Front, apparently successful at first.
Mar. 29 Marshal Foch chosen commander of all allied forces.
May 31 Germans defeated at second Battle of the Marne.
July 18 Allies launch counteroffensive, which continues till Germany is finally defeated.
Sept. 26 Americans launch an offensive in the Argonne.
Nov. 9 The German Kaiser abdicates.
Nov. 11 The armistice signed.
1919, Feb. 6–Aug. 21 National Assembly week at Weimar to formulate a constitution; great social unrest.
Feb. 11 Ebert elected president by the Assembly.
June 28 Treaty of Versailles signed.
Aug. 11 Constitution promulgated by the Weimar Assembly.
1920, Jan. Erzberger-Helfferich trial.
Mar. 13-17 Kapp monarchist putsch in Berlin.
Apr. 4 Germany sends troops, without Allied permission, into Rhine district to suppress the repercussion of the Kapp putsch,

1920 Plebiscite in Schleswig, the southern part remaining German.
Plebiscite in East and West Prussia shows large majority for
Germany; but West Prussia is given to Poland to form Polish
corridor to the sea.
National Socialist Party founded in Munich by Adolf Hitler.

1921   Plebiscite in Upper Silesia shows German majority.
French again occupy certain cities along the Rhine.

1922–23   Inflation period in Germany.

1922   Fascists assume control of affairs in Italy; Mussolini
becomes premier.

1923, Jan. 12   French occupy Ruhr district and then the entire
right bank of the Rhine from Switzerland to Holland in an
attempt to force larger coal deliveries.
Nov. 9   Ludendorff-Hitler beer-hall putsch in Munich;
Hitler sentenced to prison for five years, but is released later.

1924, April 9   Report of Dawes Commission published; insists on
evacuation of Ruhr by the French, and arranges fixed annual
payments on reparations instead of an uncertain amount,
based on a more or less realistic calculation of ability to pay.

1925   President Ebert dies in office, Feb. 28; Hindenburg elected
second president.   He appoints as chancellor in succession
the following (Hans Luther was in office when Hindenburg
was elected): May 16, 1926, Wilhelm Marx; June 28, 1928,
Hermann Müller; Mar. 29, 1930, Heinrich Brüning; June 1,
1932, Franz von Papen; Dec. 2, 1932, Kurt von Schleicher;
Jan. 30, 1933, Adolf Hitler.

1926, Oct. 16   Ratification of Locarno Treaties; Germany admitted to League of Nations.

1929   Young Plan scaled down payments on reparations; created
Bank of International settlements.

1930, Mar. 29   Heinrich Brüning becomes chancellor.
Hindenburg invokes Article 48, July 16; Reichstag revokes it,
is dissolved.

1931   Hoover one-year moratorium.
Customs pact between Germany and Austria forbidden by the
League of Nations.

1932   Hindenburg elected for second term as president, April 10;
Franz von Papen becomes chancellor June 1.
Lausanne conference, resulting in further reduction of in-
demnities.
July 20, Papen takes over the Prussian government from Braun.
Adolf Hitler offered vice chancellorship, but refuses.
Kurt von Schleicher becomes chancellor Dec. 2.

1933, Jan. 30   Adolf Hitler becomes chancellor; dissolves the
Reichstag and calls for new election.
Feb. 27   Fire in the Reichstag building.

Mar. 5   Election; Hitler gets control of 52 per cent of the Reichstag votes; communists excluded.

Mar. 21   Reichstag passes the blanket enabling act, empowering the Cabinet to rule for four years without reference to the Reichstag.

Oct. 14   Germany withdraws from Disarmament Conference.

Oct. 21   Germany resigns from League of Nations.

1934, June 30   "Blood-bath" purge of Nazi party, resulting in death of Roehm, Schleicher, and many other alleged conspirators.

Aug. 2   Death of Hindenburg; office of president and chancellor combined. Hitler becomes leader of the Reich.

PRINCIPAL DATES IN HINDENBURG'S LIFE

1847, Oct. 2   Born in Posen.

1858   Enters cadet school at Wahlstatt in Silesia.

1866   Enters Third Foot Guards at Danzig; at Battle of Königgratz he helps storm an Austrian battery under fire.

1870–1871   Adjutant to a battalion in Franco-Prussian War.

1874–1877   Attends Staff College (military) at Berlin.

1877   Joins General Staff.

1879   Marries Gertrude Wilhelmine von Sperling.

1883   Instructor in Staff College at Berlin; assists Schlieffen.

1893–1896   Commander of 91st infantry regiment.

1897   Becomes major general.

1896–1900   Chief of General Staff of Eighth Army Corps at Coblenz.

1900–1903   Commander 28th Division at Karlsruhe.

1903   General in command of Fourth Army Corps at Magdeburg.

1911   Retired at age of 65.

1914   War breaks out; at first passed over, he is given command of Eighth Army in the East, with Ludendorff; wins Battle of Tannenberg.

1916   Supersedes Falkenhayn in position of Chief of Staff.

1916   Becomes Field Marshal in command of all military forces of Germany.

1918   Organizes demobilization; supports new government.

1925   Elected president.

1930   Begins to govern by decree, independently of the Reichstag.

1932   Elected president for second term.

1934, Aug. 2   Dies; Aug. 7, is buried at monument to Battle of Tannenberg.

BOOK ONE

THE FIRST FLAG

The Germans are quite decent men,
Each one declares: I want what's right;
But right must now and always be
What I and sires appreciate.

—GOETHE

3

HINDENBURG

THE FIRST FLAG

I

EAST PRUSSIA is by no means a cheerful country-side, and if one would love the landscape and the people, he must have been born and bred there. Broad plains, interspersed with low hills and down-land, with wide expanses of heath and sandy dunes stretch away to the Baltic, which only just fails to be an immense lake. There are fine woods of beech trees, though most of the estates are composed of fields tilled in the flats. Even the so-called castles are not built upon the heights; they are big mansions, domestic strongholds in the plain, with heavy iron gates behind which the inmates live as if entrenched.

If a Junker's country mansion was of modest appearance, this was not because modesty withheld him from cutting a dash, but because he felt perfectly secure in his possessions. Lacking culture, knowledge, and experience of the world outside his Gotham, the Junker dared not venture upon such luxuries as adornment or architectural beauty. The best he could think of in this line was to set up two cannon by kind permission of the king, his liege, one on either side of the front gate, in commemoration of some battle or other. Apart from such trophies, there was nothing to tell the wayfarer of the ceaseless battles which had been fought over the length and breadth of the province; nor would one guess that, to a man, the gentry were army officers, were it not for their passionate love of good horsemanship and their skill in the equestrian arts.

Speaking generally, no natural peculiarity differentiated these far-flung stretches of cultivated soil from the fields of corn and the bands of woodland and forest across the Russian and Polish frontiers, for they formerly belonged to and are still homogeneous with the neighboring Slav landscapes. Roads and habitations were in better repair; otherwise everything was as it always had been. Agricultural methods were as of yore; the class strata of gentle and simple, of knights and workers, continued to be graded as in feudal days; the peasant still vainly endeavored to improve his lot, while the Junker was able, in spite of straitened financial circumstances, to live in style, managing his property and his estates, or mortgaging them just as his fathers had done before him.

The Hindenburgs, who in olden times had borne the name of Beneckendorff and had lived for five hundred years under that patronymic on their manorial lands in the Mark of Brandenburg, had migrated thence to carry on the work of colonization in West and in East Prussia. Thus they became what are known as East-Elbian Junkers. They lived in the homes of their ancestors, and in spite of their poverty (they were sometimes poorer than a well-to-do Westphalian farmer) they kept up the state of country gentlemen and came into contact only with their blood relations and with their social peers. When, in the eighteen fifties, our young hero spent his holidays with his grandparents on the family demesne of Neudeck, he slept in an attic room. Of a morning, when he stepped forth from what was not much better than a simple farmhouse, he would have the customary peasant's breakfast inside him. Ducks and fowls followed at his heels, for, though constantly shooed away, they were always to be found pecking about by the front door. Lilac bushes grew as freely and beautifully as they listed, seeing that no professional gardener was available to prune them, and Grannie had as much as she could cope with in housewifely avocations, in cooking, in dairy chores, and in seeing to the poultry. A maid may have tidied up the lad's room, and his grandfather's old groom probably gave his horse a rub down; but he himself was expected to bridle and saddle his mount, and this task he performed willingly enough since it was done behind the closed doors of the stable.

No sooner had the ten-year-old boy led his horse into the yard, passing under the selfsame lintel beneath which his ancestors had gone with their steeds so many generations before him, when the whole picture changed. Swinging himself into the saddle and setting out to scour the countryside, the child became "Young Master." A servant would be holding the gate open, cap in hand, and murmuring, "'morning, Herr Baron." —"Young Master," raising his crop to the salute, would cry back in a shrill falsetto, "'morning, Gustav." The man might already, or would certainly in a couple of years' time, be using the deferential "Sie" when addressing the youngster, whereas Old Master or Young Master would continue to address the ancient retainer all his life long with the familiar "du." The boy rode down towards the stream, skirting the dusty flock as it meandered bleating along the road. The shepherd had his greeting pat; so had the villagers, male and female alike, for they were children of serfs and some of them had even been born bondsmen, as were still the Russian peasants away there over the border.

Had there been any appreciable change since 1807, the date at which serfdom had officially been abolished? Hindenburg's younger and more romantically minded brother, endeavoring to give a tone picture of Neudeck, the hereditary estate, spoke of "the old, untiring bell, which never changed, and which for a century or more had daily called the laborers to their work early of a morning and again after the noontide rest." When Hindenburg, aged ten, rode out of the stable yard, this same bell summoned the peasants with their wives and children to the daily toil; his brother in later years still heard it echoing over the fields, and could not bring himself to believe that it would ever cease to call his people to their tasks while he remained master as heretofore. He was still "the master," even when in the day's course he himself should do this or that to forward a job, when he put a couple of dozen recruits through their paces, or when he drilled a few hundred soldiers.

In 1860, if a Junker paid his workpeople for their labors, the payment was not much more than a small gratuity, almost as freely conceded as in bygone days the alms of his forebears. The lord of the manor wielded then, and still wields today, such considerable power within the confines of his own jurisdiction that he could render intolerable the life of an unruly peasant. The Junker took precedence of everyone else in the district; he exercised jurisdiction in his own right over tenant farmers, copyholders, and such like. If the

taxes pressed too heavily upon him, he had the means
for retaliation ready to his hand.　He installed the
parsons in their livings; he chose the schoolmasters;
he decided what was to be the local daily wage; he
ruled the county council through a nephew-councilor
and governed the whole province through an uncle-
lord-lieutenant.　For the Junker was protected by the
mightiest man in Prussia—the king in Berlin.　Why
was he protected by the king in Berlin?　Because the
Junker protected the king from his subjects.

The king was the wellspring of life; his hand was
upon the Junker; and so long as this was so, the
Junker would have to remain loyal to his suzerain, for
had not his ancestors sworn fealty to the sovereign
when he passed out through the portals of the military
training college with the rank of cavalry officer or
lieutenant in the foot guards?　It was to the king
they owed it that they were the first in the land, and
if they occasionally murmured against him, nevertheless they and their ruler came to terms with one another;
for always in the end the treaty between them held
good, unwritten but accepted by oath: that king and
Junker mutually protected and honored one another
so as to keep burgher and peasant from becoming
rebellious, from remembering those new ideas which
had rushed in from abroad, ideas which the mad French
had scattered over the world.　That was why the
Junkers were fond of repeating the jingle: "Absolute
shall reign the king, obeying us in everything."

Grandfather was over eighty when the seven-year-
old child took his seat on a low stool at the veteran's
feet in order to hear what his elder had to say.　This
ancient head was far handsomer to look at than was

that of Hindenburg's own father, and when the old fellow told tales about Napoleon, the youngster pricked up his ears. After a meal Granddad might sit smoking his pipe, comfortably ensconced on one of the sofas in the dining room, from whose walls the portraits of ancestors looked down. Thus had he sat for fifty years, ever since as a man of thirty he had inherited the Neudeck estate. He had not been a famous soldier, having laid aside his uniform to devote himself to agriculture. Moreover, the distress among the countryfolk was so acute in the early decades of the nineteenth century that, though he was no more than six-and-thirty, he had never returned to the profession of arms, preferring, even while the king was a refugee, to continue his life at the manor. He could now tell his grandson how he had sought out the great Napoleon in the castle of Finckenstein to beg the war lord to be less exacting in his levies of supplies from the district; but the wicked Frenchman roughly repelled such pleading, and dismissed the petitioner with the declaration that armies had to be fed. These French gentry had actually come to Neudeck, and shots had been fired through the attic window.

When his grandson asked about the faded pictures on the walls, the old man, speaking from the depths of his sofa and probably punctuating his discourse with pinches of snuff or puffs of smoke from his pipe, would relate that the Beneckendorffs, during the hundred years of warfare in Brandenburg and in Prussia, had lost twenty-three sons on the battlefield; that an ancestor had been chancellor to an elector; that many had served as officers in the armies of Frederick the Great. But the forbears of these forbears could trace the line back to the ancestral keep at Quedlinburg, a stronghold which had been attacked and destroyed during the peasant wars following the Reformation. Wild times were those, the like of which would never be seen again! Where did the name come from? "Ben" meant gallows, and "Ecke" meant an oak: the gallows-oak of justice, which the family bore in its coat of arms, thus proving that justice and power had been theirs from time immemorial.

You want to know what "Hindenburg" means? The animal standing in front of the green tree painted on that escutcheon over the door—is a hind ("hind-castle"); but perhaps the animal was meant to be a *hund* (hound), to indicate *hundert* or *hundertschaft* (hundred, a political district), the tree representing the tree of justice: "leader of the hundertschaft," the administrator of justice, the lord and master. But the name of Hindenburg, the old man would explain, pointing with his stick to another picture, had been in the family only these sixty years. When the last, unmarried, Colonel von Hindenburg lay on his deathbed, he bequeathed the twin estates of Neudeck and Limbsee (oh, yes, Limbsee used to belong to the family, though now it has fallen into the claws of the Dallwitz clan!) to his great-nephew Beneckendorff, with the stipulation that the heir was to conjoin the name and arms of the noble family of Hindenburg, which would become extinct after his death, with that of Beneckendorff. The king, in 1789, graciously gave his consent to the wishes of a dying man.

And how did the last of the Hindenburgs come to own these estates? They had been bestowed, of course, by the king. Was he such a brave man, then? Undoubtedly, for once as he was riding beside the great Frederick on a battlefield, a cannon ball shattered his leg. That was during the Seven Years' War. To compensate for the destruction of a leg, and out of gratitude too, since that same cannon ball might very well have killed the king instead of merely wounding an officer in the Prussian army, our generous sovereign deigned to give these two estates to the deserving veteran.

Next, the grandfather asked the children to bring him a little box, a key, and his spectacles; and when the box had been opened with much ceremony, he would read what was written on an ancient sheet of paper now crumbling to pieces, while those of the children who had learned to read would lean eagerly over the old man's shoulder to follow the words with him. It was the farewell message of him whom they had to thank for the estates they lived on and for the name they bore:

"I am unworthy the mercy and favor thou hast vouchsafed to bestow upon thy servant. When I crossed the Vistula, I had naught but a staff in my hand, whereas now I am master of two estates. Who am I, Lord, and what my house, that thou shouldst have brought these things to pass? . . . I know that my Redeemer liveth, and that he shall stand at the latter day upon the earth: and though, after my skin, worms destroy this body, yet in my flesh shall I see God."

Grannie had quite other stories to tell, and even when she told the same stories as her husband, they sounded different. At that time, when the youngster came to spend the summer vacation at Neudeck, she was barely seventy years old, and long outlived the grandfather. The Hindenburgs and the Beneckendorffs were a sturdy race, untroubled by nerves and spiritual scruples, spending their lives in the open air, and little addicted to intellectual activities. They usually, therefore, attained such ripe ages as seventy, eighty, or eighty-five without difficulty. Hindenburg's grandmother, whose maiden name was Brederlow, was the only other one to possess an interesting head, if we are to judge by the portraits of the family now extant for our inspection. Her picture shows a handsome, proud, and strong-minded woman with dark eyes and wearing a white cloth that suggests a nun's coif, her hand resting on a Bible. She looks resolutely down on us from the canvas, collected, alert, standing solidly upon the earth, her head and figure as if carved out of wood, and of the build which she bequeathed to her grandson, the field marshal of our day. Fourteen children did she bring into the world, and yet she is depicted as upright and straight as a candle.

She took pleasure in showing her grandchildren the cottage to which her husband had brought her as his seventeen-year-old bride. Here they had dwelt until the present manor house was built; here she had been taught how to cut up the carcasses of oxen and of pigs; from here she had gone out into the fields to help in reaping the crops of flax, or down to the sheepfold for the shearing; here she had spun and woven the cloth which was to be cut into dresses and suits for her children. The little table which she used for her sewing was not varnished, and she would delight in telling her grandchildren how, during the days of the Napoleonic wars, she had learned on this very table

how to manipulate a heated knife to spread plaster
upon the dressings for wounds.   One of the men she
had nursed at that time had long remembered her
kindness with gratitude.   Another Frenchman, an
officer, had snatched a golden snuffbox from her work-
basket, and, before her very eyes, had taken a pinch.
She was twenty-two when this had happened; though
when recounting the incident she did not mention that
she was pretty, but that she had rung for the servant
and ordered him to throw away the contents of the box.
The French were intolerably arrogant in those days!

When she went over to the chapel to see whether all
was as well ordered for the dead there as it was for the
living in the mansion, she would point out the grave of
a sister of that last Hindenburg who had bequeathed
his estates to the Beneckendorff family.   This Lady
Barbara had given precise instructions as to how she
was to be buried, up to what point the village teacher
was to go with his pupils, and had left a bequest of five
hundred talers in perpetuity, out of which the schoolmaster was to be paid five talers a year for sound
religious instruction.   The village children would
awesomely tell one another that old Barbara haunted
the place, and how, riding a goat, and wearing golden
spurs, she was wont to gallop about the manor house.
The endowment which the pious spinster had left was
not administered as she intended.   The local education
authorities, balking at the disbursement of five talers,
wanted to reserve to themselves the right of deciding
how much they would pay, and wrote in the contract
of a newly appointed teacher: "If Herr Schiller conducts himself in the way a good teacher should, he will
receive a generous gratuity at the end of the year."

But Grandfather Hindenburg evidently considered
even this too great a concession, and since, as Junker,
he was a higher authority than the education committee, he inserted with his own hand the words: "an
unspecified, but generous, gratuity."

This anecdote has been given to us by Hindenburg's
brother in his delightful little book; it would undoubtedly not have been told to her grandchildren by old
Grannie Hindenburg; for it is precisely such significant
details that grandparents and parents fail to divulge
and the field marshal's biographers pass over in silence
today. They are interesting because they illumine the
ambiguous relationship in which a Junker stood towards
his king—that peculiar relationship upon which, in
Prussia, the power and the lives of both depended.

Not that I mean to imply that the Hindenburgs were
more selfish than their peers; the peculiarities in their
story can be found duplicated in other family histories.
Since the days of Frederick the Great there are three
noteworthy incidents recorded of them in Prussian
history books. The first occurred at the battle of
Kolin (1757), when Frederick sustained a decisive
defeat. The general who paved the way to the victory
of the Austrian forces against the king who was idolized
by the rest of the Beneckendorff family was a certain
Count Ernst von Beneckendorff who had been born
in Ansbach under the Hohenzollerns, but who had subsequently been given a commission in the Saxon army.
He has left a description of the attack which was to
decide the issue of the day against the Hohenzollern
monarch, and it would seem from this account that our
anti-Prussian hero looked upon the feat as the climax
of his life.

The second incident relates to a Beneckendorff, born at Reval in 1783, who entered the Russian service, became a general, and organized the famous tsarist police force which was the forerunner of the Cheka. For the East-Elbian aristocracy had been wont to swear allegiance and to fight and serve where fame and position were likely to accrue, no matter upon what terms these foreign masters and States stood in regard to the king of Prussia, who was, after all, practically of their own kith and kin.   Thus, apart from the two gentlemen above mentioned who entered Saxon and Russian service respectively, there was yet another Beneckendorff ancestor who in 1650 became Royal Polish and Swedish Chamberlain (or Starost, as the functionary was called at that time), and who bore three names which would surely get him into trouble nowadays: Israel, Köhn, von Jaski.

The third and most celebrated incident was that of a cousin of Hindenburg's grandfather, a certain Ernst Ludwig von Beneckendorff who was commissioned to defend the fort of Spandau near Berlin against a French attack.   On October 23, 1806, he had sworn as was customary "to hold the fort and only to surrender to the enemy when the building should be a ruin . . . . Next day he called a council of war, and during the deliberations all, with the exception of Meinert, a captain in the engineers, agreed to surrender the place on a number of paltry pretexts.   In 1808, Major Ernst Ludwig von Beneckendorff was condemned to be shot, though the sentence of death was commuted by the king into life imprisonment in a fortress."[1]

Such stories as these, culled from the family annals,

[1] O. von Lettow-Vorbeck, Der Krieg von 1806–7, vol. II, pp. 219 and foll., Berlin 1892.

would naturally create a ferment in the mind of an honorable young descendant wishing to take up the same profession. We may assume that Ernst Ludwig's treachery was calculated to spur on the field marshal of later days to a desire to rehabilitate the warlike renown of the family, a renown which had been in a chronic state of eclipse ever since the day when that other ancestor had had his leg shot away.

A further episode from far earlier times is worth mentioning. A Beneckendorff who had become a Teutonic Knight was given home leave in 1330, and had used his horse for the journey. The grand master took him to task, pointing out that the knights of the Order, having sworn a vow of poverty, had no longer any property of their own, and the horses they brought with them belonged to the Order's stud. Beneckendorff was so greatly aggrieved by the reprimand that he determined to avenge himself. As the grand master came from hearing Mass, the knight stabbed him—or as another tradition has it, he killed his superior in a hand-to-hand fight. Thereupon Pope John condemned him to lifelong imprisonment. This tale was first divulged to the German people by the field marshal's brother, and it would appear (since no adverse comment is made upon it) that a vengeance of the sort did not seem out of place even to a descendant born more than five hundred years later. Field Marshal Hindenburg was having his portrait painted during the war. Making conversation, the painter asked him why his ancestor had stabbed the grand master. The sitter's answer was laconic: "Oh, I suppose he was annoyed."

II

A Junker's thoughts and feelings concerning right and violence, king, freedom, and service, are peculiar to the tribe, and if we fail to understand them, we shall likewise fail to understand Hindenburg's character, which is entirely that of a type, and hardly belongs to an individual man at all. We can only explain Hindenburg in the days before he became famous if we have a thorough knowledge of the psychology of a Prussian who is at one and the same time Junker and army officer; but the explanation is more than sufficient.

The soil of the eastern marches was lacking in fertility; its geographical situation was disadvantageous, seeing that on the land side it was surrounded by alien States. The result was that the first electors of Brandenburg, coming into their inheritance from the more fertile districts of Franconia, found themselves compelled to treat it as a military colony and to look upon it as a breeding ground for soldiers—much as Egypt does in regard to the Sudan. Since war service took precedence of agriculture, the feudal system developed here along more authentic lines than elsewhere, for mutual aid was essential to defense. Autocratic princes, conquerors, and so forth could extract the bread they needed from their peasantry only if they were able confidently to rely upon the knighthood to keep these menial subjects disciplined and submissive. The farther eastward they pressed beyond the right bank of the Elbe, spreading over this uncultured land, and the nearer they got to the Russian border, the less forcible was the opposition they met with from the indigenes, from the dull and age-long oppressed laborers and burghers.

The civilization and culture which the Prussian aristocracy brought with them into the eastern marches was not much superior to that already enjoyed by the primitive inhabitants; and, since, among the German aristocracy as a whole, the Prussians had at all times been the least endowed in the matter of culture, their colonizing activities in the east could not raise the standard above the level of what they themselves boasted of possessing. It was only in such a country, only in this particular corner of Germany, which well on into the eighteenth century cultivated neither the arts nor the sciences, that the Junkers could have any success as rulers; for, as Lessing in the days of Frederick the Great declared, it was "the most enslaved land in Europe." In very early times, at the outset of the aristocratic invasion, the peasants of the sandy Mark of Brandenburg had wandered by the thousand over the Elbe eastward, not for the same reason that urged the pioneers in North America to journey ever farther and farther to the west—because other and later settlers were pressing upon their heels—but in the hope of preserving the tiny particle of freedom which they still retained. They were fleeing from the Junkers.

Among the princes who were trying to raise their heads after the distresses of the Thirty Years' War, the Hohenzollerns were having the easiest time of it, precisely because their territories had suffered the most, because energy and desire for opposition had been completely broken, and any who should promise help and protection against the marauding soldiery was given a welcome. Thus the standing army which had been created during the seventeenth century in an endeavor to protect the princes, was acclaimed by

3

the burghers of the devastated and helpless provinces
of Brandenburg and Prussia; whereas in Austria
where the estates of the old landed gentry had been
preserved, this same army was whole-heartedly detested.   The absolute power which a standing army
gives a sovereign was more difficult to fight against on
Prussian soil than anywhere else, and, indeed, it was
never successfully overcome there.

The electors and kings had created, after the Russian
model, an aristocracy that should protect the ruler
against any uprising of his subjects.   Tsar Nicholas
declared those families extinct which no longer served
competently in the army or in the State, ennobling
others to slip into their places, thereby creating the
paradox of an "aristocracy of service," and endowing
with ancestors those who in the ordinary course of
events could merely look forward to having descend-
ants; and the monarchs of Prussia followed the same
course.   The country-bumpkin Junkers, poor and
having nothing particular to do, were keen to enter a
service that was easy, lucrative, and honorable.
Since every one of them could ride and shoot, and had
learned to command men, they were chosen as teachers
and leaders of small troops of soldiers, proving themselves trusty in war, and receiving, as recompense for
a successful cavalry attack, another estate in the East.
In the winter, they took their wives to Berlin that the
ladies might attend a court ball; among themselves
they grumbled about the king, but over the Burgundy
they would become enthusiastic as they dreamed of
the glory which would be theirs after future battles.
When war came and they were called upon to practice
their profession, to do the thing they had been all the

time paid for doing, they would say that they were
going forth "to die for the king."

These Junkers, incorrigible spongers that they were,
did not fight shy of making claims upon their liege, so
that if at first they were allowed five hides of land free
of tax, they very soon raised this privileged exemption
to twenty-five hides. The margrave, elector, or whatever the ruler happened to be, did not venture to
protest, seeing that these were the only knights he had.
Moreover, he was compelled to grant them special
manorial privileges, which meant the right of disposal
of the peasants, who bore every conceivable burden
and only differed from the Negroes of Virginia in that
they were not sold into slavery on some distant shore.

Even in our own day, the manorial estates still go
by the name of "dominium"; and down to a hundred
years ago no peasant could quit his holding, or marry,
or practice a handicraft, or sell a cow, without the
Junker's permission. The Junker might beat the man,
and throw him into jail on the slightest provocation.
Even if the poor fellow behaved well, doing nothing
that was against the laws and customs of the land, he
still had to pay his lord taxes on everything; on sheep
and bees, on flax and hemp, on the water he took from
the stream, on the wick he burned in his lamp, actually
on the mire in front of his house. There were no
fewer than seven hundred fifty items upon which the
feudal lord could exercise his rights of levy and extor-
tion. On the other hand, the peasant possessed but
one right: to pray for his lord and master of a Sunday.
But there were limits to what a Junker was privileged
to do. He could not mix with the burghers on equal
terms; nor could he become a member of a guild (the

learned professions came within this category) or marry
a commoner, without losing caste.

Hindenburg's grandfather had exercised all these
rights when still a youngish man, and he told his
grandson how they were gradually curtailed and withdrawn. Was it not natural that the old man should
be alarmed by the introduction of newfangled democratic ways—"abuses," he probably called them—;
was it not natural that, in order to safeguard the boy's
pride of birth, he should impress upon him the importance of the principle which led the king to reserve commissions in the army for trustworthy persons of noble
birth? Thus only could the possible revolt of underlings be prevented.

Frederick the Great once wrote: "The promotion
of a burgher to the status of army officer is the first
step in the decline of a State." As the pressure of
alien peoples round his kingdom increased, the more
obvious became the necessity to keep up a strong
fighting force. This spelled a further growth in Junker
dominance, and new estates in the East bestowed by
the king in payment for Junker services. The freshly
created company leaders came to be nicknamed
"entrepreneurs in an arms company"; for with every
company brought into being by these soldier kings as
a means of self-protection in the first instance and
subsequently in order to carry on their campaigns of
conquest, the Junker caste received another manor.
This promoted a war mentality, a love of acquiring
booty, and, above all, loyalty to the king.

The recently inaugurated "aristocracy of service,"
which constituted a third of the Prussian aristocracy
and which on the whole belonged heart and soul to the

king, was likewise the ruling and most socially distinguished factor in the State; while the burgher and the peasant, together with university professors, musicians, craftsmen, and the like, were suspect, and, anyway, were an inferior class of human beings altogether. These fellows were called "cannon fodder" ever since the time when Frederick William I had introduced his cantonal system, a sort of corvée, or tax paid in man power, whereby the burgher had to serve in the army if he were unable to buy himself off. In this we see a beginning of the idea of compulsory military service, now universally known as conscription. When, after the third partition of Poland, Prussia was yet further enlarged, the broom squires found themselves drilling persons superior to themselves in culture and education.

Since the Junker caste completely monopolized commissions in the army, they needed only to protect themselves against local talent and energy by forcing the king to continue recognizing their ancient privilege of seniority. A couple of dozen families, looking upon the State as "pension provider," blocked every avenue to promotion on the strength of a prior claim; and should a burgher, by some strange chance, be occupying the post of advancement, the Junker aspirant had merely to skip over his head into a superior position— just as the knight does in a game of chess.

As the army grew, so did the takings of the Junkers grow. The lump sum each received from the royal treasury to pay the men of their company and to provide them with clothing, uniforms, and food, was for the most part pocketed by themselves. A majority of their recruits would be given home leave lasting many

months.   By this device the Junkers reacquired their
serfs who were promptly put to cultivating the
manorial estates.   Other economies which advantaged
their own purses were effected by making the tunics
more skimpy, by doing away with sleeves to the waist-
coats, by keeping on their lists of supplies the names of
persons long since dead; so that in 1780 Field Marshal
von Boyen said of the Prussian Junker officers, "they
are no longer soldiers but usurious shopkeepers."   Even
Old Fritz was powerless in their hands; and when, at
the conclusion of his wars, he provided twenty-four
million talers for the reconstruction of the country, a
kind of "internal reparations," the municipal authorities and the peasantry received as little and the
Junkers as much as they did in 1930 when the so-called
"Eastern Aid" (Osthilfe) was distributed.   In politics,
since they and their ancestors had constantly occupied
positions of power for many hundreds of consecutive
years, they had acquired an artfulness and a cunning
that were hard to beat.   In 1807, Baron von Stein
introduced his reforms, including the emancipation of
the serfs.   Five years later, the Junkers cheated these
same peasants, depriving them of their newly acquired
rights.   For four hundred years, no king and no form
of government had ever been able to cope with the
mulish slyness of these Prussian Junkers.

The burgesses never handled the Junkers more
roughly than did Baron von Stein, who was their equal
as regards ancestry and service, but as a Christian and
a nobleman expected the utmost from kings and
princes, and in 1808 wrote: "The aristocracy of Prussia
is a burden to the nation, because the members of this
caste are found in great numbers, are poor and full of

claims, receiving emoluments, occupying official posts, and demanding privileges and precedence of every kind. One form a Junker's poverty takes is a lack of education; another is that he is forced to be brought up in military academies which are badly equipped for the purpose, and whence he issues utterly incapable of competently filling the superior posts. . . . This enormous mass of half-educated and insolent persons rides roughshod over the sensibilities of fellow citizens in the exercise of the twofold function of noblemen and officials."

But even Baron von Stein proved impotent in his dealings with these prickly gentry. The rancor of the burgesses and the peasants grew apace up to a point, only to fizzle out once more. When some of the Junkers, through treachery and cowardice, surrendered land and forts into Napoleon's hands during the latter's 1806 campaign, the burgesses rejoiced greatly over the defeat of these "swashbuckling knights." Similarly, in November, 1918, when they calmly allowed the marks of distinction to be stripped from their uniforms, the commonalty believed their power to be broken. But in each instance, burgesses and folk were mistaken.

III

Nevertheless, by mixed marriages between Junkers and members of the middle classes, noteworthy leaders were produced from time to time, men who combined the best qualities of either caste in a happy equilibrium. Such were Bismarck, Gneisenau, Bülow, to mention but three (sons of marriages between Junkers and middle-class maids) who were able to raise themselves above the intellectual level of their peers because of the finer mental training and education bequeathed to them by their maternal forbears.

Hindenburg, too, had burgher as well as Junker blood in his veins, and the difficulties which beset his German biographers were alleviated only when they were able to call his mother "a soldier's daughter" and to describe his grandfather as "a surgeon-general." The field marshal and his brother, though they plumed themselves upon their noble lineage, never wrote a word in their memoirs relative to their maternal origins; and it was not until after Hindenburg's death that an investigator, who was himself of noble birth and parentage, undertook researches along these lines.[1] No anecdote of his youth ever refers to this delicate matter; Hindenburg's bourgeois grandmother, Schwickardt, told the children about the French wars, and also that her husband had crossed the Beresina as an army surgeon. Otherwise the fact that a streak of commoner's blood flowed in the youngster's veins was carefully hushed up. And yet the family, not a member of which had done anything he need be ashamed of, had absolutely nothing to hide!

Among Hindenburg's burgher progenitors we find masons, nappers and shearmen, herring fishers, rope makers, farriers, and even parsons. They were originally West Germans and Catholics who did not migrate eastward until later years. The most notable among these sires was the field marshal's great-grandfather, Grenadier Schwickardt, and it was from this man and not from his Junker stock, which was of shorter build, that Hindenburg inherited his height. That fine fellow probably owed his career to his stature,

[1] Cf. Peter von Gerhardt, Stammtafeln berühmter Deutscher: Hindenburg, 1934.

for he measured nearly six feet two, and served for thirty-nine years among the tall grenadier guards of Frederick the Great. Subsequently he became sexton to a Protestant cemetery in Berlin (though he himself remained a Catholic until the end of his days). All these petty bourgeois threw in their lot with the religion which at the moment seemed best fitted to promote their aims, just as the Junkers rallied to the side of the prince in whose service they might reap the best advantage; to a man, they were realists, whether they were the possessors of a blazon or not. The grenadier in question wedded Marie Puhlmann, washer-woman to the Princess Wilhelmina; and Gerhardt, my authority for these details, adds: "When and where Schwickardt the grenadier married her cannot be ascertained. His [or, rather, her] son Johann Franz, who was born in Potsdam in 1773, is described in the garrison church's register as 'illegitimate,' whereas the same observation regarding Karl Ludwig, the field marshal's grandfather, who was born in 1780, has long since been crossed out."

The latter boy became a doctor of medicine, and then a surgeon in the army medical corps. During the battle of Kulm, fought against Napoleon in 1813, young Karl Ludwig led a leaderless company back into the firing line, and this exploit was rewarded, not with an estate in East Prussia, but by his general presenting him with a case of silver spoons and forks for his future bride. This is about the only tale his soldier grandsons care to tell of his doings, although that happened to be the one day in his whole life when he was guilty of slaying fellow men, whereas, on thousands of other occasions he had cured the sick of their ailments.

Thus Hindenburg's two great-grandfathers may very well have met one another in the palace at Potsdam: the one, tall, standing to attention at the gates, as the other stepped down from his private coach on his way to a court ball. One of his great-grandmothers may have washed the linen of the other who had remained in the palace as a guest of the sovereign. By an amusing accident neither knew the other.

From both elders, from the lieutenant who later became a major and from the daughter of the doctor, the children, as they trailed from one little garrison town to another in the wake of their parents, learned about their religion, received a smattering of geography, and a working knowledge of French. More important still (as Hindenburg writes in his old age) they were taught "to love the Prussian monarchy, a love we came to regard as the strongest buttress of the fatherland." The boy's parents, too, following the example set by the grandparents, served up nothing but militarist and warlike anecdotes of their young days (unless we are to believe that both brothers, since they have retold only suchlike tales, forgot all the others). When the field marshal was twelve months old, the revolution of 1848 broke out in Posen, the province where he was born, and the army officers became extremely uneasy. "Each of them felt he was dogged by an assassin who at the suitable opportunity was to carry out his deed of darkness. When my parents went out of an evening, an ominous figure keeping within the shadow of the trees crept after them." Orders were issued by the victorious revolutionaries that every house was to be illuminated and decorated with black-red-gold flags to celebrate the event; but

Hindenburg's mother withdrew into a back room, sat down by her baby's cradle, and then recalled that this very day was the anniversary of the birth of the Prince of Prussia (later William I) so that, for her, "the lights in the windows of the front room were in honor of him."

Such stories, poured into their ears from earliest childhood, taught the boys to hate every grant of liberty to the people, and filled them with a passion of resentment towards those who dared to rebel against the king and against the Junker caste, and who had the temerity to raise the black-red-gold banner against the fatherland. At the same time they learned when it was wise to knuckle under to a victorious foe: one stuck up a few candles in the window, just as Mother had done during those days of revolutionary upheaval; yes, one could do this with a quiet conscience so long as, while compromising thus with the enemy, one still harbored loyal thoughts in his mind.

Children who watched their father every morning while he drilled his company, who were constantly having to say farewell to the comrades of their age because Father was transferred from garrison to garrison, came to look upon such things as a necessity, not a gloomy necessity, but a condition imposed by destiny. If a boy should ask sadly why they must pack up their trunks again and take up once more their everlasting pilgrimage, the answer was a simple one—"The king's will, my son!"

The restlessness provoked by such a nomadic childhood, a childhood which never knew the meaning of a fixed abode, found its one solace in the untroubled peace of Neudeck, which the boys came to look upon as their true home and which was inevitably associated in their minds with holidays. After Grandfather's death in 1863, Hindenburg's parents went to live on the manorial estates. The father, after thirty years of service, was pensioned off; the children were happy because here they were free and because they became "Young Masters," and the connection between service and command was made clear to them through the paternal example. Since he was the son of a lord of the manor, he had been able to join a smart regiment and win a commission in the army. True, he had not been very generously rewarded from the financial point of view, but he knew that the little he received sufficed for his needs and would guard him from want for the rest of his life. Thus from the time he reached his fifth decade he dwelt upon his own lands, managing them and, though forever poor, keeping up the style of a member of the ruling class.

Hindenburg's father had had no experience of active service; his peace-time duties amply sufficed him, and when he retired from the army, he took up a commanding position in the exiguous circle he had quitted as a youngster. In all these proceedings, the king was the motive force, sometimes visible, sometimes invisible. The play between obedience and command, between service and government which was so characteristic of Junker existence, presented itself to the growing boy under the sign of the king from whom the gifts of life flowed and to whom, therefore, life must be consecrated. The eldest lad, a sturdy youngster, started early on his prescribed career of service and command; for at eleven years of age he left civil life, and took up his allotted task in the ranks of the officer caste.

Cadet, 1860

Lieutenant, 1866

Lieutenant and
Adjutant, 1870

Colonel, 1878

Major General, 1897

Field Marshal General,
1916

Hindenburg as soldier, 1860–1916

His departure to the cadet school must have been taken very seriously by young Hindenburg, for he solemnly wrote his will, quite spontaneously, just before he set out. This testament is indubitably a genuine document, for we have the original in the author's own handwriting. He bequeathed his toys to his brothers and sister, arranging that one of his poorer schoolfellows should continue to be provided with the roll for breakfast he himself had been in the habit of giving in the past. "I hereby affirm that I have written the above in all truth and sincerity." Then, in a corner he wrote: "Peace and quiet is what I pray may henceforward be granted me."

This addition, with which he touchingly lays aside the rôle of testator, discloses the man's fundamental trends: the will-to-quiet, calm, no excitement, together with the enjoyment of the magnificent health which for eighty years stood him in good stead. These are the foundations upon which he built an existence never to be troubled by nerves.

IV

We are given to understand that in 1717 the soldier king reëstablished the Cadet Corps (abolished in 1919) and centered it in Berlin in the hope of arousing in his "effeminate" son, who was later to be known as Frederick the Great, an interest in the military sciences which as a stripling he despised. There were eight of these academies scattered throughout Prussia, and here the youngsters were trained until their seventeenth year, when they were transferred to the finishing school at Berlin. The wealthier nobles were accustomed to send their second and third sons to these institutions, while the poorer Junkers consigned *all* the boys of the family to their tender care; and since by the time they were eighteen they automatically rose to be lieutenants, they ceased to be a charge upon their fathers, whereas ordinary students at the universities continued to depend upon the paternal purse up to the age of twenty-five or more. Thus a Junker only "sank" to the point of entering the diplomatic service or becoming a professor if there was something physically amiss with him.

The attraction of the Cadet Corps lay, then, not in the brilliant future it might dangle before a lad's eyes, but in the fact that the career of army officer afforded security for a lifetime. In order to relieve the monotony of institutional life, the young men were assured that they would attain to the highest posts the State had in its power to bestow, posts to which persons of noble birth and lineage alone could hope to aspire. During its best days, from about 1770 to 1890, the Prussian officers' corps was so poverty stricken that its members were forced to look upon honor as a sufficient substitute for wealth; and they accepted the barrenness of their external life because they felt compensated by being the undisputed rulers of the country. The honor of an officer—which had nothing in common with the ordinarily accepted honor of a soldier—was "safeguarded" by a court of honor and a council of honor that persecuted "opinions and doctrines" after the manner of the Inquisition, for the officers' corps was a guild, though membership in this guild was not voluntary. The more their caste sentiments were stimulated, the greater was their contempt for the commonalty. "The consciousness of a special

and personal relationship to the king, the loyalty of a
vassal to his liege," wrote Hindenburg in his memoirs,
"permeated the whole life of an officer and compensated him for many a material privation. . . . The
motto 'ich dien' [I serve] thereby acquired a very
special significance."

At the time when Hindenburg joined the Cadet
Corps, in 1859, most of the officers in the Prussian
army hailed from the ranks of the aristocracy; no
burgher was permitted to enter upon the higher posts,
nor could he acquire a commission in any of the crack
regiments.   Out of a total of 2900 officers, no fewer
than 1800 had passed through the Cadet Academy;
and among the 2900 there were 2000 of noble birth.
According to the actual percentage of nobles among
the general population, the number of blue-blooded
commissioned officers should have been no more than
80, so that the nobility was twenty-five times as
strongly represented as the bourgeoisie.   In the first
foot-guard regiment, practically all the officers were
sons of aristocrats, whereas the six medical men who
had risen to commissioned rank were of bourgeois
birth and breeding.   That same year, 1859, in the first
foot-guard regiment of the French army, out of ninety-
four officers only eleven were the offspring of aristocrats.   In Prussia at that date one fourth of the
68,000 nobles were on the military rolls, receiving pay
from the State budget, and thus supported at the
country's expense.   When, in 1900, a bourgeois citizen
was given a general's commission, the monarch hastened to confer on him the rank of nobleman.   The
other bathers thus threw this poor Adam a pair of
bathing drawers!

The scornful attitude of Prussian cadets towards the masses of the population is described as follows in Roon's biography: "In the Cadet Corps, he breathed an atmosphere utterly alien to the political notions of the era of reform and the Wars of Liberation; the cadets were warned to fight shy of 'Burschenschaft' ideals, such as liberal nonsense about freedom. . . ." As a whole-hearted supporter of absolutism, Roon despised the political strivings of the German people. Three days prior to the collapse of absolutist rule in March 1848, he described the popular upheaval as "the machinations of hired and besotted handicraftsmen, . . ." and nicknamed the Frankfort parliament "a political menagerie."

The same spirit reigned in 1860 when cadets were instructed to nurture a special distrust of the rank-and-file soldiers, concerning whom a certain Baron von Manteuffel wrote: "It is a dangerous, aye, an intolerable fact that Prussia's fate and the Prussian monarchy should rest upon the more or less good will of 50,000 young agricultural laborers."

The finest feelings called into existence by the training at the military academies—esprit de corps and comradeship, virtues upon which a man may rely without their solving the bread question—surrounded as with a garland those sterner requirements of cadet education, readiness to obey and capacity for command. While unconditional obedience was inculcated, an obedience carried to the extreme of personal effacement, the desire to command was likewise sedulously fostered. The many painful hours and years passed within the walls of the military academies were rendered tolerable by the realization that, on a day to come, each young

Hindenburg (standing) as a lieutenant, with his parents, brothers, and sister, 1866

man would be placed in a position to command, were it only over a platoon of twenty men, and that henceforward this privilege would never be taken away from him.   Such a Spartan form of upbringing was the exclusive lot of the sons of noblemen, who looked upon themselves as a body of the elect.   Since this was the case, any sense of abasement or mortification was annulled at the outset, and the authorities might bellow at the youngster, they might thrash him or lock him up to their heart's content, and he could always console himself with the thought: We are the noblest people in the nation, the great penultimate step of the pyramid, upon whose apex stands—The King.

Through blind obedience the cadet was trained to become a commander; all ideas were purposely shut out, so that character might be developed; and the whole procedure was called—Service.   Thus the foundations were laid for the production not of a conquering but of a serving soldier; the concepts of duty and courage were nurtured; and the whole process was designated "giving your life for king and country." Since the king ruled by divine grace, the medieval ties between throne and altar were restored; service to one's sovereign was enhanced to become a religious duty, and the ladder to God's own self was constructed. "The views of life I reached while serving in that great school of duty, the German army," writes Hindenburg in his autobiography, "reached their highest expression in the adages, 'duty takes precedence of right,' and 'at all times, and especially in times of stress, one for all and all for one must be the rule.'"   The formula, which recalls the rules of religious orders save that God's place is usurped by the figure of the king, shows

4

us how blind an obedience was demanded; and, naturally, boys thus educated acquired the feeling that
they must never assume responsibility when there were
orders to obey, but only when there were orders to give.
Upon such moral principles, the Military Academy
could train men excellently for service. If, however,
they were creative by temperament, they had to put
the curb upon their talents until that later day when
they might develop into General Staff officers. The
Military Academy never turned out a commander of
more than second-rate ability.

How did Hindenburg pass his days during the seven
years he spent as a cadet within the walls of the
institution, which he never left except when he was
going home for his holidays?

In an unwarmed dormitory, twenty to thirty cadets
are roused from their slumbers in hard and narrow beds
by a bugle sounding the reveille; they wash in icy
water, shuffle quickly into their clothes, and, at the
first word of command which reëchoes through the desolate barracks with their bare, stony walls and their
emptiness, run down into the yard for morning drill.
They are always rushing from one occupation to
another, for every quarter of an hour is occupied in an
allotted task. A demoniacal speed seems to keep the
teachers perpetually on the go at a smart tempo as if
danger were constantly threatening, and as if any
pause for contemplation or reflection were forbidden.
Quick march to a plateful of porridge, with a scanty
morsel of butter; at the word of command the youngsters fall to, their spoons clattering in the effort to
swallow the ration within the prescribed three to four
minutes. "The more juvenile cadets," wrote Hinden-

burg's brother, "had to crumble scraps of bread from their meals, and collect them in a box, which they kept concealed on their knees lest an officer should come on a round of inspection and catch them. In the refectory next day they would empty these hoards into the common tureen and mix them into the porridge." Breakfast, and the other two meals, were eaten so fast, and the hall they were eaten in was so cold, that the cadets could dream of nothing but food and warmth when they wrote home. Hindenburg was no exception, and just before the vacations, would beg his mother to have his favorite dishes ready.

Lessons were given by officers, following much the same curriculum as that of a civilian high school, and were attended by six to ten cadets in each classroom. The pastor who saw to the religious instruction was a semiofficer. The bare room contained, in addition to the writing table and lockers, a small iron stove, a spittoon, a clock, and a portrait of the king. In the course of a lesson the classroom door might be flung open and an officer of higher rank would enter; every chair scraped backward on the floor, while the senior boy yelled, "eight cadets to the room: eight cadets present," and the books were promptly clapped together with a bang. Thereupon the officer would wrench open a locker, at random, to see whether, in the four compartments each lad was provided with for his kit, every article was in its proper place: in compartment number two the tunic, folded with its lining outside and its sleeves within; in number three, the canvas fatigue uniform, likewise neatly folded; in number four, brushes, comb, and sewing materials.

The top compartment of the lockers was the only

corner where a cadet's personal fancy was allowed to
find an outlet, and that within strictly defined limits:
a sanctuary where photos, shells, and other mementos
could be arranged.   When Hindenburg was thirteen
years old, he wrote home: "I want to arrange my
knickknack shelf as follows: at the back against the
wall, a big Prussian eagle; in the middle, Old Fritz on
a pedestal surrounded by his generals, with a group
of Black Hussars below; right in front, a chain stretched
from side to side, behind which are to be some cannon,
and before which must be two sentry boxes occupied
by two of Frederick the Great's grenadiers.   So far I
have not the materials to carry out my scheme; I set
my hopes on Christmas."

Should even the minutest article not be in its precise
nook or allotted line, the officer would ruthlessly
bundle everything out of the locker, and, under stern
supervision, give the offender a minute or so to put the
mess straight again.   If a boy laughed or if he had
blotted his copy book, he was punished in the following
manner.   He was compelled to take the knickknack
shelf out of his locker, laden as it usually was with such
treasures as lead soldiers and figurines, and, gripping
one arm of an open pair of compasses between his heels,
the other arm pointing upward, he had to bend his
knees until his hams nearly touched his calves, holding
the shelf for three minutes so steadily that none of the
objects on it rattled.   Any awkwardness meant that
the compasses would prick his rump or his heels.

Thrice daily the cadet had to polish his boots and
the buttons on his uniform coat.   While the boy was
being drilled, his officer would examine these buttons
to see if they reflected his face like a mirror, and if a

button seemed a trifle loose it would be turned and twisted until it came off. Suddenly the yard emptied itself, the youngsters rushing up to their rooms, changing their uniforms, and, in five minutes, standing once more in their places for roll call. Then the officer, using a meter measure, would assure himself that the black band which fitted inside the collar protruded the prescribed one and a half centimeters above the coat collar. If it projected more or less, the negligence was a punishable offense.

The interminable rushing from one occupation to another, the constant shouting, the loud and strident voices raised in command, kept the lads all day long in fear and on the alert; unceasingly they were upbraided and told to "stand still," to "sit up"; "eyes right" was bawled at them; or, again, "first company stand to attention," this meaning that the feet were to be placed, not at an angle of ninety degrees, but at one of eighty-five. "Hands to your sides" meant that the middle finger of each hand was to lie along the outer seam of the trousers. "Chest out," "belly in," "chin on the neck stock," "eyes steady," "shoulders back," "body upright with a slight bend forward." As they were drilled in small squads, they had to stand eight paces apart; to salute, you took three steps forward and three backward, while the hand flew up to your cap. Three minutes were given in which to burnish eighteen buttons so bright that you could see your face in them—but beware if you let a particle of powder drop on to the uniform cloth! They were made to fetch, to carry, to dress, to undress, hustled almost beyond endurance; church-going, walks, every task had to be fitted in at its exact second; nothing was to be

done in leisurely fashion, but always at breakneck
speed as if the boys were about to deliver the latest
intelligence concerning an enemy's movements.   A
cadet's legs might tremble, his hands become clammy
with perspiration, rage might consume him—but his
mouth was forever and under any conceivable provocation to remain silent.

In the evening they were allowed half an hour wherein
to write letters (which were subject to censorship); then
a drum would be beaten, and the boys fell into rank and
were marched off to the dormitories.   In three minutes
they had to be in bed, with their clothes neatly stacked
on the chair by the bedside; silence.   Meanwhile an
officer had been superintending their movements
through a hole in the wall.   In the night, he would
pass down the dormitories, and if he found so much as
a sock out of its precise place he would rummage the
whole heap of clothes, scattering them to right and to
left while ordering the culprit, shivering in his night-
shirt, to put them back as they should be.

Can we be surprised that young Hindenburg, as his
brother relates, had once refused to leave the manor
at the end of the holidays, screaming, "Never again"?
That did not prevent him, next time he wrote home,
from telling his parents that the school had been honored by the visit of an exalted personage, no less a
man than the crown prince.   To which Hindenburg
added: "For nearly all of us, this was the first time
we had seen a member of our royal house.   Never
had we raised our legs so high in the goose step as when
we paraded that day."   These cadets, it will be seen,
recognized and honored but one godhead—their king.

At sixteen he was to see his supreme master in the

flesh; for, having reached the lower fifth form, he was transferred to the Central School at Berlin. But, as was seemly in a fervent believer, the first vision of his deity was from afar. Appointed page to the queen mother, he received from her a watch which he wore for the remainder of his life. Then, "at the spring review . . . and later at the autumn review I was at length permitted to have a glimpse of my most gracious master, King William I." Having successfully passed his initial examination for a commission—an examination in which many of his comrades failed—he, together with other lucky candidates, was personally presented to the monarch; and he does not omit an enthusiastic comment on this glorious moment. Bismarck, who in 1863 was the leading personality in Prussia, is ignored in Hindenburg's letters of that date. This silence shows how great was the Junkers' mistrust of their adventurous peer; and, in general, anything intellectual was looked upon by this caste as not in very good taste. In a letter to his younger brother, who was of a more studious and contemplative disposition than the elder, Hindenburg, then sixteen, wrote mockingly of his "learned studies. . . . Besides, I hope you will give up the idea of becoming a civil servant or a landlord, and prefer to throw in your lot with the military estate."

At this time, when he had become a monitor and thus placed in a position to command instead of to obey, one of his comrades described him in the friendliest spirit. "He was severe towards himself, kindly and good-natured towards those under him. The new-comers felt comfortable and sheltered under his guardianship. Such could not be said of all the monitors. Frequently, he closed his admonitions with the solemn reminder. 'You want to become an officer!' He was not in himself very humorous, but had an excellent appreciation of and understanding for a merry prank and a good joke. . . . He was permeated with a sense of the importance of his high calling."

Into the world of this seventeen-year-old stripling now came a roll of war drums; three of the older cadets went off to the Danish campaign and actually took part in the storming of the lines of Düppel. One of the lads sent his things back, and, in a letter home, Hindenburg adds: "The tunic he wore during the assault is now being worn by an N.C.O. as an object lesson kept continually before our eyes. Prince Charles told us that after the attack he asked a bombardier whether he was tired, and the man answered: 'How can I be tired when our officers are so brave and our young cadets so courageously run ahead of us!' By royal command all this is to be written up in our archives."

The fresh young innocence of this letter with its typical anecdotes of honorable deeds, courage, and the spirit of emulation, shows us the boy, Hindenburg, contemplating war from afar. Nor are we surprised that he should wish for another war to come speedily. He had not long to wait. Hardly had he turned his eighteenth year, and had tried on his new uniform at Neudeck, proudly strutting before his parents' gaze, when he was called up for active service—for this was the year 1866, and Bismarck had decided that Germans should shoot Germans on the battlefield. But before the campaign, Hindenburg had to go through a ceremony which can only be likened to the taking of the habit by a monk: he had to swear allegiance to his king.

This oath was an institution of recent date. The German tribes had never taken the military oath, because wars were carried on by volunteers, and the old-time mercenaries only swore in "for duration." Army officers and civil servants were not expected to swear obedience to king or emperor for a lifetime. Vows in perpetuity of loyalty and obedience were freely taken by those who wished; he who did not feel inclined to take them because his commander failed to suit his taste, could stay at home. Not until the empire had become disintegrated and many separate countries were set up and the sovereigns had forced their subjects into war service, so that there was no longer free contract between soldier and ruler, did the voluntary oath become a compulsory one, a "military oath" in the modern sense. An oath of loyalty to the monarch was invested by the priests with a solemn ritual, that soldiers might be intimidated against flight and desertion.

Hindenburg swore as follows: "I, Paul Ludwig Hans Anton von Beneckendorff und Hindenburg, hereby personally swear to God the Omniscient and Almighty that I will faithfully and loyally serve His Majesty the King of Prussia, my most gracious sovereign, on every occasion, on land or at sea, in war and peace, and at every place whatsoever: that I will further the All-Highest's best advantage, while averting from him injury and disadvantage; that I will closely abide by the articles of war, which have been read to me, and precisely obey the orders I receive; and that I will so conduct myself as becomes an upright, fearless, dutiful, and honorable soldier. So help me God through Jesus Christ and His Holy Gospel."

When he was eighty-five, Hindenburg spoke of this military oath to a visitor whose acquaintance we shall make anon. Having been brought up to a belief in the king, glowing with a sentiment of pride in his calling as officer and vassal, he endowed the ceremony with its full symbolical meaning, and never forgot what he had lived through during those moments.

In his old age he was destined to have a struggle of conscience over the oath he had taken with all the ardor of his youthful soul.

V

"I am glad when I think of the future, with its variety of experience and its movement; for a soldier, war is the normal condition of affairs; and, anyway, I am in God's hand. If I fall, my death will be of the most honorable kind; if merely wounded, I shall have to make the best of it; and if I return uninjured, all the better . . .

"If I were asked what were my feelings before the battle, I should say: first of all, a certain sense of pleasure that I was at last going to smell powder, followed by a disquieting nervousness lest so young a soldier might fail in his duty. But the sound of the first shots produced a feeling of elation (they were greeted with scattered cheers); I said a short prayer, gave a few thoughts to the dear ones at home and to the ancient name I bear, and then Forward March! The number of wounded caused my enthusiasm to wane, and to give place to cool-headedness, or, rather, to indifference in face of danger. One is not fully stirred until the fight is over, when one has more time to contemplate the ghastliness of war—but I do not wish to dwell upon this. . . . My aim on the battle-field has been achieved, I have been given a smell of powder, I have heard the bullets whistle by, bullets of every kind, shells, grapeshot. . . . I am slightly wounded, and am, therefore, an interesting person. I took five cannon!!! Etc., etc. Above all I have come to realize God's grace and lovingkindness; honor to Him for ever and ever, Amen!"

In these extracts from letters written by the gallant young officer during the campaigns of 1866 and 1870 he opens his heart to disclose faith and fatalism, sense of duty and pride of blood, delight in victory, and horror at sight of the dying. If we add to this self-revelation what he tells us of the battle of St. Privat, that he timed its important incidents watch in hand, and that he took delight in his first decoration (being now about to earn another), we get the picture of a thoroughly efficient officer whom no mistaken desire for smartness will lure into overstatement. The key-note is duty in the best sense of the term. How greatly he was urged onward by caste consciousness is revealed in a letter he wrote immediately after his first fight and when still a subaltern of eighteen: "It is high time that the Hindenburgs smelt powder once again. Our family, worse luck, has been greatly neglected in this respect." One reads between the lines that the youngster was still smarting from the dishonor brought upon the family name sixty years before by the cowardice of Major von Beneckendorff at Spandau.

When he was wounded at Königgratz, he wrote: "A bullet went clean through the eagle on my helmet, grazed my head without causing any serious damage, and passed out behind." The field marshal kept this

helmet on his worktable till the end of his days. Before
their son had left for the war, the parents had taken
the eagle off the helmet and had secreted a text from
the Bible behind it, and the devout father, who was
attached to an ambulance throughout the campaign,
wrote to his wife: "O God, what a rod of discipline is
the firebrand of war in Thy hand! Praised be Jesus
Christ that our beloved child has been so graciously
saved and has not had to enter that place where the
face of horror stares down on one and the tears of woe
have flowed so profusely and are destined to continue
to flow so long!"

Simultaneously with this letter from her husband,
Frau von Hindenburg read one from her son. "You
must be feeling very sore at the separation from dear
Father, but he has gone to perform a noble, knightly,
Christian duty. It is wonderful to reflect that the
wounds which the son causes may be healed by the
father—and yet both are fulfilling their duty."

An honest young officer, son of generations of officers,
might go so far, but no further, in his reflections upon
the absurdity of war morality. But having set forth
in one single sentence the whole of the paradox of the
Christian war ethic, can a lad of eighteen be expected
to go further, and penetrate to the heart of the conflict
between God's commands and those given by the
king, to set one up beside the other and to make his
choice? Hindenburg had in this letter already reached
the utmost limit of his powers of thought and feeling,
and will vainly endeavor, sixty years later, to reconcile
such antagonistic duties as those towards God and king,
or those towards people and king.

In the political sphere, too, the foundations of his

outlook were laid at this period when two campaigns led him along with the Prussian armies from victory to victory. In the first, the South German foe wore an armlet sporting the black-red-gold tricolor. Hatred for these colors, which his father and mother had instilled into his mind through their stories of the revolutionary epoch, must have filled his soul as he saw these same colors of revolution and democracy flaunted by the enemy. Now he was expected to kill men with whom, four years later, he would be marching shoulder to shoulder against France. After such an upbringing as he had received, this fratricidal war of German against German must have been as puzzling as was the contrast between the son who killed and the father who cured. His actions were guided by his king's commands; service was the law; duty was the order of the day, and remained the rule of his life.

While Hindenburg was in Versailles during the siege of Paris, Thomas Couture did a delightful little portrait of the handsome lieutenant, whose slender figure pleased the painter well; this picture was another of the treasures invariably found adorning the field marshal's worktable. It shows us a somewhat romantic-looking youth who had gained in manliness since the photos taken of him in earlier years, but as yet none of that rigid self-control which became so noticeable a decade later.

After Sedan he began to speak more like an habitué of battlefields: "I have to admit that the French fought bravely. . . . A curious feature of the engagement was that, since we were approaching from the northeast, we had to take care not to trespass on Belgian territory." Do we not foresee a moment when the fate of the German empire might have hung upon Hindenburg's endorsement of German trespass upon Belgian territory?

Four months later the young lieutenant stood in the Hall of Mirrors at Versailles, for he had been ordered to represent his regiment "at the coronation [*sic*] of the emperor. . . . At one o'clock court reception . . . and proclamation of emperor and empire, after which we were invited to dinner." On this occasion, too, Hindenburg's eyes and heart were wholly directed towards his king; and fifty years after, when writing his memoirs, he is absorbed in his enthusiasm for the king, whereas Bismarck's name again is conspicuous by its absence. How greatly the soldier in him took precedence over the politician is shown in his level-headed comments on Sedan and Versailles, circumstantial and without any phrase making; but when Paris surrendered, he suddenly gave vent to his feelings, writing to his parents, "Hurrah, Paris has capitulated!"

VI

He now wore two decorations, and had twice marched with victorious troops through the Brandenburg Gate. Chance had willed that he should rise quickly in the ranks of a profession which is known for its dilatoriness in promotion, thus avoiding the tension usually experienced by ambitious young military men. By the time he was twenty-three, Hindenburg was satiated with victories and visions of horror; for the remainder of his life he could no longer desire war. The heroic epoch of his career was over. Followed forty years of peace-time avocations, of study in the arts of war, of theory.

With all the more force of feeling and thought must he have reverted to the days of his youth as he grew older and broader in the beam. His fortunate escape from many battles must have strengthened his faith; and though his simple Protestant beliefs protected him from feeling he had been saved because he was intended to carry out a mission, still he could not fail to look upon himself as a lucky fellow and one predestined to success. As the wars of his youth were haloed by memory, it was natural that this man whose intelligence was by no means profound should come to feel that during the period in question his country had reached a climax both socially and politically. For him, the seventies had been Germany's apogee, and this conviction strengthened the natural conservatism of a Junker, to which was superadded the personal conservatism of one whose emotional life neither expected nor experienced intensification. He had seen the emperor of the French taken prisoner, had witnessed the capitulation of Paris, had watched his king become German emperor—all with his own eyes aglow with the ardor of youth. How could such a man be expected, after these beginnings, to recognize the dangers that were besetting the empire, or the corrupting influence of power and of money upon the officers' corps and upon the dynasty? For forty years his spiritual life circled (as the starry heavens circle round the polestar) round the day when he had been privileged to be one of the conquerors who rode into the capital of the hereditary foe.

How scanty his inner experiences during the four decades were is shown by the fact that no more than twenty pages of his memoirs are devoted to that

period. The king and the flag were the symbols in which his life of feeling found sufficient expression; and one may suppose that (like William himself) in the emperor he continued to revere the king, and in the German flag to honor the Prussian. Sober-minded old Prussia was the only country in the world which had a colorless flag—black and white, so correct, coldly juxtaposing night and day. Now a red streak had been added, the cunning Bismarck having explained to the king that this came from the red and white of the Brandenburgs, the Hansa States, and the Holsteiners. Hindenburg renewed his oath of fealty to the banner which had thus come into existence; but at heart he remained a Prussian, without foreseeing under what amazing circumstances he would be compelled sixty years later, in extreme old age, to take sides for the German realm and against Prussia.

The only notable event in his life during those forty years was his marriage at the age of thirty-two to a general's daughter. It brought him an abundance of happiness and content, and for nearly the whole of the four decades gave warmth to an existence in which the gray days of service were not adorned by friendship or travel or study. His temperamental tranquillity was confirmed and deepened by his conjugal experiences; and though, as he grew older, the physical traits of his blue-blooded paternal grandmother began to show themselves, especially in the development of his huge square skull, his expression bore witness to some degree of peasant shrewdness, which seems to have been a most useful heritage from his mother's petty-bourgeois ancestry.

In the routine of peace-time service which occupied

Hindenburg with his wife

thirty out of these forty years, Hindenburg had no
more opportunity of distinguishing himself than any
other officer in such piping times.   Although the
ordinary course of promotion made him a general, not
one of his biographers has been able to disinter a
document, an utterance, or a proposal which was
worth recording.   He did not impress anyone as being
a man of exceptional powers; yet we note that he is
never alluded to as having been supercilious or arrogant,
as were so many of his colleagues.   Indeed, he is
universally described as patient, good-natured, dispas-
sionate, and thoroughly efficient both as teacher and
organizer; as never undecided, because never nervous;
as always firm and simple, like a woodcut, as we see in
his portraits.   "The austerity of his nature," writes
one of his comrades, "was shown, not so much in his
words as in his way of holding himself and in his eyes,
which then assumed a peculiar harshness. . . . If, on
inspection days, the judgment of other chiefs had
seemed to him unduly severe, he would tone down the
criticism, or even say something to counteract it altogether."   His favorite horse, a light chestnut, was
named Patience.

Since he was never a mere routinist, but always
moved like a patriarch among his satellites just as if he
were dealing with his underlings upon the manor, he
could often be seen even as an elderly general putting
young recruits through their musketry drill, or lying
in the trenches side by side with his men showing them
how to take cover.   In matters of dress, however, he
was extremely severe; and if on a hot summer's day
there was any negligence in the adjustment of collar or
neckband, the offender would come in for a rough

reprimand, for such untidiness was contrary to army discipline. That he was deemed an excellent officer is shown by the fact that he was called upon to occupy one of the twenty-four highest posts in the army, for each of which there were always two candidates of the rank of lieutenant general. Such posts were given him in spite of the bourgeois streak which had come to him from the maternal side, though he had no money and no special patronage from the emperor, and never danced attendance upon court officials nor stooped to place hunting—for throughout life Hindenburg had little ambition, though much pride of caste.

In his middle fifties he became corps commandant in Magdeburg, and there his palace was guarded by two sentries and their boxes, such as he had wished long ago in his cadet days as ornaments for his knickknack shelf. His position was now so high that he took precedence even of the lord lieutenant of the province, and he acquired the habits and enjoyed the comforts of a great gentleman to the utmost capacity his superb health allowed. All this could not fail to be extremely gratifying to a man who delighted in his ancient lineage.

Under a young king, such high posts were by no means without danger to the holder, and Hindenburg's patience and calm in these strenuous circumstances became proverbial. For a Prussian general, the great imperial maneuvers were as exciting as a war; but he got through the most dreaded reviews with the utmost imperturbability, in spite of the capricious temper of his imperial master; he was able to take a nap on a hard chair in the midst of a noisy company, and to wake up at the appropriate moment refreshed and alert. Referring, in the course of a debate, to General

Bernhardi's long-drawn-out deductions, Hindenburg merely said: "Things don't happen that way in actual war." At mess, he would sit happily over his wine or a mug of beer, allowing and enjoying good jokes; but he never permitted filthy stories to be told in his presence, being too clean-minded to countenance such improprieties.

This monotonous career was enlivened by eight years on the General Staff, which was open only to officers of exceptional ability, the way being blocked by a series of difficult examinations. Hindenburg began preparing for these ordeals at the War Academy into which he had been accepted in 1873, and where he continued his studies until 1896. The course of study at this institution had just been thoroughly remodeled; the instruction in the art of war and tactics, the history of war, and military law being increased, whereas the history of literature was cut down by half, and philosophy was entirely expunged from the curriculum.

Concerning his years spent on the General Staff in Berlin (1885–1893), a dramatic and eventful period in German history, Hindenburg has so little to tell us that he is able to get it all, including some anecdotes, into four pages of his autobiography. He was no more interested in great statesmen and scholars—access to whose society was open to any officer on the General Staff—than in the lower orders. Bismarck, who was hated by the Junker caste, and who in the end fell from power through their influence, must have been as uncongenial to Hindenburg as he was to the latter's friends. Though it was owing to Bismarck's policy that the officers had been given a chance to unsheathe the sword, these circles chose to contest the fact or to ignore it; not the Iron Chancellor, but the sword, they held, was responsible for the foundation of the young empire, which in those days loomed so large in everyone's thoughts.

Bismarck was a regular reader of the *Kreuz-Zeitung*—as was Hindenburg himself until the age of sixty; Bismarck was suspect to the practicing Protestants because he had secularized the schools, and had introduced civil marriage and other ungodly liberal practices; Bismarck kotowed to parliament and had sanctioned popular participation in government. In addition, they were envious of this peer of theirs, in that he had been raised to the rank of prince and had acquired considerable wealth. Bismarck writes admirably concerning this Junker jealousy in his memoirs. Not a single member of the General Staff recognized how insecure the new realm was in case of war, for the monarchy was neither a constitutional nor an absolute one; it was nothing but a Bismarck-State, wherein the rights of the Hohenzollerns were hereditary, but unfortunately not Bismarck's outstanding endowments. None discerned that the realm had been set up by a dictator, and would have to share the fate of all dictatorships—decay after the death or downfall of the dictator—a fate which, in this case, was postponed for a quarter of a century by the mere chances of history.

The outlook of the General Staff was well expressed in 1909: "The Peace of Frankfort only in appearance brought the struggle between Germany and France to an end. Even though the weapons are lying on a shelf, a condition of latent war persists. One of the two opponents may discover a quicker-firing rifle, a longer-range gun, a more powerful high explosive . . .

but the other will cap these with an even quicker-firing rifle. . . . A State which desires to have a say in European and in world politics dares not remain far behind the two States which set the pace in these matters, and needs must keep the arming of its soldiers up to date."

These words were written by one of the ablest men of that generation, by Count Schlieffen, who was chief of the General Staff during Hindenburg's time of service on that body, and was in every point the antithesis of his predecessor, the elder Moltke. Hindenburg found Moltke, who was eighty-five years of age, a man to admire. The old fellow knew how to hold his tongue, which pleased the taciturn officer. There is but one cursory mention of Schlieffen in Hindenburg's memoirs; the reason being that, as is well known, Hindenburg had no liking for his brilliant and versatile chief.

Schlieffen, the very antipode of Hindenburg, was a grand seigneur; incisive, sarcastic, a man of the world, creative by temperament, ready of tongue and of pen; a type always disagreeable to the Germans, and to whom scope is only given because a spark of genius is indispensable even on a General Staff. "Before everyone who wants to rise to high command," wrote Schlieffen, "there lies a book entitled *The History of Warfare*. It begins with the duel between Cain and Abel, and is by no means finished with the storming of the Lisbon cloisters (the last event of military importance when Schlieffen was writing). I must admit that it is sometimes rather a dull subject of study, . . . but one acquires a knowledge of facts."

How could Hindenburg stomach such a man, who

used pretty phrases of this kind, and went on to insist: "A commander must have genius, . . . must feel the divine fire stirring within him. . . . 'No,' said Moltke, 'genius is hard work.' This is the perfectly reasonable utterance of a man who for sixty-five years toiled unceasingly, until, in the evening of his days, he had the chance to give the knock-out blow to two great powers."

To Hindenburg, insistence upon the need for divine fire was disagreeable. Strategic problems, which he had of course studied, did not come under his ken during the eight years on the General Staff. They concerned him only during maneuvers, and in connection with the war game, upon which, as troop leader, it was his duty to lecture. In Berlin his work was confined to technical details; and he describes as one of his "most stimulating tasks" the drafting of a Memorandum upon the Use of Heavy Artillery in Field Warfare.

VII

If, nevertheless, as a serious-minded officer of high rank, he was, like all his colleagues, much occupied in the study of the next war, Hindenburg, in the oral and written discussions that went on within the walls of the big red house on the Königsplatz, found that two problems were perpetually recurring, and seemed to monopolize the strategic thought of the General Staff. The first of these was—"Will attack, or defense, be preferable in the threatening war on two fronts?" Schlieffen was strongly in favor of the offensive.

"Take the offensive, like Alexander, Hannibal,

Julius Caesar, Gustavus Adolphus, Turenne, Eugene, and Frederick! Read and reread the history of their eighty-three campaigns; imitate their procedure: that is the only way to become a great military commander. . . . Do not look to half-successes, but to immense and crushing blows. No war should be long-drawn-out until one army's strength is exhausted by the other army. . . . Wars of attrition . . . are impossible in an epoch when the nation's very existence depends upon the continuous maintenance of commerce and industry. A quick decision will set a-going once more the wheels which have been brought to a standstill by the outbreak of hostilities. A strategy which aims at undermining the resistance of the enemy forces is unsuitable when supplies for millions of men demand the expenditure of billions." Thus, in the big red house, no one was troubling to study war-time economics or preparing for war eventualities.

The second problem which was occupying the minds of General-Staff officers was Schlieffen's idea of a war on two fronts which was to be decided in the West. Moltke's plan to occupy a defensive position against the French in the fortresses on the western frontiers of Germany, and meanwhile to make a big attack in the East from the right bank of the Vistula against the Russians, was turned the other way about by Schlieffen. Since the string of French fortifications prevented a direct advance, he wanted to see the issue decided by a battle on the large scale along the line of Verdun-Lille; therefore the right wing needed to be strengthened to the uttermost, whereas in Alsace four and one half brigades and in Lorraine only three and one half corps were to be left on guard. All the reserves of the Landsturm and other auxiliary troops were to be sent in support of the right wing, and thus an advance on Paris from the north could be successfully undertaken. Speed was of primary importance; three days more or three days less might be decisive for the issue of the war.

In order to accelerate the carrying out of this scheme, it would be necessary to march through Belgium and even through Holland. No German statesman of that date seemed to have a clear vision of the consequences. Bismarck had known very well that if Belgian neutrality were infringed, England would immediately resort to arms, but his successors seem to have forgotten that obvious fact. Was it through frivolous indifference or through arrogance that the General Staff failed to hold council with the political leaders in this matter? In those days, the dangerous axiom held good at the War Academy: Never must politics influence the conduct of military operations!

"In order to take the first step in the offensive against France," wrote Ludendorff in a secret memorial under date December 1912, "it will be necessary to infringe Belgian neutrality. Only if we advance over Belgian territory can we hope to attack the French armies in the open field and come out victorious. On this route we shall have the English expeditionary force to encounter, and the Belgian troops as well— unless, beforehand, we have been able to come to an understanding with Belgium. Nevertheless, such an operation is undoubtedly more full of promise than a frontal attack on the forts along the eastern frontiers of France. This latter method of onslaught would give the war the aspect of a siege; it would cost a lot of money; and would deprive our army of the impetus and initiative which we shall need all the more, the more numerous the foes we have to reckon with."

This extract, significant as it is even to the words "we have to reckon with," and which clearly demonstrates the fact that Germany knew that war with England was inevitable, should have led to a consultation between the emperor, the chancellor, and the General Staff. Nothing of the sort took place.

No blame could attach to the General Staff for this state of affairs. For whereas throughout the world, and even in Bavaria, the chief of the General Staff is subordinated to the War Office and thus to the government, and among the Entente powers from time to time was replaced, in Prussia he was responsible solely to the monarch. We shall learn in the sequel how this anomaly, which dated from the campaigns of Bismarck's day, led during the world war to the dictatorship of the High Command and thus decided the issue. At the outset of hostilities Bethmann-Hollweg, the chancellor, received the order "to take political measures according to the needs of the plan of campaign, which must be regarded as unalterable. . . . The civil government has not been consulted in its drafting." In a militarist State, war plans are fixed and unchangeable. Germany did not mobilize with due regard to the special form the enemy coalition had taken at the moment when hostilities were declared, for mobilization took place according to Schlieffen's plan which had been drawn up twenty years earlier.

Such a policy of aloofness elucidates the bumptiousness of the General Staff in Berlin; its scorn of "civilians," among whom the political leaders of the empire were included; and its contempt for international law.

What experts thought of the matter, even in the epoch of the German republic, is shown in the writings of a hundred-per-cent German professor (Johann Hohlfeld, 1926).   He argues that the march through Belgian territory was "a measure wholly independent of Belgium's behavior; . . . and Schlieffen even contemplated the possibility of infringing Dutch neutrality. The only valid excuse for this deed of violence would have been a prompt decision of the war. . . . The wrongdoing would have been accounted a virtuous act if the consequences had been a speedy success for German arms; in that case Germany's action would have been declared thoroughly justified by results."

Since this view secured the sanction of professors of law and history, it led to the invasion and occupation of Belgium with the approval of the German nation, which was indignant that King Albert, instead of yielding without a struggle, defied Emperor William in a letter that the Germans deemed arrogant, though history will speak of it as immortal.

VIII

It is universally found that the civilian population is looked upon with contempt by those who wear a military uniform, and that diplomatists are scorned by members of the General Staff.   Therefore, only by the exercise of intellectual courage is a civilian able to keep the men of war within bounds.   A commander despises the minister for foreign affairs, looking upon him as a kind of libretto writer able to compose a suitable text for elaboration; but if the text submitted appears inadequate, our military expert will proceed to alter it according to his tastes.

In Germany this natural antagonism arises from an antithesis between mind and State which has led to the cleavage of Germany into two camps—a cleavage which may be traced through four hundred years, from Erasmus to Freud.   The aloofness of the German burgherdom from politics, which before our very eyes has led first to the disruption of the empire and then to the collapse of the Republic, is not the upshot of an innate lack of political instinct on the part of Germans. They are just as well endowed in this respect as are other, more politically active, peoples.   This aloofness can be charged to the fact that their political faculties have been palsied through centuries of disuse.   The dominance of militarism is the tragical result of an agelong estrangement of the Prussian princes from their subjects, and of the concomitant estrangement of the circles which hedge the royal power about.   If the monarch bestows the highest posts in army and State upon his Junkers because he distrusts the free burghers, and if this process continues a couple of hundred years, the burgher very naturally washes his hands of State affairs, gets absorbed in business, art, handicraft, and science, and leaves those on the seats of the mighty to continue in command while he himself is quite satisfied to be freed from all responsibility.

How can it be expected that the bourgeoisie can persist in fighting for its rights when it is uninterruptedly looked at askance by the superior classes?   Of course it will prefer to lead a quiet life—until war comes to disturb it!   Moreover, are we entitled to be surprised at the increasing arrogance of a ruling aristocracy so long as its military knowledge is guarded like some secret chemical process which is beyond the powers of a layman to understand? Up till the great war, not even the historians in Germany troubled to learn something of the science of war, and although in this militarized State everyone expected a war in which the life of his sons would be staked, people were content to leave to the military caste the care and the disposal of the instrument of war.

With distrust not untinged with admiration, the bourgeois representatives gazed at the building surrounded by sentries wherein was housed the General Staff, while the military gentlemen looked with scornful distrust upon the Reichstag over the way where the deputies never voted the army a sufficiency of troops. The minister for war, who in other countries makes his appearance in parliament wearing civilian dress if he has to vindicate any of his actions, in Berlin came with spurs clinking and with challenging mien, and was regarded with stealthy approval by those who had ventured to oppose him. Three months before the war, Falkenhayn, who was war minister at the time, uttered the following drastic words from the rostrum of the Reichstag: "If cultural progress signifies that we can no longer count upon our army in case of war, culture may go to the deuce for all I care." Twenty years later these words were re-echoed under the auspices of the Third Realm: "Whenever I hear the word *culture*, I release the safety catch of my automatic!"

The general in command was but a step lower. From one year's end to the other, this functionary inspected troops, prepared for maneuvers, played the leader in mimic warfare, organized for mobilization, with visible and overweening pride, with the

gesture of a condescending superior to the lord lieutenant of the province who was the civilian ruler of
practically the same area. Continuing downwards in
the hierarchy, we find at the base of the pyramid the
captain contraposed to the professor, the former taking
precedence in social functions, while a lieutenant was
the darling of the girls, just as nowadays is a male
film star. Men of international renown would en-
hance their social status by having printed on their
visiting cards after their name "Leutnant der Reserve,"
and even the ablest head harbored modest visions of
some day winning an order or a decoration.

And yet there were men of exceptional talent who
might have pointed to new paths. Field Marshal
Moltke was for many years in the East, studying and
lecturing, was an expert at archaeological excavations,
wrote imaginative works; General von Podbielski was
a deputy and minister for agriculture; Haushofer had
himself transferred to Japan, and subsequently became
a professor of geography; von der Goltz carried on
successful labors in Turkey; others participated in the
Chinese campaign; others, again, embarked for the
colonies in order to share in war experience there;
while yet others had posts in the German embassies
abroad. Their comrades cracked jokes at their
expense at mess. The typical Prussian general is far
better represented by Hindenburg than by all these
fish-out-of-water men.

"We are simple soldiers," he wrote, "who do not
vent their feelings in many and racy words. I am not
a writer; for literature and commandership are two
fundamentally different things. As a rule talent for
one does not imply talent for the other, nor should

the two talents be combined in the same person. There is an essential difference between word and deed. A valiant deed is now as heretofore more to be esteemed than any of the subtleties of the intellect. Presence of mind and firmness of character hold a higher place in the warlike arts than any delicate perceptions of the intellect."

Such expressions, showing us far into the inner nature of the writer, show us a man who was born and bred, as he himself recognizes, to fill a secondary rôle; a man who gave his services and did his duty single-heartedly; who, in his own words, lacked the main ingredients for creative activity. It is childish to talk about great soldiers as simple men in whom brains and eloquence play a minor part. The history of great commanders plainly shows that courage and resolution are not enough, since intelligence and the power of logical thought, eloquence and imagination, comprise half the personality, and usually more.

Thanks to so unimaginative an education and such unimaginative aims, there resulted for Hindenburg, as for almost all his colleagues, a political outlook which made them interpret (and therefore misinterpret) the complicated modern State after the manner of a so-called "simple" soldier—that is to say, after the manner of an autocrat, of a martinet.

The main essential was to despise the civilian who, being looked upon as the getter of money and the possessor of brains (there seemed to be very little difference between the twin functions to the military mind), must be kept at all costs from any post of importance in the army. Although no bourgeois could dream of becoming an officer in the Guards and no socialist could become even so much as a night-watch-man, no one ever thought of the possibility that if the old regiments were decimated through battles on a giant scale, the Landwehr officer who came to fill the vacant place would be such a bourgeois or even a socialist. Although it was solely in private conversation that he ventured to speak so openly, Bismarck, as an old man, was the only Junker who foresaw that, should the Germans suffer a defeat in war, the establishment of a republic was inevitable. He even mentioned by name the three parties which thirty years later were to found this republic. While, during Bismarck's supremacy, more than a thousand years of detention and imprisonment were meted out to socialists at one time and another for political offenses; while, moreover, under William II the franchise was widened so that the extent of the electorate increased from one and half million voters to four and a half; concomitantly with this growth in the electorate, the hatred of the Junker caste and of the generals for the laboring masses very naturally increased likewise, since the customary, traditional, and patriarchal methods no longer worked. The General Staff set its hopes upon the wholesome political and moral influence of the three years' service to bring the common man to heel; and so far as the upper classes were concerned, they could always rely upon the superlative training at the cadet academies to produce the proper sort of officer.

Although the income from the Junkers' estates was steadily diminishing because the owners never dreamed of introducing modern implements and methods of production to compete with new agricultural areas in the Americas, they comforted their souls by repeating, "soldiers alone are capable of dealing with democrats," forgetting completely that many of the soldiers in a conscripted army were necessarily democrats and socialists. A county councilor, himself an officer in the reserve and a brother or a cousin of officers, could be counted on to bring "his" peasants to vote as they should. If they refused to be guided, there were other ways of keeping an eye on them. The only circles of civilians that the General Staff could tolerate, and, on occasion even mix with, were the barons of heavy industry, since these were responsible for the manufacture of war material. Under William II, indeed, marriages were arranged between the offspring of these magnates and members of the officer caste, so that there ensued a diminution in the haughty aloofness which for generations had been the prerogative of the poverty-stricken Junkerdom. Hindenburg did not err when he wrote, "In those days, the Prussian officers' corps was not blessed with worldly goods—and that was an excellent thing. Its wealth consisted in its frugality."

Hindenburg, whether on his hereditary estates or in his companies or in his divisions, had never driven or sweated those beneath him; but he nonetheless held fast to the patriarchal foundations of the philosophy of life prevalent at the date of his birth, and further consolidated by family tradition and the experiences of his youth—following the ninety years' example set him by his first king and master. But when, after the brief reign of Frederick (a man of lofty character, with whom, however, Hindenburg had little in common), the first William's grandson, arrogant and neurotic, came to the throne, Hindenburg and his colleagues were quick to recognize the danger. None were so quick to recognize the danger constituted by the character of young William as was the General Staff. It should be particularly noted that in the memoirs written by members of the Staff, and most clearly of all in those of Field Marshal Waldersee who was chief of General Staff at the time, the thought of getting William declared incapable of managing public affairs found far more drastic expression than in the writings of the bourgeoisie or the socialists.

Nevertheless the sense of kingship was so deeply imbedded in these men's hearts that it was precisely they whom Bismarck had to fear when for a moment he toyed with the notion of playing the part of a Pepin ousting the Merovingian dynasty. But William was stronger than Bismarck, for he was backed by the sturdy "kingship idea" which reigned supreme in the cadet academies; and the chancellor, a very old man, assured his monarch in one of the last interviews they were to have together: "So long as the officers' corps remains loyal, Your Majesty can continue to reign in all tranquillity."

Hindenburg found it impossible to harbor any such thoughts. As page he had kissed Queen Elisabeth's hand; as stripling he had hailed his king as emperor; and when William I died, Hindenburg, then a man of forty, had been chosen to form part of the guard of honor that kept vigil over the body. On this occasion his feelings were so strong that he begged to be given a block of gray marble, part of the paving in the cathedral upon which the coffin of his beloved master had rested. This piece of stone was always to be found on his writing table, a pendant to the perforated helmet.

e

William II wholeheartedly reciprocated Hindenburg's dislike.   It was not to be expected that a nerve-ridden, restless, theatrical creature could appreciate a quiet, limpid, and simple nature such as Hindenburg possessed.   Just as the field marshal found William's histrionic logorrhea unbearably irksome, so was the latter, a man with a crippled arm, irritated at sight of the hale and mighty form of Hindenburg.   According to William, sentries alone had any right to be of an outsize among men—like that Potsdam grenadier of long ago who had served the emperor's ancestors and from whom the field marshal had inherited his magnificent proportions.   Yet in spite of innate aversion, Hindenburg's sentiment for kingship and the memory of his oath of allegiance kept him clear of such dark thoughts as were occupying the minds of Waldersee and his friends.

IX

Which was more out of touch with the commonalty, the king or his officers?   William II, who possessed both nationalist ambitions and socialist sympathies, and therefore in the end fell between two stools, had hazy notions about sultans who visited the huts of their poorest subjects and strewed pieces of gold as they departed; but if one of the hut's occupants murmured a complaint, the royal benefactor would like to have the rascal shot.   The officers made mock of these eccentricities which were so typical of the weakling, laid hands on their sword hilts, and prayed to the God who had created iron.   The old-time relations between king and Junker were resumed: the officers' corps protected the king while the king went in fear and trembling of his officers, and he curbed his initial popular leanings, since he felt secure only within the shadow of the guns. During the ceremony of taking the military oath, the emperor addressed his troops as follows:

"A soldier must have no will of his own; you must all be animated by one will, and that is my will. . . . Perhaps, during the present socialistic agitation, I may have to order you to shoot down your own relatives, your brothers, nay, maybe your parents—which I hope to God may never be. But even so, you are obliged to carry out my orders without protest."

Not a voice in the officers' corps was raised, be it never so softly, and not even in the most intimate circle of comrades, against these words, spoken in imitation of the Roi Soleil nearly two hundred years after he was dust and ashes. Was it not, rather, that the Kaiser, who by nature was feeble and fearful, was trying to impress his own officers by the use of strong words? Who else, indeed, was there whom a Prussian ruler needed to fear? Soldiers, not the arts and sciences, had built up Prussian greatness. It was not by chance that, among the most musical people in the whole world, the spirit of music should wilt and wane the farther north she traveled in the German realm, whereas quite the opposite phenomenon took place in the case of the war spirit. To the north belonged the drum, and Bernhardi was voicing the temper of the General Staff when in his book he declared war to be "the highest expression of true culture." Germania's ear had long since grown accustomed to this tone, so that she did not hear it any longer; but the world was alarmed when, a few months prior to the outbreak

of hostilities, it suddenly reëchoed throughout the
land.

In Zabern, a small garrison town in Alsace, a twenty-
year-old lieutenant, a Junker, railed at certain recruits
and offered a reward for the cutting down of every
disobedient Alsatian.   As soon as this was bruited
abroad, schoolboys would lie in wait for the young
gentleman and would jibe at him and tease him to
such an extent that in the end he could not walk
about the town unless accompanied by soldiers.   Naturally the school children found the guard of armed men
intensely ludicrous.   Thereupon his colonel, also a Junker, detailed fifty men with fixed bayonets and ball cart-
ridges to parade the streets.   The crowd of infuriated
civilians grew apace, especially after he had stated that
he hoped blood would flow.   Those who ventured to
laugh were arrested and locked in the barracks coal
cellar until the following day, when they were had up
for trial.   Among the prisoners was the public prose-
cutor himself.   Since the boys with their young and
nimble legs were always able to elude their pursuers,
it so fell out that the armed emissaries of the worthy
colonel bagged a crippled shoemaker, whom the lieutenant wounded so severely on the head with his naked
sword that the man fell to earth in a swoon.

When these events became generally known, excitement rose even higher, and the supreme military
authorities felt that they must take a hand in the game
"in order to teach the civilian rabble respect, and to
show how slack was the civilian government in Alsace."
The Junker colonel was told publicly to praise the
activities of the young lieutenant, the Junker general
publicly praised the colonel, the Junker War Minister

publicly praised the general. This so infuriated the Reichstag that, for the first time in German history, a vote of no confidence was passed against the chancellor and the war minister. Thereupon the emperor openly declared his confidence in these two officials. In the columns of the *Kreuz-Zeitung* the Junker Chief of Police announced that the officers responsible for the affair were legally exonerated from all guilt. In the subsequent court-martial the officers were set at liberty without further ado; while the three recruits, who had meanwhile chattered about the lieutenant's promised reward, were placed under arrest, and the governor of Alsace was dismissed his post.

Against all the rules of the theater, this farce was played before instead of after the tragedy of the war: a State philosopher might have recognized therein the elements which went to bringing about the final collapse. The Zabern incident showed the mentality of the officers' corps to be anachronistic, and so remote from any understanding of the people that its dominance in the State could not go unpunished. Since such were the thoughts of the German military command, how was any mutual understanding possible between the private in the trenches and his officer? What could be expected when men who had approved the ruling of a court-martial in the matter of those obstreperous officers now took over the government of a huge population at war and beset on all sides by manifold dangers? War Minister von Falkenhayn's conduct in the affair won for him the special favor of his emperor; and, had it not been for "Zabern," he would not have been raised in the course of the next few months to the position of head of the military command.

X

During this period, Hindenburg was no longer on the active list. For four decades, whenever he had had a vacation, he had gone for refreshment to Neudeck, where first his parents lived, and then his remoter kin. The manor house had been further enlarged, windows let into the gables; and the adjoining estate of Langenau had come to the family by marriage. But the more house was added to house and field to field upon this and other estates eastward of the Elbe, the more did things get in a bad way. As the knowledge of agriculture and the willingness to give time and trouble to it declined among the Junkers, the amount of mortgages grew, and visits to Berlin were of longer duration. By swank, by social amenities, and by making "good marriages," they tried to do on the grand scale what had been done before on a small one by shrewd marketing of their harvests. A cousin on the county council must pull strings to get the land taxes reduced. Any member of the family who had gone into the Church must play the same game with the tithes. The youngsters were sent to the Military Academy. Just as in the great domain of the empire, under William II, German power was being undermined (though few German statesmen were aware of the fact); so, in lesser domains, the Prussian landed estates were decaying through lack of initiative, industry, and knowledge.

Hindenburg, being merely a guest at Neudeck, had no concern with these matters. How did this soldier, this slave to duty, prefer to pass his time during vacation? Only in his brother's memoirs do we find references to the beauties of nature. Hindenburg's chief amusement was to play at soldiers with the children. When his

small son was still an infant in arms, the father lifted
him high in the air and said: "Little man, I am already
looking forward to the time when I shall sit beside you
at the camp fire in a war against the Russians!"
This anecdote, recorded by the brother, shows us a
soldier who always thought of himself as a military
commander, a hunter, and a scout; who wanted to
carry on war in the old style, with the rain beating
down on him and the wind whistling round his ears.
During the siege of Paris, doubtless war had still been
conducted in some such fashion. A dozen years later,
when he was playing with the boy, the romance of war
was on the wane, and when, later still, as General-Staff
officer, he was elaborating his monograph on the use
of heavy artillery in field warfare, there must have
been more talk of electric priming than of camp fires.
Old Blücher, the swashbuckler, whose picture hung on
the wall beside Hindenburg's writing table, was more
congenial to him than Gneisenau, so that the best thing
that could be wished for him and for his country was
that Blücher's mantle should fall upon his shoulders.

The brother records that, at Neudeck, when the
children (two girls and a boy) grew older, they had to
load a cart with stones and do "field service." "Of
course the enemy had improvised obstacles. At the
entrance to the wood stood an isolated birch tree,
regarded as an outpost. In times when the war game
was not being played, this tree was styled 'the forest's
janitor.' . . . But in war time it was an enemy post.
Hindenburg's little son was ordered to make sure
that the building materials were delivered without
hindrance.

"'Herr Leutnant, you will ride in advance, take

note of the morasses along the route, discover the best
way of getting past them, await our arrival, and then
report to me.' Highly honored by the commission,
the child straddled a stick and 'rode' off to fulfil it. . . .
The enemy was outmaneuvered, and thereafter the
hostile position was once more a peaceful tree."

In this lively episode, which has the ring of one
of Schumann's *Forest Scenes*, we can recognize Hindenburg's soldierly nature more plainly than in the speeches
of a later date. The same tone echoed in the words
with which he announced his retirement to his son,
now a grown man: "Have just retired, but am
retained *à la suite* of the Third Regiment of Foot
Guards. His Majesty has graciously bestowed on me
the distinguished Order of the Black Eagle. May this
come your way too! Warmest greetings! Father."

This communication, written on a post card at the
close of a successful career in which he had done better
than he had expected, displays a calm and resolute
mingling of modesty and pride. No ambition is voiced,
and no wish is expressed. The message simply announces the close of a forty-five-year term of service
on the part of a man of sixty-four, still enjoying robust
health, who is leaving one of the highest posts in the
army almost without a backward glance.

At that time, three years before the war, Hindenburg
was not appointed army inspector, although there were
six army inspectors, and the usual practice had been to
give this titular rank to commanding generals on retirement; nor was he instructed to regard himself as one of
the army leaders in the event of war. Still more remarkable is it that he was first gazetted as leader of a
reserve corps in the event of war, and that then the

Hindenburg on an elk hunt in Courland, 1915

appointment was canceled. No matter whether this happened because he was not regarded as efficient or because of the emperor's personal antipathy, the cancellation was a slight to a healthy and capable man, and it left him justly embittered.

As a haven of rest, the general chose Hanover, perhaps the quietest among the chief towns of Prussia— a place where he had served for a time as lieutenant. The only foreign trip, campaigning apart, he made in his whole life, was to Italy when he was sixty-five. Otherwise, his sole pleasure was shooting.

Not being well enough off for the more expensive forms of this sport, he had brought down his first stag when he was sixty years of age. Now, since he was a man of distinction, the landed magnates in the vicinity of Hanover made him free of their estates, and he soon became known as an excellent shot. His record from 1904 to 1924 shows that, in addition to minor game, he shot 104 wild boars, 76 roebuck, 27 red deer, 24 does, 6 black cock, 6 chamois, and, further, during the war, one bison and one elk. His game book and the trophies on the walls of his house meant as much to him as sleeping and eating; they were the only true delights of a man full of life and vigor, whose professional duties had drawn to a close.

It is strange to note that, while his memoirs contain detailed reports of his shooting trips, there is no mention of a dog, a horse, a tree, or the glory of a dawn— matters often alluded to in Bismarck's letters to his wife.

In his massive repose, he spent his time (when not out shooting) in the old Prussian city, reading the newspapers, keeping track of his cousins' and his friends' promotions, and fretting over the emperor's speeches. His son had become a cadet, and then an officer in his father's old regiment; his daughters were married off to Junkers; the family estate was in a bad way, but was still the family estate.   His was a long-lived line.   He and his wife were in excellent health.   He might look forward to twenty years of tranquillity in his Hanoverian home.

The last thing Hindenburg anticipated, still less wanted, during these three years, was the coming of war.

BOOK TWO

THE WAR FLAG

In war, one plays the bold, the destructive, and then, by turns, the gentle, the restorative rôle; one accustoms oneself to use phrases which will arouse hope in the heart and will invigorate the mind amid the most desperate circumstances. Thus arises a kind of hypocrisy which has a character all its own, differing completely from ecclesiastical hypocrisy, courtly hypocrisy, or any other form of hypocrisy you please to mention.

—GOETHE

THE WAR FLAG

I

EXCITEMENT PREVAILED at the German General Headquarters in Coblenz. News had come to hand that the North-eastern Army was withdrawing across the Vistula. East Prussia was to be abandoned to the invading Russians. The date was August 21, 1914. The army commander, General von Prittwitz und Gaffron had, the day before, been driven back by the enemy's First Army, and was simultaneously threatened by a flank attack from the Second Army. These tidings of retreat in the East were serious, but Schlieffen's plans allowed for such possibilities. After all, the decisive issue was to be fought out in the West against France even at the risk of Russian invasion in the East. Since the German armies in the West were still advancing as planned, there was no reason for panic.

But at the head of the German armies were two neurasthenics, William II and Count Moltke. They were being harassed by East-Prussian Junkers who had been compelled during the last three weeks to abandon portions of their province and of their estates forthwith to the enemy. At the same time, persons who were unfriendly to General von Prittwitz were busy convincing the emperor that this commander was incompetent; and William, like most princes, was more interested in persons than in facts. Since, to those whose hopes outstripped events, the game seemed already won in the West, pride and fear (the two main elements of

the neurotic character) made the emperor and the
commander in chief decide upon the immediate transfer of two army corps and one cavalry division from
the West to the East. They did this to strengthen the
eastern front, although, according to the general plan
of campaign, that was not the place where a decision
was to be sought, and the maneuver would weaken
the all-important western front.

The measure was premature, and the excitement ex-
aggerated, for General von Prittwitz had not yet absolutely decided to withdraw across the Vistula. Telephonic communication is more open to misinterpreta-
tion than telegraphic. Prittwitz had merely wished
to convey that he might be compelled to withdraw.
But since one unduly nervous man is likely to in-
fect another with his fears, Moltke got the impression
that retreat was unavoidable; and it indeed was in a
panicky moment that he had called up the commander
of the Eastern Front from Coblenz.

During the next few hours, the position of the army
in the East changed; or, at any rate, there was a change
in the commander's views as to its position. What
had happened? The trouble had begun through a dispute between the commander in chief and one of his
generals. The war which the German nation had entered into strong of heart, and convinced that it was
fighting in a just cause, began, as far as the leadership
was concerned, with disobedience in the East and with
an attack of nerves in the West. Reports and memoirs
concerning this war have much to say about nervousness, both as regards friends and foes. This is the
way in which mechanized warfare takes vengeance
upon the men whom mechanism has deposed. Hin-

denburg remained the only commanding officer in Europe who had no nerves.

The Russian forces, compelled by the Masurian Lakes, to march up with one army to the north of them and the other to the south of them, could only be attacked separately. General François, however (in this "war of the nations," as it was supposed to be, the German general had a French name, and the Russian Rennenkampf a German one), did not approve of his chief's plan, and preferred, on his own initiative, to strike with his army corps at the Lakes, in order to protect Königsberg, without reporting his intention to headquarters; whereas Prittwitz made for the Russian army whose headquarters were at Vilna.

While the second in command was discontinuing his successful but prohibited advance, the commander in chief was informed that the other Russian Army, that of Warsaw, with a strength of from four to five army corps, had crossed the German frontier.

The strongest personality on the eastern front, as far as the Germans were concerned, was neither Baron von Prittwitz nor his chief, but General Hoffmann (then no more than a lieutenant colonel). What was Hoffmann's first thought on receipt of the alarming news? To humbug his commanding officer? "I was afraid that the message would be too much for the nerves of the commander and for those of his chief of general staff." Those fatal nerves!

But it was too late. Prittwitz had already received the news, and had promptly decided, or been on the point of deciding(?), since he was now afraid of being attacked in the rear, to withdraw his army across the

Vistula, and he announced this intention when Moltke telephoned to him from Coblenz. Hoffmann opposed the notion, showing his chief, with the aid of a map and a pair of compasses that it would be necessary to fight before the army could withdraw across the Vistula, since the left wing of the Warsaw army was nearer that river than the Germans. The Warsaw army must be held up by an offensive against its left wing. "Prittwitz, who, like Waldersee, had lost his nerve for the moment"—this is what Hoffmann wrote about the matter later—"saw the necessity for the measures we proposed. He still remained of opinion that the attack on Rennenkampf must be called off; but abandoned his idea of withdrawing across the Vistula, and acceded to our opinion that the best thing would be to lead an offensive against the left wing of the Warsaw army. Owing to this change of views, on the evening of the 20th orders were issued which led to the battle of Tannenberg. Matters were now in train."

This turn of events, which, by universal consent, took place exactly as above described, was of supreme historical importance. Owing to the fit of nervousness from which the commander on the eastern front suffered, and owing to his report to the nervous commander in chief at General Headquarters, there was a change in the supreme command on the Vistula, and two new generals were sent thither whose employment there and under such conditions had not been provided for in the German plan of campaign. Since these two generals were in due course to decide the political future of the country as well, the fate of Germany was settled by the course of events in the East three weeks before the Battle of the Marne.

For when Prittwitz now telephoned to Coblenz that he had changed his mind and would give battle to the Russians, the emperor had already decided to depose him from command. William's agitation was shown by the bluntness of his procedure. Prittwitz's second decision, following the first within a few hours, was simply pushed aside. On August 22, a wire was sent cashiering the commander on the eastern front and his second, and informing them that their successors would arrive next morning by special train. Who were the successors?

The first officer, who had come upon the scene earlier in August, was a major general who had, when still quite a young man, shown exceptional capacity as a strategist in charge of the operation section of the general staff. Such officers who were adepts with the pen and a pair of compasses were, at the beginning of the war, naturally eager to show themselves equally competent with the "sword." Since the German coup at Liége was already in a bad way, this General Staff officer skilled in the use of maps and telephones attached himself "as onlooker" to one of the columns which was marching on the Belgian fortress. When the commander of this brigade fell, Ludendorff took over the leadership and stormed the principal fort. It was a personal victory such as later in this war was possible only to aviators or the commanders of submarines. The name of Ludendorff was in the mouths of all Germans when reports from the front extolled the brave officer who was nearing fifty, and announced that the emperor had conferred on him the order *Pour le Mérite.* The conspicuousness of his deed, its romantic character, which fitted it for rela-

7

tion in schoolbooks, and the glory of being the first in war to win this much coveted order, gave him a popularity but for which he would scarcely have been called to high command, being suspect as son of a bourgeois father and able to boast noble blood only on the maternal side.   However, Moltke now appointed him successor of the cashiered Count Waldersee.

A few hours after his appointment in the town beside the Rhine, Ludendorff was studying the map of East Prussia, measuring, combining, adding. Since he knew nothing of the new orders issued by his predecessor, he decided, after his own manner, to continue the campaign he was to lead on the morrow much as an orchestral conductor, replacing another, might take charge of an unfamiliar score.

The question arose at Coblenz whom this trained strategist should be given as army commander. The relationship between two such men in the German army is denoted by their respective titles. The senior, the commander in chief, calls his subordinate his "chief," since the latter is "chief of general staff." Thus such a pair enter history after the fashion of a married couple at a reception. The lady goes first, has all the honors, is more splendidly dressed; but her husband, who follows in her train, really has the deciding voice, since he wields money and power. She holds a representative position, sits on the right, is served first; he walks in the second place with the confident tread of one who settles every issue, and is glad to know that she will be responsible to society if anything fails to "click."

Exceptionally intimate knowledge of human nature is therefore requisite to choose a strategic couple for such wedlock as we are now contemplating. The couple for service on the eastern front had been selected long before the war; but, now that they were cashiered, a fresh union had to be improvised within a few hours, since the new men had to start eastward forthwith. "General Ludendorff is an extremely capricious person," said Moltke and the emperor to themselves. "Whom can we best appoint to serve with him?" Since there was no time for the development of an acquaintance, since marriage was to follow directly upon betrothal, the risk was all the greater, and safety could only be found by the selection of a man with a tranquil temperament.

Well, the minds of those with whom the decision lay both turned toward one whose handwriting was before them. A few days earlier, General von Stein had received the following letter: "One request. Don't forget me, if, as things develop, a commanding officer is needed anywhere! Both in body and mind I am robust, and was therefore considered for active employment last autumn, although I am on the retired list. You can imagine to yourself what my feelings were when I saw men of my own age going to the front while I had to sit at home twiddling my thumbs. I am ashamed to show my face in the street . . . Von Beneckendorff und Hindenburg."

This was the veteran Hindenburg, famed for his imperturbability. He had lived a very long time in the eastern provinces, devoting far more attention to administrative matters than to style; so much the better, for he would be the less likely to vex his quick-witted and talented chief. Besides, his distinguished name would serve as cover for the bourgeois deficiencies of the other. Above all, "nerves" never troubled him whatever happened. This letter of his had brought him to mind, as the Liége affair had brought Ludendorff to mind. "Let's try old Hindenburg!" A wire was sent to Hanover to ask if he was willing.

The old general, since the outbreak of the war, had sat at home reading the newspapers, without knowing whether to be more pleased or annoyed. According to the reports, during these first three weeks things had gone well, but they had gone well without his having a finger in the pie. Was he at sixty-seven too old to be of any more use? Had he not dreamed of sitting at the camp fire in a war against the Russians with his son by his side? Now his son and his sons-in-law were at the front, smelling powder, taking enemy guns, perhaps soon would win decorations. Was it really hard upon fifty years since he had taken enemy guns at Königgratz? The old helmet with bullet holes in it was within range of his eyes, and recalled the legend of his youth.

Among the generals mentioned in dispatches from the front, were many men younger than himself. What crime had he committed that, last year, his name had been struck from the list of those available for active service in the event of war? Every time he moved a little flag forward on his map of the fighting front, he could not but sigh that he was only playing a game, like the war game he had so often played when still in service. Now, when at length a stupendous reality might have crowned the labors of a lifetime, he had been shouldered aside like an elderly actor, who must look on from the stage box, while a novice is acting the part he had been wont to act, and, moreover, probably playing it badly! Not once had the authorities thought proper even to let him know how his Memorandum on the Use of Heavy Artillery, to which he had devoted the best years of his life, was standing the test of war experience!

On August 22, at three o'clock in the afternoon, when he was sitting over his coffee in this disgruntled mood, a wire was brought him, the red line on the envelope showing that it was an official message. Was he willing? He called his wife, showed her the telegram, and wired back, "Am ready." The household was greatly excited. What was in the wind? To which front was Father being sent? On what mission? Where was his field uniform? Was there plenty of woolen underclothing? Great bustle and confusion! The telegraph messenger came three times more. Second wire: "Major General Ludendorff will fetch you tomorrow morning by special train." Third wire: "You are to command the Eighth Army on the eastern front." Fourth wire: "The special train will pass through Hanover station at three o'clock in the morning."

Excitement grew. It was not a reserve corps he was to command, not an army corps at all, but a whole army! He had never dreamed of anything so big as this! In the East, too, his native province! Prittwitz, whom he was to supersede, was his wife's cousin! What sort of fellow was this Ludendorff, his new chief, of whom he had heard, indeed, but whom he had never seen in the flesh? They hadn't summoned him to G.H.Q. at Coblenz, but had instructed him to be on the platform at Hanover and to get into the special train for the East. That meant that a battle was raging. He had no general's field uniform, so he had to wear black trousers and a loose gray fatigue-blouse. He said good-by to his wife, and told her not to be afraid, for the commander of an army was never in the firing line. At three o'clock in the morning, the special train steamed in. It consisted of two carriages, the front one being rigged up as a map room. Out of the other stepped the younger general, who saluted and gave his name. Instantly the train resumed its journey.

In the carriage, the pair began to talk matters over. For thirty hours, Ludendorff had been kept informed about the situation in the East and the progress of the battle there, whereas Hindenburg had to be given the news. Thus, from the outset, the situation between the two men was a topsy-turvy one. "To begin with," writes Hindenburg, "he explained to me the situation of the eastern front. . . . Before long I and my new chief of staff were at one in our view of the situation. Before leaving Coblenz, General Ludendorff had been able to issue the first, essential orders, designed to secure the continuance of operations on the farther side of the Vistula. Everything else had to be, and could be, postponed until we reached headquarters at Marienburg. Our talk cannot have lasted much more than half an hour. Then we betook ourselves to rest, and I made the best possible use of my opportunity for this. Thus we traveled together towards a joint future. . . . For years, thenceforward, we were to be united by joint thoughts and joint actions."

This first deliberation was but a prelude to similar

ones which went on from day to day throughout four years. Ludendorff had studied and prepared everything; he put his views before Hindenburg, who approved them in the course of half an hour. The man's iron nerve enabled him, during the four troubled years that ensued, to sleep peacefully no matter how eventful the day, just as on this occasion.

Next morning (the men they were to supersede had already departed crestfallen) the new commanders found a much more favorable situation than they had anticipated. The plans of Hoffmann, which had already to some extent been put into execution, and had been amplified by Ludendorff's telegram from Coblenz, were reconsidered and endorsed; and were carried out on the 23rd, on the lines arranged after the panic of the 21st had been overcome. When, on the 24th, one of the divisions of the German right wing, hard pressed by the Warsaw Army, retired into a more favorable position, this partial retreat was "of decisive importance to the subsequent progress of the battle." For now the Russians believed the Germans to be in retreat all along the line. Their orders to follow up this supposed retreat were intercepted by the Germans. The instructions "with incredible carelessness," had been transmitted in plain text instead of in cipher, "thanks to which blunder, the conduct of our campaign on the eastern front was greatly facilitated, and, indeed, in many sectors, only rendered possible thereby." Furthermore, the two Russian army commanders were at feud, with the result that one of them, perhaps deliberately (as had happened under like conditions in 1905), exposed the other to a catastrophe—for in no other way was the former's inertia explicable. These two circumstances promoted the success of the outflanking of the Russian Second Army, which the new German commanders now decided to undertake in the grand style, transcending Hoffmann's plans. Telegram to Coblenz: "Concentration of the army for an enveloping attack in the region of the twentieth corps planned for August 26." There now developed one of those brilliant battles which Schlieffen had called "Cannae battles," and had planned for long in advance. It was possible because as yet the forces under arms were not numbered by millions. As in earlier days, about 150,000 Germans were fighting against about 200,000 Russians.

But, once more, in a critical moment, the struggle was decided by a calm mind as against "nerves." When François wanted to get together his widely scattered army corps, before attacking, and thus lost precious time, so that the first German onslaughts were repulsed; when suddenly the German troops began to withdraw, driving numbers of prisoners before them, and thus giving the impression that the Russians had broken through their lines, according to credible reports, Ludendorff's nerve gave way, and he proposed to transform a battle of annihilation into a frontal attack. If this story be true, it was Hindenburg's self-control which saved the situation, for he stuck to Ludendorff's original plan.

At the end of the Battle of Tannenberg, the Russian army had been annihilated. Its commander, Samsonoff, was the first and last leader in the world war who, feeling it impossible to live down the dishonor of a defeat, blew out his brains.

II

Hindenburg had already attained the rank of lieutenant before Ludendorff was born. The latter had attended the same military academy as his senior, and had served on the same General Staff; but he had not had the experiences of Sedan or of Versailles; and, not being of aristocratic blood, he had never formed one of the entourage of the old emperor. His training had come under William II. A strenuous worker, an able specialist, he was regarded on the General Staff as one of its best intelligences, but was not personally liked. As chief of the strategical section, three years before the war he had demanded the establishment of a new supplementary reserve of 600,000 men, declaring that, in default of this, Germany would be defeated in a war upon two fronts. In the ensuing conflict with the minister for war, Ludendorff was dismissed from the General Staff and demoted to become a regimental commander—a position from which he looked back wrathfully to the days when he had been regarded as a master of strategy. When the war opened, the man who was to be the leading German strategist throughout its duration was nothing more than a brigadier.

In any case, being a man with ideas of his own, he was not liked by the emperor, who found his unquestionable ability irritating. Moltke, on the other hand, esteemed him so highly that, in summoning him to Coblenz, the commander in chief said: "I know of no one in whom I have such unmitigated confidence as yourself. Perhaps you will be able to save the situation in the East." By these words, and by sending for

Ludendorff in preference to anyone else, Moltke in-dicated that Ludendorff was to be the actual leader on the eastern front.

By their respective characters, and in view of the distinctive influences which had formed these char-acters in youth, Hindenburg and Ludendorff, although educated in much the same way, were very different, and supplemented one another, thanks to these same differences. Everyone who writes about the men refers to Hindenburg's "character" and to Ludendorff's "intelligence." The terms are never transposed. While no recorder has anything to say about Hinden-burg's having had a flash of insight, whether in military or personal matters, not one makes mention of a cordial or friendly trait in Ludendorff. Hindenburg's con-tribution to their partnership—imperturbability—was complemented in Ludendorff by a number of qualities which Hindenburg lacked. Writing of the two, Foch said: "Ludendorff, *c'est un général;* Hindenburg, *c'est un patriote.*"

In bodily frame these differences between them were emphasized. As compared with the mighty, sturdy, herculean figure of Hindenburg, so well fitted to inspire respect, Ludendorff, who was shorter, but somewhat stocky, looked ill-proportioned; so that there was not an agreeable bodily contrast between the two, as, for instance, between Sickingen and Hutten. Hindenburg, healthy until he became a septuagenarian, and then again until he was eighty-seven, slept, ate, and moved throughout his long life in accordance with precise and well-tried rhythms, which none of his occupations, interfered with not even during the war. Ludendorff, on the other hand, who had suffered shortly before the outbreak of hostilities from an attack of neurasthenia, and whose pallid countenance and flaccid cheeks during the war years were the result of his strenuous exertions uncompensated by sport or recreation, was never at ease, never satisfied. Hindenburg, who looked like a picture, was always impressive with his simple and rather cumbrous lineaments. Ludendorff, with a protruding chin and an aggressively distrustful expression, seemed to be trying to produce an effect. In the former, everything was relaxed; in the latter, everything tensed.

Mind and character were in keeping with these bodily differences. A certain emotional depth, which we often find in hard-headed persons, and which is apt to delight the Germans, was part of Hindenburg's composition, although it never interfered with his ideals of service and duty. It is shown in his early and uniformly successful marriage, and in his relations with his children; also by the fact that he had no enemies (although, before the war, he had no admirers either). Since he was never fretted by ambition, he could not have enough of country life, association with his family, and his favorite sport with the gun. Nevertheless, he did not allow these things to interfere with his devotion to the service.

Ludendorff, continually on the lookout for new opportunities for distinction, had no time for private life. Only once did he depart from this rule, when he saw a pretty woman seeking shelter from the rain in a doorway, begged her to share his umbrella, walked home with her, and soon afterwards married her. The anecdote seems to belong to one of the novels of the period. By this marriage, Ludendorff, then forty years of age, acquired three stepchildren, for the lady, in order to marry him, had to divorce her first husband—and, according to German law, this was possible only when the latter had been proved unfaithful. This step was all the more remarkable since Ludendorff, a man who was so keen to get on in the world, might have been expected to try to compensate for his middle-class origin on the paternal side by marrying above his station, whereas the lady of his choice was also middle-class, the ex-wife of a man of business. The club gossips made fun of him on that account. Now Hindenburg, who also had middle-class blood in his veins, would never have dreamed of marrying any woman who was not the daughter of a Junker. Ludendorff, who was authoritarian by nature, had, before the war, insisted upon his wife's sitting silently by his side while he worked half through the night, for he liked to have her near him. She sometimes complained of this exaction to her friends. Much later, when he was approaching sixty, he divorced the lady whom he had married under such romantic circumstances. If he had had any children, he would certainly not have played the war game with them, like Hindenburg, for he thought about figures rather than about camp fires.

Nobody ever saw Hindenburg out of temper, and nobody ever saw Ludendorff laugh—indeed his comrades at Düsseldorf declare that during the years spent in that town he never even smiled. "Unpleasantly dictatorial in conversation; harsh, obstinate, and opinionated," is what Karl, the chief of the emperor's Cabinet, writes of him. Whether it was because a temperamental skepticism had extinguished in him all feelings other than ambition, or because increasing experience of his fellows intensified his nihilism, this much is certain, that Ludendorff believed in nothing, and therefore believed in luck. There was no God, and he had never come into contact with a true king, since William I had already become a myth when Ludendorff swore fealty. War of the old kind, as it had still been fought in the year 1870, was unknown to him. As far as he was concerned, a modern battle consisted of three elements: the mathematics of the commander in chief; the excellence of the munitions; and the courage of the troops.

Hindenburg, on the other hand, grounded his life upon faith in God and the king, the latter being God's anointed. All his army orders began or ended with a reference to God; and after any important decision, he added: "With God's grace!"

The contrast which had puzzled him—when he was eighteen—the contrast between himself as a son who was a slayer, and his father who was trying to heal the wounds that son inflicted, no longer disturbed him after half a century of service had steeled his mind. In his memoirs, he writes concerning the British blockade of Germany: "They want to starve our women and children! If God will, that cannot fail to have an effect upon husbands and fathers at the front, if not immediately, still by slow degrees!" He goes on, complainingly: "Thus can men think, and nevertheless continue to pray!" This lapidary addition shows the naïveté of pious generals who can condemn an unchristian enemy while themselves, as patriots, justifying and ordering measures which involve the drowning or deportation of thousands of enemy women.

Important practical consequences resulted from the divergent moral foundations of these two men. "Many," writes Hindenburg, "degrade the war from its lofty altitude to regard it as a mere game of hazard. I have never taken that view. Its course and outcome, even if the outcome should be unfavorable to us, have always and everywhere seemed to me the expression of an inexorable logic. He who seizes his opportunity, has success on his side; he who fails to do so, loses." This, the only philosophical reflection in Hindenburg's autobiography, is clarified somewhat by a critical observation of the French General Buat, who writes: "Hindenburg never believed that the happenings of a war can be anything else than a uniform succession of consequences, closely interlinked with one another. Through the whole of the long campaign he never recognized the workings of the omnipotent god of chance."

Ludendorff, who once appealed to "feeling" against irrefutable figures, was, like every professed rationalist, impelled from time to time during the war as in his indiscreet marriage, to resolves whose illogicalness attracted him. These were romantic deviations into a forbidden realm; and for this reason, before his last great offensive, he actually appealed to the god of chance. Though this inconsistency may make him more congenial to some, it did not help him to victory; but it enables us to understand better why he was subject to fits of depression.

These two men, thanks to their differing capacities, had acquired differing characteristics in the military academy which made them an admirable pair to run in harness: one of them, qualities, the other, talents; one of them, constancy, the other, knowledge; both of them, staying power and sense of duty; both of them, incorruptibility. However, to command ten million soldiers and to guide a population of sixty-five million persons, a wide knowledge of the world and a good understanding of Europe were indispensable— things not to be acquired on the General Staff. Over and above devotion to the service and a sense of duty, there were requisite some of the gifts peculiar to genius: insight, fire, imagination.

Such being their respective dispositions, impulses, and acquirements, the active relationships of the two men called to serve together in high command could not but pursue a favorable course. The chief was glad that the other could bestow on him so abundant a wealth of knowledge as to free him from the need of disturbing his own balance by studies and vexations; the subordinate, who would never have put up with an effective commander for a month, was delighted that he could take refuge behind the other's signature. Whereas the older man had long since come to regard his career as closed, and had only resumed active service prompted by his sense of duty as an officer; to the younger it seemed, as soon as the war broke out, that at last his time had come. The former had had his fill of war in youth; the latter had been waiting thirty years for a war, and, to quote a phrase of Bismarck's, "would almost have ceased to be a useful soldier if he had not longed for a war." To Ludendorff, the war was the third act of his life; for Hindenburg, it was an epilog.

Since mutual jealousies were excluded by the elder man's huge size, advanced age, and temperament, the younger man was glad enough to leave the honor and glory to his senior; for he was more interested in power than in laurels. At the same time Ludendorff, in so far as he was capable of such feelings, was certainly glad to have so nerveless a regulator at his side; one who, when he himself was dashed by the withdrawal of columns, by bad news, or by unmistakable reverses, accepted everything with equanimity; for such temperamental calm and self-confidence is invaluable in a commander, especially when, at long last, he wins the fight.

This relationship between the army commander and his chief, one that was wholly the outcome of personality, tact, and character, has never taken so happy a form in any other couple. It was, in truth, an anomaly; for the Prussian spirit is continually organizing, that is to say artificially constructing that which is not by nature organic, while trying to slay by mechanical determination that which is organic. Both men, in later years, were to write guardedly about their mutual relations.

Hindenburg: "One of my most noteworthy tasks was, so it seemed to me, to leave as free scope as possible to the brilliant thoughts of my chief of staff, to his almost superhuman powers of work, and to his unwearied energies. I had to be to him a loyal comrade in war, as I had been taught in the folk tales I had heard in my youth."

Ludendorff rejoins in his book: "After talking things over with my colleague, I frankly told the field marshal my ideas as to the best conduct of operations, and laid definite proposals before him. It was a great gratification to me that, invariably from Tannenberg to the time of my retirement, he agreed with my ideas, and approved my proposed orders. . . . Our views concerning the peace were equally harmonious. I honored him highly, served him faithfully, esteeming his lofty sense of honor no less than his loyalty to his king and his joyful sense of responsibility." After these remarks, the name of Hindenburg disappears from Ludendorff's memoirs, and thenceforward he speaks only of himself.

According to Hindenburg, during the four years of the war Ludendorff worked from seven in the morning till midnight. He himself went to see Ludendorff at nine every morning. "Our conversation seldom lasted long. In many cases a few words were sufficient for us to come to an understanding." Then Hindenburg would go for a walk. Subsequently he would deal with the dispatches from his chiefs of section. The commanders would have their meals together: midday dinner, afternoon coffee, and supper at half past nine—peace-time customs.

Ludendorff's activities, on the other hand, are disclosed by his edicts and his memoirs. They display the amazing energy of a dictator who was, at the same time, his own commander in chief. No one did more than he during the world war. A vignette of 1918 shows him telephoning to the C. O. in Lille about the course of the great battle there; being called away into the next room during the conversation because Bucharest had rung him up and he wanted to let the people there know his views about peace negotiations; then he got back to the first phone and sent instructions concerning the movements of German divisions against the Lys.

8

General Hoffmann, one of the chief witnesses, tells us that Hindenburg, during the daily conversation with Ludendorff and the staff, was mainly a silent partner, merely saying at the end: "Has any of you gentlemen anything to add? No? Then, God willing, let us go ahead!" Colonel Bauer, when he speaks of the "commanders," is obviously thinking only of Ludendorff. In private conversation, Hoffmann declared that, after hearing people say that Hindenburg had won the battle of Tannenberg, he himself had ceased to believe in the existence of Caesar or Hannibal.

Even if the plans and decisions were chiefly Ludendorff's, it does not follow that Ludendorff was alone responsible for them. Training at the military academy had strongly impressed upon Hindenburg the notion that joint responsibility is joint responsibility; and in his own memoirs, though Ludendorff had attacked him, he never repudiated his share in the responsibility. If he harvested Ludendorff's glory, he loyally shouldered also the burden of the latter's mistakes; though he had never sought power, he regarded himself as having issued the orders signed by his name; and it would obscure our image of Hindenburg's character were we to ascribe to Ludendorff alone any of the resolves which, during this period, settled Germany's fate.

The testimony of their collaborators confirms this view. Again and again, General von der Schulenburg tells us how Ludendorff said he could not decide this or that until he had asked the field marshal. General von Wetzell, who worked for a long time hand-in-hand with the two commanders, giving evidence later before the commission of inquiry, said: "In the year 1918, the field marshal was in full possession of his mental and bodily powers. His carefully pondered judgments, ripened by age and extensive military experiences both in war and peace, had a moderating effect upon the impetuous energy of Ludendorff."

In view of these utterances, what ground is there for doubting Ludendorff's own statement that he and Hindenburg worked together in perfect harmony? With carefully chosen words, Ludendorff goes on: "The field marshal allowed me to participate in his fame. The commander in chief bears the responsibility. He bears it before the world; and, what is harder, before himself, before his own army and his own fatherland. As chief and first quartermaster general, I was fully co-responsible, and never failed to bear the fact in mind."

Such being the assignment of rôles, a favorite comparison of Hindenburg and Ludendorff to Blücher and Gneisenau cannot hold water. What maintained old Blücher's self-respect though Gneisenau did all the thinking—namely the cavalry attacks, camp life, hardships at the front in wind and storm—were the very things which Hindenburg had to forego. Nowadays a commander in chief conducts the war with the aid of telephones and wireless from a villa or country house a hundred miles or so behind the fighting line, and sees much less of the hard knocks of war than the so-called common soldier. Whereas in old days, generals in need of rest and change during long campaigns, would retire to their headquarters and lie upon a sofa, Hindenburg had to go out shooting by way of recreation, in order to get relief from the air of stuffy rooms. Once at G.H.Q. William II even set to work sawing wood in order to stir his muscles a little—at a time when five millions of his subjects had no reason to complain of lack of bodily exercise.

III

What really severed the two commanders was the Hindenburg legend. For reasons deep-rooted in the German character, the populace gave to only one of them a glory which in reality was due to the other. But for this legend, the course of the war would have been very different, and probably its upshot altogether different as well. Inasmuch as the legend in question was originated and fostered by the populace, its dangerous consequences recoiled upon those who desired a leader after their own heart.

The origin of the legend was the victory at Tannenberg. This was the first German victory in the war; and was, indeed, the only German victory as the common people understand the term. The enemy had been surrounded, his army annihilated, more than one hundred thousand men had been taken prisoner; thousands of cannon and hundreds of flags had been captured; a whole province, which had been lost to the foe, was regained—and all this three weeks after the opening of the war, almost without losses or unfavorable repercussions. The church bells pealed joyfully throughout the country; the schools held high festival; the captured guns rolled through the Victory Gate in Berlin. The rescuer, the great unknown, received the heartfelt gratitude of a nation which believed itself to have been shamefully attacked. Everyone was asking: "Who is this man?"

The first thing the Germans learned was, that Hindenburg was a huge fellow, as strong as Siegfried, and at the same time as gentle and lovable as a child; there was a rough shell round a tender kernel. His great head was one which seemed to invite reproduction in plaster casts and in sugar; his tranquil eyes, his big mustache, his hard-bitten, soldierly face, convinced everyone that he was an eagle of a man—old and yet powerful; gray, titanic, and genial. When they heard that he had been brought back to active service from the retired list, the Germans went crazy with delight. A man who had been undervalued, and yet had not been soured thereby—how touching! Besides, his name had an agreeable ring, for after the battle of Tannenberg he had for the first time omitted the "Beneckendorff" and signed simply "Hindenburg." He was thus a combination of all the traits which inspire reverence in the Germans: authority and repose, the obvious lineaments of a man born to command, and the invisibly impressive qualities of the good husband and father.

While Hindenburg thus possessed all the characteristics likely to make his compatriots regard him as a hero, there was nothing about him to make a German citizen uneasy. Men of genius like Goethe and Schiller, Frederick the Great and the first Moltke, could not achieve popularity during their lifetime; and Bismarck was definitely unpopular until the day of his dismissal, although his strength and greatness had been generally recognized. The two men who, during centuries, had really won the hearts of the Prussians had been Blücher and Wrangel. It was to them that Field Marshal von Hindenburg was henceforward compared—and his new rank, conferred in November, 1914, contributed to the growth of the legend.

When some of his additional distinctive qualities became generally known, the adoration of the populace was intensified. He was deeply religious, modest, a silent man—these features confirmed the picture of the laconic man of action. Hindenburg, therefore, needed no pretenses to make himself pleasing to the Germans; and, for the very reason that he had never posed as a great man, it was easier for him to be accounted one. The few words he uttered roused enthusiasm; and when he said: "The war suits me like a visit to a health resort," he had definitively achieved the conquest of this military-minded people.

Inasmuch as Ludendorff lacked all the aforesaid qualities—being neither big of frame nor eagle-like, nor well up in years nor a successful paterfamilias nor a tender kernel in a rough shell, but endowed with genius and inventiveness, a passionate temperament, inscrutability and ambition—he was looked upon by the Germans as one of those necessary personalities who, like a prince consort, seem indispensable for the maintenance of established institutions. Since he was not commander in chief, he also lacked that position of supreme authority to which the Germans look up with so much reverence. The belligerents (not the Germans alone) were at this stage of the war expecting an outstanding general to be its hero; not a soul in the early days had the remotest inkling that, when the trouble was over, monuments would everywhere be erected to the Unknown Soldier.

Legend made Hindenburg a popular hero without his having done anything to pose for the part. The circumstances of his first victories contained those romantic elements without which a great reputation never comes into being in Germany. "Tannenberg" was already romantic enough, because at this spot five centuries before the Poles had inflicted a grievous defeat upon the Teutonic knights. Hardly anyone remembered as much, but since attention was now drawn to it in the newspapers, the widespread feeling was that the honor of the Germans had (although somewhat late in the day) been made good as against the Slavs. The name "Battle of Tannenberg" had as rhythmical a sound as the name of Hindenburg. In his report to the emperor, the field marshal recommended that this name should be officially adopted. Neither he nor the public at large stopped to think that the name might be offensive to the Poles, whom it was a part of German policy to placate. Everywhere it was declared and believed that the new commander had pursued his studies at Tannenberg.

The leader of the other Russian army managed to avoid a second devastating blow, withdrawing before the German advance, and quitting the region of the Masurian Lakes, where, early in September, many more Russians, tens of thousands of them, were taken prisoner.

These lakes became a new focus of the legend. Their waters were peopled with elves and nixies; in the popular imagination, will-o'-the-wisps moved over them. These were the souls of the Russians who had been drowned in the dark waters; and, since the region was known to very few Germans, all the more quickly did it become a land of fable. Had not the field marshal been garrisoned there in youth? The newspapers, having got hold of this "fact," bruited it abroad as follows, with numberless variations.

"After being put on the retired list, the veteran spent his summer holidays every year among the Masurian Lakes. Borrowing a cannon from Königsberg, and a company to serve the gun, he went with them into the marshes. From morning till night, he had the heavy piece dragged from one quagmire to another, measuring how deep the wheels sank in the bog, and how many horses were needed to extricate it from difficult places—twenty beasts being sometimes insufficient. He took notes, calculated, made sketches. When autumn came, he returned the cannon with thanks, and went home." Although there are no "quagmires" in that part of the world, such stories were told and believed, not only by ordinary citizens over their beer, but even by such an intellectual leader as the playwright Gerhard Hauptmann.

When, after a few months, Hindenburg's triumphs came to an end, the legend was firmly established, and the Germans, who cling so long to an authoritative pronouncement, did not read until after the war in the field marshal's memoirs: "Before this day I had never seen the battlefield which proved so fateful to German civilization in the East." Meanwhile his name had been widely popularized in streets and squares; statues of him in marble and wood, life-size and larger, had been erected far and wide throughout the realm. One read "Hindenburg" on bills of fare and wine-lists; while to his house in Hanover there came a steady stream of tokens of affection, cures for every imaginable ailment, and talismans of one sort and another, including a wonder-working bean which an Indian was said to have picked for him at an altitude of 20,000 feet.

Within a few months, Hindenburg had completely replaced the emperor as the idol of the populace. Too long had it been necessary to put up with William's restlessness and talkativeness. Now, at the head of affairs, was an equable man who knew how to hold his tongue and to keep his important thoughts to himself, or, when a foundation stone had to be laid, appeared as a mighty figure and hit the nail on the head with a few pithy words. The falling away from the emperor, who no longer sought the limelight, was prepared among the German people by the growth of their devotion to Hindenburg, which the latter did nothing to cultivate.

Ludendorff was not jealous. What Bismarck had endured from his king, Ludendorff tolerated from Hindenburg, who publicly referred to the chief of staff as his 'loyal assistant.' Subsequently, in a vein of sarcasm, but not with reproach, Ludendorff wrote: "A distinction was drawn between the field marshal's actions and thoughts and my own. He was supposed to incorporate the principle of good; I, that of evil." Richard Dehmel, writing from headquarters, reports: "Ludendorff is more admired, but less venerated; the admiration for Ludendorff is cold, or tempered with irascibility; the veneration for Hindenburg is warm-hearted. People have absolute faith in him, whereas Ludendorff arouses unstinted hopes. . . . Manifestly Ludendorff is a master of calculation, who relies upon the simple shrewdness of his more primitive colleague to safeguard him against miscalculations."

The legend which thus came into being in the autumn of 1914 has persisted to this day. It had immense influence throughout the next fifteen years of German history, deciding the war and the fate of the republic. Since Hindenburg was the first and the only German who gained a victory in the World War in open fight, his compatriots looked to him alone for success in the struggle, and, being tenacious, continued to believe in the Hindenburg legend even after the final catastrophe. This is in keeping with the temperament of the Germans, which makes them prone to regard intellectual problems in an emotional light, inclines them to build less on genius than on character, and to give the palm to simplicity.

Only in exceptional instances are they dazzled by a contrasted type, the histrionic, as that of the emperor.

IV

When Schlieffen, in his eightieth year, lay dying, he said, "Strengthen the right wing!" With these authentic last words, he left to his successors a final instruction as to what had always been his chief concern. A year later, his successors weakened the right wing; and thus they lost the decisive battle of the war and with it the war as a whole.

Against his own will, the younger Moltke had been made chief of the General Staff. A man of culture, devoid of warlike ambitions, who for some years before the war broke out had been neurasthenic and otherwise ailing, he would not take over the position until the emperor made a personal appeal: "I want once more to have a Moltke in supreme command. Should matters take a serious turn, I shall myself be on hand to lead!" In the early days of September, just after

Hindenburg's victory at Tannenberg, the German westward advance was arrested at the Marne, in a battle about which, at the time, the German nation was not fully informed. The story of the Battle of the Marne, which lies beyond the scope of the present book, can be described only in outline as an appendix to the account of the victory on the eastern front.

According to the military critics, one of the three or four reasons for the defeat on the Marne was the removal of three army corps from an extremely important position between the First and the Second Armies on the right wing. The panic aroused in Coblenz by the telephone message from the eastern front on August 21, led to the transference of these troops from the western front to the eastern at a time when a decisive forward movement in the West was being prepared. The error was persisted in, although the sending of new leaders to the East had aroused fresh hopes. When, after the victory at Tannenberg, Ludendorff was asked to what point the three additional army corps were to be directed, he, being far away in the East, and dominated by Schlieffen's basic notion of a strong right wing in the West, said that the reinforcements in question were not absolutely indispensable to him. If there were difficulties in the West, they might just as well stay where they were, since in any case they would arrive too late to help himself and Hindenburg in the battle now going on. Since in spite of this generously worded answer, the three army corps were nevertheless dispatched, and were therefore lacking on the Marne, one can only suppose—to repeat—that panic and arrogance must have been the mingled motives at G.H.Q.

The two other main causes of the defeat on the Marne can only be explained psychologically, as resulting from the deliberations of neurasthenics. If Moltke botched Schlieffen's plan of campaign, if he strengthened the left wing in Alsace, thereby weakening the right wing which was all-important, this was because he wished, under the emperor's eyes, to safeguard prestige, which might suffer from a temporary advance of the French in Alsace, one of the chief bones of contention. Yet Schlieffen, when drafting his plan, had been quite unconcerned by the thought that the French might advance into Alsace and even make their way across the Rhine. "Should they do that," he wrote, "after our enveloping victory between Lille and Paris, they would simply fall into the Germans' arms." The third reason for the defeat, the sending of a lieutenant colonel without written orders to the front, where, on his own initiative he was to decide whether this momentous battle should be continued or interrupted, was also the outcome of panic and confusion at General Headquarters. Neither the commander in chief nor the chief of general staff went to the front to study the situation on the spot. They were 125 miles behind the firing line, waiting upon events in a pleasant villa in Luxemburg, not even in telephonic communication with the advancing armies, passively awaiting information as to the views of the several army leaders instead of sending them explicit orders.

All military critics, the French included, agree that the Battle of the Marne was decided, not by the strength or skill of the Allied forces, but by the blunders of two nervous chiefs on the German side. In the official German history of the war we read: "During the noon hour of September 9, the chief of the General Staff in Luxemburg suffered a serious collapse owing to the receipt of tidings of disaster, some actual and some imaginary. . . . Almost at the very hour when our battling army had gained a great victory, he decided upon withdrawing the whole of the German western front. . . . In the year 1910, he had suffered from a severe illness, since which his bodily strength and his nervous tension had been slowly declining."

Although the German people were not allowed to learn anything about the check on the Marne, it was at least able to note that a victory had been gained only on the eastern front. Awareness that there they were the sole victors, and the echo which their success aroused from the people, could not fail to strengthen the self-confidence of Hindenburg and Ludendorff during these early weeks, so that they naturally began to look forward to attaining the highest positions in the army. Their new rival was not of such a caliber as to impress them.

General von Falkenhayn, whom the emperor had now appointed commander in chief, may be compared with Prince Bülow: adroit, cultured, courtly; less shrewd than Bülow, but more of an adventurer. He had left the service early, had become an army instructor in China; then, during the German expedition to China, had again entered the service, and had at length become minister for war, since the emperor had a personal liking for him. Falkenhayn, though his hair was gray, had the slim figure of a lieutenant; he could speak several languages fluently; and these

qualities, with his elegance and polish, impressed
William. Falkenhayn's conduct in the Zabern affair
had also shown that he had a contempt for common
folk which is proper to the aristocrat. Younger than
any of the other army leaders who now became his
subordinates (the ruling princes who were nominally
in high command being left out of consideration),
though by no means so young as he looked, he exerted
on the emperor a charm similar to that exerted by
Bülow; and he seemed destined to thrive upon the
favor of his gracious master, which he had admirable
opportunities of cultivating day by day in the isola-
tion of G.H.Q.

V

Hindenburg's life as field marshal on active service
has been admirably described by the artist who painted
his portrait, and shows how a man whose head was not
easily turned could gradually adapt himself to the
rôle assigned him by the world, since the rôle was an
agreeable one. We see a straightforward, self-dis-
ciplined, and cheerful army administrator transforming
himself at the nation's call into a celebrated commander
without any abatement in the fundamental kindliness
of his character traits. But the modifications he
underwent were amazing in a septuagenarian. The
man grew to fit himself into the place fashioned for
him by the great myth.

In his new position Hindenburg remained what he
had always been, good-natured and genial. There is
no account of his ever having stormed at his underlings; all reports agree in describing an equable, nay,
considerate chief. The man without nerves, who

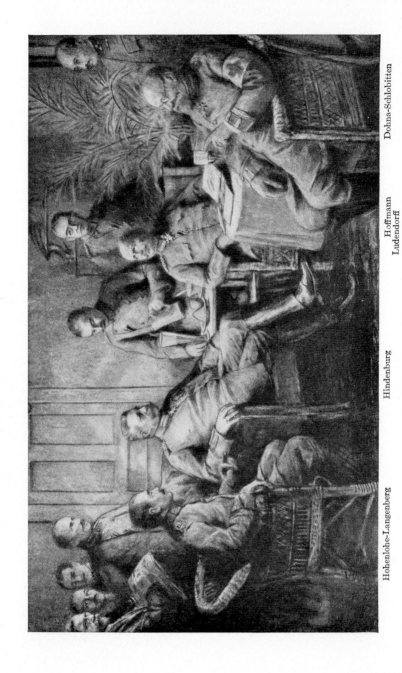

Hohenlohe-Langenberg   Hindenburg   Hoffmann   Dohna-Schlobitten
                                         Ludendorff

A social evening at Headquarters

could always sleep soundly and whose appetite never failed, diffused over the agitated life at headquarters the tranquil illumination of a planet which, since it borrows its light from another source, never blinds anyone by its rays. No reverse, no darkness of the situation, could disturb his night's rest. In the reports which describe Hindenburg week by week throughout the war, but one day is mentioned (in May, 1915) when his countenance was overcast with gloom, and when he said that he had many cares. This item stands alone, and his visitors were never weary of extolling his equanimity, even during the last weeks of the struggle. When penning his will as a boy of twelve, had he not written: "Peace and quiet is what I pray may henceforward be granted me"? Did he not succeed in maintaining this equanimity after he had lost the war? Such natures, spared but also denied the profoundest spiritual perturbations, are, like Hindenburg, touched to the core only late and through the most intimate losses.

At headquarters, Hindenburg diffused severity of mind when work was in progress; and when the tasks of the day were over, he proved an unfailing comfort. His reports and conversations are primarily concerned with eating and drinking. Eels, rusk, and a pyramid cake, his favorite articles of diet, were supplied to him wherever he went; also old brandy and champagne, which had to be of German manufacture. The table talk, renewed throughout the four years of the war at midday dinner and supper (for, except during one illness, Hindenburg was always at mess), was such as might have been heard at any manor house east of the Elbe. When it did not turn upon the war or on personal matters, jokes from the front or experiences when out shooting were retailed. The field marshal was a great admirer of Schiller's *Wallenstein*, which appealed to his veteran's heart; on the other hand, he disliked Goethe, justifying this sentiment again and again on the ground that Goethe had admired Napoleon, had failed to understand the German revival, and, besides, had behaved badly to his mother. When the Goethe Society, which was unaware of these sentiments, begged a friendly word from him, through contrariness he sent them a quotation from Schiller: "Ans Vaterland, ans teuere, schliess dich an!" (Cling to your dear fatherland!), but his aide-de-camp prevented the sending of this dispatch. Hindenburg's judgment on Goethe was to be given on a later day!

Nor did he like Wagner's music, though he was fond of Mozart. If, when he was having his portrait painted, or when he was out walking, he whistled to himself, it would generally be a military march. The only pictures that interested him were those of the chase or of battles, or those that depicted scenes from German history. He was outraged that Hodler, "a French-Swiss," should have been chosen to paint the pictures of the German War of Liberation, and that Marteau, the violinist, should have had a call to the Berlin Academy—"The man is a French reserve officer!" He had a special fondness for a small phoenix palm, which he always liked to have as a table decoration, and which, carefully packed, followed him to wintry Poland. He knew the family tree of every Junker, the relatives, the landed property, and the careers of every clan; knew in which regiment every nephew of a Prussian nobleman was serving; and would ask such sprigs of the aristocracy after the health of their kith and kin by name. He kept up a regular correspondence with his own people. When out walking, he picked flowers to send to his wife; gave orders as to the photographs that were to be posted to her; inquired what she had had to eat when she dined out in Berlin; but would not allow her to come to headquarters, since this was forbidden ground for women, and he would not make an exception in his own case. Still, she might stay for a while at a neighboring country house.

To ladies who came by day for an hour, he was always extremely courteous, kissing hands after the German manner; he wrote extremely polite letters, and, as king of this field-gray court, pushed his complaisance so far that when entertaining he never gave the sign to rise from tables, even if the youngest lieutenant in the air force was one of the guests. All who enjoyed his hospitality were abundantly supplied with motor cars, servants, furs, and other luxuries; and he made it his personal business to see that their sleeping accommodation was satisfactory and that they had flowers in their rooms. On birthdays, there were birthday cakes with candles, also garlands and speeches. If anyone asked him a foolish or indiscreet question, he did not show temper, but, in his heavy bass, gave so amusing an answer that the matter was turned off with a laugh.

To the eternal question, "When will the war be over?" from 1915 onward he always gave the same answer, "Soon! Soon!" When the Italians declared war, he said: "That disturbs me very little. Italy will have one reverse after another. A beautiful country, but its inhabitants are fanatical and

9

presumptuous people." Concerning Wilson: "A doc-
trinaire fellow! Spots danced before my eyes when I
read his 'fourteen points.'" About the English:
"England has come into the war only for business
reasons. Now she has found out that it is a bad
business for her, and she would like to make peace."
As regards matters of long ago, no less, for instance
about Napoleon as a great campaigner, the opinions
in his table talk were such as may be found in any
German schoolbook. During his long life, certain
opinions had become petrified in him, and among
these was what he thought about wounds and death
in battle. When, one evening, after supper, General
Hoffmann reported heavy losses, Hindenburg said:
"Yes, very sad, but inevitable." After a day of
extreme tension, General Ludendorff's eyes followed
Hindenburg who was leaving the room, and he said
to the painter: "That chap has the nerve to go quietly
to sleep just as if nothing had happened!"

Very remarkable was Hindenburg's moderation as
regards the question of peace terms, even after his
first victories. Herr von Oldenburg-Januschau, an
East-Elbian Junker, who was later to play a decisive
part in his life, insisted at table that the Germans,
in the peace treaty, must acquire every inch of the
land where German soldiers had been buried. To
which Hindenburg replied: "We must take no more
than we can digest without damage to our German-
dom! We need Liége whatever happens, but only to
round off our frontiers. Don't let us overestimate
our successes!"

On other occasions: "The Pan-Germans will ruin
the peace for us with their preposterous demands."—

"This war is like the third waged by Frederick, when he only preserved what he had already acquired."—"How could we take Antwerp without annexing a large part of Belgium?—And that would be a great mistake!"—"To annex a large slice of Poland would be a schoolboy's blunder." He repeated as much again and again in the year 1915, but never in the presence of Ludendorff, whose influence in political life did not begin until later.

Speaking generally, it was Ludendorff's insatiable appetite for work which gave the field marshal a chance to hand his views down to posterity; inasmuch as Ludendorff vanished into his office directly a meal was finished, and only once, on his fiftieth birthday, sat on at table until ten p.m. The result was that Hindenburg, with his court and his guests, remained to rule the roost. Then, and during his daily constitutionals, he could express his opinion freely, without being disquieted by Ludendorff's lion-tamer look which the chief of staff was apt to direct at the commander through his monocle. Such externals, trifling as they seem, are of great importance.

For what Hindenburg had now begun to acquire at the eastern headquarters, the new element in his being, was *fame*, with all its consequences. If without internal convulsions he was to endure a popularity more overwhelming than that which had ever accrued to any other German, he needed to preserve that equanimity which service, his aims, and an affable disposition facilitated. But he would have had to be a philosopher to withstand such an onslaught without turning a hair, and to divert it, so to say, upon the deviser of his battles. Army regulations stood in the way. He was superior officer, and therefore the stage was his, much as William I had had to accept the credit due to Bismarck's successes.

Soon after the Battle of Tannenberg he wrote to his wife somewhat sarcastically: "Perhaps your old man is going to become famous!" Now he read in the papers that he, who had never deemed himself anything more than a fairly efficient General Staff officer, was, all at once, "the greatest strategist of the century." Nor was it in the newspapers alone. Day by day his adjutant had letters to sort by the basketful; letters sent to the general who had been an unknown man yesterday, and who now received homage, gifts, advice, and requests by the score. The manager of a zoo sent photographs of a new hybrid type of beast of prey which he wished to call "Hindenburg"; and a midwives' association urgently begged him to bring the war to a close as speedily as possible because, in the absence of the men, no children were being procreated, and they (the midwives) were therefore out of work. Although so much adulation from his compatriots could not but tickle the old gentleman's vanity, he remained the man of station, so that amid the pother, his ears were attuned to the rustling of the wings of the great eagle known as posthumous fame.

In these circumstances, Hindenburg began to mold himself more or less upon Blücher; to deliver pithy answers; to address common folk in a paternal way, and to couch his edicts in the traditional style: "Now we shall let ourselves go and slash the fellows until they have had enough of it!" Or, "I shall be on hand to make the English sit up!" Or, again, on receiving

The Field Marshal and his staff at Tannenberg, 1914

news that four thousand Russians had been taken prisoner: "Excellent; we must never give those chaps the least glimmer of success, or they may get used to it!" That was the sort of way in which the commander in chief of the German armies during the World War spoke and wrote—Blücher to the life! Had not nature fashioned him in the same mould? Was he not extraordinarily like his predecessor?

Posthumous fame actually crossed Hindenburg's threshold in the form of a painter. Journalists, men of letters, visitors from neutral countries, demanded from him wit and eloquence, qualities foreign to his temperament. But a painter—he was the herald of immortality; and, in very truth, the head of the taciturn Hindenburg was worth looking at. When connoisseurs asked him whether he would sit to Liebermann, the greatest portrait painter of the day, Hindenburg refused. He had no taste for highly colored pictures. He loved historical clarity, genuine uniforms, every detail perfectly accurate, as in the great historical canvases he had been wont to admire in the castles where he had spent his youth. But when the historical painter Vogel arrived—a man better acquainted with the story of the house of Hindenburg than with the history of art—and at once proceeded to depict Hindenburg as Blücher, the field marshal felt that at length recognition had come his way. "That is a different sort of thing!" he said, of Vogel's first sketch, as compared with earlier essays. "That is not a picture for home consumption; it is genuinely martial."

This was on February 15. Thenceforward he would not part from his portrait-painter-in-ordinary, keeping Vogel employed until the end of the war; and then once more when he had become president. Contemplating an extremely artificial portrait which showed him with a warlike air from which all the kindly qualities had been expunged, he said, "That is how I should like to go down to posterity"; and he wrote his name and the date beneath the daub. For weeks, now, morning after morning, at the eastern headquarters—less frequently, afterwards—he sat to his "little professor"; by no means a silent model. Again and again he had a word to put in. He never failed to come to the studio of an afternoon, "to inspire" the artist; would order a change of position; and was above all deeply interested in the buttons, the gold braid, and the decorations displayed in the portraits. "You have never served," he said to the painter. "A cloak without a button is like a flower without scent." He would write letters as well as talk about the arrangement and equipment of his uniform; and once, in the studio, he sat down in front of the picture and, with his own hand, painted in a pair of spurs.

In a letter to Vogel, Hindenburg writes: "The paletot has still six buttons, not five; but the tunic has eight. Put them in a row, and show the buttonholes. According to army regulations, it is essential to have an officer's sash for the attachment of the field marshal's baton and the binoculars. In the uniform of the 147th regiment there is neither a yellow tab nor a white band on the collar, so that this, as everyone knows, is gray right up to the red border." Half a dozen letters which the painter publishes, always with humorous comments, deal with the important question of buttons; the penultimate of these epistles, a holograph document, is dated March 16, 1918, a few days before the great German offensive. This letter, indeed, is more especially concerned about Hindenburg's trousers at the Battle of Tannenberg: "My trousers are not dark enough! There is no reason why black trousers should not be most impressive. Then you mustn't forget to paint in the stripes of a General Staff officer. Jack boots, black, with box spurs—not brown gaiters!"

Most of these comments relate to an out-size picture representing Hindenburg with his staff at the battle of Tannenberg. The Junker vitality in him was dominant then; for while the war was in full blast, six months after Tannenberg, he made the staff come with him to an appropriate hill, that the painter might make a sketch in the open, while the models were shivering with cold—although at Tannenberg in the previous August the weather had been blazing hot. Then Vogel was sent to the actual seat of operations, accompanied by an officer who had played an active part in them, to study things on the spot. So many modifications in this particular canvas were needed that it was not completed for two years. Hindenburg was even more interested in a picture painted in accordance with his reminiscences. It concerned the day of his arrival at Marienburg, when, just before the battle, a huge figure in a cloak, he was standing on the river bank near the castle lighted up by the red glow of the sunset, while he watched the women refugees from beneath his bushy eyebrows. Such portrait, at once virile and moving, being thoroughly accordant with the Germans' idea of their hero and appealing as they did to the taste of the man in the street, were eminently calculated to favor the growth of the "Hindenburg legend." The old man knew this well enough, and traded on it. For once, when standing before his picture as Blücher, he said to Vogel:

"Here I look as if I were saying: 'I shall not rest until I have downed all the Russians. Not one of them shall escape me!'"

Since at this time, in the spring of 1915, there was still active movement on the eastern front, and a great battle was expected from day to day, he urged the painter to work "double time" at the great picture and came with a measuring rod to make sure that the decorations were to scale. He provided rubber galoshes for his painter of battle scenes; was continually asking about Ullstein's color prints of his pictures; took all his royal visitors to see them; but when one evening some of them said it was too dark to look at pictures, he gave orders, "See that the studio is well lighted within a quarter of an hour!" Thereupon his guests were able to parade in front of the canvases before a row of privates standing at attention and each holding a lamp.

"What?" he once asked Vogel in semi-feigned indignation, "you will need a year to paint such a picture? The whole battle lasted no more than five days, which were a lifetime. Do you mean to tell me that it is harder to paint pictures than to win a battle?"

For the field marshal, moreover, the painter-in-ordinary acted as a sort of Boswell, to whom the great man disclosed his most private thoughts. One of these thoughts comes again and again, and is an immense contrast to what other noted commanders have said about the art of war: "The general should only lay down the broad lines, leaving details to his subordinates. . . . But all responsibility falls upon the general's shoulders. It is not so easy to manage a battle as you might think. Nor does it suffice to issue orders like—'Advance the guns; forward, quick march!' Not a bit of it, you have to maneuver here and there." (When speaking thuswise, he was playing the new Blücher so much to the life as to assume the Berlinese dialect which did not come naturally to his tongue.)

One morning at eight o'clock he entered the studio, sat down, and said: "Well, I've brought a measuring chain with me, and we'll plan out a battle on the floor!" This was the tone which found an echo in every true German heart.

But there was trouble when Vogel wanted to depict Ludendorff and Hindenburg on the same .canvas. Ludendorff had neither time nor inclination. Whereas Hindenburg (so the painter writes) was "all on fire" about these paintings, Ludendorff was cold, and thoughtfully remarked:

"I would rather wait to have my portrait done until this job is finished. Popular favor and the fortune of war are extremely fickle. The goddess of war is a sorry baggage."

When, at length, Ludendorff gave way and came alone to the first sitting, the artist's preliminary sketch infuriated him. Hindenburg had wanted Ludendorff to be looking at him, thereby creating the impression that the younger man was receiving orders from the elder. This was too much! "Ludendorff," writes Vogel, "said that such an arrangement of the two portraits was derogatory to him in respect of his military relationship to Hindenburg. During the conversation that ensued, he became so much excited as to declare that, regarded as a historical document, my picture would be inaccurate. By degrees I was able to appease him sufficiently to let me begin painting. . . . Everything passed off quietly, but the atmosphere was somewhat chilly." That evening, before supper, Ludendorff came up to the painter to give him a cordial handshake. The group was modified as Ludendorff wished.

This is the only recorded occasion on which the proud and silent subordinate openly claimed his share in the glory. It was not surprising that Ludendorff should be a trifle sore; for, although the field marshal always treated him with extreme consideration, it must have been galling to be perpetually spoken to and spoken of by Hindenburg as "my loyal assistant." When, on Ludendorff's fiftieth birthday, Hindenburg drank his health, the toast was still to "my loyal assistant! . . . I can only say, 'Your Excellency, no one could replace you!'" Why, on this noteworthy occasion did not the field marshal say, and why, in his memoirs, did Hindenburg never write of the man whom he had to thank for so much, "my faithful comrade"? Why did he give this title, fifteen years later, to an untried gentleman-jockey [Papen] whom he made chancellor? Because an additional star on the collar marked an additional gradation; because service and rank were the hands of the clock face in Hindenburg's life.

The completion of the pictures was continually being postponed, for there was always some detail to modify—not because an art critic complained of anything in the composition or the coloring, but only because there was an insignificant error in one of the uniforms, or what not. Of a picture of the two commanders with their collaborators, Hindenburg said carpingly that the representation of General Ludendorff was "too meditative," an amazing criticism in view of the relationship between the two men during all these years.

The emperor had criticisms peculiar to himself. When the pictures were to be exhibited to his majesty, the court general insisted that there must be a red satin background to set off the gold frames in accordance with William's taste. That evening the painter scoured the tiny town of Pless on the hunt for red satin. At length he found some in a middle-class household where a betrothed young lady had a fancy for being married in a room hung with red satin, and was radiant when requested the loan of this room for the exhibition of a picture of Hindenburg and Ludendorff before the august eyes of the Hohenzollern.

Next day the emperor said that Ludendorff's mouth was too tightly closed, "but in other respects I am well pleased. The way you have made Hindenburg's figure dominant is most commendable." But William was not satisfied with the Tannenberg picture, for Ludendorff was too near the field marshal. "This gives a false impression, since it was the field marshal who won the battle!" When Vogel tried to defend his composition, the emperor silenced him with a curt: "That is my will!" Subsequently a court general whose only knowledge of war had been derived from pictures of Frederick the Great's battles, and who therefore had slumbering memories of field howitzers, rushed into the fray with the suggestion that the background would be considerably improved by a battery which had just ceased firing. Vogel made no objection, but Hindenburg vetoed the idea, saying, with an air of finality, "The picture will be painted in accordance with my wishes!" (The worthy artist prints all these humiliations in his book.) Hindenburg's last letter about the Battle of Tannenberg is dated November 7, 1918!

Nor was it possible to arrive at unity about the battle. Each of the two commanders had his own version of the public's favorite aria, the "Song of Tannenberg," and neither would admit that there was any other possible interpretation than his own. No one had ever heard Hindenburg or Ludendorff speak of the famous battle in the other's presence. In referring to the matter, each of them was accustomed to open with the words: "At the time when I won the battle of Tannenberg . . ."

Whereas, during the most critical periods of the war, Hindenburg arrived at table punctually on the stroke of one and of eight, always cheerful and always sharp set, there were days when Ludendorff did not turn up at all at meals; or, if he came, he would be pale, would bite his lips, and, while gulping down a morsel or two, would eagerly ask the news, and then seize upon the earliest opportunity to leave the dining room. One of his favorite gestures on such occasions was to pull down the corners of his mouth. "He pulled them down more and more," records the adjutant mockingly, "although one might have thought they had already been pulled down as far as possible." If

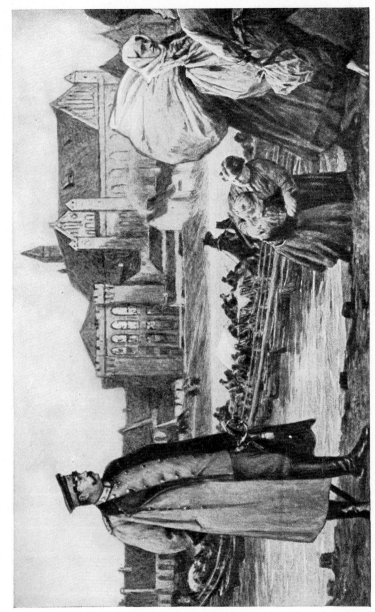

Hindenburg on the evening of his arrival in Marienburg, August 23, 1914

he rolled bread pills slowly, with one hand, people knew that his mind was at ease; if he rolled them quickly, the weather was stormy; if he made them with both hands at once, there was the devil to pay.

When sitting to Vogel, at first he continually yawned and groaned. But when in a joint picture of himself and Hindenburg, Ludendorff was to be represented as bending over a war map, the painter had provided a veritable map, whereupon Ludendorff, thinking always of his plans of campaign, picked up a pair of compasses, devoted himself to contemplation, forgot the picture, and thus naturally assumed the tense expression Vogel desired. On one occasion, however, after sitting for a few minutes, he jumped up, exclaiming: "Today the fate of Germany is being decided in the West! I am too much disturbed in mind to sit for my portrait!" We see Ludendorff, in the East, intensely agitated about a battle that is going on in the West without his participation. There are some who admire such nervousness more than they admire imperturbability. But when that evening the painter told Hindenburg what had happened, the field marshal said:

"Quite. Tranquillity is the main requisite today. Those who have the best nerves will win the war."

Such answers, such a demeanor, such infallibility, had a most impressive effect upon everyone in those days. From year to year, they magnified the Hindenburg legend, although the outcome of the war was far from being a direct confirmation of his theory about nerves. Still, there have always been simple folk who, even after the patient's death, have been ready to praise the doctor for continuing to encourage the sick man by assuring him he would undoubtedly recover.

Intoxicated by his reputation as an invincible commander, Hindenburg in due time came to believe in the Hindenburg legend. Now he began to compare himself to Napoleon. "You know my principle," he said to the painter; "never to sacrifice a soldier needlessly. That was Napoleon's principle as regards his French troops; so, as far as possible, he sent foreign levies into the firing line; but I can't do that, since all my men are Germans." Once more demonstrating the battle of Tannenberg on the map, he referred anew to the victory of the Poles five centuries before. He pointed to a region with his finger nail, saying: "At that time the battlefield where the Teutonic knights were defeated was of the size of my nail. But the battlefield on which I defeated the Slavs is as large as my hand. It is a great joy to me that I was able to wipe out that disgrace."

The way in which life at headquarters intensified the old general's good opinion of himself had subsequently a marked influence upon his decisions. What a change! An impoverished Junker who had found it hard to keep his head above water, he had for a few years occupied a good position as general, and had inspired considerable respect. His influence had been limited to the region of Magdeburg, among the petty magnates of the province of Saxony, where he was able to cut a dash perhaps a dozen times during the winter at receptions and banquets. Now, day after day, he sat at the head of the table, nearly always with distinguished guests to right and to left, persons who had come to enjoy the privilege of meeting him. Evening after evening there were formal receptions, introductions, toasts, expressions of gratitude. Men of high station, ruling princes and kings, Chinese and other orientals, were sharing the hospitality of one who until hard upon seventy had remained practically unknown. Owing to his mighty physique, he stood out in any company; and, since every dispatch from the eastern front made a point of referring to this bodily detail, he once more had good reason for offering up thanks to the memory of his burgher ancestor, King Frederick's tall grenadier, whose biological legacy was responsible for the impression aroused by the first glimpse of Field Marshal Hindenburg.

Freed by his assistants from the necessity of cudgeling his brains in search of original ideas; an officer of exalted rank, admirably cared for; the object of persistent veneration on the part of the populace, and in continual receipt of admiring letters and gifts; adulated by the distinguished persons who came to visit him—Hindenburg may be regarded as the happiest man in wartime Germany. Among all the commanders for whose personal gratification (for this is the essential truth) the war was carried on, no one had so few vexations to put up with as he.

VI

What could be more natural than a clash between the popular hero and a court general? Would not a dramatist have had to invent one, if history had not spontaneously brought it about? Distrust of Falkenhayn, the failure of Schlieffen's plan on the Marne, the natural desire of every general to push the attack against the enemy confronting him (the Russians, in this case)—all these conspired to quicken the opposition between Hindenburg and his new chief. The disastrous aspect of the situation was that this necessarily involved a clash with the emperor as well.

While many millions of Germans continued to believe in the wisdom and efficiency of their leaders (would they otherwise have persisted in sacrificing themselves?), they became the victims of jealousies, court intrigues, and quarrels about precedence. Only after long years are data concerning these matters arising out of the piles of documents in which they have been entombed; arising like the spirits of the slain, who ask, reproachfully, "What did we die for?"

Because Hindenburg was the popular hero, and, since nothing decisive was being done in the West, he endeavored to settle matters in the East where he had been victorious, Falkenhayn, with redoubled tenacity, continued to throw away the lives of German youths at Ypres, without the remotest prospect of breaking through there. Because the German emperor had come to an arrangement with the Austrians before the war broke out that he, a German, was to be the supreme commander of the troops, and because Conrad von Hötzendorf was in revolt against this compact, Falkenhayn elbowed his way into the dispute between Hapsburg and Hohenzollern and allowed Conrad to take independent action which would weaken Hindenburg's position. When the German field marshal marched on Warsaw, the Austrians hung back, so that 60 German battalions were facing 224 Russian ones; the roads to Breslau and Berlin were practically opened to the Russians, and Hindenburg was compelled to effect a rapid withdrawal. Some military critics speak of this retreat as the most important of the joint operations of the two commanders. The art of war is the strangest of the arts; when it is the instrument of victory, the commander is great; but when it is the instrument of a clever retreat, he is even greater. In all the other arts, failure is censured.

On two subsequent occasions, Hindenburg and Ludendorff wished to strike an annihilating blow at Russia, but the emperor and Falkenhayn, alarmed by their own failures, would not permit the offensive, agreeing only to a "war of attrition." Beyond question, jealousy was not the only motive that actuated them; but that it was a contributory factor is shown by the passionate way in which Falkenhayn in every respect the emperor's tool, tried to thwart and injure the popular commanders who were his subordinates. Had he not learned as one of the main principles of strategy that the enemy's forces must be divided in order to strike at them in separate sections? What if he were to detach General Ludendorff, the dangerous and ardent man who was the moving spirit of the eastern front, from old Hindenburg, thus leaving the latter unaided to show the German people how much genius he possessed? He therefore commanded Ludendorff to organize a Southern Army, and to take command of this himself. That was the emperor's first blow directed against the popular hero.

Thereupon the veteran servant of the king arose in revolt against his master. Hindenburg's letter of dissent, which in point of form it was an impropriety to send, has never been published. It must have contained a protest, not only against this last order of Falkenhayn's, but also against the commander in chief's whole attitude, for on January 15, Moltke

10

wrote to Hindenburg: "I know how hard it must have been to a man of your loyalty to communicate to His Majesty in your letter my own thoughts concerning General Falkenhayn, and your judgment of him. I hope to God that your action may be successful! This man is tending to bring us all, the throne and our fatherland, down to destruction. . . . No one but you could have written as you have so rightly done. . . . I congratulate Your Excellency, and I shall stand and fall with you."

Moltke was reputed pious. Is there not a false ring about the introduction of God's name into his intrigue? Having been long since superseded, he could not stand with Hindenburg; and since he was collaborating with the disgruntled generals, we need not wonder that Hindenburg's letter was speedily followed by an emissary from the eastern front, Major von Haeften by name, who was to be instrumental in persuading the emperor to reinstate Moltke.

Already, three months after Hindenburg's rise, the emperor was almost the field marshal's prisoner. True, he promptly dismissed von Haeften, and would not hear a word about the reinstatement of Moltke, with whom he had been so greatly disappointed. But William did not venture to push the scheme of detaching Ludendorff from Hindenburg. He countermanded Falkenhayn's order to separate the two men, thus recognizing the field marshal's right to communicate with him directly. In diplomatic phraseology, this likewise was one of those retreats of which the critics will approve; but it was the first retreat of the aging emperor who, soon after his accession to the throne, had dared to "drop the pilot"—to depose Bismarck.

The empress, his brother, and his son, but above all
Bethmann, brought their influence to bear on him in
the matter. They were united in the conviction that
the popular hero must become supreme, but William
was to dally for another eighteen months before making up his mind to an appointment which would
thrust himself into the background.

"Hindenburg's fame," reported Prince Hohenlohe,
the Austrian ambassador, writing at this juncture from
Berlin to Vienna, "gives Falkenhayn no rest. . . .
Beyond question that is why Falkenhayn is so eager
for a great offensive in Galicia in the hope that a victory
may be won there without Hindenburg having any
part in it. . . . An element in the affair naturally is
that Emperor William, for all his appreciation of
Hindenburg's services, cannot suppress a certain
amount of jealousy on account of the immoderate
increase in the popularity of the field marshal. Nevertheless, he cannot fail to rejoice that this man, whom
he appointed to high command against the advice of
many distinguished officers, has been so conspicuously
successful. Hindenburg's intervention against Falkenhayn has served only to raise the latter in the emperor's
esteem and to secure for him exceptional distinctions."

Such were the underground intrigues which led to
battles, forced movements of troops and defeats in
which hundreds of thousands of patriotic Germans did
their best, trusting in the utterances of their leaders,
and innocently believing that they were risking or laying down their lives for the welfare of the fatherland.
The battles have been forgotten and which of the
two factions was right, those who wished to strike
an annihilating blow, or those who wished to continue

the war of attrition, is only of interest now to writers of the history of the Great War. That does not concern me. But the struggle between types of character is important for all time.

First, we see a king, who for twenty years has been clamoring to the world about his mailed fist and his shining blade, but has never learned the art of war. Now that the war which he has unceasingly threatened is upon him, he loses his nerve, and has to take refuge behind the backs of veteran generals who are trying to save his throne for him. But he becomes jealous of them when they are too successful and his subjects acclaim them, so that he tries to stop their triumphant advance. He prefers to place his troops at the disposal of their rival, a man of his own finding, one who makes such charming obeisances, and accredits the monarch with the glory resulting from victories, thus confirming the royal master's perspicacity before the world. Second, we have a sickly general, who, because he is a neurasthenic, loses the decisive battle of the war, but who, three months later, instead of resting content with his favorite study, theosophy, wants to climb back into the office of commander in chief by standing on the broad shoulders of the new popular hero. Next we have a favorite, who, when the realm is at grips with fate, wants to modify the ground plan of the German war in such a way that the Austrian ally (also detested) shall gain a victory rather than the much envied popular hero. In a world of such intrigues, and when we are faced by such documents, must not our sympathies return to the two commanders who, in contradistinction to all others, at any rate know how to win battles?

In front of his Posen Castle, 1915

Their subsequent dangerous omnipotence will be incomprehensible except to those who have investigated the story of their struggle against their chief, Falkenhayn, and against the emperor. While Hindenburg is proposing to seize the Russian army in a vise in Poland and Galicia, and, with the support of the Austrians, to annihilate it, Falkenhayn, by counter orders, holds them in check, until at length, in May, 1915, the break through the Russian lines at Gorlice is effected by another general than Hindenburg, namely by Von Seeckt—a matter which, later, was to result in other politically important enmities. Then the emperor, wishing to keep the popular hero under better control, moves G.H.Q. to Posen (where, as it happened, both Hindenburg and Ludendorff had been born), establishing himself in the East, although the decisive battle is not to take place in that part of the world. Falkenhayn will not provide enough troops and munitions for another great advance in the direction of Kovno and Grodno. In the face of all these absurdities, Ludendorff, for the first time, makes a scene in the emperor's presence, so that the empress has to intermediate.

Falkenhayn, meanwhile, was trying to win his laurels in the lowlands around Verdun, sacrificing half a million men in the attempt. During this holocaust, he compelled Hindenburg to spend the second winter of the war inactive. When the field marshal made fresh complaints to the emperor, Falkenhayn rejoined: "Whether Your Excellency approves the views of the Army High Command does not matter now, since His Majesty has decided. In such an event, every part of our armed forces has unconditionally to adapt itself to the plan of the High Command. As to the other points in your telegram, I must decline to bring them to His Majesty's notice, since they take the form of irrelevant historical comments with which, in these serious days, I could not possibly trouble the Supreme War Lord."

He did not reply, "I, the supple court general," although, in his own person, he was the High Command, and although His Majesty's decision was given merely by a nod of the head before luncheon; and although the emperor, who must not now be disturbed was delighted to receive any and every visitor, being so much bored during the war that his courtiers were continually on the hunt for something to amuse him and occupy his mind. The two commanders, however, were condemned "to almost complete inactivity" throughout this winter. While before Verdun the youth of two nations was being slaughtered, the leading strategist of the war was organizing the conquered provinces, and the popular hero, who wanted to fight an annihilating action and to win a great victory, was glad to relate the shooting of a mighty elk, a fallow deer, and a bison in January, 1916, in the Russian forest of Bialovich. The black head of the bison had been prominent for six centuries in the family coat of arms.

During the secluded life the two commanders led in their comfortable quarters, they knew nothing of the feelings and thoughts of their troops, and yet these "common soldiers" were not mere machines—or, if machines, were such as would one day fiercely resent the work they were being put to. Now and later, Hindenburg and Ludendorff lived apart from the commonalty. It was in accordance with the established

order of things that they should not personally experience the working of the enemy's chief weapon,
hunger; but they never even saw a private soldier or
a workwoman who was undernourished. In Hindenburg's memoirs, indeed, there are frequent references to "the wonderful achievements of our excellent
army;" but the words sound like those in which a
Junker had been accustomed to commend his serfs
after the gathering of the crops. He liked to speak to
his men in a partiarchal tone, asking them whether
the bean soup was good, and these grateful Germans
always answered with a smile: "*Jawohl, Herr General-
Feldmarschall!*" Not a word in his book records a
spontaneous saying, the look upon a face, an answering glance, from any member of this gray, infinitely
numerous people's army. As late as October, 1918,
when the populace, long held in check, was beginning
to mutiny, Hindenburg, in conference with the imperial chancellor, vetoed the proposal that officers and
men should have the same rations.

But one little encounter is sketched. In the autumn
of 1915, accompanied by his painter-in-ordinary, the
field marshal went for a constitutional in an eastern
area which the Russians had invaded during the early
stages of the war. They met a countrywoman, ac-
costed her, and asked her how she had got on during
the Russian occupation. The woman remained mute.
At length Hindenburg impatiently demanded, "I want
to know what happened to you, how you got on
during those days."

The woman answered, "Herr Hindenburg must not
ask what happened, but what did not happen!" With
a burning blush, she escaped from the colloquy. This

encounter, recorded by Vogel, has no epilog added
by the painter turned courtier. We are not told that
Hindenburg was dumfounded by the incident, or that
he inquired what terrible distress the poor woman
must have witnessed or endured to make her answer
as she did. He tells us nothing either of this or of
the hundreds of other answers that must have been
given him. During the evenings, at mess, where
amusing anecdotes from the front were frequently
retailed, there is no word about any such answer.
The people are there to answer whatever questions
may be asked them. When a woman is stubborn, becomes impudent, and runs away, the old hag can thank
her stars if she escapes arrest. What had happened?
Nothing had happened, neither to Hindenburg on the
day of the interview, nor to the woman during the
Russian occupation—nothing of moment.

More and more voices made themselves heard, however, through the newspapers, concerning the need for
handing over power to these two conquerors who were
being kept out of action against their will. "There
is only one way," wrote Tirpitz as early as March,
1915. "Hindenburg must become imperial chancellor,
chief of General Staff, and chief of the admiralty, all
in one. . . . I have little personal knowledge of him,
and do not know whether he has any political insight.
But he seems to be a shrewd, sound man; while
Ludendorff has certainly the proper spirit for bold
and venturesome enterprises in the East." Such were
the ideas of one of the most powerful and independent
men in the realm, who was destined later, again, to
play a decisive part in Hindenburg's life. Today he
knows little of Hindenburg, but he has absorbed the

Hindenburg legend, and, not being a court admiral, he dreams of a dictatorship.

But eighteen months were to elapse after Tirpitz's anxious utterance before Falkenhayn had earned enough discredit to make his disappearance from the scene essential. The attempt to storm Verdun, which cost 225,000 German lives, had failed. Rumania had entered the war. The chancellor Bethmann, another weakling, when urging Hindenburg's appointment, was seeking an authority on which he could rely, without foreseeing that the man would be strong enough, not only to support him, but also to overthrow him. We have come to August, 1916, two years after the battle of Tannenberg. The emperor, afraid to meet the eyes of his unsuccessful favorite, did not personally inform Falkenhayn what was afoot, but told another court general to telephone to Hindenburg summoning him and Ludendorff to G.H.Q. Falkenhayn heard nothing of the matter. The emperor in cheerful mood received the two commanders on the castle terrace (William's state performances during the war, as previously, always took place upon terraces, in a park, in reception rooms; and were always associated with luncheon parties), and appointed them to the supreme command of the army.

Their titles were traditional, but their powers were new. Ludendorff was given the right, in case a difference of opinion should arise between him and his colleague, of appealing directly to the emperor; Hindenburg's powers were left undefined. He had not pushed himself to the front, and he did not know at this moment to what extent he and his colleague were to become Germany's dictators. It is true that both of them had fought against Falkenhayn and believed they could make a better job of things than he was doing. Moreover, Ludendorff's ambition made him aim at supreme power.

Hindenburg, however, was simply wafted upwards by the legend.

VII

On this day in August, 1916, at Pless Castle in Silesia, for practical purposes Bismarck's constitution was thrown upon the scrap heap. Since the establishment of the empire, the emperor had been the Supreme War Lord, to whom the chief of the General Staff was responsible, as the manager of a business is to an owner who can dismiss the manager at any time. Now the emperor had two chiefs, himself becoming no more than a decorative personality like the king of England, and actually unable any longer to dismiss them. Furthermore, in view of differences between the political and the miltary arms which might be expected to arise from moment to moment, the post of supreme judge had slipped from his grasp. William II, who received his power directly from God, who had so long challenged the world as an almighty and all-capable genius, was degraded to the position of a shadow. In a panic at the outset of the war, he had sent two men to take command of the eastern front; if they failed in the great enterprise now intrusted to them, the emperor would lose his crown.

Hindenburg somewhat reluctantly, but Ludendorff eagerly, seized the fourfold dictatorship. They sent their opponent Falkenhayn as commander in chief, not into the desert, but to Rumania, where, by speedy victories, he acquired fame; manifestly he was one of those born to succeed in the second rank. A fundamentally new plan was drafted by Ludendorff, not along the line he had been urging for years, but, to the astonishment of the experts, aiming at the delivery of the chief thrust in the West. Was it that France, customarily regarded as the hereditary foe, exerted a magical attraction on every German supreme commander; or was it that Ludendorff already anticipated the Russian revolution? The development of the next two years showed indecision as regards the distribution of the troops; but always the preponderance of force was directed towards the West where the commanders expected the final decision and where they ultimately failed.

The second dictatorship was turned inward, where hitherto the delegated General Command had ruled in accordance with the constitution under the orders of the chancellor. Now the two army commanders took control, and therewith the management of the slowly reviving political parties, of preventive arrests, of the censorship, and of all the other matters which decided the mood of the country. Since they were also responsible for the supply of munitions, they became dictators of economic life as well.

The fourth dictatorship concerned the problems of the war aims, those of the offer of terms of peace, and in due time the actual conclusion of peace; for these matters would now be left to the High Command. This meant, since henceforward the emperor's wishes might be considered of no account, that they were in the hands of the two commanders, who therefore wielded the dictatorship of foreign policy.

What competence had Hindenburg and Ludendorff to function as dictators in any field of public life with the exception of the military one? What preliminary training had they had for such undertakings? Did they really know anything about the economic life of Germany, the social structure of the country, or the composition of the various classes? When had they studied the characteristics of foreign lands, their make-up and history, or the causes and consequences of the alliance against Germany? What knowledge had they of such matters as compared with Lloyd George or Clemenceau, who, though subject to some sort of control, and therefore far less effective dictators in their respective countries than Hindenburg and Ludendorff now became in Germany, still exercised a considerable measure of independent power as opponents? I will let Hindenburg answer these questions.

In his memoirs he speaks of himself as having "an unpolitical nature. I had no inclination to occupy myself with contemporary politics. Perhaps this was because my liking for the rôle of political critic was too small; or perhaps it was because my soldierly feelings were too strongly developed. To the last cause, doubtless, must be assigned my dislike for diplomatic negotiation. Of course it may be said that this dislike was due to prejudice or to lack of understanding. . . . However that may be, my feeling was that concern with diplomatic matters was in some way fundamentally alien to our German character." During the war "I never felt the need or the wish to occupy myself with contemporary political questions more than was absolutely indispensable." He quotes

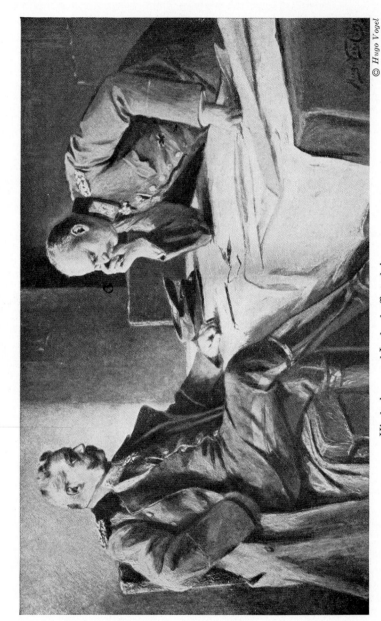

Hindenburg and Ludendorff studying a war map

Moltke: "During his operations, an army commander must think first of all of military success. How his victories or defeats may react upon the political world is no affair of his, inasmuch as the turning of the former or the latter to account is the business of statesmen alone."

"On the other hand," Hindenburg continues, "I should have had an uneasy conscience if I had not made my views effectively felt whenever it seemed clear to me that the activities of others were driving us into dubious paths; if I had not insisted upon activity whenever perplexity or inertia appeared to me dominant; if, finally, I had not emphasized my views as to the present and the future when it seemed to me that the conduct of the war and the future military safety of my country were being endangered by political measures. . . . Whenever my opinion was asked, whenever a question arose to which an answer from the German side was not forthcoming though an answer was essential, I saw no reason for holding my peace."

It is here that tragical complications begin. We have a soldier who repudiates interest in politics and declares that he has no talent for such matters; who insists that the Germans in general are averse to or without gifts for diplomacy; who approvingly quotes the utterance of one whom he regards as his master, to the effect that the political utilization of the successes or failures of the commander in the field must be left exclusively to professional statesmen. Yet, almost in the same breath, he declares that his conscience would prick him if he should fail to enforce his own policy upon a perplexed and inert government; if he should refrain from answering unanswered questions; if he should not intervene to insure the future safety of his country, this implying the need to participate in settling the terms of peace. Since Hindenburg had not wormed his way into his high position or struggled to attain it, but, literally, had been lifted into it by a popular fiat, was he therefore entitled to regard himself as executant of the national will? Was a man who was such a slave to duty entitled, merely because his king was a weakling, to play the part, not only of Blücher and Gneisenau, but—in defiance of Prussian tradition—also that of Hardenberg the statesman, to whom Gneisenau had always subordinated himself? Was Germany's political situation like that of a house on fire, where, when the professional firemen are tardy in coming to the rescue, any stout-hearted layman will take charge of operations and do his best to save the inhabitants.

But what if, from among the depths of the people, other ideas and demands should arise; if, through the mouths of their parliamentary representatives, classes estranged from the two commanders should run counter to the opinions of these popular heroes, and demand an understanding with the enemy instead of conquest and a fight to a finish? By what moral right (since there was no written one), did he, having declared his antipathy for "politics," exclude from influence the new energies which were perhaps forming themselves beneath the "perplexity and inertia" he decried? Was he entitled, by threatening to throw up his position, to stifle proposals for seeking safety along lines to which he was averse? Granted the weakness of the emperor, the chancellor, and the

Reichstag, it was nonetheless presumptuous for a man who knew himself to have no gift for politics to venture upon the decision of political questions that were supremely important; and the best that can be said by the historian concerning the political dictatorship of these two commanders is that they acted conscientiously according to their lights.

Although when a common soldier makes a mistake it may be accepted as a valid excuse that he did his best according to his lights, such an excuse is not accepted either by the law courts or by the public when a doctor commits a blunder; and the plea of "patriotism" is no less inadequate as exculpation in the case of kings, ministers of State, or army commanders. As regards the actions of persons in so high a position, the question is not whether they acted according to their best lights (why should they do anything else?), but whether their lights were good enough. No one's lights are good enough to deal with all great problems simultaneously.

Undoubtedly our two commanders were sufficiently shrewd in respect to many matters that were outside their competence to leave the formal leadership to others. Ludendorff, though he had a taste for politics, telling us that he had often been recommended for the post of chancellor, goes on to say, "But, if I was to carry on the world war, I had to control the instrument of war. This alone demanded exceptional capacity for work. It would have been unthinkable to take over simultaneously the management of the cumbrous machine of government. Germany needed a dictator whose activities would be centered in Berlin and not at G.H.Q." But how long would Ludendorff have put up with a civilian dictator, since he could endure even a military chief only because the latter was a man who seldom had a word to say? How was it possible to draw a hard-and-fast line between campaigning and politics, seeing that, during the long-lasting encirclement and blockade of the Central Powers, every economic problem was interlaced with the problem of the war, and in any case a soldier who has won a victory finds it hard to renounce the fruit? What about Hindenburg? Did he perhaps remember those days after the battle of Königgratz, when, a lieutenant of eighteen, he and his comrades used to look through a telescope at the tower of St. Stephen's in Vienna, and when these young hotheads had gnashed their teeth because the political leader who had begun the whole business, had sounded the bugle for retreat? But may not Hindenburg have subsequently come to recognize the wisdom of Bismarck who in the Truce of Nikolsburg had prudently renounced the fruit of victory?

The fact was that, side by side with the Hindenburg legend, it was the lack of a Bismarck in Germany which made the essentially unpolitical Hindenburg a political dictator in conjunction with Ludendorff, who also regarded himself as "a soldier and not a statesman." Their mistake was not that of seizing political power, but that, feeling themselves incompetent to exercise it, they were not sufficiently enlightened to renounce it. Although Hindenburg disliked Bismarck, one can hardly doubt that the field marshal must have read the following passage in the ex-chancellor's memoirs: "The establishment and limitation of war aims, the consultation with the monarch about such matters, are and remain during the war as they were before it began a political problem; and the way in which this problem is solved cannot fail to exert an influence upon the conduct of the war."

In faint tones follows the voice of Bismarck's anæmic successor, Bethmann, who, after having advised the dictatorship of the two commanders from the eastern front, was frightened by his own rede, and said to his collaborator: "Now we have replaced Falkenhayn by Ludendorff. Certainly this is good strategy, but I am afraid he will ruin my whole policy."

Subsequently Bethmann testified to the fact that these forebodings had been justified by events, writing: "There was hardly a single political question concerning which Ludendorff and the High Command did not merely insist upon a say, but also upon the exclusive right to decide the issue, . . . always alleging that otherwise the war would be lost, and that Hindenburg would throw up the sponge. Beginning with the adoption of personal and business relationships which made harmonious collaboration practically impossible, and going on to open conflict with the political leaders of the country, the circumstances of the July crisis led to a régime which unquestionably culminated in an autocracy of the military command."

But what if Hindenburg became the really effective dictator, occupying a unique position in the German political world? "Ludendorff," testified General Wetzell before the Commission of Inquiry, "was not in a position to do everything he wanted. Between him and the Supreme War Lord there always stood the iron figure of the field marshal—in political matters no less than in military ones."

II

"The emperor as a person," wrote Bredt in a report to the same Commission, "had retired into the background, and the true War Lord of the German armies was Hindenburg. Not only was the entire fighting force of Germany controlled by this one personality, but, in the last resort, the decision always rested with him." General von Kuhl wrote, "Although Ludendorff was co-responsible, and however great an influence may be ascribed to him in theory, in actual fact Hindenburg was responsible."

Hindenburg never denied this. If he plumed himself upon the victories won by Ludendorff's military genius, he subsequently accepted the reproaches leveled against Ludendorff's policy. In one of his threateningly subservient letters to the emperor, Hindenburg went so far as to demand the right to decide "everything which touches the life of the German fatherland." By now his power had become so overwhelming that Bismarck in purgatory must have turned green with envy as he read the reports of it. Thus neither of our two commanders had any right, after defeat, to ascribe their failure to errors of statesmanship on the part of Germany's politicians—a thing defeated commanders are so fond of doing. If Hindenburg, as the particulars show, had the final word in all political questions, if he signed the two main decisions in January, 1917, and in October, 1918, he must bear the blame as well as wear the laurels.

That was why, being an upright man, in the beginning of the year 1918, when he was at odds with the emperor, he wrote that he himself and Ludendorff were actually, though not legally, responsible "before the German people, before history, and before our own

consciences, as regards the terms of peace. . . . His
Majesty's decision cannot override the promptings of
the generals' consciences." In extreme old age, moreover, he said to a confidant, "I lost the greatest war
in history. How will posterity judge me?"

VIII

There were three powers in Germany which might
have been competent to resist the dictatorship of the
two commanders. In August, 1914, a power had been
assigned to the emperor vaster and more compre-
hensive than any enjoyed by the belligerent sovereigns. Since his formula, "We have been shamefully
attacked," was universally believed by the Germans,
himself not excepted; and since, for a long time, the
political parties had practically ceased to exist, William II was mightier than the kings of Prussia had
been for a century. Constitutionally and by popular
approval, he was in very fact the Supreme War Lord.

But a neurasthenic who though in safety perceives
danger on all sides, collapses as soon as danger comes
close. When a parade-ground show became a mobilization, when maneuvers turned into genuine battle,
the change was too much for the weak heart of this
war lord, and the man completely broke down. The
futility of the previous conduct of his life became
painfully conspicuous now that he had to forgo the
diurnal round of banquets and receptions, the laying
of corner stones, official visits, and speeches, concerning which Bismarck had written, "The emperor
would like to have a birthday every day." When the
dictatorship of the two commanders had become estab-

lished, William's daily work was reduced to half an hour. At noon, Ludendorff reported to His Majesty, while Hindenburg stood by. "On these occasions," writes Hindenburg, "Ludendorff gave a picture of the situation. When important decisions had to be made, I myself took the floor, requesting, whenever this seemed necessary, the imperial approval of our plans. The great confidence the emperor placed in us rendered the specific assent of the All Highest needless as regards matters that were not fundamental. . . . For the rest, even as concerned proposals for fresh operations, he was usually content with my explanations."

The courtly gloss of this phrasing does its best to conceal the utter boredom of this half-hour conference. To accelerate the despatch of business (since not only had the war to be carried on, but the whole German realm to be ruled), "the time of our daily report to the emperor was in many cases likewise devoted to conferences with representatives of the government."

This lamentable background, which ought by rights to have been a strong foreground, must never be lost sight of when we are contemplating in the rôle of dictator His Majesty's most loyal officer, who was subsequently to be raised to the emperor's own position. "We are vassals," he had once quoted; "we fight the king's battles, we obey. He commands, wills, and does whatever is right." All the while the dictators continued to keep up appearances before the king, in order to save his Majesty's face; and to the question why he did not go a step farther, Ludendorff replied: "I am still too much of a cadet to want to play Cromwell's part."

The second power in the realm, the chancellor, whose abilities had not impressed anyone during the five peaceful years in which he had been the leading statesman of the German realm, had, during the first days of the war, become world-famous through two utterances. When the British ambassador, taking leave on the occasion of the British declaration of war, referred to the German infringement of the Belgian treaty, Bethmann did not trouble to ask whether England had never broken treaties—though such blunt truths as these come readily to the lips of a born statesman when war breaks out. Falling into the Englishman's snare, he described the treaty as "a scrap of paper." In any other country than Germany, so gross an error, spoken in a private diplomatic interview and promptly trumpeted throughout the world, would have sufficed to sign a minister's political death warrant. The same day, before the Reichstag, Bethmann said, "Necessity knows no law." The truth of these two remarks, which the Allied Powers underlined again and again during the war by their own breaches of international law, is no excuse for Bethmann's stupidity. In Bethmann-Hollweg's case, as in the case of Sir Edward Grey (afterwards Lord Grey of Fallodon), statesmen's ignorance of the foreign nations with which they had to deal led to misunderstandings which took on the magnitude of catastrophes. Perhaps the whole war might have been avoided if the ministers of State in Europe had known the nature, the language, the typical civilizations of the countries they were salaried to know and understand.

Bethmann's weakness was a German weakness. He

worshiped the invisible gods in the Königsplatz, the
all-giving, all-destroying General Staff whose mys-
terious powers, whose incomprehensible but mortal
brains carried on their wonderful activities in the
twilight between war and peace, to emerge from dark
clouds as suddenly and as terrifyingly as a thunder-
storm. Since the chancellor, like the emperor, had
proclaimed to the world that Germany had only
drawn the sword in self-defense, it was the former's
easy task to confine himself to this aim. But when, in
November, 1914, General Hoffmann declared that
Belgium would have to be surrendered in the peace,
Bethmann rejoined: "You are the first soldier who
has expressed to me the view I myself hold. But if
I were to say as much in the Reichstag, a hurricane of
public opinion would sweep me from my place."
Such was the height of selfishness reached by Germany's leading statesman. Five years later how much
virile self-confidence he possessed was shown before
the Commission of Inquiry of the Reichstag where
he had to testify under oath. When asked whether
he would take the oath or would prefer to affirm,
he answered hesitatingly: "I should like . . . to
testify in the same manner as Count Bernstorff."
Who can be surprised that Bethmann, during the
year 1917, in the interval between these two utterances, agreed to everything which he had previously
opposed!

The third power in Germany, the Reichstag which,
by the constitution, still retained a voice in war time,
had, for practical purposes, abdicated. Even the
socialists, whose habit it had been for the last thirty
years to distrust every government, believed the words

of the White Book which declared that Germany had been shamefully attacked by a foresworn tsar. Thus the very men who, only three days earlier in Brussels, holding conference with their French comrades, had pledged themselves to resist the outbreak of war "*par tous les moyens,*" now unanimously voted the credits for a war as to whose origin they must, at least, have been skeptical. The only one among them who was inclined to take another course, Karl Liebknecht, complied with the will of the Party, and held his peace.

No doubt the tsar as one of Germany's enemies had complicated the situation; and the socialists recalled the words of their deceased leader Engels, who, in the eighteen eighties had written a wonderful prophecy of the war:

"Prussia-Germany can no longer engage in any war that will not become a world war, and, indeed, a world war of unprecedented extent and violence. From eight to ten million soldiers will be at death grips with one another. The devastation of the Thirty Years' War will be compressed within the space of from three to four years, and will be diffused over the whole continent. Famine, pestilence, general confusion, arising from urgent poverty, will be spread throughout the army and the populace; hopeless disorganization of our highly artificialized economic system as regards commerce, industry, and credit alike, ending in universal bankruptcy; a collapse of the ancient States and of their traditional statecraft, proceeding so far that crowns by the dozen will be rolling on the pavement, and no one will care to pick them up."

This amazing prophecy, in which even the figures were correct, was printed by Engels in December, 1888, thirty years before the end of the war. He acclaimed its coming, as certain to lead to the liberation of the Russian and the German workers—of course under the control of the government.

Thirty years later, the Reichstag allowed its worthy teacher, the imperial government, to take this control out of its hands; for as soon as the well-behaved children had voted five billions, they were given a holiday, being strictly forbidden to assemble, to speak above a whisper, or to complain of their good teacher. They all went obediently back to their homes at the word of command; but whereas the citizens spoke of what was now inaugurated as the "truce of parties," the generals called it a "state of siege." Whilst in the other belligerent countries criticisms in the press and uttered by the representatives of the people were able to compensate for the mistakes of the generals and statesmen by securing dismissals, and by the refusal of the "subjects" to do as they were bid (for even in the first sitting of the Duma after the outbreak of war, the opposition had something to say), in Germany and Austria all that commoners had to do was to hold their tongues and to fight. Indeed, most of them found it easier to die for their fatherland than to think for it.

Could anything more be expected from the Germans? Had they not, in Prussia at any rate, for the last two centuries left the task of political thinking to that class whose members had been trained, not indeed to become capable rulers, but to exert the will-to-power—trained upon their estates on either bank of the Elbe, in the military academy, and on the General Staff—receiving from the king their lands as guarantees of power? If, after the war, the crown prince of Germany complained that the Germans had lacked a Clemenceau—it was his own father, nay it was Bismarck, who had made it impossible for such a man as Clemenceau, sprung from an obscure bourgeois family, to rise to power in Germany. Clemenceau and Lloyd George were summoned to lead the war by the voices of their respective nations. The only thing which the German people could give freely, its favor, was given to a man who was at once Junker and general, one who a few years later, was elected to become the head of the State.

Habituated to love order more than liberty, the Germans were, to begin with, happy in their passive rôle; they would never squabble after the manner of their enemies across the Rhine, where the Chambers had actually cashiered a general; and when they spoke of the "truce of parties," it aroused in their minds a comfortable and homelike impression such as that produced by an apple dumpling. At this stage, no one troubled to ask whether a nation which was paying for the war with its money as well as with its blood (for those billions were the people's own money) might not have the right to utter a word through the mouths of its parliamentary representatives; for the Prussians were used to a suffrage which gave a rich man as many votes as a hundred or a thousand poor ones. As far as democracy went, Germany was a century behind the times, and elsewhere in the world people could hardly believe that as late as 1918 the Prussian peasants and workers voted in the third "class" while their landlords and employers voted in the first. Meanwhile the workers had to fight and fall in the first ranks while their lords and masters often stayed at home, leaving their obscurer brethren to sweat in the munition factories, making barbed wire or shells for their benefit and for that of the country. No one dreamed in these early days of the party truce of trying to abolish such inequalities.

When, after the revolution of 1688, England was for many years at war with the *Roi Soleil*, there was no talk of truce between the Lower House and the House of Peers. When, a century later, France had to defend the young Republic against foreign onslaughts, the Jacobins did not swear a peace with the nobles or the wealthy bourgeois but drove them out. By fighting for rights at home while at war against foreign foes, these critical but enthusiastic nations intensified their impetus, instead of having it stifled by smoldering discontent. The Germans, being used to having the traffic held up in their streets when companies or regiments were marching to parade, remained, even in war time, standing like good children on the sidewalk, declaring the great boulevard of the class struggle closed to allow the passage of troops. In the last great speech he ever delivered, Bismarck said that wars were decided by impetus and fire; but, as far as the Germans were concerned, during the World War this impetus was repressed by the heavy hand of the military authorities. While Germany was being starved by the blockade, was being treated by her enemies as a beleagued fortress, those who ruled within were themselves maintaining a "state of siege"; their subjects must be shown that cloud-bursts and avalanches made no difference to the fact that a German's chief duty was to obey.

Such was the internal situation. Since neither the emperor nor the chancellor nor the Reichstag continued to exercise power, the two dictators had a free hand.

IX

Their activities were, above all, political. After the speedy subjugation of Rumania—a sort of brilliant overture performed by their deposed adversary—the new commanders were stalled both in the West and in the East as their predecessors had been, and seemed determined to improve the desperate war position by political measures. Faced by the same gloomy situation as everyone who had held power before him during the war, Hindenburg should surely have realized that his only hope was to relieve the pressure upon Germany by sowing division among its enemies. He must win over Russia or England or both, and must avoid raising up any fresh adversaries. After the conquest of Rumania, this would have been possible, by being conciliatory to Russia in Poland, to England in the vital question of Belgium, and to the United States as concerns the privateering supply of munitions to the Allies. The two commanders took the opposite course, and within five months had made it impossible to dream of conciliating any of these three countries. The old saying that the pen frustrates the conquests of the sword now acquired new significance, when the same hand was holding both pen and sword.

Peace with Russia; that was every German's wish-dream, since neither sentiment nor tradition impelled

Germany to aim at the conquest of Muscovy. For centuries the two countries had been friendly neighbors. But while in Stockholm German emissaries were negotiating with the vice president of the Duma in the hope of paving the way for peace with the tsar, who was known to be weary of the war, and while the new Russian premier (misnamed Stürmer) was hinting his readiness for an amicable arrangement, the two commanders decided to establish a kingdom of Poland, thus destroying any chance of a separate peace with Russia. They did not want such a peace. They hoped to deliver a crushing blow upon their particular enemy, to whose defeat at Tannenberg they owed their glory; and they therefore mobilized Polish soldiers against Russia. In August, 1915, Ludendorff had written: "We shall not make a separate peace with Russia. We do not need one, for we are strong. If I can't do what I want in Poland, I must found another kingdom in Lithuania and Courland." Still more emphatically, in October, 1915, he declared "that Poland must on no account be restored to Russia, nor must it go to Austria, but must become a more or less independent State under German tutelage. We must safeguard our own future; . . . and this becomes more difficult the less we now take advantage of our opportunities to weaken Russia." July, 1916: "Since the Austrians fail us, I turn my eyes once more towards Poland. The Pole is a good soldier. Let us make a grand duchy of Poland, with Warsaw and Lublin, and then drill a Polish army to fight under German leadership."

Now, having risen to power, the two commanders insisted upon the immediate establishment of a king-

dom of Poland, in which the German governor of
Warsaw had promised to levy a million soldiers, or, at
least, four divisions.   Vainly did Bethmann and Helfferich, the chancellor and the vice chancellor, who were
working for a separate peace with Russia, try to hinder
this scheme.   Ludendorff was continually dreaming of
Polish divisions; the dictators insisted upon the foundation of the new kingdom, and got their way in two
months.   "In view of our war situation," writes
Hindenburg, "how could I possibly have made myself
responsible for the refusal of such auxiliaries? But if
I was to get them, there was no time to be lost."

Here is disclosed one of the field marshal's character traits which was subsequently to decide the fate
of Germany, namely the weakness of a man otherwise
so resolute when matters he did not understand were
in question.   Down till the autumn of 1915, whenever
Hindenburg spoke of peace terms, he insisted upon the
need for moderation.   Then came a sudden change of
tone, although there were no fresh victories to justify
it.   As early as October, 1915, he said: "We must make
our position so overwhelmingly strong that no one
will venture to attack us for a century.   Colonies are
of the utmost importance in this matter."

The language of Ludendorff!   The voices of the
Junkers, the kindred and the comrades who, over their
wine at headquarters, had made clear to him what
their loyal hearts expected from a victory!   Taking a
sharp curve, Hindenburg, who knew nothing about
such questions, allowed his sound instinct to be led
astray, and accepted whatever was pumped into him
by his caste.   Fifteen years later, the same trends
were to recur when he was chief of the realm.   Yet he

writes retrospectively, "The discussion of these countless political questions and counter questions served
only to give me uncomfortable hours, and strengthened
my aversion to politics."

The upshot was the enrollment of from eight to ten
thousand Poles under the German flag—and Stürmer's
remark that this action "killed" the possibility of
peace with Russia.

Without fear of uncomfortable hours, and despite
his aversion to politics, the commander thought it his
duty to attack, forthwith, a new political problem.
A number of civilian voices had made themselves heard
in the land, declaring that the integrity of Belgium
must be restored as the chancellor had promised when
war broke out. There seemed a good many reasons in
favor of such a view.

The wound to international morality dealt by the
German invasion of Belgium (the wrongfulness of
which the Allies were perpetually dinning into the ears
of neutrals) could be cured by an unambiguous pledge
to withdraw from Belgium as soon as peace should be
made. As far as England was concerned, strategical
as well as moral considerations came into the question.
England had entered the war on professedly moral
grounds; but Napoleon had declared Antwerp to be a
pistol aimed at England's heart, and that had been
said in days when long-range guns could fire only a
few hundred yards. Furthermore, since the occupation of Belgium there had been a falling-off in German
victories, German forces, and German raw materials.
Whereas in the West, at the outset, 1,700,000 Germans
had faced 2,300,000 enemies, the respective forces at
the beginning of 1916 were 2,300,000 Germans against

3,500,000 foes. As time passed, the blockade restricted the import of wool, cotton, copper, rubber, lubricating oil, and other raw materials. During the third winter of the war, after a bad harvest, it became necessary to replace potatoes in the rations by turnips, and the allowance of bread on the food cards was reduced. The German soldiers, badly fed, clothed, and armed, continued to hold back the enemy in four theaters of war, but were unable to assume a vigorous offensive; and, being fitted and trained for a war of annihilation, were no better at defense than their adversaries.

The surrender of Belgium, since the Belgians were not hereditary enemies and the conquest of their country had not been one of the war aims, must necessarily come next in a German leader's mind to the possibility of peace with Russia. But in this matter the spirit of the Military Academy took precedence of reason, and the idea was rejected on grounds of safety and honor. "Shall we surrender like poltroons a country which, if we did not annex it, would certainly be annexed by the French, a land in which our soldiers were butchered by cowardly francs-tireurs firing at them out of the windows? Shall we give back the Flemings, who are pure-blooded Teutons, to the rule of the Walloons, under which they have so long groaned? Besides, what would happen in the next war if we were again shamefully attacked? The captains of industry would be perfectly right if they were to protect our country forever—by making Belgium's stores of coal and iron their own!"

In the House of Commons, Ramsay MacDonald appealed to the Germans to declare plainly: "We do not want Belgium; we will evacuate it as soon as peace is made. As our chancellor said, our invasion of the country was nothing but an act of military necessity."

In their memorial of April, 1917, the two commanders replied: "Though Belgium still exists, she must be kept under German military control until she is politically and economically ripe to enter into an offensive and defensive alliance with Germany. . . . But, for strategic reasons, Liége and the Flemish coast, together with Bruges, will remain permanently in German possession, or ours under the terms of a ninety-nine-year lease. The cession of the parts and places named is an indispensable condition of peace with England." In his pose of a sterling German soldier, Hindenburg had coined the pithy phrase: "The aim of politics is to injure an adversary by all possible means, including the strongest."

Among the civilians who spoke of peace, Wilson was better understood in Germany than anyone else; for his political morality was derived from or accordant with certain Kantian arguments. But as far as the two commanders were concerned, he, too, was suspect. Now was reaped the fruit of expunging philosophy from the curriculum of the Military Academy. When, at G.H.Q., news came to hand (in December 1916) that the president was preparing a peace move, the emperor countered the move with the parody of a manifesto in which, before all the world, William seemed to be offering to shake hands with his enemies. Since, however, while making this gesture with his right hand, he continued to hold fast with his left to all the territories on which he was firmly planted with both feet, his "friendly offers" were rejected by ten States.

Wilson, whose favor the Allies had been wooing for a year, responded by yet another attempt to keep his country out of the war from which it was benefiting so greatly as a neutral. The long-standing friendship between Germany and the United States could be imperiled only on the high seas; not, as in the case of England, by direct rivalry in naval armaments, but by naval sniping. Germany, whose fleet was only one third as strong as the united fleets of the Allies, could defend her coasts, but could not break the blockade; and was, therefore, as the weaker sea power always is, compelled to fall back upon raiding exploits of cruisers. In this field she achieved wonders, recognized as such even by her enemies. Whether the comparatively new weapon of the submarine was entitled to sink a merchant ship without warning, was still a moot point of international law. Morally, too, the problem was unsolved and perhaps insoluble. Hindenburg had good reason for writing: "Our enemy is bombarding us with American shells. Why should we not sink their transports? Have we not the means of doing so? Law and right! How are our enemies observing law and right in these matters? That is what the soldiers are asking on our fronts." Tirpitz adopted the same view; and in such a situation, every Englishman would have taken an identical line had the country at which the question was pointed been an adversary instead of being the most powerful of all the lands which still remained neutral.

The chancellor, however, impressed upon the naval staff, and upon the two military commanders at the time of their accession to power, that no submarine must sink a neutral vessel. The civilian minister got

12

his way in this matter only because the sinking of
the S. S. *Lusitania* in May, 1915 and of the S. S.
Sussex in March, 1916 had caused great excitement throughout the world, and had made the entry
of the United States into the war extremely probable.
In this matter, as in certain others, the moral indignation of the Allied Powers had a false ring, for the
Lusitania was carrying munitions, and therefore, according to American law, ought not to have had any
passengers on board. The valid reasons against unrestricted or "ruthless" submarine warfare were not
humanitarian at all; they were questions of power,
which in this case signified "questions of caution."

Four months later, when the two commanders had
come to realize that by land fighting they could not
make any more headway than their predecessors, they
had recourse to what Hindenburg described as "The
only means which were still at our disposal in the
beginning of the year 1917 for achieving a German
victory." In support of the hazard, it was merely
necessary to prove that the sinking of British ships
would "force England to her knees" before the Americans, who were also concerned in the matter, would be
in a position to strike an effective blow in Europe.
Of a sudden everyone in Germany began to speak
about tonnage; and, while four million Germans were
occupying the widely scattered trenches, for months
it might have been fancied that Germany was chiefly
engaged in conducting a naval war.

Since it was essential to justify the great resolve, the
naval staff published long tables showing that unrestricted submarine warfare would "do for" England
in six months, whereas the Americans could not bring

a powerful force across the Atlantic within one and a half years. "The Americans have no soldiers," said Admiral Capelle, secretary to the navy, in the Reichstag. "They have plenty of man power, but no officers or noncommissioned officers to train their men. Even when they have trained their soldiers, these can only be brought to Europe in numbers too small to play an important part in the war; nor will American troops be able to land here, for our submarines will sink the transports. From the military point of view, therefore, America counts for nothing, and once again for nothing, and a third time for nothing!" (The fourth time, 1,900,000 men crossed the Atlantic and decided the war; only one transport was sunk.)

These asseverations worked! An admiral had pledged his professional honor. The Prussian Finance Minister asked in the Reichstag whether anyone expected the American reinforcements to swim across the seas or fly over them. Who cannot hear in these stout-hearted words, the vigor of a man of open-air life; who can fail to sense the sanguine expectations, racy of the soil, appropriate to the common sense of one who has never been sophisticated by the niceties of the understanding?

The naval authorities did what was necessary to convince the two commanders, after the manner of company promoters who need money for the building of a factory and can produce figures showing a sure yield of ten per cent or more. The commanders believed what they were told, with the trifling drawback that they were not capitalists, but only executors.

For this method of warfare, moreover, there had been discovered a happy name, which is a very important thing in Germany. It was spoken of as "ruthless" submarine warfare, with the implication that hitherto the war had been carried on with undue consideration. The snappy phrase secured millions of new adherents. Before the decision, whose importance was clear to everyone, the two commanders must speak a decisive word. In view of their training, how could it be expected that they could regard the blockade as anything more than an economic problem? In the great red house in the Königsplatz, where for forty years a thousand brains had been busily at work preparing for the war, there could not have been unearthed a single document to describe the starving-out of the dangerously placed Germany by an enemy with superior sea power. What they wanted now was to work out the figures that would prove the ease with which Britain could be starved by the activities of German submarines. Then all that remained necessary was the calculation of the political consequences.

How they judged these issues is shown by two priceless documents, in which both commanders give tongue at once, whereas Hindenburg mostly kept his own counsel and let Ludendorff speak. His memoranda were written by Ludendorff and other collaborators; his *Aus meinem Leben* was not really the work of his own pen; and quotations from these documents, which must often be made because of the consequences of what purported to be his utterances, have an artificial tone which makes them veil his nature rather than disclose it. There exists a "brief official report" of the

conferences held on January 8 and 9, 1917, to decide
about the submarine campaign, and this report I shall
abridge yet further.[1] At the head of the first document, reproduced from shorthand notes, is written:
"Strictly private, from hand to hand!"—this manifestly implying that anything merely marked "Private" would speedily become common knowledge.

On January 8, at Prince Pless's castle in Upper
Silesia, the two commanders held a council with
Admiral von Holtzendorff, chief of naval staff; there
were also present Captain Grasshoff and Colonel
Bartenwerffer, here playing the part of the Muse of
History, since he took the notes:

Holtzendorff: The chancellor is coming again tomorrow.

Field Marshal: What is his grievance?

Holtzendorff: The chancellor wants to reserve to
himself the diplomatic preparations for the ruthless
submarine campaign in order to keep America out of
the conflict. In the case of America, he has described
the note about armed steamships being "traps for
submarines," as likely to precipitate a conflict.

Ludendorff: The chancellor knew about this already.

Holtzendorff: The Foreign Office believes that if
North America comes into the war, South America
will likewise. They will all be thinking about what will
happen when peace is concluded.

Field Marshal: Well, we've got to win before we can
make peace.

[1] Urkunden der Obersten Heeresleitung, 1920, pp. 322 and foll.; signed "F.
d. R. von Bartenwerffer."

Holtzendorff: What shall we do if the chancellor refuses to join hands with us?

Field Marshal: That question has bothered me a good deal, too.

Holtzendorff: Then you must become chancellor.

Field Marshal: No, I can't and won't. I can't negotiate with the Reichstag.

Holtzendorff: I regard Bülow and Tirpitz as inadmissible, owing to their relations with the emperor.

Ludendorff: I don't wish to overpersuade the field marshal.

Field Marshal: I cannot speak in the Reichstag. I refuse. What about Gallwitz?

Ludendorff: Do you think he is in favor of the submarine campaign?

Holtzendorff: The chancellor inspires great confidence abroad.

Field Marshal: Well, anyhow we must stick together. The submarine campaign must go ahead. We are counting upon war with America, and have made all necessary preparations. Things can't be worse than they are. Everything possible must be done to shorten the war. . . .

Holtzendorff: State Secretary Helfferich said to me: "Your plan will lead to catastrophe." My answer was: "You are letting us drift into catastrophe."

Field Marshal: I agree. The main thing from my point of view is that the submarine warfare will not weaken us anywhere from the military standpoint.

Next day there were seated at the same table Hindenburg, Ludendorff, Bethmann, and once more Bartenwerffer as reporter. The two naval men, whose expert information ought to have been considered decisive, were no longer consulted by the military commanders; nor was the emperor to have a voice. The dictators were alone with the chancellor, and the three of them had to make the greatest decision in the world war. The chancellor, who came to warn, or, probably, after having vetoed the scheme for months, to resign, spoke first:

Chancellor: If His Majesty commands the ruthless submarine campaign; the chancellor is to do his best to see to it that America keeps out of the war. . . . In fact, however, we must reckon upon America's entry against us. . . . Neither Holland nor Denmark will come into the war, at any rate unless events make them believe that our submarine warfare will not be successful. As regards Switzerland, we have to bear in mind that the Allies, if there should arise a shortage of food in Switzerland, will bring pressure to bear upon that power to allow the passage of French troops, or perhaps even to join the Alliance. . . . The upshot depends upon the efficacy of our submarine campaign. Admiral von Holtzendorff expects that England will be in a bad way before the next harvest. . . . On the whole, the prospects for the success of an unrestricted submarine campaign are extremely favorable. Of course the issue cannot be regarded as certain. We have to bear in mind that, in view of the military situation, we are not likely to achieve a successful issue by great victories on land. Submarine warfare is our last card. We are faced with a very grave decision. But if the military authorities think the submarine campaign indispensable, it is not for me to stand in the way.

Field Marshal: We are equipped for all eventualities; against America, Denmark, Holland, and even Switzerland. The submarine campaign can merely serve to bring about a moderate increase in our previous successes. We need the most energetic, most ruthless action attainable, and therefore the unrestricted submarine warfare will begin on February 1, 1917. The war must be brought to an end as speedily as possible, although we can hold out for a long time; but we must end it for the sake of our allies.

Chancellor: Is it not conceivable that the submarine campaign may postpone the end of the war?

Ludendorff: The submarine campaign will improve the position of our army. If, in England, there should arise a shortage of wood for pit props and a slackening in the supply of coal, the manufacture of munitions will be retarded; and this will ease matters for us on the western front. . . . Russia's offensive power, likewise, will be impaired by a lack of munitions due to scarcity of transport.

Chancellor: Should the United States come into the war, American aid will take the form of the supply of food to England, financial help, the sending of airplanes, and of volunteer corps.

Field Marshal: We shall be able to deal with that. The chances of a submarine campaign are more favorable than they ever will be again. We can and must undertake it.

Chancellor: Yes, if success beckons, we must act.

Field Marshal: We should have good grounds for

reproaching ourselves in later days, were we to miss this opportunity.

Chancellor: Certainly the situation is better than it was in September.

Ludendorff: The measures of security against neutrals will not take a provocative form, but will be purely defensive.

Chancellor: What if Switzerland were to come into the war against us, or were to allow French troops to pass through Swiss territory?

Field Marshal: From the military standpoint, that would not be unfavorable to us.

X

These documents, the most important German State papers between the declaration of war and the armistice (for this day the war was lost a second time), reveal the characters of those engaged in the conversations recorded, reveal them both as personalities and as symbols. Although hundreds of conversations of the same kind took place at the various headquarters during the war, only these German documents disclose so clearly the civilians' dread of the military authorities.

The day before, the gods of land and water (the air was not yet organized) had joined forces to keep the chancellor in office—not because he pleased them, but merely because no substitute occurred to them. The only other person proposed for the office was a general of artillery mentioned by Hindenburg. When, thereupon, the navy made a move to push the chief of the

army into the chancellorship, Hindenburg refused—
not with the customary excuse that he was no more
than a soldier without talent for politics, but solely
on the ground that he could not deliver speeches.
The two army dictators were so sure of their power
that they did not even ask the emperor's opinion; but
Hindenburg, when requested by the second great
power in the State, the navy, to become chancellor, was
content to declare, with virile brevity, "I refuse."
Even Ludendorff, who did not wish to be deprived of
his valuable umbrella, advised the field marshal
against acceptance. Why, taking it all in all, was the
decision in favor of ruthless submarine warfare now
arrived at? Hindenburg tells us with his customary
straightforwardness and simplicity: "Things cannot be
worse than they are. Everything possible must be
done to shorten the war, . . . so long as the
submarine campaign does not weaken our military
position."

On the second day, the refractory civilian is brought
to book. Since the emperor prefers to hold aloof,
there is no need for courtly periphrases; and if anyone
wishes to form a considered judgment regarding the
question of life or death for the German nation, there
can be no better way than by a study of this hour
when the conversation took place in the absence of
witnesses of higher or lower rank. In very truth, the
only person present when the military dictators came
to their momentous decision, apart from the under-
ling who acted as secretary, was an official who was
convinced that the scheme was disastrous, but was
determined to hang on to his position by the skin of
his teeth. He knew that the two tin gods in uni-

form needed merely to wave their hands, and he
would be thrust away from his place on the seats of
the mighty.

We must remember that, though Bethmann had
little real power, he had been longer on the seats of the
mighty than Hindenburg and was only a few years
younger than the field marshal. We must recall that
for eight years in succession he had been chancellor
of the German empire; that throughout the war he
had continually operated under cover of the emperor;
that he had been longer in power and more effectively supported from above than any of his war-
conducting colleagues. Recalling these facts, the
reader will need to bear in mind the peculiar characteristics of the Prussian theogony to understand
the chancellor's pitiful attitude. After explaining to
the two commanders that their new decision would
bring the greater part of the powers that still remained neutral into the war against Germany, he
suddenly drew in his claws, purred like a placated
pussycat, and said, "Well, I am not in a position to
oppose your wishes."

How different are the manly tones of the popular
hero! Although he recognizes the position of Germany to be so bad that it cannot grow worse; although
the two dictators' policy in the Polish matter has
made peace with the tsar impossible, and in the Belgian matter has made peace with England no less
impossible—our aging leader is undismayed, and, with
the lion's splendid tranquillity determines to show his
teeth to four additional States. Let them take sides
against Germany if they dare! Like a hot-headed boy
he exclaims, "We must have speedy recourse to the

new weapon, that the war may be more quickly brought to a close!"

The statesman's modest protest that perhaps a ruthless submarine campaign will serve only to protract the issue, is answered by the cold voice of Ludendorff, who speaks with his customary concreteness and clarity. The calculator and specialist, who carries in his head a clear picture of all the figures that bear upon the case and of all the paths of communication, is ready in this instance, as throughout these four years, as a loyal assistant, to hand building materials to the field marshal, to the military architect who is his colleague. What obstacles stand in the way? America has long been supplying the enemy with money and munitions. Now there will be men as well? The statesman had included among his objections no more than a casual reference to "volunteer corps," much as in peace time well-bred diplomatists are accustomed to speak of the possibility, not of war, but merely of "complications." To talk of troops, a million or even two, turning up in due time on the western front, and perhaps able to decide the issue of the war and secure a victory for the Allies—this would be harsh and disagreeable language for a civilian to use to the military commanders. "Volunteer corps" conveys a romantic sound to the ears of these men who dispose of lives by the million. There is even a faint undertone of mockery.

With the easy gesture of a king by right divine, the hoary warrior waves away objections, and produces the historic utterance, "We shall be able to deal with that!" There is no need to supply lengthy justification by figures and dates such as his assistant is always ready to supply. Tranquillity suffices! "Well, we've got to win before we can make peace!" How overwhelming must have been the effect of this iron figure of the field marshal! Notice that the statesman, having discharged his duty, and having made the necessary protests in the presence of a stenographer who was recording for the benefit of posterity, now went on to rejoin almost graciously that the alluring prospect of such successes must certainly not be renounced—all the more seeing that the general situation was now better than it had been four months ago when he had still interposed a veto. Only with a hurried last warning, does he questioningly introduce once more the word "Switzerland." The prompt retort of the field marshal is amazing. Hindenburg actually appears to want the Swiss to join the enemy Alliance, saying, "From the military standpoint, that would not be unfavorable to us." The resolute military dictators did not trouble to contemplate the prospect that next year the "volunteer corps" of well-equipped Americans would be present in the flesh on the plains of Flanders.

Had they, then, thrust their way forward to dictatorship? Had they forcibly usurped political power? Almost without stirring a finger, Hindenburg had been uplifted by the legend; by a chorus of requests from the populace. The power of final decision had been, so to say, laid upon his mighty knees in the form of two dice which he was to shake in the famous helmet of Königgratz so that his throw would disclose the voice of destiny. He shook this strange dice box in his powerful warrior hand, and lo! the decision of America to enter the war was the upshot!

According to the testimony of the document (Bethmann's report), unless a ruthless submarine campaign
were immediately opened, "the two commanders
would not accept responsibility for the further military conduct of operations. On the other hand, if
their wishes were acceded to, they were prepared to
accept responsibility for all the military consequences,
even for the consequences of intervention in the war
against Germany on the part of the European neutrals
and of America. As far as this last was concerned,
they did not think that the intervention of America
would be of much importance."

We can readily understand that the military commanders did not let the German people know how
grave was the situation of their country. "Things are
drawing to a close," said Hindenburg to his painter-
in-ordinary during these days. "One more vigorous
blow, and we shall be able to make peace." The most
amazing thing was that they were humbugging the
emperor as well as the people! Von Lersner, of the
Foreign Office, writes: "To his appeal in favor of a
ruthless submarine campaign, the emperor had secured
a large measure of approval; but I learned, in strict
confidence, that this approval was largely engineered
by Hindenburg and Ludendorff in order to convince
the world how unanimously the German people supported the emperor."

Until yesterday, both the chancellor and the vice
chancellor had been strongly averse to unrestricted
submarine warfare. What will they do now? Such
is the question which forces itself into our minds.
How will their wish to retain high office accommodate
itself to their sense of self-respect? How will their

longing to cling to dignities comport with the dignity which a statesman wishes to maintain before posterity?

For such situations, diplomacy has two useful words, "caution" and "self-sacrifice" which, in specious combinations, serve to mask any amount of self-deception, In this instance, the vice chancellor rallied chivalrously to the support of the chancellor, obviously trying to excuse himself by finding excuses for his chief. Bethmann's first thought had been to resign, reports Helfferich. "Still, he was able to convince himself that, though this would have been the easier course, he had no right, in such a way, to shuffle off responsibility. . . . He could not have accepted the burden of preventing the submarine campaign, even if he had been competent to do so. . . . I, likewise [Helfferich, admonished by Bethmann], had to consult my conscience as to whether I ought to make a demonstration by resigning. . . . But this would sow confusion among our own ranks and discourage our allies. It was, indeed, the most difficult decision of my life. . . . Go, or stay—continue to fight at my post as a general does, even though, during the discussion of the plans of operation, he has not been able to make his colleagues adopt his own scheme? I parted from the chancellor with the assurance that I would help him, as far as in me lay, to advocate the submarine campaign before the Reichstag."

Thus when two men who are nominally governing the empire foresee that a decision of the military commanders will lead to its defeat, they do not attempt to avert this decision either by putting up vigorous arguments against it in conference, by memorials to the emperor, or by threats of resignation. They care less for the welfare of Germany than for keeping up appearances; although in the enemy countries, the pressure of public opinion was continually leading to ministerial crises and to crises in the military command, that a more vigorous prosecution of the war might be insured. In the authoritarian State, the supreme object was to maintain the semblance of unity, the picture of the party truce; in the militarist State, the Hindenburg peace must be safeguarded. During his examination of conscience, the civilian was rescued from his dilemma by a military parallel derived from the days when he had been an army officer; he salved his scruples by regarding himself as a general who must stick to his post. Although he had to make the most difficult decision of his life, he did not trouble to ask his wife's advice, nor did it cost him a sleepless night. The answer came as pat as the firing of a pistol; within ten minutes, the question was settled; both Helfferich and Bethmann decided to sacrifice themselves for the sake of the fatherland. Not until they were alone, one of them in his office, the other in his automobile, did the chancellor and the vice chancellor draw deep breaths of relief. Once more threatening fate had been gracious to them; the military commanders had not frowned at them; the civilian rulers might go on ruling.

XI

Self-deception was complete; the chances of peace were ruined in three directions simultaneously. At the time when the foregoing decision was made, the chancellor declared that there were no further hopes of a revolution in Russia. Within six weeks, the Russian revolution had begun. Simultaneously, the determination to conduct an unrestricted submarine campaign destroyed any chance of making peace with England at this juncture. At that time, being at their wits' end, they had asked Ballin, the Jew, who was thought more of in London than he was in Germany, to get in touch with the British shipping and banking world. "In the beginning of January," so writes Ballin's collaborator, "his efforts had been so far successful as to bring about direct communications between the hostile parties. But the announcement of the intended submarine campaign ruined everything, since the Allies were certain that this would induce the Americans to come into the war on their side."

Finally, Wilson had been sounded with regard to his conditions, and had just made a proposal which seemed likely to be the subject of favorable consideration by the Allies. Thereupon Ludendorff, wishing to put a spoke in this wheel, announced the intention to push on with the submarine campaign and begin it three days earlier than had been planned. What could Wilson, upon whose favorable attitude so much depended, think of the German proposals, when, while he was being asked to act as intermediary, he was at the same time, as chief of the mightiest neutral power, threatened by the German government? The disclosure made plain to all eyes that there was a cleavage between German militarism and German statecraft; or, to put the matter in other words, between State and spirit among the Germans.

The shade of destiny still loomed indecisive between the contending parties. During these January weeks

13

of the year 1917, Wilson was honestly working on
behalf of peace.   On the 28th he again offered to
mediate in Washington.   On the 29th, Bethmann,
delighted at a turn of affairs which might relieve the
burden on his conscience without imperiling him in
any way, begged the emperor to cable the most conciliatory proposals possible.   Thereupon great indignation among the military!   Their pistols, they said,
were loaded and aimed.   Were they suddenly to be
told not to shoot?   As in *The Magic Flute*, there came
to the helpless and lonely civilian from three portals,
shouts of "Stand back!"   The military commanders,
the naval staff, and under their pressure the emperor
as well, would not accede to the chancellor's suggestion.
The admirals entrenched themselves behind "technical grounds," the classical pretext of specialists who
cannot refute a layman's reasonable objections.   The
submarines had already been despatched under specific
orders, were at their posts, and no longer attainable.
Would not Bethmann rejoin, "But are you not in
touch with them all the time by wireless?"

No, what seemed best to him was to play a double
game, and simultaneously to threaten the Americans
with torpedos and to offer them an olive branch.   On
January 30, the German ambassador informed Colonel
House, Wilson's friend, of the peace conditions; but
on the 31st the same ambassador had to hand the
secretary of State the German note about the intended submarine campaign.   War was the upshot.
When Bernstorff, who had foreseen what would happen,
got back to Germany in May and explained that at
the end of January he had wanted to arrange terms of
peace, Ludendorff replied: "Yes, but *we* did not want

anything of the kind! Now, within three months, we shall settle matters by our submarine campaign."

When the failure of the submarines had become obvious, Bethmann, too late, in an acrimonious document, plumed himself upon the foresight displayed in the objections he had ventured only to whisper. Hindenburg answered him on July 7: "It is impossible to foresee the precise moment at which the whole war economy of our enemies will collapse; but I am certain that it will collapse, and that before very long." After the war, referring to this great blunder, he wrote in his memoirs: "If a leader's blow fails, he is unquestionably exposed to the curses and the scorn of weaklings and cowards. But the aim of our German military education was to produce the courage which enables a man to face such responsibilities."

In the epilog directed against his critics, whom he termed cowards, the fundamental problem of the man's life is once more disclosed. As cadet and as General-Staff officer trained to independent resolve (but always backed up by the decision of his Supreme War Lord), a man with so strong a sense of duty could do wonders as long as he could look up to a guiding authority. But when night has fallen, when the starry heavens are veiled in clouds, when the polestar has become invisible, how can the captain guide his ship if he stands alone upon the bridge in stormy weather and with no knowledge of the coast and the reefs? The emperor had ceased to function as War Lord, and had also ceased to function as arbiter between the government and the army. Thus there was nothing left for Hindenburg but to make these decisions of outstanding historical importance with the aid of his own common sense, and lacking the reinforcement of his knowledge and talents by those of any other intelligence. When persons of such a type put their trust wholly in God, their tranquillity does not depend upon the success of their actions but solely upon the conviction that they have done their duty—and that consolation was left to Hindenburg.

XII

The first thing the two commanders did after the failure of the submarine campaign was to overthrow the chancellor, whom they had chiefly to thank for their own high position. Did he seriously expect that he would be able to weaken their political influence because of this failure? They were army officers, and had relied upon the figures produced by the navy. To replace a refractory government by an obedient one, they had to threaten resignation, a means to which Bismarck did not have recourse until after a decade of remarkable successes, trying it on only thrice in fifteen years, whereas the three commanders did so thrice in a single year. Since the emperor clung to his chancellor lest he should find himself helpless under the dictatorship of the two commanders, they sought an ally, and found one in the Reichstag, suspicious though they were of that corporation. Bethmann, like everyone who tries to be all things to all men, lost everything in the end. The moment came when the two dictators were to learn to know their Germany.

Since the outset of the war the party of the Junkers, agrarians, and officials had continued to send members to interview the two commanders, so that

A picture showing an excellent likeness of Reichspresident Field Marshal von Hindenburg, taken during the World War in the General Headquarters

again and again some representative of the Center
had been received at G.H.Q. But what a social
democrat looked like, a member of the strongest party
in the State, a representative of those engineers and
munition makers upon whose activities the issue of the
war depended quite as much as upon those of their
brethren at the front, was hardly known, even from
photographs, to the commanders, the emperor, or the
crown prince.

In the Reichstag, and far beyond its walls, the failure of the submarine warfare had aroused disquiet,
increasing the self-confidence and magnifying the demands of parliament, so that now from the left likewise, Bismarck's constitution was gravely threatened.
Yet, even so, perhaps nothing untoward would have
happened, if, in the spring of 1917, a young deputy,
dining with a general at the front, had not had an
after-dinner conversation. This man was Erzberger,
a member of the Center Party, one who, believing
that the war reports spoke the truth, had hitherto
unfailingly supported the policy of conquest. General
Hoffmann, whose nose had been put out of joint
because he regarded himself as having been neglected
by Ludendorff, confided to Erzberger truths which
were in general sedulously kept from the ears of German civilians. Erzberger, being a shrewd man, proceeded to make a careful study of the war map and
the figures. Thus equipped during these July days,
he publicly expressed doubts as to the accuracy of the
figures published by the naval staff, adding that the
supreme army command had also erred. Victory could
no longer be achieved in the open field; it was essential
to work for an understanding among the belligerents;

and, indeed, the Reichstag must do this, since neither the commanders nor the chancellor would try to do so. It would be possible to secure a democratic majority for a resolution endorsing the words uttered by the emperor in the opening days of the war, "We have no desire for conquests." This bold political filibuster went so far as to say that, instead of continuing the fight, it would be cheaper to lock up twenty-five thousand Pan-Germans in hydropathic institutions.

To prevent the passing of such a resolution, the two commanders now hastened to Berlin. On July 13, 1917, the pair of them for the first time looked Germany in the face, and probably even offered to shake hands with it. In the hitherto unapproachable red General Staff building in the Königsplatz, the place from whose windows they had often looked mockingly at the Reichstag, the two commanders (who, naturally, being military chiefs, could not demean themselves by going to visit civilians) received, in detached groups, two or three delegates from each party—much as, at a dentist's, two or three members of the same family will be summoned from the waiting room to the operating room, treated, and then sent away. The treatment was left to Ludendorff, who assured the members of each party in turn how well things were shaping at the front, and what a lot of harm talk about proposing peace terms would do the country. Then he went on to answer a few questions put by the anxious patients, such as: "How long will the pain last?" "Can you guarantee a cure?" "Can the trouble be cured by medicine, or will the knife be necessary?" Old Hindenburg looked on silently, as if he held a watching brief. The interviews ended in mutual astonishment. The representatives of the people had found the generals to be not such roaring lions as they had hoped; and the generals had found the representatives of the people to be less wolflike than they had feared. This, moreover, was the only time when Hindenburg and Ebert met.

A few days before, Bethmann had been able to prevent this encounter. With the courage of a man at bay, he explained to the emperor that it would be unconstitutional for the commanders to try to exert an influence upon the representatives of the people. This intrigue was the final cause of Bethmann's overthrow in the Reichstag. But when he wished to resign, the emperor demurred mainly because the chief of his majesty's cabinet could not suggest a successor. For two days, Bethmann continued to hope, offering as a gift to pliable deputies the establishment of equal electoral rights in Prussia—a proposal which the emperor refused at first to indorse and then approved by telephone. Hindenburg, who had already gone back to G.H.Q., wired the emperor that any declaration in favor of peace by negotiation was inadmissible at this stage. The emperor protested, and rang up headquarters, whereupon Ludendorff was content to say that he had already sent in his resignation. "This time," he added, after reporting over the wire, "I shall not give way, but shall abide by my decision!" The emperor was in a fine rage. It is particularly trying to the temper of princes that they make their vassals great and yet cannot get on without such confidential agents even when these prove refractory.

"Your Majesty is aware," wrote Ludendorff in his missive of resignation under date July 12, "that it is impossible for me, as a responsible member of the High Command, to retain that confidence in the imperial chancellor which is essential to our effective coöperation, . . . since the war is not to be fought to a finish. Such a lack of mutual confidence cannot but be disastrous to our country. Your Majesty's commands and attempts to smooth matters over, can no longer prevent disaster." Hindenburg, writing simultaneously, explained that he had the gravest objections to the proposed resolution. "With due consideration for the army, I must humbly beg Your Majesty to prevent the civil government from making such a declaration." Only a week before he had still been writing to Bethmann declaring, "We can escape a helot's existence if peace terms can be arranged."

When Bethmann's head was simultaneously demanded by the representatives of the people, the military commanders, and the crown prince, the only choice left to the worthy emperor was which executioner it would be best to employ; and, since he did not wish to encourage the idea that he was acting under pressure from the Reichstag, he gave a hint to Bethmann that the best way would be to accept the silken rope from the hands of Ludendorff. Obediently the chancellor declared it to be "a matter of course" that the two commanders must stay at their posts, and his own resignation was accepted next day.

The commanders, however, who for a long time had failed to gain any such brilliant victory as this one in the battle of the Wilhelmstrasse, found, when they came again to Berlin and received some more deputies, an "ungracious master," who informed them that, as officers, they would have done better to remain at headquarters. Since, however, they showed no inclination to take this broad hint, their timid War Lord submitted to them a list of three or four candidates, a bill of fare from which, having eaten the chancellor, they were to choose the next course. The name of an undistinguished imperial commissary or courtier pleased them, perhaps because it reminded them of the "German Michael"; they marked this name with their finger nails, and next day a hitherto unknown man named Michaelis became the ruler of the German realm. His suitability for the post was thus worded by himself in conversation with a deputy, "Being always busy, I have hitherto merely run as a contemporary alongside the chariot of politics."

More experienced drivers of the imperial chariot at once took charge. With this end in view, Hindenburg composed a memorial summarizing all Bethmann's defects: lack of propaganda, pessimism, injury to monarchical prestige. It was incumbent on the new chancellor to avoid these errors. The deputies, too, were given their instructions at the first reception of the new chancellor. Hindenburg wanted the proposed peace resolution to be "gingered up," saying that it would discourage the officers if there were any question of renouncing the conquests that had been made. The emperor, on the other hand, wishing to take vengeance for his defeat, and, after his manner, choosing the populace as forum, said to the deputies, while the vice chancellor was handing round cigarettes: "Europe, united under me after the peace, will conduct a second war against England. Where the Prussian guards set foot, there is no democracy!"

A strongly nationalist historian, Professor Delbrück, has described the whole affair as "General Ludendorff's mutiny"; and Hartung, an equally ardent nationalist, professor of history in Berlin, writing under the supervision of the Third Realm, speaks of the matter as "an unquestionable incursion of the High Command into the political domain. Nay, it was more than that. Since the emperor, in view of the general situation, had no recourse but to answer his generals' proposed resignation by the dismissal of Bethmann, it was likewise an infringement of the rights of the throne, for Hindenburg made common cause with Ludendorff. . . . It has also to be remembered that, although Hindenburg and Ludendorff wished to enforce the dismissal of a chancellor, they had no successor to offer." In fact, Ludendorff, the army officer, was surprised to learn that a successor to an imperial chancellor was not always kept in reserve just as for a general, who, in former days, might have been killed during an onslaught, and, even now, might fall through a regrettable oversight.

The two generals' motives were different. As far as Hindenburg was concerned, such an infringement of the rights of the crown would have been inconceivable if he had, at bottom, still regarded William as his sovereign. He must, therefore, have built up in his mind some eccentric theory of his duty—a card house of sorts, with royal-popular pinnacles. Somehow or other, he must have persuaded himself that he was doing all he did for his king's sake.

Ludendorff, on the other hand, who, beyond question, already despised his king, was thenceforward double-faced in his political exactions. As a connoisseur (perhaps the only German connoisseur) of the military situation, he had, since assuming the reins of power, become fully aware of Germany's impotence; but he did not want to be the man to make an unsatisfactory peace. Colonel Haeften, who was his collaborator, testified subsequently before the Commission of inquiry, "He needed imposing war aims to maintain the spirit at the fighting front; for soldiers lack the requisite impetus if they think that they are only battling for a negotiated peace." To quote Delbrück once more: "The resolute face upon which the High Command insisted was assumed at the cost of the government, and, finally, at the cost of the War Lord as well. The High Command, resentful of the implication of slackness, . . . wished to shuffle this charge off upon the diplomatists. . . ."

The two commanders erred because they were out of touch with popular feeling. No one could blame them for that, in view of their training in the Military Academy and on the General Staff; but the upshot was disastrous to the cause they had at heart and of which they were the supreme leaders. During the third year of the war, "conquest" had become a dead issue to the privates in all the trenches, whether manned by Germans or by others. No longer could any French soldier be stimulated by being told to fight and suffer in order to gain a victory over the Prussian Junkers; nor a Russian, by the war aim of reëstablishing the golden cross on the summit of what had once been the basilica of St. Sophia; nor an Italian, at the cry of "*Italia irredenta*," by the longing to recover the Trentino. All who went on fighting did so merely because they had to, or inspired by the natural

wish to defend their homes. It was in the belief that
he was defending his home that the German soldier
had taken up arms, and if, in this year of crisis, the
French front had been at the Rhine, the Germans
would have continued to fight with as much élan
as the French showed in the occupied regions of
France.

But now the Germans were far advanced into Flanders and Poland, into Serbia and Rumania, into Palestine and Armenia; and the more the German lines ex-
panded, the more plainly did the men who held the
German trenches realize that what they were holding
was nothing more than a greatly distended air balloon.
When Hindenburg writes that in 1917 all parties in
Germany would have made it a point of honor to fight
to the last gasp for the sake of Alsace-Lorraine, we
hear the voice of the blue bloods who assembled every
evening at his supper table. Then, as today, both
the German people and the French were weary of the
unceasing quarrels over two provinces of mixed na-
tionality.

At that time, in the autumn of 1917, it was once
more possible for the German commanders to make
peace. On August 30, the papal nuncio transmitted
to Berlin a proposal made by France and England.
Belgium was to be surrendered by Germany, but
there would be no claims for reparations; there was to
be a referendum in Alsace-Lorraine; the German
colonies would be restored. The official who ruled
the empire as representative of the generals referred
the matter to G.H.Q. Thereupon the emperor declared that the Hohenzollerns "would stand or fall"
with the Imperial Provinces (*i. e.*, Alsace-Lorraine,

Hindenburg, the Kaiser, and Ludendorff studying war maps at General Headquarters

and, later, the Hohenzollerns were to fall with them).
The military commanders demanded in addition Liège
and the Flemish coast. Aware of the weakness of
their own military position, they regarded the enemy
offer as a sign of weakness on the other side. Lloyd
George, however, not being even vouchsafed an answer,
shook off his anxieties, regarded the silence of Berlin
as a personal affront, and said: "Germany must first
be smashed!" Ten years later, when unveiling a war
memorial, he declared: "At the end of the third year
of the war, four out of the seven Allied belligerents
had been beaten to their knees, their armies were defeated. Had German statecraft been equal to German
military efficiency, the United States would never
have come into the war, and England and France
would have stood alone to fight the most formidable
military machine known to history."

A dense fog enwrapped the German people. The
common folk continued to believe that they were
fighting for their lives, as the captains of industry
were fighting for the mineral resources of Longwy and
Briey; the Junkers, for estates in Poland; the army
commanders for coasts and fortresses in Belgium: and
all joined with their camp followers to form a "Vaterlands-Partei" whose grandiloquent name excluded
from the fatherland everyone that did not belong to
this party. The nobility and gentry, the cousins and
the comrades of Hindenburg, showed him in his comfortable headquarters the German people as seen in
the mirror of the master class; but the common soldiers
only saw the field marshal as he rolled by them in his
automobile, or from the ranks in a review. Never
did the German private in those days see the com-

mander in chief sitting by the roadside eating bread
and sausage as his prototype, old Blücher, had sat in
days of yore. It was just as well that the common
soldiers did not see the official documents that concerned their hunger and the pay of their comrades who
were working at munitions. If they had seen these
documents, there might have been mutinies.

The private soldiers might have read in one of Hindenburg's dispatches, penned in March, 1917, that
they and their civilian comrades must learn to endure
the increasing pinch of hunger: "Our authorities will
have to see to it that such tuition is forthcoming. I
shall regard it as a great blunder if this tuition be left
to the trade unions and to certain press organs (read
Vorwärts of March 18); that would be to set a
fox to mind the geese." He might have read also,
this private soldier, that as late as June, 1918, Hindenburg considered that it would be inevitable to raise
the officers' pay when peace came. "Recently, indeed, I have come to question whether we can possibly
await the conclusion of peace before raising the officers'
pay." Having referred to the general rise in prices,
the commander in chief went on: "Necessarily this
led to an extraordinary increase in the cost of living."
Twelve days later Hindenburg takes up his parable
against the working class. The output of the munition
workers is declining because "wages are too high, so
that poverty no longer drives people to work nor stimu-
lates them to earn bonuses."

But even though the common soldiers heard nothing of these complaints, their discontent could not but
be intensified by some of the measures adopted by the
two commanders who knew nothing of the life of the

people. A good many of the items of the "Hindenburg Program" had to be discarded because, as Helfferich put it, "Quantities of valuable material and still more valuable labor power remained in a state of industrial ruin, being partly never completed and partly incapable of full utilization. Had matters been more carefully considered, . . . our economic life might have been spared numerous shocks which cut at the roots of our nation's powers of resistance."

For at this juncture the patriarchal ways of the Junkers, who, on their estates, were accustomed to bring their people to reason by good wishes and turnips, were to be applied to a famine-stricken industrial country; and the common man who, amid his fatherland's distresses, was not expected to think for himself but only to give his life at another's command, must go on fighting for the extension of his country as far as Lake Peipus. He was to be fired by martial ardor, not because he was defending the land of his fathers, but in order that certain coal fields eastward of Gleiwitz and Beuthen should become German, and the subterranean frontier posts in the eternal night of the Davy lamps should be thrust farther to the east.

The officers' custom of insisting upon blind obedience from the troops was to be extended to a people's army in which there were no longer 30 per cent but only 3 per cent professional soldiers. The continuance of the Old Prussian drill (which Field Marshal Boyen, a century earlier, had rejected as "poisonous to the Landwehr"), was now to be utilized to produce fervor and self-sacrificing zeal alike in callow volunteers and in bearded veterans from the Landsturm. Those who remained alive from among the blue blooded of the prewar officers' corps (many of them had fallen gloriously at the front) did not fear death, but feared the loss of their position in the State. They may be compared to lions of a circus menagerie, accustomed evening after evening to appear in the limelight and to be loudly applauded while obedient only to their royal lion tamer, but who now find their menagerie invaded by common buffaloes. Surely this could not fail to weaken the prestige of the lions?

Whenever he came home on furlough, the private soldier learned that the ruling class was still reluctant to grant equal suffrage to the lower orders. Everything was to be arranged patriarchally by an "Easter message" from the king. With Hohenzollern punctuality, three years too late, equal suffrage was to come from above as a gracious promise to pay, a reward for meritorious service—and there was no likelihood that the promise would ever be fulfilled. Since the two commanders regarded the "idea of the State," and not the people, as their fatherland, they gave the fullest support to the "Vaterlands-Partei" which considered that equal suffrage would be a disaster, and resisted parliamentary government as derogatory to the crown. In his memoirs, Hindenburg is still complaining of what had been "extorted under pressure of the war." Ludendorff was an open adversary of electoral reform, and favored a scheme of the Junkers by which they wished to make sure, in any event, of the inviolability of their feudal estates. There was a storm about this matter in the Landtag on March 14, 1917. The same evening, an item of wireless news startled the world: revolution in St. Petersburg!

Even when the second war credits were voted, some of the German socialists had broken away from the main body of the party. But as late as March, 1916, when in all other parliaments socialists had long been demanding peace without victory, the one member of the Reichstag who ventured to voice the same demand was refused a hearing because what he wanted to ask for was in accordance with the realities of the situation. When, in April, 1917, a minority of "independent social democrats" detached themselves from the party, this same Haase was fiercely attacked. In such circumstances, how powerful an impression must the Russian revolution with its Workers' and Soldiers' Councils, have made upon the German workers! The German naval "mutineers" of July, 1917 did not seize any of their officers, nor did they demand the cessation of the war; they merely went ashore without leave, returned to their ships in the evening, and, in a pronunciamento, demanded peace without conquest just as Wilson had demanded it two years earlier with the approval of most of the Allied ministers of State. Their second demand, the same rations for all, was the expression of the daily pinch of hunger from which millions were suffering in beleaguered Germany. But the two commanders did not hesitate in the third year of the war to apply the harshest measures to these bluejackets, with the result that there were two death sentences, 181 years of major imprisonment, and 180 years of minor imprisonment inflicted upon those whose vision of peace, had it been accepted, might have delivered their country from the Peace of Versailles.

14

XIII

There was no lack of warnings. During the fourth year of the war, hunger brought back half the Germans to the motives that had inspired them during the first year; the only thing they could think of was how to save their country and their lives. Not only burghers and civilians at the rear, but also powerful army leaders, implored the two dictators to bethink themselves.

The crown prince, who doubtless was still one of the comparatively small minority of Germans who had a breakfast to eat every day, joined the defeatists. "If within a definite time the submarine campaign does not achieve its ends," he wrote in a secret memorial, "the struggle must be broken off. Our losses can no longer be made good, whereas our enemies are continually able to call upon fresh reserves."

Yet more remarkable was the testimony of Prince Rupprecht of Bavaria, another of the army leaders on the western front, who, in the critical days of July, 1917, wrote in a four-page letter to Count Hertling:

"Even if the troops still needed on the eastern front should be liberated for service elsewhere, they would not suffice to decide the issue in the West. . . . It now seems clear that our submarine campaign is unlikely to starve England out, or will, in the best event, take a very long time to achieve this. . . . In the course of the present year the filling of gaps in our ranks is likely to become increasingly difficult. . . . It is, therefore, of extreme importance that before autumn we should conclude peace with Russia, renouncing any idea of annexations or war indemnities.

. . . As regards the help the Allies can receive from America, this must not be underrated. . . . From the late autumn onward, we should in my opinion, do our utmost to negotiate with our adversaries. . . . The possibility of making peace must not be wrecked by insisting upon the return of our colonies."

Let us suppose (quite a plausible supposition!) that in August, 1914 this army commander, in view of his royal birth and high rank, had been summoned to take charge on the eastern front instead of Hindenburg—with Ludendorff as chief of staff. In that case Prince Rupprecht would have become the official "victor of Tannenberg." Having achieved this great success, which he was quite as competent to achieve as Hindenburg, and having the additional advantage of his royal rank, and the universal popularity inspired by his victory, it is likely that he and Ludendorff would have acquired supreme power. But he would not have yielded to Ludendorff's ideas. He would have pursued reasonable aims as one of the two dictators, instead of being, as he now was, no more than a powerless on-looker writing to the no less powerless Bavarian premier.

The two commanders, determined to fight to a finish, treated such documents with contempt. Though various similar warnings came to hand, they insisted, as part of the peace terms, upon the surrender of Poland, Courland, and Lithuania, the Flemish coast, and parts of Rumania. This was in the summer of 1917, when mutinies in sixteen French army corps and the disorders in Russia had aroused much discouragement in Paris. "We can regard the military situation," declared Hindenburg, "with great confidence, and we

are in a position to carry on the struggle even without
the aid of Austria."

The field marshal's demand for the permanent retention of the German conquests was reinforced by his
belief in the king's declaration that Germany had been
shamefully attacked. By the annexation of coal beds,
iron fields, and agricultural lands, he wanted to safeguard the realm against any repetition of such an onslaught. It was not the industrial magnates and the
Junkers whose advice the two commanders were following in this matter; Hindenburg and Ludendorff,
who knew how desperate was the military situation,
and nevertheless, after the manner of soldiers, were
persistently animated by the desire to extend their
conquests, decided the historical issue. At a meeting
of the crown council held in September, 1917, they demanded as basis of a peace by negotiation that Germany should acquire an extension of territory in Upper
Silesia, that she should retain the iron fields of what
had been French Lorraine, and that such vast areas
of Belgium should be annexed that that country
would herself be impelled to seek a union with Germany.
"As a result of this, Holland would also be attracted
into the German orbit." Thus Germany would occupy
all the North Sea coast confronting England, and must
also have a big colonial empire in Africa. This memorial, which was composed by Ludendorff, but bears
the signature of Hindenburg, is described by the latter's
nephew, Gert von Hindenburg, in an apologia for his
uncle as the outcome of the confused thoughts of a
general playing at politics. Gert continues: "These
war aims were preposterous, a most undesirable example to set for subsequent conquerors. Bethmann

had solemnly guaranteed the complete restoration of
Belgium. The field marshal himself considered that
the economic annexation of Belgium would be fruit-
less without a long-lasting military occupation. . . .
The High Command completely failed to grasp how
exhausted were our troops. . . . One cannot but
be amazed that the High Command never stopped to
think how much these German war aims (by no means
unknown to the enemy!) were responsible for the
Allies' determination to fight to a finish."

In this epoch, for whose description the methods of
a war of attrition are applied even against the reader,
the strategy of the two commanders became more and
more incomprehensible; and we shall therefore do well
to allow the aforesaid nephew, Major von Hindenburg,
to speak for us, quoting from the book which was intended to promote his uncle's honor and glory. He
writes that he cannot understand "why Hindenburg,
after being appointed commander in chief, did not
immediately try to secure what he had hitherto so
eagerly advocated, namely a decision in the East.
After the defeat of Rumania, . . . a decisive blow
could surely have been struck in this quarter."

No less disastrous, in young Hindenburg's opinion,
was the inertia of the High Command during the summer of 1917. "It would certainly have been better,
even at the cost of withdrawing as many troops as
possible from important sectors of the western front,
to deliver smashing blows upon Russia, dispersing
there the forces of an enemy no longer able to resist,
and quickly compelling the Muscovites to make peace.
. . . According to the opinion of outstanding authorities upon military matters, the German troops

could have occupied St. Petersburg in less than a week without a serious struggle. The whole course of history would have been changed. In view of such a German success, . . . Kerensky would probably have been willing to sue for peace, and he might have been able to suppress the bolshevik revolution." After going on to show that like considerations apply to Italy, Gert von Hindenburg insists that his uncle made the very mistake which, when commander on the eastern front, he had so often blamed Falkenhayn for making."

At about this date, Haber, a Jewish professor, made an invention which strengthened the German armies much as, Rathenau, another Israelite, had saved previously the country by the concentration of raw materials and by finding substitutes for some of the more important ones that were lacking. Haber warned the two commanders against the use of his new poison gas unless they were sure of being able to fight the war to a finish within a year. After the lapse of a year, explained the inventor, the French would be able to imitate his gas, while protecting themselves against German gas with rubber gas masks, which the blockaded Germans could not manufacture. Ludendorff nodded assent, and the victory of the Austrians over the Italians on the Piave was mainly ascribable to the surprise effect of the new gas. Since the French took sixteen months to imitate the gas, and could not foretell when the war would come to a close, they prepared fifty thousand tons of poison gas for use in the anticipated winter campaign of 1918–1919.

How can these signs of mingled presumption and dread in Ludendorff be explained; how can the repeated sins of omission interspersed with perpetual fresh attempts be explained—how otherwise than by a profound conviction that victory was impossible? This feeling seems to have taken possession of him when he assumed the leadership; for previously, when in opposition, he had been as confident of victory as can be any man who is aware of possessing greater gifts than he discerns in his superiors. At a later date, he touched lightly on this problem in a noteworthy utterance: "We extended our lines all over the world without establishing them firmly in Europe. . . . We manifested ourselves prematurely when we had not developed an adequate national consciousness." Since his ambition would not allow him to settle the war by an understanding but only through a fight to a finish, and since, nevertheless, knowing the numbers and forces as he did, he could not but doubt the possibility of victory, he continued to incite the Germans to attack, counting on the likelihood of some lucky chance, on the caprices of the war goddess, displaying a gambler's mood unsuitable to a cadet; for when a Prussian grows dithyrambic, look out for squalls! One can hardly doubt that from time to time he envied the field marshal, his coadjutor, for the latter's simplicity and untroubled faith.

XIV

Once more fortune smiled on the two commanders. A bold thought had induced them to have Lenin sent across Germany from Zurich to St. Petersburg in the hope that this man would exude a spiritual poison gas which would lay his compatriots low. Taking a short view, their calculations were sound; taking a long one, they were insuring the victory of their archenemy. No one could foresee how this amazing journey would end, least of all Lenin himself, when, accompanied by thirty friends, he set out northeastward from Stuttgart in the third-class carriage of the sealed train, and drove across Finland in a sleigh to the frontier of his homeland. At the railway station in St. Petersburg, he was received as a national hero. Six months later, he had risen to supreme power, and, in contradistinction to Kerensky, was determined to make peace.

It was then that Trotsky sent through the ether his immortal appeal, "To all!" A new tone echoed round the world. Lenin's underground periodical had been called *Iskra* (The Spark), and it was the spark of the wireless which carried one of the first messages of the bolshevik revolution to the remotest lands of the globe. It was, indeed, a spark of the spirit, a spark of passion, which appealed to all the belligerents by the same name. If not the greatest, it was certainly the most sublime moment of the war. For the first time those who spoke such multifarious tongues were summoned to regard themselves once more as brethren.

What an incredible thing had happened! One of the four chief powers which had for three years been battering at the gates of the huge German fortress was ready to make peace, presumably on any conditions, for its new leader thought of the Russian people rather than of Russian territory. Russia, the special foe of the two commanders and yet the least detested among Germany's enemies, could be won over within a few days by three or four paragraphs of a peace treaty. More than a million German soldiers could be withdrawn from the eastern front and transferred to the western before the American auxiliaries of the Allies arrived.

But the two commanders were busied in ruling Germany. First of all they must drop their latest creation, Michaelis, who had been no more than a camp follower, "a little boy running alongside the chariot of politics," and had therefore suited their purposes as chancellor of the German empire. Now the dictators chose two new men, whose most striking characteristics were that one was very old and one very young. Was it their design that the seventy-four-year-old imperial chancellor should be rejuvenated by the forty-four-year-old secretary for foreign affairs, or was the latter to be held in check by the former? This much only is certain, that the old man had been "born a mummy," and that the latter had mummified himself in order to be "in the swim." In itself, the combination of a philosopher with a man of the world would have been agreeable enough to the Germans; but this time the two commanders had selected weaklings who could not compare with themselves in vitality—this being what seemed to them of supreme importance. The gigantic Hindenburg would have been able to carry the count, a man four years older than himself, out of the Reichstag on his sturdy shoulders; and even Ludendorff could easily have thrown the younger man in a wrestle. The days when Herr von Kühlmann, as a young attaché wearing an uhlan's uniform, had, in stormy weather, climbed a rope ladder up a ship's side, were over and done with, since this exploit had started him on his career.

For the rest, Kühlmann, had he not been too cynical, might well have thought that his understanding would

enable him to save Germany in the year 1918. Never
was a name better suited to its bearer.

On the other hand Count Hertling, a Catholic, was
ill-suited to his name, if it was derived from "hart"
(hard); for he was so pliable, so prone to compromise,
that he had based his philosophical studies "upon the
foundation of Greek philosophy, in the sense of the
Christian Fathers and of the teaching of the Middle
Ages"; and only twice in his life had seriously opposed
anything or anyone—on the first occasion, when he
demurred from Bismarck's policy and advocated papal
infallibility; and now, forty years later, when he was
opposed to the notion that Hindenburg was infallible.
Feeling that the ship was sinking beneath his feet, the
ship he had been summoned to steer, he promptly
haled from its innermost depths two unknown stokers
and placed them on the bridge, so that, when disaster came, they could absolve him from responsibility.

After the democrats in the German Reichstag had for
decades, and recently throughout three years of the
war, vainly demanded a share in the powers of government, they naturally felt flattered at being allowed to
participate in steering, though they entered upon their
duties so shortly before the shipwreck. They ought
to have known better, and to have refused to become
confederates instead of sufferers. However, Hertling,
as the first chancellor selected from the Reichstag,
took a couple of democrats into his cabinet, appointing
one of them vice chancellor.

As far as the two commanders were concerned, their
first step towards popular government was a sort of
re-insurance in the event of disaster; and subsequently

in a decisive hour, they greatly developed this catch-penny notion.

The military commanders had sworn a truce with the bolsheviks without consulting the statesmen, for what conqueror can resist the chance of making this mingled gesture of pride and grace to the conquered, this gesture of which he has dreamed since the firing of the first shot? A defeated general, indeed, is less gratified in accepting it. Since, however, in this instance, the commanders were the real rulers of the German realm, they insisted that they must have the chief say as regards the terms of peace, though that matter is usually left to statesmen. They sent General Hoffmann to represent them at the table round which the negotiations were to be conducted, manifestly wishing to brighten it up with a uniform. In any case this table must have looked rather paltry in the abandoned house which the negotiators had taken possession of at Brest-Litovsk, a little Jewish town on the Polish frontier, a place which had been nearly destroyed during the war. It was customary for princes and diplomatists to conduct peace negotiations in gay palaces or impressive castles. Now, for the first time in history, parleys were taking place in the gray environment of a foresaken inn among the snowdrifts of a wilderness. But whereas of yore at such conferences, inquisitive ladies had vied with one another in holding receptions during which they fluttered their fans, and the terms of peace had really been settled not during the official sittings held in the daytime, but in the bedrooms where amorous dallyings went on by night—here, at Brest-Litovsk, apart from the obscure stenographers, the only woman present was a Russian of

the working class who had come on equal terms with
her male comrades. A new age in history was heralded
by these characteristics, which it would be futile to
dismiss as mere externals, for they were emblematic.
The epoch of Brest-Litovsk was a symbolic epoch, and
here was arranged a peace less imposing to the eye
than previous ones, but offering more to the ear, inasmuch as the negotiations between the two States
were held in public, and for the first time every word
of the proceedings was wirelessed all over the world.

The content was as new as the form. There was to
be neither victor nor vanquished, were to be neither
conquests nor indemnities; the people were no longer
to be thrust aside by kings, but were to determine
their own destinies. These ideas, whose emergence has
been the only result of the World War, were, at about
the same date, summarized by President Wilson in
Fourteen Points drafted along the lines of his earlier
speeches, and accepted in the main by Count Hertling
and Count Czernin in their respective utterances in
Berlin and Vienna. Russian territories were to be
evacuated according to the sixth point, and Russia
was to have the right of self-determination and was to
be accepted into the League of Nations. After all,
the precise wording did not matter much; the important thing was the inauguration of a new international
philosophy which, towards the end of this almost
interminable war, mankind was everywhere beginning
to adopt.

To affirm the new philosophy before the whole world
was now incumbent on the Germans, for it had been
they who in word and deed had hitherto so obstinately
repudiated it. Should they do what was expected of

them, should they, as the first conquerors in the
World War, show themselves to have been modified by
the new spirit, the people of all the enemy countries
would heartily acclaim them, and would be given
unanswerable arguments to use against their own die-
hards and chauvinists. Would the two commanders
recognize, during these Christmas days, that history
had intrusted the threads of fate to German hands as
a sign that the Germans were to begin the new deal?
Would they now, in this region where for the past two
years they had suspended the offensive, seize this unique
opportunity?

Banished to a typical Russian wild, the distinguished
German negotiators had, perhaps, for the first time an
unmistakable conviction that a war was still in progress. Being well-bred persons, however, they tried to
compensate themselves for the loss of the customary
Christmas festivities and for exile from their palaces
in Berlin and Vienna, by the observation of amusing
details. Thus they describe in their memoirs that a
Russian delegate, a peasant, when at table picked his
teeth with his fork; or that another, who was later to
become Russian ambassador in Berlin, openly declared "that everybody would be well off under communism, and some (among whom, I presume, he
counted himself) better off than they had been."
With as much zeal as the Germans displayed in making
such notes for future use, did their adversaries take
advantage of the negotiations to deliver lengthy
orations which should make their ideals known to the
workers of the world. When Yoffe, in his logical way,
or Trotsky, in metallic tones, had expounded the
new doctrine, Kühlmann, with his tired voice, would

drawl out a few platonic phrases in the hope of saving
European civilization.

After the first few days of the conference, voices
from afar, if only by telephone, began to mingle with
those of the negotiators present in the flesh at Brest-
Litovsk. The two commanders were horrified to
learn that the secretary of state was actually approv-
ing some of Wilson's Fourteen Points, which the
German dictators had only pretended to recognize as
the basis of negotiations. What the devil was General
Hoffmann about? In a letter to the chancellor, Hindenburg now formulated his conditions. The occupied
areas were to be annexed as firmly as possible to the
German empire; and along the west of Poland a corridor of German territory inhabited by nearly two million Poles, was to extend to the Baltic in order to
safeguard the German frontier.

These demands of the military dictators, which
conflicted with the conditions agreed to in the armistice, led to a crisis. Negotiations were broken off, and
the Germans took train back to Berlin in order to see
the emperor. New Year's Day; organ playing in the
cathedrals; trumpeting in the streets; a great to-do!
General Hoffmann, who did not wish Poland to be
mutilated, was invited to luncheon by the emperor,
who thought that Hoffmann might strengthen his hand
against the dictators; and when the meal was over,
the general sketched for the emperor a reasonable
frontier line. Since the two commanders had not been
invited on this occasion, the emperor, next day, summoned them to look at the map, declared he had withdrawn his previous assent to conquest, and proceeded
to assert himself in the style of the *Roi Soleil:* "Here,

generals, you will see that I have drawn the future boundaries of Poland, those which as Supreme War Lord I regard as desirable, . . . supported in my opinion by a famous expert, General Hoffmann."

Hereupon Ludendorff lost his temper:

"I cannot endure that Your Majesty should browbeat me by quoting the opinion of one of my subordinates. I refuse to recognize this frontier."

Hindenburg tried to mediate. The emperor closed the painful scene with the words: "I will wait a little while, then, to receive another proposal from the High Command." Without having come to an agreement, the parties quitted Schloss Bellevue, and went their several ways, without having arranged, as did the witches in *Macbeth*, for a further meeting.

Next day the two commanders once more proffered their resignation, less than six months from the time when, by this means, they had secured Bethmann's dismissal. Hindenburg's letter, under date January 7, 1918, began in a nettled tone (we recognize Ludendorff's style):

"Your Majesty gave General Ludendorff and myself the right and intrusted us to the duty of seeing to it that the outcome of the peace should be accordant with the sacrifices and achievements of the German people and the German army. . . . The impression I have derived concerning what went on at Brest leads me to think that the German negotiators have been more diplomatic than vigorous. . . . In the Polish question, Your Majesty has thought fit to regard General Hoffmann's opinion as more valuable than mine and General Ludendorff's. Hoffmann is my subordinate, and has no responsibility as far as the Polish question is concerned. What happened on January 2 has been extremely painful to myself and to General Ludendorff. We take it as a sign that Your Majesty has no regard for our opinion upon a matter which concerns the life of our German fatherland.

"It is Your Majesty's exalted right to decide. But Your Majesty will not demand that straightforward men who have faithfully served Your Majesty and the fatherland should participate with their authority and their names in proceedings wherein they cannot honestly participate because they have a profound conviction that these proceedings are injurious to the crown and the empire. Your Majesty will not demand that I should support Your Majesty's proposals for operations which are among the gravest in history when they are not necessary for the attainment of certain definite military and political aims. I humbly beg Your Majesty to decide the issue after due consideration. My person and General Ludendorff's must play no part where necessities of State are concerned."

It had come to this with the king of Prussia, whom the writer, when a cadet, had so much idolized! With what feelings was the septuagenarian field marshal animated when, making the usual flourish, he signed his name beneath this letter—a letter which was such a terrible one for an officer to write to his king?

When, next day, the chancellor read Hindenburg's letter, the veteran count felt outraged at the dishonor done to his master, insisted that the two army commanders were being undisciplined, and, in conversation with the emperor and having consulted Kühlmann by wire, they arranged with him a new statement, from which the two commanders would, as the slang phrase goes, "get an earful." In an eight-page memorial to the emperor, Hertling, an old man who had no wish to cling to office, took up a position which the two weakling chancellors who had been his predecessors had for three years hesitated to assume, for he wrote:

"The military authorities can always voice their demands on their own initiative, but only as suggestions or advice for consideration, never in the form of instructions which the imperial chancellor must accept. . . . It does not seem to me permissible that Hindenburg and Ludendorff should make the continuance of their indispensable military labors dependent upon the fulfilment of political demands concerning matters whose decision is exclusively the affair of the crown and its constitutionally responsible advisers. If the degree of confidence which the two commanders have inspired in the German people is to be utilized without reserve in political matters also so that their political wishes must be acceded to without demur, this can only mean that the whole conduct of military and political affairs has been laid in the hands of the gentlemen in question, who are made solely responsible. . . . Such a transfiguration of the government of the empire would be likely to have serious internal consequences."

Here was a silvery gleam flashing athwart the German darkness—these words of protest, the only ones that were ever ventured (and of which a copy was immediately sent to the two commanders). More than this—they came from a philosopher! They were indications that Berlin was accessible, not only from Potsdam, but also, though more slowly, even from

15

Weimar. For this utterance expressed a protest of the spirit against the everlasting dominance of military uniforms. Thus fortified by the philosopher, and all the more because the philosopher was a count, Kühlmann, the man of the world in the inhospitable East, now ventured to assert himself against the two commanders; and the emperor, delighted because he had at length secured support against the dictators from two different sides, left the much censured General Hoffmann at his post where the negotiations were being carried on, and sent to Hindenburg an answer which some successor of Bülow's would seem to have written in oil instead of in ink:

"I cordially thank you for your soldierly candor and for the unqualified clearness with which you have defended your conviction. . . . My trust in the two of you cannot be shaken by the fact that I and my political adviser, the imperial chancellor, differ from your views in many respects." But, the emperor went on to say, he expected that any further opposition from this quarter would cease, so that the writer of the letter of protest would be able to devote himself imperturbably to his further duties in the actual conduct of the war. "Rest assured, my dear field marshal, that you will always find my ears open to anything you may wish to say, and that nothing could be further from my mind than to disregard your valuable advice without duly considering it. Let me expressly beg you to give me the benefit of it in future. I remain your well-disposed and grateful king, William R." And now, anyone who has listened breathlessly to this horrible tale will ask himself what could stand in the way of negotiations which should establish upon the

basis laid down by Wilson a peace of mutual understanding, which would put an end to the continuous
foreign accusations that the Germans were a "mili-
taristic and conquering people," and thus deprive the
Allies of one of their chief reasons for continuing their
cannonade? Would not reason at length triumph over
the military mind?

Not a bit of it. There came a happy ending to the
quarrel among the German leaders, which had been
nothing more than an old-fashioned intrigue. The
two civilians had not lost their tempers because they
wanted to come to an understanding with the Russians
in a reasonable way. They were just as keen upon
conquest as the two military commanders, for a German statesman can be as militarist as a German
soldier. Both the philosopher and the man of the
world were of noble birth; they had both worn the
king's uniform; and they were both ready to accept
Hindenburg's pithy definition of politics as "injuring
an adversary by all possible means, including the
strongest." The only thing they had objected to
was being hectored; and the whole interlude was the
outcome of jealousy between rival authorities. What
are the Russians making such a fuss about? In the
armistice, we promised that there should be no forcible
annexation? Yes, under the tacit proviso that our
other enemies should also negotiate for peace. What's
that you say? The German workers, encouraged by
the new tone sounding across the frontier, have become
restive? There are threats of strikes in Berlin, and
strikes already in Vienna?

Against such disturbances, whether at home or
abroad, a Prussian minister of State appeals to the

god of battles, especially when he himself is engaged in peace negotiations and wears a general's uniform. At Kühlmann's request, therefore, and not because of a direct order from the two dictators, General Hoffmann suddenly jumps to his feet in the dingy council chamber at Brest—or, to be more precise, he ostentatiously remains seated in his chair—and informs the Russians, "We are the victors, and don't you forget it!" The words that for thousands of years have been dinned into the ears of the vanquished. Hoffmann denies having thumped the table as he thus spoke. In any case, his threatening voice echoed round the world; and when the Russians again ventured to speak of Wilson, the Germans broke off negotiations. The campaign in the East was resumed. Without encountering any resistance the Germans marched into Russia, occupying Livonia and Esthonia in a few days. The capital was in imminent danger, and Lenin sued for peace. When Trotsky wanted to put up a fight, and demanded a referendum, Lenin, waving his hand in the direction of the retreating Russian armies, answered: "Our men have already voted: with their feet!"

The dictators, who had hitherto been in a bad humor because of the above quoted letters, were ready to shake hands now that a happy ending was in sight, and they demanded "the annexation of Lithuania and Courland, including Riga and the islands, since we need more land to feed our people." In the Napoleonic style, acceptance of these conditions was demanded "within forty-eight hours, by courier." When the Russians accepted by wireless, General Hoffmann imposed yet harsher terms, and insisted upon their being signed within three days. As late as August 1918, supplementary concessions were extorted, the Russians having to renounce all rights in Livonia and Esthonia, and to pledge themselves to the payment of six billions of gold marks.

Kühlmann, having now got into his stride, went to Bucharest, and there, during the spring of 1918, forced upon the conquered Rumanians the terms demanded by the two dictators: the State domains were to be ceded; Germany was to have a ninety years' lease of the oil wells, was to own the railways, was to exercise economic control; the Rumanian army and the supply of munitions were to be reduced; the country was to be occupied for five years; there were to be deliveries of grain to Germany; the Dobrudja was to be made over. What was the upshot? Wilson began to speak in a new tone. To peace treaties of such a character, the answer must be the unrestricted use of force, "until all self-seeking dominions should have been crushed!"

But our valiant German commanders were undismayed. They did not foresee the day when the mailed fist of their enemies would impose the same sort of peace upon themselves—a tributary peace, a slaves' peace, a shameful peace. What they held, they would hold fast. They sent an expedition to Finland; stabilized German rule in Poland to replace the Austrian and Polish dominion; set up a despotic government in Ukraine; treated Russia as long ago Julius Caesar had treated the Gauls, and, in the intoxication of conquest, exclaimed: "Germany's power extends from Finland to the Caucasus!"

XV

While the German commanders were reveling in their conquests, the German people was starving. For two years, now, the forces of conquest and starvation had pulled Germany in two directions, until, at last, the rusty chain had to snap, and the State fall with a thud to the ground. When Liebknecht was imprisoned on May 1, 1916, it was for having demanded in his leaflets and his speeches nothing more than the emperor and the chancellor had declared to be Germany's motives on the first day of the war—defense. During his trial, fifty thousand workers went on strike; and when, in 1917, there was an increasing shortage of bread, two hundred thousand downed tools in Berlin.

Trotsky's speeches at Brest-Litovsk, sounding always nearer and louder like the clear signals of the Leonore overture and overtopping the rest of the orchestra, had aroused yet louder echoes in the heart of every sufferer. In a dramatic crescendo the two motifs of the World War had reinforced one another; and, issuing from the gray conference chamber at Brest, had become audible to the whole world. In all the belligerent lands the generals and the magnates of heavy industry, the officials and the war profiteers, wanted conquests, and had been able, by suggestions and promises, to arouse the necessary feelings of hatred in part of the populace; but the masses in general, wanting to combine in a class stratification instead of remaining racially severed, were longing for unity, whether achieved by the League of Nations or by the world revolution. Horizontal and vertical folk movements inevitably intersect. During the days of Brest-Litovsk, the mission of this war, planned by destiny but hitherto secret, for the first time became plain.

Roused by the aforesaid signals, in the end of January half a million workers revolted in Berlin; if you add to these the malcontents in Vienna and the rest of Germany, they numbered nearly one and a half millions. It was the first great rising of the populace, not against defeated generals, but against those who had been only too victorious. No one, at this juncture, demanded a socialist republic; the demand which made itself so widely heard was one for renunciation of conquests. The commanders had recourse to "strong measures": arrested the ringleaders; militarized the great industries; suppressed *Vorwärts;* dispersed meetings; and degraded military service (for which, three years earlier, countless youths had volunteered) to become a punishment, threatening that "all strikers fit to bear arms" would be "sent to the front." The system was called "intensification of the state of siege," to indicate, like the phrase "ruthless submarine warfare," how gentle had been the measures hitherto used.

But the reader must not suppose that the veteran field marshal was moved by an antisocial spirit. His patriarchal intentions—those of an aged Junker who, at Neudeck, had been accustomed graciously to answer the salutes of underlings born into serfdom—disclosed themselves in one of Hindenburg's memorials. "All that is possible must be done to insure that childbearing shall no longer be a burden for the poor, but a delight. . . . To heal our wounds, it is essential that we should promote the formation of settlements, and make it easy for everyone to found a family. What I should like to see is every workman established in his own house with a nice little garden, where he can enjoy himself with his family when the day's work is done."

In this reference to a "nice little garden," do we not hear echoes of the paternal magnanimity of past centuries during which the Junker tried to mitigate the hardships fate had imposed upon his serfs? In heaven we are all equal; and, here below, one can, at Christmas, give the children of the poor a box of lead soldiers! How similar this fancied world seems to that of the bolshevik leader, at any rate as reflected in the head of a Prussian general—"a world in which everybody would be well off, . . . and some (among whom, presume, he counted himself) better off than they had been."

Such being the situation, growing more and more difficult both at home and on the fighting front, the two commanders formed the most arduous of their resolves. In March, 1918, a year and a half after they had risen to supreme power, they ventured upon another blow westward, hoping to decide the issue of the war by breaking through on the western front where the German advance had been stayed for two years. Public criticism, and especially that of the Commission of Inquiry, was subsequently concentrated upon this offensive of the spring and summer of 1918. The matter is plain enough to anyone who troubles to study the documents. Since, however, the question how far military errors of judgment led to the destruction of the German people cannot be answered by a layman, I shall be content to quote the opinions of experts.

As to the preliminaries for the great offensive, Major von Hindenburg, the field marshal's nephew, writes: "The army no longer has the martial energy of 1914; the troops are badly fed and badly clothed; war-weariness is general. . . . The subalterns have to mind what they are about, being well aware that they can no longer handle their men with Old Prussian strictness. The High Command, however, has not yet fully grasped this fact. Things are being hushed up so that Hindenburg and Ludendorff overestimate the capacity of our forces. Without spells of home leave, without time to take breath, the same trust-worthy shock troops are hustled hither and thither, and kept at it until they are absolutely exhausted." Since the munition factories had been depleted of workers in order to man the fighting front, with the result that munitions were scarce, Major von Hindenburg spoke of the offensive as a desperate hazard. Even the Allies, with forces nearly doubled in the last two years, had not been able to break through; for the lines were deeply zigzagged, and could be easily reconstructed if breached. Would not the High Command take all this into consideration before venturing on a forward movement not made under compulsion? While Wilson and Lloyd George were holding peace talks in immediate expectation of the offensive, Hindenburg was publicly declaring, "The victory essential for Germany's political and economic future can no longer be snatched from us." A year before this he had privately told the admirals that things could not well be worse.

The trouble was that the dictators' will-to-conquest ran counter to the generalship of the commanders—

although dictators and commanders were the same
pair. Only if every possible man had been withdrawn
from the eastern front by February, as was done,
too late, in September, could a decision in the West
have been secured. Instead, fifty-three divisions were
left in the East to hold the conquests in that part of
of the world. "It was a disastrous error," such is the
younger Hindenburg's judgment upon his uncle, "to
leave these forces in the East. . . . Instead of con-
centrating all forces in the decisive hour, they were yet
further scattered. In Finland, in Turkey, in Macedonia, in the Caucasus, in the Crimea, there were an
additional million of German soldiers. By a bold
abandonment of the East we could, in March, 1918,
actually have secured a considerable numerical superiority, and in that case we should probably have
been able to compel the enemy to negotiate." This
view was subsequently confirmed by General Haig,
who declared that in those March days of 1918 the
Germans, if they had had two or three more cavalry
divisions (then inactive in Ukraine), could have
made a breach in the Allied lines and compelled a
withdrawal.

However that may be, Ludendorff, during the winter
of 1917–1918, transferred forty-one divisions from the
eastern front to the western, so that when the offensive
was resumed it was with a force of 3,600,000 men on
the western front—twice as many as at the opening of
the war. He hoped that these troops would enable
him to get the better of the enemy before the arrival
of the Americans—for the near prospect of this, which
when the ruthless submarine campaign was initiated
had seemed to the two commanders no more than a

Hindenburg, Hoffmann, and Ludendorff planning the Eastern Campaign

trifling danger, was the only reason why the offensive was begun as early as March.

As regards the technique of the offensive, General Hoffmann considers that its whole strength should have been concentrated upon one chosen point instead of being delivered northward and southward of the position on the Somme. "In the spring of 1918," writes Major Hindenburg, "the position of affairs was the opposite of that which had prevailed at Tannenberg. . . . The strong fortresses of Metz and Strassburg were by no means competent to hold up the French forces in Alsace-Lorraine. But, for political reasons, the German High Command did not dare to surrender the Imperial Provinces even temporarily to the French. Neither in the East nor in the West were they willing to abandon occupied territory. Every salient on the front, however many troops its defense would need, must be retained." Ludendorff had in view a peculiar kind of offensive, which was to stretch from one sector to another, and might need a considerable time before success could be achieved. "But the calculations upon which this scheme has been based are the gravest blunder of the High Command. In view of the courage and strength of the German troops, partial successes are, of course, possible; but the great decision cannot be achieved in the West. . . . The gain of a few miles here or there is of no avail."

Here we see Ludendorff famous technician, nihilist, and desperate gambler, venture a last hazard. Since he would not admit the failure of his policy or the strategic impossibility of victory, since he would not even see that the sources from which his troops were supplied were drying up, he hurled himself into this enterprise, no longer full of hope as at the outset, nor yet a doubter such as he became later, but in desperation. He must certainly have been familiar with the sentences written by Field Marshal von der Goltz in the year 1901:

"The boldest onslaught, guided by the best generalship in the world, will lead to destruction if the available forces are insufficient to effect the occupation of a position whose occupation can alone make a satisfactory peace possible. We see this most plainly in the fate of great commanders, from Hannibal to Charles XII and Napoleon, who failed only in this one point, and were thereby ruined. They resembled a clever company promoter whose financial resources do not suffice to enable him to carry his speculations to their limit, with the result that some failure, trifling in itself, renders nugatory all the brilliant successes hitherto achieved."

The psychological determinants of these mistakes of the two commanders, nay of the general failure of Prussian strategy, were significantly indicated by an anonymous General Staff writer in the year 1920, as follows: "Our army school had entered its Alexandrian epoch, in which the absolute takes the place of the relative, and the panacea that of the specific remedy. . . . Ludendorff had immoderately enlarged the huge machine which he found ready to his hand. In peace time, this machine had worked without friction; but in war time it broke down, since it was not adapted for war service. . . . It could not fit itself to unforeseen circumstances—which arise when the first soldier falls into line; it could not allow for what the enemy would do. All that was possible

was to give an initial thrust; should something new
stand in the way, this thrust must be canceled since
the impetus was incapable of being modified. . . .

"Herein lies the vast difference between the conduct
of the war upon the eastern and the western fronts
respectively. The small and purposeful General Staff
of the Eastern Army was a competent war machine.
. . . Thus in the East, we see even Ludendorff, after
making a general plan, modifying it as circumstances
vary. In the West, such modifications were impossible, for the machine devoured time. . . . Every
defect in the apparatus was enormously magnified, so
that the excellence of the commander, his intellectual
mobility, his capacity for turning the peculiarities of
the situation to account could not overcome these
mechanical defects. . . . Since, in the West, Ludendorff had formed no general plan, he did not feel
the need for a mobile apparatus. . . . In the end
he could not even use it to carry out minor plans. One
who went into a war with such an apparatus was fore-
doomed to defeat."

This account, designed, in large measure, to exon-
erate the two German commanders by dwelling upon
the defects of the German military machine, is, really,
a technological criticism of the Prussian State, and can
be transformed into such a criticism by changing a few
substantives. Perhaps the two magicians' apprentices
really were swept away by the millions of besoms they
had conjured up. Again and again, at this turning
point in destiny, we note the working of the spirit of
the Military Academy, which forebade its pupils to
lay a finger upon the almighty organization. These
two royalists were able to overcome their king; but

the military machine, the god enthroned high above the king, showed in the end that it was stronger than they. Being its thralls, they could not control it.

The king, who was less concerned with the thunder of the battles than with the gentle rain of orders and decorations that followed them, was able, this time, to sow confusion even in so subaltern a field of activity. He rewarded the first technical successes of the offensive, so that the populace believed that the breakthrough had at last been successful, that the enemy front in the West had been shattered, and that, substantially, the war had been won. Hindenburg received the resuscitated Order of the Iron Cross with Gold Rays for winning the "greatest battle in history"—a decoration which, before him, only Blücher had been granted for the victory over Napoleon at Waterloo. This and the exaggerations of the bulletins diverted people's thoughts from strikes and a peace by mutual understanding, and aroused for the nonce universal cheerfulness. Naturally the ultimate failure of the great offensive would prove all the more crushing.

Still, even though such fearful mistakes were being made, they might do good in the end by teaching—at too high a cost, it is true!—that no victory on the western front was possible. "On the day," writes General Hoffmann, "when the High Command decided to abandon the offensive against Amiens, it should have informed the government that the time had come for opening peace negotiations. . . . In any case, it should have been recognized that there must be no further offensives. To take the offensive involved terrible losses in men and munitions, losses which could no longer be replaced."

Yet the incredible happened; in the summer there was a fresh offensive! At this period the reports of the two commanders speak of a monthly loss of 200,000 men, replaced by no more than 120,000, among whom were 80,000 described as "cured of wounds."

Then the tanks arrived. "One cannot but reproach the High Command," writes Major Hindenburg, "for having failed, until too late, to recognize the importance of tanks. Today it seems hard to understand why the High Command did not, immediately after the battle of Cambrai (November, 1917), devote its best energies to the making of an efficient tank. The German armament industry, being at a very high level of technical development, would have been quite equal to the occasion. . . . The Hindenburg program provided for more field guns, rifles, and machine guns than were needed, but in other respects was extremely lame. . . . Industrial circles had devised plenty of schemes for the making of armed and armored automobiles, but the High Command had turned them down."

The ablest critics declared that the loss of subsequent battles was due to the Germans' lack of tanks. Later, young Hindenburg writes: "When, during the German attack on Amiens, a gap of ten miles yawned between the British and the French forces, and the English army had already been ordered to withdraw, the Germans would have won a smashing victory if they had been able to thrust a squadron of tanks into this gap, thus opening the way for the German infantry." Whereas Ludendorff, in retrospect, continued to declare that the effect of the tanks had been insignificant, Major von Hindenburg, who had been at the front when the tanks were at work, bitterly rejoined, "The German officers and men who had practical experience of the devastating effects of the tanks will not be likely to indorse General Ludendorff's views."

Such criticisms must not be dismissed as no more than posthumous words of wisdom. According to trustworthy reports, the numbers, the experience, and the efficiency of the Americans were increasing day by day. It was in June that the Germans first encountered these quasi-mythical adversaries whose coming had been expected for a year and a half with mingled mockery, doubt, and dread. Even now, the German people would have heard nothing of the matter had not men from the front on home leave spoken of the admirable equipment of the first American prisoners, who really seemed to have come from another world.

Warning voices multiplied. An initial peace move had already been made by the German crown prince; then, in June, Rupprecht, heir to the Bavarian throne, spoke in favor of opening negotiations. The extraordinary thing is that, although Ludendorff was shaken by these admonitions, as we learn from the subsequent avowals of Prince Rupprecht and of Colonel von Haeften, neither he nor Hindenburg would stop the proposed offensive. "The fact is," according to evidence given before the Commission of Inquiry, "that he really failed to understand the spirit of the nation and that of his own army. It was disastrous that he neither could nor would see how exhausted our troops had become. Ludendorff must answer for his failure to make offers of peace at this juncture, and for the fact that drunk with the lust for conquest, he intrusted the destinies of the German nation to the possible intervention of a *deus ex machina*, and having consequently sacrificed hundreds of thousands of lives."

"In like manner," writes General Hoffmann, "he closed his eyes to the menacing signs from the Allied front. . . . Since the High Command had failed to secure a German victory in the West, it ought at least, in the summer of 1918, to have sent German reinforcements to the Bulgarian front. Such reinforcements were obtainable from the Eastern Army. . . . Moreover, among our people in general, no one really grasped how serious was the situation. . . . Even we, even the headquarters of the Eastern Army, were not informed about the heavy losses in the West. . . . Everyone was convinced that the Western Army could hold out whatever happened."

In his memoirs, Hindenburg admits that there was no adequate strategic reason for the summer offensive of 1918. The aim, he tells us, was, by attacks here and there, to shake the hostile lines in such a way that "accidentally, so to say," a collapse might be brought about. Marshal Foch termed this "buffalo strategy!"

At this time, when the last German levies were being wasted in purposeless offensives, the rulers had discovered a novel game. Even during the Brest-Litovsk crisis, Hindenburg, having had to stomach the previously quoted letter from the emperor, demanded the head of one of the latter's highest officials, Valentini, the president of the Crown Civil Cabinet, whom the field marshal regarded as responsible for the policy of renouncing conquests. "One of Your Majesty's confidential advisers," wrote Hindenburg in those days

16

to William, "is sowing misunderstanding between
Your Majesty and the people. It is essential that a
new one should be chosen, who will frankly and boldly
report the actual condition of affairs to Your Majesty
and put Your Majesty once more in touch with the
people, who earnestly desire this." Did the people
know who Herr Valentini was; who his successor should
be; or even who the emperor was?

In the beginning of January, 1918, the last-named
felt himself so completely forgotten that he penned as
marginal note to an article the words: "This has
come about because both sides ignore the emperor!"
That is the soliloquy of a man who before long will
abdicate. Now, in the summer of the same year, he
was taking a more cheerful view of the world. Fresh
diadems were to be allotted; there would be newfangled uniforms; and reviews and processions. In
order to revive the tradition of the Teutonic Knights
(and what, in 1918, could seem more desirable to the
Germans?), the king of Prussia was to become Duke of
Courland; and, lest this new dignity for his royal
rival might pique the king of Saxony, the latter was
to be made Duke of Lithuania. That seemed simple
enough, but proved, after all, to be an almost insoluble
problem because of the claims of the king of Würtem-
berg, who for four years had likewise amused himself
with playing at work in the Red Cross and similar
organizations. Perhaps it would be better to make
him Duke of Lithuania? Then what about the rulers
of Bavaria and of Baden? Would not the other kings
and granddukes be mortified if they were left out in
the cold? We might let them have fragments of Alsace as a possible solution of a long-discussed question.

But as for Finland, that, decided the emperor, must be assigned to a Hohenzollern prince!

During these weeks the man of the world, secretly supported by the philosopher, ventured a peace move. The secretary of State had not heard a word about the threads which Colonel von Haeften had spun, in the previous March from The Hague towards America. Ludendorff had kept the report of the matter locked up in a drawer. At this juncture, however, Kühlmann felt impelled to make a public overture. Speaking in the Reichstag, he did not, indeed, say a word about Belgium, but, amid patriotic mouthings, remarked: "We can no longer expect the war to be brought to a conclusion in a purely military fashion without an interchange of political ideas between the contending parties."

Thereupon the wrath of Achilles burst over the head of the civilian slacker. Only the day before, the two commanders had won back a strip of disputed territory along the *Chemin des Dames*. Was this a time when the secretary of State ought to begin talking about an exchange of ideas between the belligerents? In the German G.H.Q. there were no ideas, for there the German sword was supreme! Hindenburg wired to the chancellor: "The speech has had a shattering effect upon the army." So fine was the two commanders' hearing, that, five hours after the speech had been published, they knew its effect upon their three million soldiers. New threats from the military dictators: "Choose between Kühlmann and ourselves!" The veteran philosopher tried to save his collaborator's scalp, and made excuses for Kühlmann's horrid lapse by explaining that the secretary of State

had been overtired, and had been short of time for
preparing his speech. In fact he had been too busy
even to have luncheon; that was why his tone had
lacked sturdiness and why he had produced so feeble
an impression. Thus luncheon, a meal which had
long since gone out of fashion in beleaguered Germany, had once more become an affair of high policy.
"The secretary of State," rejoined Hindenburg stiffly,
"must find time. . . . Behind him stand the *Frank-
furter Zeitung* and the *Berliner Tageblatt*."

Two days later Kühlmann spoke again in the
Reichstag. His discourse was vigorous, carefully prepared, that of a man with a savory meal inside him.
His previous utterance had been misunderstood; nothing but the dash of our troops, and so on, could decide
the war! Ten days after the ignominious withdrawal,
which obviously was nothing more than a strategic
retirement, Kühlmann was dismissed, having, with
this second speech of his, gambled away a great part
which, as monitor, he might subsequently have played
in the Republic. A certain Herr von Hintze, a naval
officer, and an intelligent man, succeeded him in the
middle of July, not accepting the post until the two
commanders had assured him that they still had
excellent grounds for believing they could conquer the
enemy.

"Yes, such is my hope," was Ludendorff's rejoinder.

"In that case, I will accept the office," said Hintze.
"Someone must be secretary, anyhow. As soon as
our position is good on all the fronts, I shall make
diplomatic advances."

The next news was of a fresh reverse at Rheims.
Hintze traveled back to H.G.Q. and "begged" the

commanders to agree to his taking preparatory steps, expecting that after a defeat he would find them in a suitable mood of depression—as he actually did.

How much during this last phase the army leadership had become a game of hazard, is shown by two well-attested utterances made on the same day by the opposing commanders. Throwing his cards on the table, the gambler Ludendorff said: "If my onslaught on Rheims is successful, we shall have won the war." On this same July 15, Foch said to Loucheur: "If the German offensive on Rheims is successful, we may lose the war."[1]

XVI

On August 8, the western powers, breaking through the German lines with the aid of tanks, gained a great victory along the road from Amiens to Saint Quentin. That was the first Allied victory in this part of the world for years, but was now only the first of a series of victories by means of which during three months the German front was steadily pushed back. A great change of attitude resulted in Germany; there was a consultation among the doctors; the patient must be regarded as on the dangerous list, and the question arose whether the family should be informed how desperate was his condition. The statesmen were summoned to G.H.Q. During the night before their arrival, says Colonel von Haeften, "Ludendorff was very grave." Next morning, August 13, Hindenburg came to see Ludendorff, and, in the colonel's presence, asked, at ten o'clock, what he was to tell the

[1] Ludendorff, Urkunden der Obersten Heeresleitung, page 494.

statesmen about the situation. Ludendorff replied: "We must let them know the whole truth." Thereupon the chief of staff gave the field marshal a picture of the situation no less frank and gloomy than the one he had given the colonel overnight.

Immediately afterwards, like an inquisitor who hopes, at long last, to extract a confession from a tortured soul, Hintze came to see Ludendorff—unaccompanied for the moment. Ludendorff made an avowal: —Four weeks ago I told you I still hoped to conquer the enemy. I am no longer sustained by that hope.

Hintze: Well, what are you going to do about it?

Ludendorff: By a strategic defensive, we shall gradually paralyze the enemy's fighting spirit. But I ought to tell you that the field marshal takes a more cheerful view of the situation than I do.

Hintze, who, after what he had heard, could only think about the impossibility of victory and not about the possibility of defeat, replied that in the circumstances he would certainly prepare peace moves. But the imperturbable Hindenburg, the man with no nerves, would not allow himself to be intimidated. In a council of four, consisting of himself, Ludendorff, Hintze, and the chancellor, the field marshal spoke confidently, saying: "We are still far advanced in enemy territory; our army is stout-hearted; the men at the front are willing to go on making sacrifices, and will continue to fight until the negotiations take a favorable turn. I have absolute confidence in the resisting power of the troops." Although when we read these words today they sound paltry enough, they certainly encouraged those who heard them at the time. For the rest, the commanders complained to the statesmen about the faint-heartedness that prevailed at home, and demanded further annexations in Belgium and Poland. When, therefore, Hintze. gave an extremely gloomy picture of the political situation, Ludendorff taunted him with playing the "pessimist."

Such being the mood of Hindenburg and Ludendorff, what were the other players in the game to do? Could the emperor and the chancellor, could the vigorous secretary of State, all three of whom wanted to face up to the necessities of the position, convince the two commanders how desperate it really was, and immediately take steps to negotiate for peace? No one seems to have suggested that an attempt should be made to weaken the enemy politically by some such step as the reorganization of Poland, by coming to an understanding with the subjugated nationalities in the East, by declaring the autonomy of Alsace-Lorraine—although these ideas had been discussed again and again since the beginning of the war.

Next day, August 14, there was a council in Spa, at which the emperor, the crown prince, and three court generals were brought face to face with the four chief actors, Hindenburg, Ludendorff, the chancellor, and the secretary of State. The minutes of this meeting also throw a strong light on the respective characters of the participants.

"After the Chancellor had dilated upon war weariness and hunger, Ludendorff insisted upon the need for stricter internal discipline, for the development of the internal forces of the country with the utmost possible energy, and for the punishment of Lichnowsky.

"Hintze with reference to the foreign situation: Increased confidence of the enemy, for whom time was working, whereas time was working against Germany; Austria was at the end of her resources, and the neutrals were sick of the war. Field Marshal von Hindenburg, went on Hintze, had defined the situation thus, that our army command must make it its aim to paralyze the enemy's will-to-war by a strategic defensive. The statesmen must bow before the utterance of the greatest commander thrown up by this war.

"The Crown Prince indorsed what Ludendorff and Hintze had said, and emphasized the need for stricter discipline upon the home front.

"Emperor: Yes, better order at home! To insure this, new instructions must go to the generals. . . . There must be a more effective combing-out to re-man the front. In Berlin there are still a lot of young fellows loafing about. . . . The enemy is suffering, too, has had heavy losses, needs raw materials and food supplies; the English harvest has been a poor one, and the tonnage has been reduced; perhaps owing to this scarcity England may gradually become inclined to make peace. We must choose a suitable moment for trying to come to an understanding with the enemy. When the right time arrives, possibly an offer can best be made through the queen of Holland. . . . It would be well to appoint a Propaganda Commission to increase the confidence of the German people. Encouraging speeches must be made by persons whose voice carries weight with the public—Ballin, for instance. . . .

"The Chancellor also referred to the need for energetic measures to maintain authority at home. . . . Diplomatic steps must be taken to force the enemy to seek an understanding, and the most appropriate moment for this would be after the next successes in the West.

"Hindenburg said he hoped that the army would succeed in maintaining its positions on French territory, and thus, in the end, would enable us to enforce our will on our adversaries."

After this conference, the two representatives of the government could not but say to themselves that the only clear thing which emerged from it was its lack of candor. Ludendorff had told Colonel von Haeften that things were in a very bad way, and that therefore steps must promptly be taken to secure a tolerable peace. But the statesmen who had been summoned on this account must only be told half the truth, and this half was divided between the elderly philosopher and the young naval officer who was now secretary of State—accurately divided, lest either should get an overdose. Before the witness whom Ludendorff was careful to keep in the room during his conversations with Hindenburg, he spoke of the necessity for telling the statesmen the absolute truth; the colonel was to hear how relentlessly the commanders intended to speak the truth.

But when the two statesmen arrived, Ludendorff begins by concealing from the secretary of State, and then both the commanders conceal from both the statesmen, how desperate is the situation. The imperturbable field marshal had been able to rally the spirits of his depressed chief of staff, so that when one of the two statesmen paints a gloomy picture, Ludendorff chides him for his pessimism. The more

serious the crisis, the more stalwart we must show
ourselves to be! The emperor has brought with him
three court generals, to protect himself against Ludendorff's nervous irritability and rudeness. In this
room, each is afraid of the others: the statesmen,
afraid to ask the generals questions which the latter
could answer; the generals, who are afraid of being
examined by the elderly philosopher, and keep him at a
distance by assuming a confidence they do not feel;
the emperor, who has been afraid of his son since the
latter issued a defeatist memorial; the crown prince
who, though he is a defeatist, does not wish to appear
a slacker in the eyes of the generals; the court generals, who want to go on warming themselves by
keeping the All Highest in a sunny mood—why,
really, have the lot of them assembled? Truths must
not be spoken in this atmosphere; a radiant mood
cannot be induced. What on earth is to be done in
so painful a situation?

They find it easy to agree upon one point, each
being a Junker or a general or both. The people, the
common folk, are to blame for everything! These
underlings must be kept down with an iron hand!
Authority must prevail; internal order must be strenuously maintained. See to that, Excellencies! Send
troublesome workers to the front! Have the young
fellows who are loafing about with nothing to do
combed out, and send them to the front as well. The
crown prince, who has made a point of visiting the
trenches, can unhesitatingly insist upon strict discipline. As for the emperor, he is delighted that the
crops in England are poor, and continues to talk
about tonnage, so that he would seem to have heard

nothing with regard to the disappointments of the
submarine campaign.   On the other hand, in the
present straits his thoughts turn to his courtier Jew
[Ballin], who is to make speeches, since the German
Michael is manifestly too sensitive to talk enthusiastically under present conditions.   Ludendorff has
discovered a prince behind whose offenses he can take
cover for his own, since it has become plain to him
that Lichnowsky's secret memorial, which was betrayed to the enemy two years before, must have so
greatly increased the enemy's fighting fervor for a
few days at Amiens as to enable the French to break
the German lines.

Of the two statesmen at the council table, one
declared only that he bowed to the authority of the
greatest of commanders; the other, that he was waiting only for the next victory in order to make a diplomatic move.   While the cloud-burst is killing the
cattle, and the experienced peasant must help to shelter them beneath rocks and trees, specialists declare
that as soon as the sun begins to shine once more,
larger byres must be built.

Among the lot of them, Hindenburg is the only one
who, chary of words as ever, can talk hopefully to
express, with his usual imperturbability, his confidence
in ultimate victory.

"God be praised, the horrible word 'death' has not
been uttered!" think the court generals, as they leave
the councilroom behind the emperor who, with serious mien, strides off to luncheon.   Hertling declared
later that no one had said a word to the effect that
the game was up.   The only advice of the military
commanders was that the enemy onslaught must be

stubbornly resisted. Hintze writes: "There was not a syllable or a hint from the field marshal or from Ludendorff to the effect that their estimate of the military situation led them to infer the necessity at this juncture for a diplomatic peace move." On the other hand, Colonel Haeften, to whom overnight and early that morning the truth had been told, but who was not present at the council, declares, "If the generals had been anything like as frank to the statesmen as they were to myself, it would have been plain to the statesmen that not an hour must be lost before initiating political negotiations." General Ludendorff was anything but frank, as far as words were concerned; and his actions conveyed a very different impression from that which would have been conveyed by frankness. At the close of the conference "he firmly pressed the hand of the secretary of State." Men of action are not fond of using many words; they are neither orators nor writers—a good handshake says all that is needed!

Before the subsequent Commission of Inquiry, Delbrück, the nationalist professor, passed a devastating judgment on Ludendorff. Hindenburg, however, was exonerated, in the following remarkable words: "The field marshal must be excused, for he no longer possessed the mental energy to expound the situation clearly, and was wholly under the spell of Ludendorff." This derogatory statement must be repudiated. When Hindenburg was seventy, and even when he was eighty-five, his mind was as clear and vigorous as when he was in his prime.

A fortnight later, to a colonel who was in his confidence, Ludendorff said in plain terms that he had thought it better to conceal the situation from the Foreign Office. "Perfect candor would have led to a catastrophe! If I had told them the truth, they would have completely lost their heads." But none of those present at the council knew, at the time, a fact which was subsequently disclosed during the sittings of the Commission of Inquiry, and one which is mentioned by Ludendorff himself in his collection of relevant documents.

When the session was over, he had the minutes, which had been initialed by the nine who were present, brought to him, that he might safeguard himself before any subsequent tribunal, were it only the tribunal of history. He had regarded old Hindenburg's contribution to the debate as lacking in firmness. Why had the field marshal said to these civilians and to the emperor, "he hoped," etc? A soldier does not hope, he declares. According to the minutes, Hindenburg had said he "hoped" that the Germans would be able to maintain their positions on French territory. Ludendorff, therefore, struck out the word "he hoped," so that the utterance ran: "The field marshal said that the army would succeed in maintaining its positions on French territory."

XVII

"We are far advanced in the defile, the living are but the remnants of former companies. The others, men to be envied, lie dead along the road. . . . We scramble through a wood which the French are shelling with heavy artillery. Through the rocks runs a little pathway which is paved with corpses. As one

might stumble over roots, we stumble over rotting
arms and legs. The wood comes to an end. Our way
leads down the declivity into the gully of death. For
a moment we stop to recover our breath, and wait to
see if the front-rank men have got through. Bang!
Crash! Forward and down! Not a tree, not a bush;
even the crags have been ground to powder by the
shell fire, to a dust into which one sinks up to the
ankles. Fragments of human beings everywhere. A
leg, a waxen hand, heads looking like turnips dropped
from a loaded cart. A human trunk burst open, with
the guts hanging out, and a swarm of hungry flies
lying across it like a black veil. Close at hand more
severed heads, contemplating the work of these flies.
Heads, one of them with a black mustache; to the
left of this, a very youthful head, whose glazed blue
eyes seem to stare at the adjoining head, of which the
face has a crooked nose. Among them the shells
arriving with a whizz continue to fall and burst. The
file leader stumbles over a dead leg sticking up from
the ground out of a clumsy ammunition boot. He
gives a loud cry, and falls. Is he wounded? Stride
over him! Onward! Bang!" [1]

By day and by night the thunder of the guns was
unceasing, and their distant rumble could be heard
even at G.H.Q. The commanders no longer heeded it.
When, each morning, they looked at the lists of the
previous day's losses, it was with eyes rendered callous
by years of experience. They looked at them as the
manager of a mine who finds on his writing table
figures concerning the output of the night shift com-
pares them in his head with the figures of the day

[1] From Vitus Heller, Nie mehr Krieg!

before, and puts away the record in his file. Of course a commander cannot be tender-hearted in war time, especially when the war has lasted four years; but if he is callous, if the losses remain for him mere figures without any human implication, he resembles a surgeon who will do half a dozen operations in the forenoon, and then go to his luncheon without a qualm. Great physicians are more sensitive.

The car of doom rolled along at a brisker rate. Catastrophe, thought the augurs, would be better than panic. During the next six weeks, the despair of the army and of the people continued to increase.

The vice chancellor, sent by the Reichstag to the commanders, begged them to agree to the abandonment of Belgium as part of the peace terms, but was told, even at the end of August, that there must first be an agreement concerning the Flanders question. When whispers about the surrender of at least part of Lorraine began to make themselves heard, the commanders tried to drown them with their famous utterance regarding their determination to defend "every foot of the soil of the fatherland." Ministers of State and generals have always been ready to defend this with their own honor and with the bodies of their compatriots. The vice chancellor was reassured by Hindenburg's confident description of the position of affairs. At the street corners people could read huge placards signed by the field marshal, "We have won the war in the East, and we shall win it in the West likewise." An admiral declared it to be "an excellent thing that there are already numerous American soldiers in France"; and another, Admiral Scheer, publicly announced, in September, "There can be no doubt that our submarine campaign will compel England to sue for peace." The parliamentary deputies were even less well informed than the workers. It was not in the Reichstag, which was being fed with false information, but from his neighbors, the Westphalian farmers, that Schücking, a deputy, heard in August, "The war is lost; the Americans have come!"

Subsequently this same deputy, a distinguished lawyer, reported to the Commission of Inquiry how an officer—in civil life a factory owner—was asked, at this juncture, by his general, to write a report for headquarters regarding the spirit of the troops. When he wrote that the spirit was as bad as it could be, the general picked up a pen: "The High Command won't like to read that!" he remarked, and wrote instead:

"The spirit of the troops is, in general, excellent. Stricter discipline will greatly improve it."

While the commanders were thus wishing to be humbugged, they passed on the fog to the statesmen. A Badenese member of the Committee of the Federal Council was officially informed that, although the situation was difficult, there could be absolutely no doubt of a German victory in the end. If these plenipotentiaries had been told the truth, which the commanders were legally and morally bound to disclose, they would have hastened to inform their sovereigns, who would have come together in Berlin and compelled a German move towards peace—for they were all sick of the war, and the lesser princes were afraid of losing their thrones. In general, people cling more anxiously to small properties than to large, for those accustomed to great wealth are apt to regard it as eternal.

Especial pains were taken to make things easy for the emperor during the last terrible weeks of the struggle. The military courtier who was his chief companion in the concluding months, writes in reports that have much to say about castle terraces, walks in parks, processions, and lunches, "All concerned did their best to divert the monarch's thoughts from the grave troubles of the day, and to discuss with him important problems of art, science, or technique.

"When the emperor took up such a theme, drawing upon the inexhaustible sources of his personal experience, the otherwise weary hours passed in a flash, and were a perpetual refreshment."

Thus did the emperor continue (though only in the realm of reflection) to fight for the welfare of the German nation. His brilliant descriptions of the excavations in Corfu or his gracious presence at the Royal Opera House were romantically accompanied by the incessant but distant rumble of the heavy guns. Simultaneously, one could hear the tread of companies still being levied for the front—too light a tread, that of lads of eighteen, stunted by lack of food during the critical years of growth.

The awaited blows were hammering on the western front. On September 2, a breach was made along the road from Arras to Cambrai. On the 12th, Foch gained another victory, for now two million Americans had joined the Allies to fight against two and a half million Germans. On the 15th, in Macedonia, the Bulgarians laid down their arms and returned to their homes punctually on the day previously announced. On the 19th, at Jaffa, the Turks fled before the British; Austria was about to make a separate

17

peace; on the 28th, Foch gained another victory over Ludendorff.

Now, at length, Ludendorff threw down his cards. "The game is up; make peace quickly!" The enemy, which for four years had been kept far from the German frontier, was drawing closer and closer. Still, the commander's brow was not clouded with despair. Although some spoke later of Ludendorff as having had a nervous crisis during these days, his actions indicated that his mind was perfectly clear, and he effected a strategic withdrawal which commands universal admiration. I speak, of course, of the political front. The military front had become absolutely untenable, for Germany was left without allies. Till yesterday he had concealed the danger. What was he to do in the circumstances?

General Ludendorff had an inspiration; indeed, one may say that at this juncture he made history, and compelled Hindenburg to join with him in the process. At the close of the war he shuffled off responsibility, much as a man of the Landsturm lays aside the uniform which the king has provided him with only for the duration of one battle.

Of a sudden, the two commanders became democrats; they discovered the advantages of parliamentary government. They decided, within five minutes, to reconstruct the constitution of the German realm, although for two years they had strenuously resisted any change. What no arguments and no strikes had been able to achieve, Marshal Foch now achieved. Education and prejudices, the Military Academy and the royal power, were forgotten. The one important thing was to make the people responsible for the peace,

whose inauguration the two commanders had postponed as long as possible by their political demands,
and whose present menacing aspect was their work.
Their main concern was, by admitting that defeat was
overwhelming, to bring about the establishment of
representative government. Obstacles must be swept
out of the way; the populace and the Reichstag, taken
by surprise, must be suddenly compelled to assume
power the instant power began to burn the fingers of
the commanders. If the Reichstag, unwilling to handle
red-hot iron, was inclined to wait, its reluctance must
be overcome. Revolution from above must fore-
stall revolution from below. That was the course
matters took! The German Reichstag did not fight
for power; power was thrust upon it by the military
autocrats—a form of revolution previously unknown
to history.

Ludendorff manipulated his puppets like a master.
On September 29, the chancellor and the secretary
of State were summoned to headquarters. They were
bluntly told that the game was up, and that the army
must have a truce within twenty-four hours. As the
public was subsequently to learn, the statesmen "were
thunderstruck." Then Hintze pulled himself together,
and said this would lead to revolution and the fall of
the dynasty. What hopes the emperor entertained
during these days can be plainly discovered from the
report of his adjutant, who writes that in this emergency, "The field marshal ought to have placed himself beside the emperor, and, as a responsible statesman, over the head of parliament, have established a
government of national defence."

If Ludendorff had really lost his head, the imperturbable Hindenburg would have taken charge, and might have been able, in conjunction with his king, to struggle to the last, as was to be expected from the family tradition and from Hindenburg's own character. In actual fact, Ludendorff behaved with unusual adroitness, since his only aim was to foist responsibility on to parliament as quickly as possible. He succeeded. Next day he declared that Hindenburg and he had come to their brilliant decision separately, not under stress of emotion, but after mature consideration; and when, in this conversation between the pair, Hindenburg continued to demand the mining district of Longwy and Briey, Ludendorff was unusually curt with him. Today he did not wish to be bothered about mineral resources. Today he wanted to rid himself of the burden he had been shouldering for so long, and to transfer it to the broad back of the German people.

What remarkable strategy! During these days Ludendorff was the unchallenged leader; he ruled, and everyone else obeyed. It was not that, as happens in other States, a capitulating general is dismissed by the king and the government, and a new one appointed in his place. Even in defeat he overthrew the government and set up a new one. The veteran philosopher curtly refused to go on playing his undignified rôle, and the naval officer was simply made to walk the plank. Two substitutes must instantly be found. A special train for the minister of finance and for a major attached to G.H.Q. Tomorrow, they will make a declaration to the Reichstag, early in the morning. As soon as possible—not an hour must be lost. In the eyes of God, four years are as a single day. Any

moment there may be a fresh breach on the front
leading to complete catastrophe.

Terrible was the anxiety aroused in Berlin. No one
in the Imperial Chancellery, no one in the Foreign
Office, had been prepared for such a bludgeoning. In
one of the committee rooms of the Reichstag, the
German nation, represented by eight party leaders
was informed by an apathetic major, who had a fine
old Junker name, that the war was lost, and that
"day by the day the situation was likely to get worse."
The eight men stared at him blankly. "They were,"
records an eyewitness, "absolutely dumfounded. Ebert
turned deadly pale, and could not say a word: Stresemann looked as if he had been poleaxed." Von Heyde-
brand, the Junker leader, who has sometimes been
spoken of as the uncrowned king of Prussia, remarked in the cloak room: "We have been lied to and
cheated!"

Unquestionably the voice of anger was heard from
all sides, but no one refused to accept the bequest.
Any Junker would have had the shrewdness to reject
a proposal that he assume such a responsibility; but
only the Socialist leader Scheidemann saw that it
would be folly to take over a "bankrupt enterprise."
Nevertheless, five days later, he was the first socialist
to become a member of an imperial cabinet. Ebert,
on the other hand, always a patriot, declared at the
end of the war as he had at the beginning, that a man
must not forsake his country in its hour of dire
need. Never did civic sense manifest itself more
forcibly than among the parties of the working class
and of the intelligentsia, which now unconditionally
assumed the heavy burden resulting from a defeat of

the Junker and military caste. It was touching. It was stupid.

Why did no one think of saying to the dictators of the realm: "Get yourselves out of the mess you have made!" Did not people know that during the last three months the hesitations and the criminal silence of the two commanders had led to the loss of 400,000 men killed and wounded—to say nothing of those reported "missing"? Did they not know that the offensive of the year 1918 had cost one and a half million Germans? Did they not know that four times during the course of the war the enemy had offered to make peace on reasonable terms? Did they not know that leading German men of business, in memorials and private correspondence, had advised peace by negotiation; and that the respective heirs to the imperial and the Bavarian thrones had done the same thing? Knowing all this, civilians accepted responsibility for the peace. These party leaders wanted to play the patriot instead of showing themselves to be men of strong character. In a few years they were to realize that they had not even acted patriotically!

On the lookout for a new chancellor, the popular government of newborn Germany hit upon a German prince. He was not a man of outstanding intelligence, but serious-minded and honest, more advanced than any of his royal colleagues, free from many of their prejudices, half Russian by blood, South German (and therefore anti-Prussian) by education, consequently of better type than the Junkers alike through training and through character, and a man who had long been suspect among the die-hards on account of his leanings towards peace. Now, Prince Max of Baden hesitated, nay shuddered, before the ominous task he was expected to undertake.

Hindenburg who on September 29, as on all critical days, had kept in the background, wired on October 1 to the acting vice chancellor: "If by seven or eight o'clock this evening it is certain that Prince Max will form the government, I am prepared to postpone matters until tomorrow morning. If, on the other hand, there is any doubt about Prince Max's forming a government, I regard it as essential to make an offer of peace to the foreign governments this very evening."

How complete and how sudden a change! The mechanical security of modern warfare had been shattered; the dug-in front had been transformed into an old-style battlefield; chance had taken the place of organization; anything was possible; the future was no longer calculable. Whereas the conduct of the war at headquarters had been as tranquil as the management of a big business, now everything was of a sudden disorganized as if by lightning, and the army commanders could hear the thunder of the approaching guns. The haste and perplexity of the dictators was shown by their hourly appeals to Berlin, whence, with a complete change of attitude, they hoped deliverance would come, while they urged cabling to America in search of safety—for all were at their wits' end.

What, in these desperate hours, had become of the field marshal's imperturbability? Why, after four years of war and four months of increasing decadence, had it become so urgently necessary to sue for peace without preliminary negotiations? Had the enemy discovered a new poison gas, a new method of aërial warfare? Had the hostile troops set free on the Macedonian front been transported to France through the atmosphere within a few days? Had not the rate of increase of the American troops been calculated years ahead? Let us see what the military experts have to say.

"The German High Command," reports Major Schwerdtfeger to the Commission of Inquiry, "itself told the Entente that the Central Powers had lost the war. . . . Without transition, the High Command, which, up till then, had continually declared the western front to be impregnable, now informed the alarmed statesmen that the strategic position had become absolutely hopeless. The natural result was an irremediable collapse of public opinion. . . . The High Command was the responsible judge of the situation. It is, therefore, even though the Supreme War Lord endorsed its actions, concretely responsible for the conditions of the peace."

But in these days, no one was bothering about Supreme War Lords! When, on October 2, all persons of influence were combining to force power upon the reluctant Prince Max, one can still recognize Hindenburg's tranquilizing touch, although he could really do nothing to help:

"When," writes Prince Max, "he entered the room with his usual self-confidence, I was confirmed in my hope that he would, in the end, side with me. (Prince Max did not wish too hasty an offer of peace to be made.) His tone was calm, as compared with that of Ludendorff's agitated messages. Essentially, he stood on the same ground. Again and again, from this or that optimistic phrase of Hindenburg's, I tried to draw the political inference, 'Well, then, the new government must be given time.' . . . But always I received the same answer: 'The military situation is so grave that no postponement is possible.' " When the prince drew Hindenburg aside for a private talk, and asked him whether the game was actually lost, the field marshal replied:

"We have resisted their attacks so far. Within a week I anticipate a further attack, and cannot feel sure that this will not lead to a catastrophe." Then he amended the word "catastrophe," saying: "Or, at least, lead to the gravest consequences."

Amid such devastating questions and answers, the hopelessly perplexed new ruler went on vainly trying to save something out of the smash instead of firmly telling, first the commanders, then the emperor and the crown prince to form a government from among their own friends—the Junkers and the captains of heavy industry, the leaders of the Vaterlands-Partei. Such persons, being well acquainted with the history of war, would have insisted that an armistice was never the work of governments, but was always brought about by parleying between the commanders of the opposing forces. The German commanders must hoist the white flag, or must wireless to Marshal Foch a message requesting a "cease fire," and an interview between the lines. What would the two commanders have said if, eight months before, Count Hertling had forbidden them at Brest-Litovsk to make an armistice with the Russians on their own initiative? At that time, a representative of the Foreign Office had had to sit modestly at the board of negotiations to express the army commanders' wishes. The breaking off of hostilities was a military affair. At Brest, each of the three allies had been represented by a staff officer. The Reichstag ought to have made the military commanders take the same line now.

Nothing of the kind happened. In the first days of their power, the representatives of the people were afraid to use it. In Germany, the suggestive influence of a uniform, of decorations, and of titles was too great; it has lasted for another fifteen years, and, to all seeming, will last forever.

The burghers who had been summoned to form a cabinet—not a noble among them—obediently sat down to prepare a note to Wilson—although, before its dispatch, Prince Max had demanded a message from Hindenburg, which he received that day in the following form:

"Berlin, October 3, 1918. The High Command abides by its request of September 29 that a peace offer should immediately be made to the enemy. Owing to the collapse of the Macedonian front, with the consequent weakness of our western reserves and the resulting impossibility of making good the heavy losses incurred during recent battles, as far as human calculations go there seems no possibility of enforcing peace upon the enemy. Our adversaries, on the other hand, are continually bringing fresh reserves into the field. The German army still stands firm, and victoriously repels all onslaughts. But the situation is growing more serious from day to day, and may compel the High Command to make very grave decisions. In these circumstances, it is desirable to cease the struggle, in order to spare the German people and its allies needless sacrifices. Every day's delay will cost the lives of thousands of valiant soldiers. Von Hindenburg."

In this historic document there is no allusion to a frustrated sea fight or to a mutiny in the army as cause of the defeat. As soon as the new chancellor had Hindenburg's declaration in his hands, he wired a request for peace on the basis of Wilson's Fourteen Points.

During the snowstorm of notes which raged during these October weeks, the behavior of the two commanders was vacillating. When there was a trifling improvement in the military situation, or when Wilson's demands were more onerous, they tried to put a spoke in the wheel which (to everyone's horror) they had so impetuously set a-rolling. Out of touch with the people as they were, they never realized how eagerly their starving fellow countrymen were listening to the tones from abroad, and they continued to speak of the "indomitable determination of the Germans to resist to the uttermost." Out of touch with their own soldiers as they were, they knew nothing of the war weariness which prevailed throughout the army, continuing in their telegrams to write of the readiness of the brave German soldiers to sacrifice themselves for their country, although these same soldiers, in view of their commanders' explicit utterances, had long known that they were defeated. A week after sounding his first note of alarm, Ludendorff showed himself inclined to sing another tune, and declared: "I was ailing then, but I am all right again now."

Not a word about the collapse of his morale! To intensify the comedy, the general procured a medical certificate to the effect that his nerves were and always had been in good order.

Previously, as the reader knows, he had declared that he and Hindenburg had, on the same day, independently come to the conclusion that an armistice must immediately be demanded. The question, therefore, arises: Which is the true version? In any case, now that a government existed, the two commanders had found a simple way of evading responsibility. At the cabinet meeting of the 21st, they announced through their representative that their assent to the note addressed to Wilson was not required, since they had no political power, but were merely army commanders. In January, Hindenburg had informed the emperor that he regarded himself as morally responsible for everything which concerned the life of the German people. Ludendorff, once more spoiling for a fight, said he hoped that next spring he would be able to resume the offensive with the aid of six hundred tanks. His euphoria was completely restored.

While the two commanders were thrusting all responsibility upon the shoulders of civilians, they were simultaneously dispatching orders to these. Consider, for instance, Hindenburg's long "Instructions to the Armistice Commission," which opened as follows:

"The military situation is of such a kind that our forces no longer suffice to hold the front securely. For a long time the new levies have not been adequate to replace our losses. . . . It is in view of this state of affairs that the offer of peace has been made. Nevertheless we must be ready to resume the struggle at any time if the attempt should be made to impose conditions destructive to our future. . . .

Should it appear that our enemies' demands necessitate a resumption of the struggle, we shall certainly fight on the German frontier under extremely disadvantageous conditions. . . . A speedy cessation of the struggle is urgently desirable in the interests of the Germany army. . . . The first essential is, therefore, an agreement to cease fighting, an armistice."

This "Instruction," which the defeated commander sends to the civilians who are acting in his stead, which a Junker hands to burghers, insists, again and again, upon the urgency of the situation. In the decisive hour, we shall see Hindenburg demanding unconditional surrender. The new bourgeois war cabinet was so strongly influenced by the suggestions of the four last years and by those of the two last centuries of military dominion, that, under pressure from the commanders, who had sent representatives to the sittings, they rejected the first full-dress speech of the new chancellor, weakening down Prince Max's political discussions with Wilson into a political chamade. Then Hindenburg suddenly altered his course, for, whereas on the 10th, during the interchange of notes with Wilson, he had agreed to the complete evacuation of occupied territory, on the 24th he ordered the troops to continue a stubborn resistance, and himself bowed before the emperor's veto.

While the two commanders expressly rejected the idea of a *levée en masse*, because they dreaded nothing so much as the "armed nation," having been accustomed all their lives and throughout the war to a highly drilled army, at this juncture two civilians demanded the arming of the nation and a mass levy.

These two distinguished Jews were the only Germans who, during the last days, continued to talk of national defense. In phrases which have become classical, Rathenau publicly declared the commanders' offers premature, advised a mass levy, and the establishment of a Board of Defense, concluding with the words, "We do not want war but peace—though not a peace of subjugation."

"This," writes Prince Max in his memoirs, "was the cry of a patriot. It moved me profoundly. . . . Not until later did I learn from friends that on October 2 Rathenau had wept like a child, and had cudgeled his inventive brain in the hope of finding some means of preventing the peace offer. If only in those days he had come to see me! . . . Rathenau's article aroused general excitement. People pricked up their ears to listen to his words of open distrust of Ludendorff and Wilson. In the cabinet, we discussed the question of a *levée en masse*."

The other Israelite was Max Warburg who, as a banker, was well informed about American matters. On October 3, summoned in council by the prince, Warburg said: "Let the soldiers do their own white-flag business. If we humiliate ourselves now, it is not the better type of Americans that will get control of the situation but the others. Wilson would not be able to resist the pressure of the party politicians. Watch out! What he is looking for is the establishment of a German republic!" In conclusion, we learn from Prince Max's memoirs, Warburg said: "I am surprised to find myself, a civilian, compelled to insist that the soldiers should go on fighting! My own son, who is now under training, will have to go into the trenches four weeks from now. Nevertheless, I implore you not to give way at present!"

Among the bourgeois ministers of State, only one was found to give its true name to the game the generals were playing. When, in a telegram to the chancellor, Hindenburg begged him to keep up a defiant tone in speeches and in the press, for otherwise the discouragement among the populace would ruin everything, Solf, the new minister for foreign affairs, described this maneuver as "an extremely dangerous attempt to shuffle off responsibility. Why," asks Solf, "is the general mood so depressed? Because the military power has collapsed—not conversely. Such an attitude is intolerable, especially when Ludendorff has rejected the idea of a *levée en masse*." This is the only recorded utterance of those days in which a bourgeois gave a clear description of the historical situation. The first socialist minister of State did not do so much. Ludendorff showed his contempt for those upon whom he had forced the leadership in a phrase, or perhaps one should rather say a mood. "Make the beggars get a move on!" he snapped out in the war cabinet. "Pitch a high note! Cannot Herr Ebert manage that?"

For the first time in Prussia a general officially mentions a workman, a saddler, as one of his colleagues. Ebert was the chief of the detested Social Democratic Party, with whom, in July, 1917, Ludendorff had been forced to shake hands. Today when he had need of such fellows, being a tactician, he wondered what sort of influence a man like Ebert could exert upon the workers. "Ginger it up!" Hindenburg had said in 1917. Now the common folk, who had been trampled upon, were to "get a move on!" Could not Herr Ebert manage that?

Ebert, no doubt, at that moment, was working upon one of the committees of the Reichstag. Would the Reichstag now seize power? What did the Reichstag do at this ultra-critical moment in German affairs? It prorogued itself on October 26, and did not reassemble before the revolution!

To be sure, that day, it had made an end of Bismarck's constitution, had subordinated the chancellor to the Reichstag, and had thus completed the bourgeois revolution, after having reduced the emperor to the level of a hereditary president with a handsome title. Two million Germans had fallen—and yet some people speak of this as a bloodless revolution!

A few days before, Ludendorff's scalp had been taken. The purifying element in the tragedy was the fall of the dictator, not the emperor's abdication. People had demanded the retirement of Ludendorff, and Prince Max had easily induced the emperor to accede. No one voiced the same demand as regards Hindenburg. The partition of popular favor of which Ludendorff had spoken at the outset of their collaboration, became conspicuous in these closing phases. The difference of the public attitude towards Hindenburg and Ludendorff respectively has already been explained as dependent upon the character of each and upon the Hindenburg legend. The emperor, too, though he detested both of them, distinguished between them in accordance with the legend. After Hindenburg's army order which meant a rejection of Wilson's reply at the very time when the cabinet was still negotiating, the emperor was in a fury. With

Hindenburg, who had signed the aforesaid order? No, with Ludendorff, who was recognized to have been the real author.

When William now summoned both the commanders to Schloss Bellevue, Ludendorff referred on the journey to the probability of his dismissal. Hindenburg rejoined that in that case he would himself resign. To the emperor, Ludendorff began by abusing the new government on the ground that it was not backing up the High Command. The emperor declared that the General Staff had made a mess of things. Ludendorff begged permission to resign. William replied: "I thank you for expressing that wish, as it makes things easier for me. I shall try to rebuild my empire with the aid of the social democrats." Next, William suggested various military measures, which Ludendorff rejected as impracticable. Then Ludendorff took his leave. When Hindenburg also expressed a wish to resign, saying he did not care to separate from his collaborator, the emperor replied:

"You are the palladium of the German people. You must not desert it in its utmost need." "My appeal was successful," related the emperor subsequently. "The field marshal agreed, after a severe struggle with his feelings."

Concerning Hindenburg's alleged struggle with his feelings, we have no other evidence, but we know Ludendorff's impression. "My husband considered," writes Ludendorff's wife, "that he had been left in the lurch by Hindenburg, with whom he had shared the joys and the sorrows of all these years, and who now allowed him to resign, while himself remaining in the emperor's service."

18

From William's lips, during these days, also, for the first time came the name of the saddler. Although before this he had openly proclaimed, "For me every social democrat is an enemy of the empire and of the fatherland," he now declared, "I should be glad to work with Herr Ebert." To this ruler who was on the verge of a crash, Herr Ebert, though still in the background, had suddenly become a person of supreme interest! Two days later William pompously exclaimed, "The emperor's office is to serve his people," and next morning fled from his people to his new capital, the Belgian headquarters. This flight decided his fate. No one would have injured a hair of his head if he had stayed in Berlin to abdicate there in favor of his grandson, who would have ridden on a fine white horse through the Brandenburg Gate. At the end of October, no one expected anything more. But William ran away. William II lost his throne as he had lost the battle of the Marne, by being too far away from the scene of the struggle.

As concerns Ludendorff, one cannot but ask why he did not, like other dictators when fallen from power, blow out his brains or at least die fighting. With him begins the series of the numerous potentates and princes who had no taste for a hero's death. Soon afterwards, disguised with a pair of smoked spectacles, and provided with a false passport made out under the name of Lindström, he escaped to Sweden, where he wrote his interesting book on the war. Later he returned to Germany, founded a pagan sect, and devoted the best of his energies to attacking Hindenburg and the Jews. When, in November, 1923, he joined forces with Adolf Hitler in organizing an insurrection which proved unsuccessful owing to the cowardice of their Junker comrades, he described it as the greatest disappointment of his life "that our leading circles have shown themselves incapable of reviving in the German people the will to freedom." His chief regret in life, he said subsequently, was that he had not deposed the emperor during the days when he was dictator. His own words give him away, "I am still too much of a cadet to want to play Cromwell's part."

Among all the Germans, during the war he was the most interesting figure and the most dangerous. Certainly he always remained the cadet, but soon ceased to be the king's servant, obviously because he was not a Junker. The splendid energy with which for two years he ruled the realm would have been invaluable under a more distinguished chief. To learn how stupendous were his exertions, one must study the volumes of his documents. It was not his fault that he was conquered, for, by the time he rose to power in the third year of the war, Germany's position had become hopeless, victory impossible. But his high ambitions blinded him to the impossibility and made him persistently unwilling to conclude a peace of negotiation. Being ambitious rather than thirsty for fame, he was plainly more desirous of shining over his envious comrades than of shining in the pages of history, so that thoughts of General von Seeckt or of General von Falkenhayn were more of a spur to him than thoughts of Foch or Haig or even of Clio. If he had had a Bismarck as political chief and a dozen Hindenburgs as assistants in the field, in the end, like William I at Nikolsburg, gnashing his teeth, he would have had to accept a peace of renunciation. Such a peace would not have given the Germans a new form of State; but would, perhaps, have introduced into the old State a certain measure of freedom which would not so speedily have been metamorphosed into its opposite as in the Republic, for which the Germans were not yet ripe.

XVIII

The convulsions which, during the next few days, led to the inauguration of the Republic, and which it is not my present purpose to describe, were not the stormy eruptions of long-repressed forces; nor is it true to say that they were the outcome of hunger. Revolutions are far more often made by well-fed men than by hungry ones. Just as the democratic régime was not achieved by the Germans, but was accepted from the hands of those who wished to fling away power, so the established authorities—the princes, the Junkers, and the generals—were not overthrown, but simply ran away. There was so little active will among the German people, that five hundred stout-hearted officers would have sufficed to maintain a constitutional monarchy after the British model such as the emperor had declared his willingness to accept. Documents are extant to show that the socialists wanted to maintain the empire. It was only because the old authorities absconded—partly from panic, partly because they were too shrewd to remain and make themselves responsible for the acceptance of such a peace as they foresaw—that new energies had to fill the vacuum. Since, however, the requisite new energies had not been preparing themselves before

Conversing with the Crown Prince at the thirtieth jubilee celebration of the
reign of Kaiser William II, 1918

and during the war, for the most part they proved
ineffective, and soon let the old ones slip back into
their places. The truth of these assertions will be
plain to anyone who studies the details of what happened between November 1 and November 9; and
there is no other way of accounting for the brevity of
the life of the German Republic.

Among all those in leading positions, Hindenburg
alone marched on with the new crowd without missing
a step. The technique of his transition from one
form of State to the other may be compared to that
of the transition from one musical phrase to another
such as we find, for instance, in Beethoven's Fifth
Symphony. We can plainly recognize the moment
when the imperial motifs pass into the minor key and
speedily become inaudible, giving place to the theme
of a new march.

When, in his second note, Wilson hinted at the de-
sirability of the emperor's abdication, Hindenburg was
in a great rage. "Never," writes an eyewitness,
"have I seen the usually equable man so immensely
excited. His Prusso-German officer's honor revolted
at even having to listen to the American's suggestion,
and, with a spontaneous outburst of enthusiasm he
shouted, 'Long live our emperor and king!'"

The incident thus reported by a certain Captain von
Wallenberg, who unfortunately does not mention where
it occurred, is unique in Hindenburg's life. A few
days later, he made an official protest against any
limitation of the imperial rights: "How could our
officers' corps, which is loyal through and through,
endure that its All-Highest War Lord should thus,
seemingly of set purpose, be deprived of his supreme

authority? The corps would thereby lose its very soul."

For two years, while the king was still there, Hindenburg had held the monarch in his grip, gently at first, but more and more firmly as time went on. The field marshal did not need His Majesty's orders, but merely to look up towards His Majesty as a symbol. What he obeyed was not this particular king, but the fluttering of the royal banner. Enough that William should be seated on the throne like an image in mosaic. The less this image had to say the better. But now, when the enemies of Germany wanted to take the symbol away, the king's old and faithful servant was enraged. The object of his worship was being removed from the altar.

Then came the marvel. Immediately after that "Long live the king!" which came as heartily from the septuagenarian field marshal as it would have come from the cadet of seventeen, Hindenburg, who was still holding the reins of power, as is shown by his continuing to issue army orders, approved without further parley the sending of an answer in which the German government uttered no word of complaint about Wilson's suggestion that William should abdicate. Immediately after his spirited protest against the removal of the "soul of the officers' corps," namely the commanding authority of the monarch, Hindenburg accepted the proposed change in the constitution. This extraordinarily rapid veering from "no" to "yes" was accordant with the man's fundamental trait, was the expression of that imperturbability which sustained him, not only in hours of danger and crisis, but also in fateful times of emotional stress. While nothing would have induced him to move a finger to impair his monarch's formal prerogatives, neither did he stir a finger when others were destroying these same prerogatives—and in both cases he called his inaction "service." Examinations, years of hard work, the summons of his king, and then the legend; had raised him to his high position; and there he would remain, tranquil whatever happened.

The main point was that the king gave him his orders. If the king had told him to fight, Hindenburg would have promptly drawn his sword. Beyond doubt, he would have done this in the literal sense of the words if a gang of revolutionary soldiers had forced its way into the villa at headquarters in order to arrest the emperor. But if his monarch had decided upon abdication, well, such were His Majesty's orders, and an officer had no right to appeal from His Majesty's personal character to His Majesty as a symbol of majesty. Thus Hindenburg's attitude towards the king during these November days was perfectly accordant with his own and William's respective natures, with his own and the emperor's idea of monarchy.

On November 1, he had still vigorously protested when Drews spoke of abdication; but at the same time he immediately recognized that Groener's private proposal to send William to the front was impracticable. When, on the 5th, Hindenburg dispatched Groener to Berlin, it was with instructions to protect the king whatever happened. On the 6th, Ebert proposed one of the emperor's sons as successor, but Groener rejected the proposal, saying that Hindenburg wished to maintain William at all hazards. That day the dynasty could still have been saved, and the man who more than any others desired to save it inspired the action which made its downfall inevitable.

What now happened as the outcome of Groener's negotiations with Ebert has not hitherto been made public; but the information has leaked through from what Groener told his friends. On November 8, at Spa, in a conversation between Hindenburg and Groener, the pair of them decided that, whatever happened, the emperor must not leave the country, but must, as Ebert's Cabinet wished, abdicate in favor of one of his grandsons. Thus on the morning of November 8, 1918, the determination to save the dynasty still prevailed; but at a later hour of the same day Hindenburg had changed his mind, and had come to share Herr von Hintze's view that the cause of the House of Hohenzollern was hopelessly lost. On the morning of the 9th, he informed Groener of this new decision, and, without further parley, asked the astonished Groener to come with him to William and persuade the monarch to abdicate and depart. Like so many other weighty decisions made by Hindenburg during the war, this one was come to on his own initiative, and yet he wished another to bear the brunt.

Presumably, in making so sharp a curve, Hindenburg was animated by the sentiments of a medieval vassal, who would rather see his sovereign flee the country while clinging to a chance of return, than hand over the throne to another even of the blood-royal. We shall see that in advanced old age Hindenburg was to avow some such feeling to Chancellor Brüning. Anyhow, it was reasonable enough that he should let William drop for he knew that the emperor was afraid; besides, the field marshal's recognition of the consistency with which William, during these weeks, and now from hour to hour, was allowing himself to be hunted out of position after position must have prevented Hindenburg from trying to hearten his master to resistance. But his sense of honor as an officer made it impossible for Hindenburg to utter the words which would send His Majesty across the frontier.

The field marshal's decision of November 9, in the morning, has become historical: "The High Command has resolved to acquaint His Majesty forthwith that, should civil war break out, the armed forces of the realm could not be depended upon to support His Majesty, and that commissariat difficulties would make it impossible for the army to wage a civil war."

Other generals, at this juncture, believed Hindenburg's views in this matter to be unsound. Such decisions belong to the realm of feeling rather than to that of precise observation, for a dozen instances taken at random cannot disclose the true mood of an army of millions, and Prussian methods are most unsuitable for the solution of psychological problems. As Hindenburg was never a man of yielding disposition, and detested breaches of discipline, he would certainly have been on the side of those who were spoiling for a fight had he not been well acquainted with William's weakness. He therefore took the right course when, a few hours later, he begged the emperor to accept his resignation, justifying himself with the observation:

"I find it incredibly painful to advise my War Lord against the thought of reconquering his homeland. My heart joyfully acclaims the idea, but I regard its execution as impossible."

He said no more, and only half believed what he actually had said. He knew well enough that his king did not want to fight. When General von der Schulenburg declared a march on Berlin to be possible without provoking civil war, and when the veteran General von Plessen supported Schulenburg, William was glad that Hindenburg's advice stood in the way.

Hindenburg now burst into tears, and ordered his subordinate, General Groener, to make the vital communication—to say what he himself was unable to utter. Half a dozen Junkers stood mute around their king, and could not bring themselves to urge his abdication and departure. It was left to a man of lower-middle-class origin, Groener the son of a paymaster, to do the needful. He was good enough for the task; just as, five weeks earlier, the new petty-bourgeois Cabinet had seemed good enough to the Junkers to undertake the liquidation of a war which Junkers had begun, conducted, and lost. Groener carefully skirted the thorny dynastic problem, being content to depict the military situation, and to emphasize the difficulties of a return march—so long as William remained as head. He went on to say, drastically: "The army will march home resolutely and in good order under its leaders, but not under Your Majesty's leadership."

Now it had been spoken, the terrible word of which the emperor must certainly have dreamed more than once. Now he was so much overcome that, after one or two attempts to speak, he went out into the park.

For a few hours, and obviously for form's sake only, the discussion continued. The emperor's silence after General Groener's mutinous utterance, and the lack of any passionate repudiation of Groener on the part of the other generals, were sufficient signs that all was lost.

Now the course of events became dramatic. There were more and more urgent appeals from the chancellor in Berlin—"Immediate abdication, or the monarchy will inevitably fall!" The emperor's answers ran: "Treason! Shameless, disgraceful treason!" or "Your Excellency, I must have this declaration from you in writing!" or "Has not the army sworn an oath of loyalty to the king?" In the interludes, His Majesty spent the time in a hall overlooking the garden, in front of a wood fire that glowed on the hearth. Sometimes he went for a stroll in the park; and, of course, he lunched. Hindenburg passed into the background once more. How rightly he had judged the emperor was shown by William's dread of going to the front, a step urged on him by Groener as late as the 9th, for the rescue of the monarchical principle—Groener being the only man who spoke frankly to His Majesty. Beyond question, if the king had decided on such a step, our doughty old Hindenburg would have mounted his horse and have ridden beside His Majesty into battle like those martial ancestors of whom he had been told as a boy at Neudeck. This romantic way of making war with a cavalry attack, for which Hindenburg had longed during four painful years, would have come as a joy to him in the end—seeking a hero's death in the old knightly fashion.

The one who would not accept so glorious a way out of the difficulty was Emperor William; and while there was still talk of a chivalrous struggle to the bitter end, His Majesty was having telephone messages sent to Holland, to prepare for flight in the morning.

Hindenburg, who was stubbornly silent, did not, as has been currently reported, beg the emperor to leave at once; that request was left for Plessen and Hintze.

"The emperor nodded assent," we read in the court report. But, when dinner was already being laid in the royal train, William, stagey as ever, exclaimed: "No, and yet again no! I will not do it! I will not play the poltroon like a captain who deserts his sinking ship!"

Thereupon a court dinner, with six or eight covers. A fresh delegate arrived, and urgently recommended His Majesty to cross the Dutch frontier. Then the emperor made up his mind, in the historic words:

"Well and good, if it must be so. But not before tomorrow morning, early!"

When Hindenburg awoke next morning, the imperial train had been for some time already on the Dutch frontier, which was only half an hour's journey distant. For form's sake, the field marshal showed surprise, but in fact he had expected nothing else. Not that he had advised William to run away, but had merely tendered his resignation. Instead, the departing emperor had reinstated him in the supreme command.

For the first time in four years, the field marshal was alone. His comrade had gone and his king had gone, both of them having run away during the last days of the great war. The motifs of kingship are growing fainter and fainter. Strange, new fanfares are sounding louder and louder. The war is finished. Today, in the enemy's camp, the armistice will be concluded. Tomorrow the army must start for home.

The white flag is waving. The royal flag has been lowered. A new flag is being hoisted. Service goes on.

BOOK THREE

THE SECOND FLAG

No matter how intelligent the legislative
authority may be, that will not help the
State unless the executive be strong.

—GOETHE

THE SECOND FLAG

I

A FEW YEARS after the crash, a prince of Prussia was selling his household goods by auction, and one of the lots offered for sale was Frederick the Great's flute. A number of Potsdam officers, determined to save this relic for the House of Hohenzollern, came to the auction, and one of them said to the prince: "We cannot endure that this treasure should fall into profane hands. We shall stand shoulder to shoulder to protect the great king's flute."

The prince looked at them coldly, and rejoined: "If, on November 9, you had stood shoulder to shoulder in front of your king, there would have been no need to sell the flute!"

The flute found its way into bourgeois hands, as the Republic had done. Upon the bronze tables of history there is inscribed no name of a Junker who, inspired by the traditions of three hundred years, died for his king, for the old flag, or because he was true to the military oath. The two naval officers Zenker and Weniger who, during the mutiny of the Kiel bluejackets, resisted the hoisting of the red flag and were shot down while defending the war banner of the "König," were of middle-class origin. These two, and an elderly general who, sorrow stricken, shot himself at Goslar in front of the Bismarck monument, were the only three heroes to realize in their deeds the oft-repeated phrases about Prussian loyalty—when loyalty to the Prussian monarch had become

disadvantageous and dangerous. One other *beau geste*
was that made by a young officer in the courtyard of
the public headquarters in Berlin, who publicly broke
his sword when the command "Don't shoot" was
issued.   No doubt this was a reminiscence of something he had seen at the Theater Royal in a perform-
ance of one of Wildenbruch's plays.   We hear nothing
more of this young man.   Another German who shot
himself from distress on account of what had happened
to his country was the Jew, Ballin.   This suicide took
place on November 9.

Otherwise, among the tens of thousands, no one lifted
a finger.   Where were all those who, a few months
later, began to agitate against the "November criminals"; the powerful army commanders, the admirals,
the field marshals, the tribunes of the people?   They
said that their king's flight had paralyzed them.   But
if the monarchical ideal was thus restricted to a single
personality, if the institution itself was not eternal, it
had been idle to claim that it existed by God's grace.
Was the sanctity of Peter's Chair forever lost because
Pope Alexander Borgia was an adventurer?

The German revolution had introduced something
new and strange into history.   The officers and the
Junkers, the king's vassals and paladins, broke troth
as soon as he left; those who remained true to him
were burghers and common folk.   With embarrassment, these good people went to those members of the
royal houses who had not fled in the first panic, and
begged them to consult their own safety by departing.
When, at Potsdam Palace, the crown princess heard
soldiers arriving, and, surrounded by her children,
recalled the fate of the tsarina, the deputy who was in

command of the troops entered the room, stood at attention, and said, in his best imitation of a military manner:

"Your Majesty is under our protection. Everything is safeguarded. We await Your Majesty's orders."

Not one of the twenty-two German kings and princes, not one of their sons, nephews, or cousins (there were about one hundred twenty of them in all), had anything taken from him by a German soldier or workman; not a finger was laid upon any of the thousands of the hangers-on at their courts; and a few weeks later a visitor to various petty capitals would be proudly assured by the citizens that their particular duke had been the last who had had to abdicate.

Only the Prince of Waldeck saved the honor of his caste by refusing to abdicate, on the ground that he was also "sovereign of Pyrmont" and therefore could be excused. His subjects nicknamed him "the stubborn"; but in the end he, too, had to go. He reminds one of the oboist in Haydn's humorous orchestral composition, during which one musician after another lays down his instrument and quietly leaves the hall, until at length, with a concluding cadence, the oboist, too, disappears.

The Hohenzollerns, likewise, were cordially requested by the people to remain. On November 6, Ebert, the leader of the workers' faction, had fruitlessly proposed to General Groener that one of the emperor's sons or grandsons should succeed William. On November 8, Scheidemann, the socialist minister of State, spoke apologetically to the Cabinet as follows: "We have
19

done our utmost to tranquilize the masses. If they have been stirred up about the question of the emperor, this has mainly been the work of middle-class press organs. It has been made extremely difficult for us to get in touch with the chancellor. But if the abdication of Emperor William does not now take place, followed by the succession of one of his sons, the question of the Republic will become acute." When, on November 9, the leaders of the social democrats appeared in the last bourgeois Cabinet, and Ebert, as their chief, demanded that the reins of power, which were already his *de facto*, should become his *de jure*, Herr von Payer asked: "Is that documentary?" This monumental inquiry from a democrat on the morning that seemed likely to mark the end of a régime which had lasted for centuries was characteristic of the orderliness of the Germans—an orderliness which stands in the way of their making a revolution. The same day Ebert vainly requested Prince Max, heir to the grandduchy of Baden, to stay on as vice regent of the empire —just as, in 1848, the bourgeois revolutionists had appointed one of the archdukes to the same office. The Germans found it impossible to conceive that a free State could get along without princely protection. Ebert would not take over power from the hands of Prince Max until he had consulted with his friends, and accepted it in the end only with the proviso that his appointment as chancellor of the realm must be made "within the limits of the constitution."

This was the most extraordinary revolution ever known—one in which the old-established potentates begged reputed traitors to relieve them of the burden of power! Wels, president of the Social Democratic

Party, on the morning of November 9, implored the workers not to quit their jobs; and, in the end, Scheidemann proclaimed the bourgeois republic from the Reichstag only because, ten minutes earlier, Liebknecht, who was quicker to move, had proclaimed a Red republic from the palace. It was a competition between the verandas which, at that noon hour, decided the fate of Germany; and, "flushed with wrath," Ebert berated Scheidemann after his proclamation, saying, "You ought not to have done that! It is the business of the National Assembly to decide upon the form of the State!"

But what about the mutineers? What about the bluejackets? When, during the last days of October, they refused to obey orders, this was only for the reason that, after spending three years in harbor, they were unexpectedly ordered to put out to sea and attack the enemy—because and although Hindenburg had called the war off. What they demanded on November 5 was nothing more than this: the liberation of their imprisoned comrades, no black marks against them in the records, uniformity of rations for officers and men, no need to salute when not on active service, and, finally, a change in the mode of addressing their officers. They were to be compelled to use the third person only at the outset: "Herr Kapitän has ordered"; after that, they were to be allowed to address him with a plain "you." Such were the demands of 80,000 bluejackets, who had 3000 officers on board with them and all the weapons in their power!

So careful were the Workers' and Soldiers' Councils to keep order, that Hindenburg himself gave them his support—whereupon in Dresden and elsewhere they

accepted officers as members.   At Königsberg, the
officers showed their gratitude by giving the men four-
and-forty geese from their goose farms.   In the great
cities, where there had been most fear that the "lower
classes" would get out of hand, it was made especially
plain, even in this chaotic hour when liberty was still
to be fought for, that Germans value order more than
liberty.   When the socialists found at Hamburg, on
the morning of November 9, that the trade-union
headquarters had been occupied by their left-wing
brethren, the independents, they procured an injunc-
tion from a bourgeois magistrate, and showed this
document to the independents, whereupon the latter
withdrew.   While Ebert's troops were besieging the
bluejackets in the royal stud house in Berlin, a truce
was declared at noon.   Everyone said: "Today is
Christmas.   We'll go home to our mothers, and begin
fighting again when the holidays are over!"   Liebknecht's forces, too, could have occupied the completely undefended buildings in the Wilhelmstrasse
had not Christmas stood in the way.

A few hundred underfed bluejackets who occupied
the palace in Berlin for weeks had at their absolute
disposal the imperial cellars and storerooms, where,
as if on exhibition, were all the articles of diet which
the German common folk had never had a sniff of for
four years.   Would you not expect them to have
seized the chance of having a good blow-out?   Instead, they appointed a committee to see that there
should be no looting, posted sentries armed with stink
bombs at the doors of these underground rooms,
gravely took possession of the books kept by the
court-commissariat officers, and made careful entries

of the rations distributed among the comrades. When they installed machine guns later at the windows of the first-floor rooms, they laid down newspapers so that the polished floors should not be scratched. After their stronghold had been shelled by the other side, they made neat piles of plaster and fragments of iron and glass beneath the shattered walls.

In like manner, after the shelling of all Germany, the citizens were ranged in three heaps or groups: the old power, the new power, and the Reds. The question in this revolution was not which party had more courage, but which was the most frightened. Since the barricades were not made of paving stones and overturned casks but of outlooks; since the weapons were not artillery and rifles but votes and speeches, there was completely lacking that impetus which had hitherto decided revolutions. The requisite élan was only present when the guns went off—to shoot the Reds; and in that case, since the many were against the few, it contributed greatly to the fall of the Republic.

Here, likewise, first steps were decisive. The fate of Germany, and therewith Hindenburg's subsequent career, depended upon what happened during these opening weeks of the Republic. So long as an adversary has still reason to dread that force will be used against him, he respects the new power. But if, listening carefully in his hiding place, he hears no sound to indicate that guns are being marshaled to destroy him, he comes forth with a smile, gets together with his comrades, and says: "Where there is nothing to fear, there is still something to win!"

II

Hindenburg—who now reigned alone, for General Groener, nominally associated with him, had none of Ludendorff's magic art—Hindenburg, while still acting as imperial field marshal, had dictated the conditions of the armistice at Spa to the civilians who were to arrange matters with the Allies in his stead. It was as imperial minister that Erzberger with his three companions met Marshal Foch at Compiègne on November 8; and an imperial government received and published the enemy's conditions, which, on the morning of the 9th, were read by all Germany. During these days the vision of the multitude was still obscured by the censorship, by prohibitions, by the state of siege, and by the notes of an unknown princeling.

Foch demanded as basis of the armistice the immediate evacuation of all occupied territory, the surrender of weapons and railway trucks, the handing over of the German fleet. In addition he required, in defiance of the first understanding, the occupation of the Rhineland, and a one-sided liberation of prisoners of war. This obviously unjust condition was contested by Erzberger, relying on Hindenburg. During October the latter had again and again declared in writing that there could be no question of any peace but a reasonable one on the basis of Wilson's Fourteen Points, and that otherwise Germany would go on fighting to the last.

Here, as in the question of the emperor, a sudden and unexpected change took place in Hindenburg's mood. On November 10, he wired from Spa to Erzberger, "In the conditions, do your best to secure mitigation of the following points." The points in question were: the grant of more time; no neutral zone in the Rhineland; fewer railway trucks; blockade; prisoners. Then Hindenburg went on, "If you can't get your way upon these matters, you must nevertheless agree to the enemy terms."

Nevertheless! Erzberger read this word with horror. He was compelled to agree to peace on any terms. This man who sixteen months earlier had been the first to give expression to the half-formed will to peace of the representatives of the people; the first civilian who had dared to declare the figures published by the Navy Department to be false and the army commanders' submarine policy to be mistaken—was now sitting, as sole German plenipotentiary. With three of his compatriots as witnesses, he now was forced to confront the hard faces of the conquerors, and was under orders from Hindenburg to agree to any and every demand. He sat as the civilian Trotsky had sat at Brest-Litovsk confronted by the hard visage of General Hoffmann. But there had been no Russian commander behind Trotsky to wire orders to the negotiator. Trotsky had fought the tsar all his life long, had fought against the war for three years—and had to play the tragic part of every new leader who takes over the reins of power when power has collapsed. But Erzberger was a civilian who three days before had been the emperor's minister, who had left the emperor in order, himself, to travel into the enemy camp, and who was, even now, acting under orders from the emperor's commander in chief.

Why did he not, like Trotsky before him and Count Rantzau after him, rise to his feet, break off the negotiations, give back his commission to the government

and to the army commander, and compel the latter to
sign the armistice himself? To be sure, some other
negotiator had to accept the inexorable terms in both
the before-mentioned instances—a Russian in one case,
and a German in the other. But the humiliation for
which neither Trotsky nor Rantzau had been responsible was left by them for other men to assume. The
legend of Tannenberg was what made Erzberger
accept Hindenburg's "nevertheless" as a command;
and his acceptance cost him his life.

Four days later, in Cassel, Hindenburg had one of
the strangest experiences of his long career. Uncertain
what awaited him, but quite prepared to be taken
prisoner by any troop of soldiers, he had, with the bold-
ness that his king and his fellow officers lacked, returned
to the center of Germany. When the train drew up
at the platform in Cassel where he intended to establish
his headquarters, he was uncertain as to how he would
be received. Would he not find the common soldiers
given up to drunkenness and lechery as had happened
in other revolutions? Would they not revile him?
The old man would have died rather than surrender
his shoulder straps! But what happened? Let his
companion, Captain von Wallenberg, tell the story:

"The order that prevailed, the cordial and respectful
reception, delighted the field marshal. The members
of the Workers' and Soldiers' Council, wearing, not
red arm bands, but black ones, reported for duty; and
he had the feeling that these men, who formed a double
row for him to pass through, wished to assure their
serious-minded and faithful leader of their devotion. . . .
In the afternoon there came a number of delegations
to pay honor to the field marshal. Numerous children

surrounded him and sang. The field marshal was greatly moved by the love these children showed for him. Tears rose to his eyes, and he said, with a break in his voice: 'Yes, the times are terribly difficult. But we will continue to put our trust in God, and then things will get better.'"

"Hindenburg belongs to the German nation and the German army," began the proclamation of the Cassel Workers' and Soldiers' Council. "Never has he stood nearer to us in the greatness of his fulfilment of duty than he does today. His person is under our protection. The field marshal bears arms, and in like manner the officers and privates at headquarters will retain them."

By this time, however, the gentlemen were hungry and wanted their dinner. Captain von Wallenberg writes: "We were properly served in the hotel. All the same, the food was extremely bad. The field marshal sat among employees and officers, consuming out of a mug some soup which left the stomach and the palate asking what it had been made of. Perhaps its badness may have been intentional, so that the commander in chief could have no doubt as to the general shortage of decent food."

Our worthy captain is obviously astonished by this soup. Being attached to headquarters, he has hitherto known about the general shortage of food only from what he has read in the newspapers. Now his stomach and palate are perplexed as to the constituents of a soup to whose taste almost all other Germans have grown used during the last two years. They know well enough what it is made of, having to stand in a queue for a couple of hours every day in order to get the needed, but very dubious, green vegetables and root crops. It is plain from his account that the gentlemen of the G.H.Q., who know so much more about war than any other Germans, are the only ones in this room at Cassel who have never consumed war soup out of a mug before November 15, 1918. While they had continued to declare that the mining basin of Briey, and the grain lands extending as far as Lake Peipus, were indispensable to the feeding of the German nation, ordinary folk had nearly perished of hunger. Had these leaders been willing to renounce conquests two years before, commoners might once more have been enjoying eggs, beef, and a glass or two of good beer, without any sense that their "honor" was thereby imperiled.

Since Hindenburg's aide-de-camp has lived afar from these realities throughout the four years of the war, he now returns to his country like a man who has been on a voyage to the North Pole. He is surprised what remarkable table manners his fellow citizens have adopted during his absence; and, although he is pleased to find them so friendly, he cannot but suspect that the cook (doubtless a Red and a Spartacist!) must have deliberately made the soup worse than usual to teach the field marshal a lesson. Had these lordly ones, in their villas or in the officers' mess, but lived for a month or even for no more than a week as common folk in their homeland were living, maybe the foul, strawy taste of the damp black bread would have given them less inclination for the retention of the coast of Flanders. Such an experience would have allowed the idea to enter their minds that it was a mistake to penalize the Germans in the attempt to make them the masters of Europe, and that it would be better to let them nourish themselves like other mortals.

Hindenburg did his best. Whereas the admiral in chief and other officers of the highest rank wired to the republican government explaining that they would not serve under it, the field marshal was persuaded by General Groener to support the new order. Hindenburg's appeal to the troops to maintain discipline made a strong impression on Ebert. The appeal concluded with the moving words: "In battle you have never left your field marshal in the lurch. I therefore have undiminished confidence in you!" When, notwithstanding this, on November 20 the radicals demanded Hindenburg's dismissal, Ebert explained that the field marshal had "given his word of honor to support the new government. The difficulties of demobilization rendered it indispensable to avoid needless disturbances in the army." Since, however, Ebert had nothing tangible to show, having merely received Groener's propitiatory assurance by telephone, the new chief of the State naturally wanted a message in writing. Hitherto, during these chaotic weeks, when no one trusted another farther than he could see, Ebert had nevertheless confided in Hindenburg, and Hindenburg had not disappointed him. Not until December, however, did the field marshal make up his mind to write as follows to Ebert:

"If I address the following lines to you, I do so because I am credibly informed that you, like myself as a true German, love your fatherland before everything, putting aside personal opinions and wishes, as I have had to do in order to help my country in its hour of need. In this spirit I have joined forces with you to rescue our people from the threatening collapse. The fate of the German people has been laid in your hands. Upon your determination it will depend whether the German people acquire a new impetus. I am ready, and behind me stands the whole army, to support you unreservedly. We all know that after this lamentable upshot of the war, the reconstruction of the realm can only be effected upon new foundations and in new forms."

Still, though no one has asked his advice upon political matters, he cannot refrain from putting in his oar: "In my view, only the following measures can get us out of our present difficulties: the National Assembly must be summoned again in December; the Workers' Councils must be done away with, and instead of them, a few representatives of the workers can collaborate with the authorities, having only a consultative voice. The government must be safeguarded by the police and the army." Hindenburg goes on to complain of "the prevailing disinclination to work, although wages are so exorbitant—just as it was last May! . . . I know that from the radical side people look at me askance because I occasionally say my say about political matters. But I take these things so much to heart that I had to write a few words to you about the matter."

This pompous official dispatch took the place of the oath which any other revolutionary government would have exacted from the commander in chief under the old government if he was to remain in the service of the new. What overwhelming evidence of the abnormality of the situation! A month had passed since November 9. Hindenburg, his friends, and his officers had seen how timidly the new power was behaving; how everyone could continue to hold the office to which he had been appointed by the emperor; how no one was being called to account, no one was being dismissed; how the new government was showing itself strong only in fighting the Reds; how much at a loss it was when compared with the old authorities. Is it not obvious that these old authorities felt themselves firmly seated in the saddle once more when only a month had elapsed, seeing that their supreme head had so condescendingly extended his hand to the new power?

We might have expected, in the circumstances, that the ruling chancellor would have written to the veteran commander in chief as follows: "You must be aware that we regard imperial generals with supreme distrust, and that your views as officer and Junker are the very ones which our victorious party has been fighting for the last thirty years. Nevertheless, in our extreme need, we intrust to you the task of demobilizing the army, since the soldiers look upon you personally as their friend. We will send someone in our confidence to stand by your side, and he will keep you fully informed regarding our will. For the rest, we must ask you to devote yourself to this work of demobilization, and to leave politics alone." Not a bit of it. It is the army commander of the old power who, quite in the tone of the grand gentleman, writes to the saddler. Hindenburg has been informed, credibly informed, that Ebert, likewise, is a true German. As regards the new realm which is to be established after the "lamentable upshot of the war,"

Ebert's first business must be to abolish the Workers' Councils, with the aid of a thoroughly efficient police.

How much more ardent is the tone of the letter in which, at this juncture, the field marshal espouses the cause of his emperor. When the enemy demanded that William should be handed over, Hindenburg wrote to Marshal Foch: "A soldier who should fail to defend the sovereign to whom he has sworn fealty, would be unworthy of the name of a man of honor. . . . On both sides, during the war, there have been splendid instances of soldierly thought and feeling. . . . As commander in chief of an army which for centuries in succession has cherished as its greatest treasure the tradition of genuine martial honor and knightly sentiment, I am sure you will be able to appreciate my views upon this matter."

This elegantly worded epistle shows how Hindenburg regards Foch, the enemy, as also his comrade; how the fact that they both wield a marshal's baton makes the Frenchman closer to Hindenburg than can the German blood of a German worker. Does not this Junker's letter go far to confirm the theory of Ebert's party, a theory which the Junkers always loathed: namely that equality in position, class, and interests often binds men more closely together than equality of blood and language? Foch cannot read the German letter, but its translation appeals to him as if it had been written by his own brother. Ebert can read Hindenburg's message, but a whole world severs him from his fellow countryman. For one is the letter of a battle-scarred, star-bedecorated officer to another of the same kidney; whilst the other is the letter of a proud field marshal to a city manual worker;

and nothing but the temporary weakness of the soldier has led him for the moment to intrust the reins of government to the workman's calloused hand. Who that has carefully read these priceless letters and compared them, can continue to believe firmly in the ties of blood and soil, of race and language?

Hindenburg is once more at Colberg, drawn thither by the disorders in the East as he had been nearly five years earlier, now to defend Germany against the Poles, who at his previous visit were called Russians. What has happened to the thunder-and-lightning paragraphs of the peace imposed by force at Brest-Litovsk? In February, the Russians occupy Lithuania and seize Riga; the Poles are in Posen; everyone is following his own bent, and the G. H. Q. (which has become an L. H. Q.) is trying to establish order among the volunteer corps and irregular levies which, in these regions, on patriotic pretexts, are camping round bivouac fires as old Hindenburg had dreamed of doing years and years before. Now he dreams of peace, but peace does not come, and any day war on the grand scale may be resumed.

While in Weimar the young republic is fighting impotently against a peace treaty which is going to be enforced upon an isolated Germany, in the breasts of the four hundred newly elected representatives of the people anxiety about their country struggles with anxiety about their personal possessions. If they glance at Paris, they see there a foe who can find excuses for a third tyrannous peace in the tyrannous peaces imposed by the Germans at Brest-Litovsk and at Bucharest. In Paris are the representatives of five great powers with differences of their own to settle but united in the resolve to subjugate the Germans. A glance towards Moscow shows the German republicans a sixth great power with plenty of brave soldiers. Here fate offers fresh chances: an alliance with the Russians. With this Germans can make head once more against the forces of the western Allies. To sign the Treaty of Versailles means many years of thralldom, but the safeguarding of private property; whereas the new chances offered by an alliance with Muscovy would mean that private property in Germany would be threatened. Since the German revolution was nothing if not bourgeois, the new rulers of Germany naturally resisted the tempting voices in the East.

Once more, however, the Weimar assembly asked whether Germany could not fight her enemies single-handed. Hindenburg denied the possibility in May. On June 20, he declared: "We are in a position, as far as the eastern provinces are concerned, to reconquer Posen and to maintain our frontiers there. In the West, however, if our enemies should make a serious onslaught, considering the numerical superiority of the Entente forces, and their power of outflanking us on both wings, there is little, if any, hope of success. A successful issue of the general operations is therefore extremely questionable; but, as a soldier, I must speak in favor of perishing on the field of honor rather than of accepting a shameful peace."

Down to the very last, at Weimar, it was uncertain how the vote would go. Both the nationalists and the communists were opposed to signing the Treaty of Versailles, but between these members of the right and of the left, opinion vacillated, and the question of dishonor was much debated. Maerker, a reactionary general who was at that time lobbying in Weimar, declared that a majority against the peace could be got together. "What finally decided the matter was a telephone call from General Groener to President Ebert, in which the former stated categorically that if fighting were renewed the prospects of a successful issue were hopeless, adding his firm conviction that in the end even the army would approve of accepting the peace conditions."

Of course Ebert wanted to talk with Hindenburg over the phone in person. Since feeling in the government was strongly opposed to the signing of the treaty, Hindenburg's yes or no would be decisive. Ebert, in view of the importance of the matter, had sent a preliminary communication to Colberg, appointing 4 P. M. for a conversation. At 3.30 P. M., Hindenburg entered Groener's office, and had a brief talk with the latter concerning the impossibility of further resistance—a question which the pair had several times discussed during these critical days. After about a quarter of an hour, Hindenburg pulled out his watch and said:

"There is no need for me to stay. You can give Herr Ebert the answer just as well as I."

Thus Hindenburg shuffled off on Groener the responsibility for this momentous decision; just as, eight months before, on November 9, he had made Groener advise the emperor to cross the frontier. Yet for fifteen years Groener was again and again, without protest on his part, to shoulder the blame for the signing of the Treaty of Versailles, being content to tell a few intimates what had actually occurred on these memorable occasions.

20

Soon afterwards, Hindenburg retired from active service. So strong was his sense of duty that he did not flatly insist on resigning. "In view of my great age," he wrote, "my wish to retire into private life will be readily understood—all the more since it is generally known how hard it must be for me, with my views, my character, and my past, to accommodate myself to the retention of my office under the new conditions." Ebert, accepting his resignation, expressed the "inextinguishable gratitude of the German people."

The field marshal said farewell to the troops in a touching order of the day.

"Recently I informed the government that, as a soldier, I should prefer an honorable death on the field of battle to a shameful peace. I owe you this explanation." Then the field marshal becomes retrospective, speaking "of the three royal and imperial War Lords whom I have been privileged to serve. There was a period of tranquil but indefatigable work in peace time; then a rapid ascent to a lofty position, glorious victories, and tenacious resistance loomed before my eyes. I think also with profound distress of the dark days of our country's downfall." He concludes: "Hard as it may be, you must put your personal wishes in the background. Only by unanimous labor will it be possible, with God's help, for our unhappy German fatherland to move on out of deep humiliation towards better times. Farewell. I shall never forget you. Hindenburg."

This document, the only one in which he signs as plain "Hindenburg" without the "von," discloses the field marshal as a veteran officer possessed of much dignity; and the fine concluding sentences sound notes pleasing to the German in him. Notwithstanding his advice to Ebert, during these eight months he showed himself a nobleman in the proper sense of the word in the way he devoted himself to the leadership of an unruly army which the two other leaders had forsaken. This epoch represents the moral climax of his life. One cannot but wish that, with the document just quoted, announcing his second retirement, the curtain had fallen on his public career forever.

III

Those who would understand why this curtain rose again six years later must have at least a superficial understanding of the defects of the German Republic. What was happening throughout these six years in Germany? What ought to have happened?

The curse of a bankrupt heritage, a curse which necessarily affects a revolution that follows upon defeat in war, could not here, as in the peasant land of Russia, be nullified by completely sweeping away the old power. Germany, whose leadership has been almost entirely intrusted to the nobility, but whose civic achievements have been mainly the work of its burgher class, could be metamorphosed only by gentle pushes and not by a violent thrust. Change had to come about gradually, and in a sort of self-deception accordant with the hypnosis of the country during the war. Had a bold group of revolutionists been able to seize power during the first moments of general paralysis, it could not have held power for long. The deep-lying reason for this is one that concerns the psychological stratification of the country, which does not correspond to the professional stratification.

Just as the court officials of the pharaohs used to build for themselves mausoleums like those of their masters, in pyramidal form but decorously smaller, so do the Germans copy the pyramid of their military state with a hundred variations. The platonic archetype which floats before their gaze must again and again be imitated; and therefore they made replicas of the pyramid on which their king stood in numberless little pyramids, ranging in size from the political party with millions of members to the bowling club. The stone which is alone and quiescent has no independent life; only when it has become part of a pyramid, sustaining parts of some stones and pressing on parts of others, has it a life worth living, a life vivified by service and command. Consequently the burgher does not cling to the burgher nor the manual worker to the manual worker; but the wealthy burgher strives by money, paying court to his "betters," and if he is lucky by marriage, to uplift himself towards the nobility, to thrust down those that are beneath him. He aspires towards the next tier, and would rather endure the contemptuous smile of his superiors than join with underlings in laughing at them. Since the skilled worker likewise tries to become a bourgeois, there is a stasis in the national life. The petty bourgeoisie, forsaken by the great bourgeoisie and courted by the manual workers, becomes an amorphous central mass. All the energy of the German stream runs to waste in the lagoon of petty bourgeoisdom, and when the current leaves these regions, it is with exhausted energies and diminished flow, like the Nile below the great morasses.

A state in which for centuries the Junkers had

dictated the laws, must, instead of breeding the will to liberty, breed the will to become law abiding. It was not because the German workers were too nationalistic in feeling that they lost their revolution, but because they were too anxious to belong to it.

A new situation arose when the lowermost Germans detached themselves from this endless body of those who were slowly and obliquely climbing towards the sun of power, and instead of pushing shoulder to shoulder with the others from beneath, wanted to assault the main body from the flank. When one Red worker after another drew away from the comrade whom he would not follow into the bourgeois twilight, he only intensified his comrade's determination to continue climbing. Nay, by resisting the attempts of the average workers to climb, the Reds compelled these workers to make terms with the upper dogs, even during the brief moments when these were no longer upper dogs, or were at least not visible as such. Thus the peaceful majority of the workers who, four years earlier, like all Germany, had allowed themselves to be forced into a war on two fronts in accordance with Schlieffen's plan, now attacked their more radical brethren in the hope that, when these had been subjugated, they would find themselves in a stronger position as against the old powers. But then it was too late; the opportunity had been lost; the old powers had in the meanwhile regained strength. You may call such a dilemma tragic, if you will; anyhow, it is typically German.

The civilians had accepted from the militarized nobles responsibility for the armistice, thereby relieving the latter of the stresses which might in some degree have

wrought a moral purification.   Now they were making
themselves responsible for the acceptance of the Treaty
of Versailles.   There was a double shift of fronts.
The bourgeoisie and the embourgeoised workers who
ruled the new State railed in speeches and manifestos,
in newspaper articles and in books against the foreign
enemy on account of the peace terms.   They never
railed against their co-nationals who had been in
power throughout the war, and whose persistent
refusal to negotiate for a reasonable understanding
had been responsible for the characteristics of the
peace.   These sometime rulers, on the other hand,
who had been accustomed to rule for centuries, were
more cunning, since they attacked, not the enemy
abroad, but the bourgeoisie at home for having agreed
to the terms of peace.   Impudence went so far that
in the new National Assembly the representatives of
the old power made their favorite motif, patriotism,
audible, voicing unctuous self-satisfaction as if it had
been a virtue.   Vast, indeed, were the moral and
political consequences of that shifting of responsibility
for the armistice upon the shoulders of the bourgeoisie,
which Ludendorff had regarded as a master stroke.

Besides, if we look for excuses, there was a grievous
lack of talent for rule in the new parties.   During
fifty years of dictatorship, first under Bismarck, then
under William II, and finally under Ludendorff, it
was inevitable that there should have been an atrophy
of political talent which had grown during the years
before and after the revolution of 1848.   The Junkers
who, though they had not learned how to rule, had
learned how to command, knew, as highly trained army
officers, how to provide for reserves and successors;

and the thirty or forty families which had actually
been in command for two centuries in Prussia saw to it
that a sufficiency of vitality and money should flow
to them from the State.   By always sending a brother
or a cousin into the government, they resembled the
entrepreneurs of Genoa or Portugal, who used invariably to dispatch one of their sons with the fleet of
merchant adventurers to watch over the treasures
which they would sell when the ship got safely home.
A minister for agriculture beside the Spree cared for
the interests of many hundreds of Junkers whose lands
were in the valleys of the Elbe and the Oder.

The new men who now came in the hope of helping
the millions of their party comrades behaved with
the force of dogmatic conviction.   What they lacked
was Siberia.   The last victims of the Socialist Law
were dead or at liberty; at any rate, very few remained
in prison or lived as refugees in foreign parts.   Since
those now in power had done no real fighting to secure
their position, and had not undergone suffering in
attaining it—for power had been forced upon them
when the State machine was at "dead point"—they
shrank from power as something which they did not feel
competent to wield.   It was not so much that they
dreaded responsibility, for readiness to accept responsibility is part of every Prussian's training; but,
literally, I repeat, they were afraid to wield power.
Being so few in number and so unpracticed in statecraft, these leaders resembled a small group of strolling
players suddenly called upon to take the star parts
because those to whom the principal rôles had been
assigned had been disabled in a collision.

Since the obliquely upward movement of bourgeois

ambition had not been interrupted by the revolution,
the result was that, during the period of national
collapse, this passion for the legitimate assumed the
hues of nationalism. Everyone was afraid of seeming
unpatriotic, and sported at least an invisible and imaginary armlet on his sleeve. Had not the workers
been railed at for thirty years as antipatriotic? Had
they not, during the long-sustained war, become field-
gray heroes? This was the time to amalgamate with
those who had actually ventured to name their
party the Vaterlands-Partei. The old empire, which
they had so long antagonized, was now envisaged by
the socialists as crowned with an aureole; and they
began to venerate Bismarck, as a son who has always
been at odds with his father will begin to glorify him
as soon as the old man dies. The very word "Reich"
(empire, or realm) acquired a magical ring; everyone
wished to participate in the advantages of this name.
While the German emperor still held sway, there had
not been nearly so much talk of the imperial government, imperial leagues, and imperial institutions. The
only word which no one ventured to utter was the
word "republic," which had painfully foreign, and
especially French, associations; and the outer world,
which translated "Reich" by "Empire," could not but
feel that there had been no essential change.

The new leaders did almost nothing to convince the
outer world that Germany had changed; but they did
everything in their power to convince the homeland
that things were not so bad after all. Continually
fighting to suppress the Reds, who were trying to
establish a socialist State, they kept up contact with
the ancient order of things, looking backward rather

than forward, and shelving any attempts at socialization by the well-tried device of appointing commissions of inquiry. They did everything in their power to spare the feelings of the bourgeois, whose left hands they grasped; and since the bourgeois were with their right hands holding the left hands of the nobles, an electric contact was maintained between the classes— only the communists, shunned by all alike, being kept aloof.

Thus there was undisguised satisfaction when it appeared that most of those who turned up in the new National Assembly had been members of the Reichstag—at Weimar, of course, not Berlin, but that made very little difference. The old Reichstag, which had prorogued itself during the revolution, had given but one sign of existence while the disturbances were still in progress. The fact that, even in the first flush of new events, not more than half of those elected to the Weimar National Assembly were socialists, gave additional proof of how fundamentally bourgeois was German sentiment. This was a great consolation to the socialist rulers of the country. Another consolation was that, even during these first elections two months after the revolution, eighty of the elected socialists belonged to the defeated right, and only twenty-two to the radical left.

All the deputies were fired with the wish to please the bourgeoisie, and all the old parties suddenly claimed the proud title of "People's Party." The new parties talked of "objectivity" (freedom from bias). This common characteristic among democracies, and one which in times of revolution paralyzes impetus, is peculiarly dear to the Germans when it can abrogate the need for decision. Aspiring to show that they had developed out of partisans into statesmen, many of the new men began by sacrificing their old party, and then went on to sacrifice the new State. In Berlin, one of the first measures of a socialist chief of police was that he allowed the taverns to remain open until dawn, which was manifestly injurious to the employees thereof. When it was proposed to make an ovation before the Privy Council to the socialist minister Severing, this same chief of police forbade it, on the ground that "demonstrations in the governmental quarters of the city are not allowed."

In later years, the socialist festival of May 1 was prohibited by a socialist minister of State. Demonstrators were not permitted to carry through the streets the national flag whose colors had been so ardently fought for; the banner must not be disclosed until the meeting place had been reached, and no incident in a comedy could be more humorous than the regulation that this banner could only be borne through the streets hidden away in a bag of black American oilcloth. Finally the socialists, who had steadfastly refused to vote the funds for every new ship wanted by the emperor, hastened to provide the republic with its first armored cruiser, in which the Germans were to seek a hero's death beneath the waters. The old potentates, who nicknamed the new ones "November criminals," had given them a title of honor which the alleged criminals did not deserve.

While the new potentates were thus renouncing the realization of their ideals, they made it easy for their adversaries to revive the old ones. Inasmuch as socialists had been excluded for thirty years from all the higher offices, the revolution made a vacuum which could be filled only by the retention of the former imperial officials. By the old laws, the so-called "non-political officials," the powerful permanent officials whom Bismarck had so much detested, were irremovable. They could not even be dismissed for gross negligence, seeing that demotion was not allowed, and there were practical difficulties in the way of transfer to an equivalent position in some other government office. No one dreamed of simply repealing these laws. Thus there was no method of coping with the stubbornness of a permanent official within his own field; least of all where payments were concerned. The permanent officials, as choir, obeyed the orders of the permanent chief of staff as choir master, and ignored the heroic tenor, who occupied the center of the stage in the limelight. This tenor, moreover, was frequently changed. Again, these permanent officials ignored the minister of State. As a result, there was, functioning in all the government offices, a passive response which was sympathetic with strictly royalist traditions and made it impossible for the new ministers to rule differently from their predecessors. Someone has called these permanent officials "the secular clergy of the rulers, forming a firm front against the ruled." Inasmuch as this system of government was disseminated throughout the beehives of the provinces and districts, it was impossible to stabilize a new spirit in the State administration. A wine cask which has not been very thoroughly scoured before being filled with new wine will always communicate a taste of the old one.

In fact, it was the chief desire of the aforesaid obliquely gradated hierarchy to preserve this old bouquet.   The king and nobles remained as distinguished as ever.   In good society, the word "republic" had an unpleasant aroma, if only because it reminded one of a moment of weakness, of defeat at home even more than of defeat by the foreign enemy.   In Germany all the court flunkeys of two-and-twenty princes were pensioned off, whereas for the most part in other lands these gentry were unceremoniously banned by the revolution.   The landed estates remained nests of Junker oppression for a full ten years, "in order to maintain a dam against the Slav flood."   Nevertheless, the great lords of the soil hired Polish workers from the eastern side of the dam, because the Poles would work for lower wages.   These decayed estates were as old-fashioned as ever.   Since no one ventured to partition them, it was one of the chief lessons of the history of this period that Germany could more easily rid itself of kingship than of Junkerdom.   By inflation, that is to say, by the consequences of the war which impoverished the common people, the landed gentry and the large-scale capitalists freed their possessions from debt, since inflation cleared off the mortgages.   In addition, the propertied class secured millions from the State for the maintenance of property. Some of these ardently nationalist and blue-blooded champions of Prussia were, with their estates, transferred to Poland by the Treaty of Versailles.   In such cases, with the best socialist will in the world, the German government could no longer give them financial assistance, but these patriots nationalized themselves as Polish citizens so that, on foreign soil, they might better "hoist the flag of Germanism."

While the aforetime potentates, transiently dismayed

by the squall, but speedily tranquilized, were re-concentrating their forces, the "objectivity" of the new magnates led them, six weeks after the revolution, to speak contemptuously of the new State in their electoral addresses. "The revolution, instead of bringing us the promised freedom, has brought us dictatorship and an intolerably arbitrary régime—instead of the promised bread, a danger of famine." They made no protest when some blockhead from the sometime governing class hastened to found a *league for the League of Nations:* nor when the First Citizen of the State, who had been publicly vilified and sought the protection of the law courts, was gloated over by the judge because the latter was able, by implication, to censure the president of the Republic. If the Germans want to make a revolution, they go to the law courts, and not to history.

When the "revolutionary" government ventured to adopt black-red-gold for the new national flag, they retained the antiquated naval banner, merely venturing to add the new colors in the form of a jack. Even when the most brutal attacks were made upon the State authority; when in the year 1920 the government was driven out, and when in the year 1922 the most influential minister was assassinated; the authorities did not deal firmly with the ex-officers who were responsible for such outrages.

These things were possible, not because the new potentates were men of especially weak character, but because centuries of subordination have predisposed the German temperament to weakness. The new men were decent fellows enough. Except for one of the Prussian ministers of State, who "bought" the ex-emperor's cellar and fitted out a little palace for himself, they kept their hands clean. None of them used their official positions to make money; none of them were involved in financial scandals. Loebe, president of the Reichstag for a decade, and in receipt of a high salary, lived very simply, gave month by month the surplus he did not spend to a Children's Aid Association, putting by no more than 2000 marks a year to provide for the education of his son. The first time Severing resigned, he did so of his own free will, although had he stuck to his post a few days longer his salary would have been considerably increased. Vainly did the old potentates try to prove in the courts that Erzberger had evaded the payment of taxes; and that one of the democratic ministers of State had accepted a gratuity from a vintners' syndicate in the form of a few cases of wine. Such revelations as were possible, disclosed nothing in comparison with the advantages which for centuries—and again after the revolution—the blue-blooded families were able to secure from the government.

What led the new men astray was not the pursuit of gain, but social ambition. Dinner jackets corrupted the Republic. These handicraftsmen, printers, secretaries, now risen to political power—men who, all their lives, had been kept waiting on the doormat outside the rooms of their well-born countrymen—had had but one dream. Their only ambition was to acquire the easy manners, the empty smiles, the smooth phrases of the lordly mortals born to wear evening dress and patent-leather pumps, or else to wear officers' uniforms. Their sense of social embarrassment was stronger than were their class feelings, although for years they had

fought stoutly on behalf of their class, and had taken
the field against the enemy order of society.

No doubt many of them were simple and straightforward enough; but very few of them were sufficiently
intelligent to realize that the man who is too adaptable
is seen through and despised, whereas one who holds
aloof is respected. They did not understand that an
experienced leader does not think first of the strength
of his adversary's following, but of the intensity of his
adversary's self-confidence; that the experienced leader
begins by measuring himself against his adversary, and
only then goes on to measure his party against his
adversary's party. What the new men wished above
all to acquire were certain mannerisms which every
hotel waiter acquires within a few weeks. In their
endeavor to avoid making one who had formerly been
styled His Excellency smile, the new potentates behaved in a way which made it impossible for them to
impress Their Excellencies. The first president of the
republican Reich, a man of blameless life, learned
to ride when he was fifty years of age, because, in old
Europe, kings were expected to appear on horseback
before their people; others learned to shoot. A gallant
lady of good society boasted of having inaugurated a
great labor minister into the secrets of love making.
The new men drove about in glittering automobiles,
and had themselves, week after week, photographed
by flashlight at banquets. The first minister for
national defense, a sometime basket maker, was so
much overcome by the glamour of uniforms that he
never noticed how the men who wore these uniforms
were conspiring against the Republic; and all hastened
to the villas of the upstart princes of the banking world,

not in the wish to make money out of speculation,
but to shine at garden parties. Instead of standing
on the tractor of a new age in order to till the fields
of an era in the making, they devoted themselves to
picking the belated roses of the nineteenth century.

IV

A strange epoch! Even those who studied it no
more than cursorily, with the fugitive glance and the
inattentive ear of the newspaper reader, perceived,
however vaguely, unusual colors and unfamiliar tones!
Two-and-twenty German princes had stepped down
from their thrones. Even the most petty of these
monarchs had worn a diadem, had had a court chamberlain, and thousands of subjects who abased themselves before him, listened eagerly for his lightest
word, warmed themselves in the sunshine of his
favor. Now influence was wielded by men who had
been born in the back rooms of history, who had
grown up under poverty-stricken conditions. The
thrones were wrapped in dust sheets, the palaces had
become museums; and common folk, wondering
whether they ought not to wear woolen overshoes
before setting foot on the polished floors, had an uneasy conscience as they trailed through the resplendent
rooms on Sundays. The mightiest of these sovereigns,
to whose words Europe had hearkened breathlessly
for twenty years, had been replaced by a square-headed
saddler, whose aims were justice and compromise
—but who could please nobody. Meanwhile the
princes, who had lost territories and power, wanted,
above all, to save their property. They would rather
be described by the unpleasant epithet of "covetous"

than renounce a few millions in favor of the impoverished wights who had formerly been their subjects, even though such renunciation might have paved the way for their return.

A civilian, a man previously of no account, had sat in an unwarmed railway carriage holding parley with the enemy's victorious field marshal; and next day the German people had read in the papers what provinces, what weapons and munitions, and what battleships and cruisers they were to hand over. With despair they read these stipulations, for their dead lay in heaps on distant battlefields in foreign lands; and they could not but ask themselves why. By myriads the German soldiers had returned from a long-lasting war, filled with amazement and bitterness when they reached their native towns, where they vainly awaited a word of gratitude, and looked askance at the gyrating couples of friends and sisters from whom they felt estranged, so that they were reluctant to join the dance.

Germany's nearest ally, speaking the same tongue as Germany and conscious of a common destiny with the German fatherland, wanted to unite its fate with the Germans, making one country under one flag. Austria, however, was hopelessly impoverished, so the German coal barons and factory lords were unwilling, and the union between Germany and Austria was a dead issue long before the Entente powers forbade it. Nine hundred men who had said nothing more amiss than had their counterparts among the enemy, were to be handed over to this enemy for trial by biased courts; and only one, an alien Jew, ventured a righteous protest. Ten thousand foreign soldiers were occupying the German Rhineland; dark-skinned

21

Moroccans roused loathing in blond German women; though shopkeepers and hotel proprietors had mixed feelings when these swarthy customers finally marched away.

To enforce the payment of reparations, Germany's western neighbors reoccupied German territory. Inspired with venomous hatred, leaderless groups of German youths began a guerrilla warfare among the factories, as if they had been in the gulleys of the Apennines. Meanwhile the great dictators went into retreat for a day, to emerge later posing as martyrs before their workmen. Twenty parties, issuing lengthy programs, endeavored to scare away confusion and poverty; and, while endless repetitions of the words "liberty" and "right" came from the throats of the spokesmen of the people, in the committee rooms anxious men were seated reckoning up votes to see if a ministerial majority could be secured. One party leader brought a suit for slander against another. For weeks all glances were turned towards the purses of the petty bourgeois; but within a few years one of them had been slain by an assassin's bullet, and the other had been burned to a cinder in the St. Gothard train.

Whereas, for four years, the blood of millions had been shed, now gold began to flow away like blood. For a long time, indeed, gold had become invisible, and had been replaced by paper currency; but now the paper faded, losing its value from day to day, so that, in the hour of its receipt, the receivers preferred to squander it upon enjoyment rather than wait till the morrow, when it would buy nothing. Of course everyone coveted the paper money of those countries in which the currency was still comparatively stable. Simultaneously, one of the patriotic phrase makers whose sharp eyes enabled him to see a little farther ahead than the rest of them, heaped up a mountain of paper money, sold his hoard across the frontier, borrowed from the State, a few weeks later returned the money which had become valueless; bought whatever he could lay hands on—ships, hotels, railways, theaters, mines—until, out of the distresses of his nation, he had forged himself an enormous ingot of gold. Then he suddenly collapsed, and, even in death, defrauded Germany of the death duties.

Thousands of young soldiers were willing to be recruited as they had been three centuries before; went to the East in search of loot and adventures; said that the title deeds of the lands they wished to settle on were written in blood; and were, in the end, driven back, to return home impoverished and to vent their disappointment in the formation of leagues against the present State. The coffers of the savings banks were emptied; insurance policies became worthless. Bequests ceased altogether; universal distrust led to the break-up of the oldest ties; and when further crashes flung thousands of the pious into poverty, they rioted against the Jews who, as aliens, must have caused these woes, and were regarded as universally rich and happy.

When reparations were not paid according to pledge, broad-shouldered Americans appeared upon the scene, calculated in interminable conferences the billions (the card houses) which future generations were to pay; and, during these conferences, while they were squandering vast sums in the hotels where they were engaged in devising a plan to stay the hunger of the masses, the number of suicides continued to increase. At the same time, greed-inspired foreigners poured billions into Germany—for these foreigners expected to earn high interest on their money, which, to their astonishment, was used only to erect magnificent buildings all over the country. Then, of a sudden, there came abortive risings—splashes like those made by somebody who jumps into the water, though the agitation speedily died away into ripples, and was succeeded by restored tranquillity.

Shots resounded; papers rustled; volunteer corps beat their drums; orators harangued; girls sang, and danced to the sound of jazz music; only those who had their ears to the ground could hear the faint groaning of the populace.

Yet, amid these strange and multifarious happenings, the new potentates were unable to revive the lost ideal of the masses. What, for all their honesty, distinguished the democrats from those who ruled this German nation before and after them was their total lack of imagination. After the gray years of the war, the people wanted light and color; after the long years of obedience, they wanted vivid impressions. Instead of imitating the variegated example of Moscow, like the dictators who followed them—instead of vivifying the new epoch for people's eyes and ears by new emblems, new names, and new music—the republican leaders, serious-minded men, worked on inconspicuous committees, trying to enhearten the masses by lectures on socialization and pamphlets on birth control!

Surely the movement had had its heroes! Why did

it not occur to any of the republican leaders to found
a Bebel Factory, to rename one of the great squares
"Liebknecht-Platz," to set up a monument to Lassalle?
Why were not the Germans reminded of the sufferings
of the pioneers, of the great deeds of the men of 1848?
Why were not Herwegh's poems publicly sung by cho-
ruses of male voices?   Why were the political programs that were issued so stupendously boring that
there was absolutely nothing fresh in tone and color
among their tedious thousands of words?   Not a
thing was done to give the workers the self-confidence
they needed to make them feel that they themselves
were the State.   There were no demonstrations to
tickle the fancy of the bourgeoisie.   Why, the very
Reds named their faction from that of a slave rebel in
the days of classical Rome—a name which could not
be expected to appeal to German ears as might that
of Hutten or Engels have appealed!   No new songs
and no new flag; no new orator and no new author;
no fresh costume and no unwonted gesture—nothing
to stimulate the masses who had been robbed of their
traditional emblems.   In the long run a State cannot
live without ideas; and it cannot, without emblems,
start with a rush on a new career.

V

Had it not all happened before?   Seventy years
prior to this revolution, a Prussian officer, Rüstow by
name, who had escaped from prison and in due course
became a brigadier in the Swiss service, wrote about
the revolution of 1848: "The army of the people was
designed to protect popular rights, but within a few
days a routinist reaction set in.   The gaze of the

bourgeoisie, of the upper middle class and of the lower, was turned away from the sins of those in high places to concentrate upon the terrific image of a threat to property. Communism, which had already been a specter haunting the minds of Prussian generals, with lightning speed became a Red Specter for the German bourgeoisie as well. The armed counter-revolution was ignored, although it was raising its head everywhere. The folk movement suddenly assumed a new aspect, to become one for the defense of private property, and the armed people was stunted into a militia."

Seventy years later, the defeated potentates were no less shrewd. Habituated to rule, they were quick to perceive what would be the best line to take. After a preposterous rising had failed in the year 1920, the old-time authorities decided that, since the new State was not laying about itself vigorously on account of this affair, it should not be prematurely attacked in the open, but should patiently be mined from within. They succeeded in achieving their end in the course of a dozen years.

Was not the Treaty of Versailles the best point at which to begin driving these mines? You need only talk to people about outraged honor, and they would be ready to listen to you! In Weimar the representatives of the nation had accepted the Versailles Treaty with reserves as regards culpability for the war. Since Clemenceau had insisted upon their signing, and had threatened a new war, the Germans had accepted under compulsion, declaring in set terms, "that the honor of the German people was not impaired by what was thus forced upon them." This protest had been a matter of common knowledge, but had been forgotten

by all the world next day, so that the imperial
potentates could stump the country with the cry—
"The Republic has sold our honor!" At the same
time they interpreted the universal German repudiation
of Germany's sole culpability for the war as equivalent
to Germany's blamelessness as regards the war, and
proceeded to instil into the minds of their compatriots
that Germany had neither begun the war nor lost it.
The authorities made no murmur of denial when these
views were voiced in hundreds of books and speeches.
No one, indeed, would have bothered to refuse the
defeated army the title of the "unconquered army"
if it liked to delude itself in this fashion; but those
who were thus compliant failed to recognize how
serious the outcome would be—that after a decade of
false suggestions, a credulous generation would have
grown up in the belief that Germany had been innocent, that her enemies had been inspired by malice,
and that vengeance would be right and desirable.

The sun in whose rays the officers and the Junkers
could warm themselves once more was the recently
created Reichswehr. What was to prevent their
serving under the new flag? The military oath?
William had publicly and expressly absolved his
officers and officials from their oaths of allegiance.
Surely that sufficed? It did not seem to occur to anyone that there must be two parties to a divorce; that
one of those who have sworn a pact may have stronger
feelings of loyalty than the other, and may continue
to keep an oath which the other repudiates, because
his heart and conscience are involved. A Jesuitical
artifice enabled these officers to retain their sense of
honor while serving under a detested flag, which they

despised as the symbol of revolution and as the emblem
of those who had destroyed the royal authority.   If
the former oath could be so readily annulled, why
should one not swear a second oath with mental
reservations?   Later the Nazis declared that, in such
circumstances, it was an actual duty to commit perjury.

Since there was no Trotsky in Germany, the imperial
army officers were welcomed with open arms, and very
few new ones were appointed.   In the year 1913, the
proportion of men of noble blood in the Prussian
officers' corps was 22 per cent; by 1921, it had risen
once more to 21.3.   Manifestly the extent of the
victory of the revolution was comprised in this difference of 0.7 per cent.   Since, by the reduction in the
size of the army, thousands had been left out in the
cold, the republican State was, in this matter likewise,
doing its best for the old officers; no pensions were
reduced, and no privileges were withdrawn.   A reduction in the percentage of the nobles by 0.7 was the
measure of the advance.   By the end of the Seven
Years' War, a noncommissioned officer had become a
general; after the World War and the revolution, the
highest rise achieved by a noncommissioned officer was
to the rank of captain.

Noske, the first minister for defense, gave the reason
when he said: "I prefer one who makes no attempt to
hide his convictions to one who plays the republican."
It never occurred to him that genuine republicans, and
perhaps none but these, ought to be made officers in the
present army.   The officers had to accept proletarians
as messmates, and paid them due honor—until in the
end they could roast them on their sword points and
gobble them up.   The minister for defense felt himself

to be admirably protected against his hostile brethren by such splendid officers as these. When a volunteer corps was being swiftly marched before President Ebert, General Maerker heard the minister for defense say to Comrade Ebert, "You can be easy in your mind now, for all is going well again!" When someone wrote a letter warning Noske against this general, Noske sent Maerker the letter as a mark of confidence. Why had Noske confidence in Maerker? The general had once said to him, "For you, Minister Noske, I would allow myself to be hewn in pieces, and my jägers as well!" The worthy burgher general not only wrote this down, but subsequently had it printed. Was it not to be expected that, after such protestations of loyalty, the minister for defense would be eager to comply with any and every demand put forward by the officers? Every estate in the republic was criticized and derided, except the military estate, which during fourteen years was immune! If, in the Cabinet, anyone ventured to utter a derogatory word, the minister for defense would roundly assert that should such things be said he could not answer for the conduct of the troops; and no resolution of the Cabinet was ever passed against the veto of the minister for defense. Thus he and the Reichswehr secretly ruled the country, and behind him ruled an invisible major.

As regards this first minister for defense, it is true that, if not his neck, at least an arm, was speedily broken by an abortive rising. A certain Herr Kapp, a Prussian civil servant (who had, of course, been a member of a students' corps and was an officer in the reserve), had joined forces with a discharged and therefore mortified captain and with a major from the

Baltic volunteer corps. They were joined by another
captain who wanted to play at war-making once more;
and finally won over the general of the Reichswehr in
Berlin. These conspirators were determined to make
short work of the Republic. With a couple of battalions
from the Eastern Marches, they succeeded in occupying
the government offices in Berlin. But in these times,
for it was only 1920, the workers were still willing to
down tools when the State was in danger. The general,
who had expressed his willingness to be cut to pieces
for the sake of the minister for defense, was more or
less involved in the affair. The government fled;
there was a general strike; the government came back;
and soon everything had blown over.

In the trial which ensued before the Supreme Court,
which lasted for a whole week in the red-gold hall,
almost all of the old potentates and almost all the new
ones appeared to give testimony, disclosing the existence of a political jumble whose composition was no less
inscrutable than had been that of the soup served to
Hindenburg in Cassel. There was a socialist minister
for finance who had been in treaty with the ringleaders
of the revolt, being determined to have a foot in both
camps. There were generals, too, who had hedged as
gamblers hedge when betting on a horse race. There
were secretaries of State whose memories were extremely untrustworthy; there was a whole forest of
Excellencies! The most remarkable of all the witnesses
was General Ludendorff, who testified that, "quite by
chance," on that March day he had taken a walk
to the Brandenburg Gate, at seven o'clock in the
morning, the very hour when the rebels were making
their noisy entry. The great comedy of this trial was

the prelude to the tragedy of the Republic, just as the Zabern affair had been the prelude to the World War. In the end, one of the Junkers was sent to a commodious fortress, where he stayed but a very short time, and the other gentlemen were set at liberty. There had been very little stir. All the Excellencies continued to draw their pensions.

Things were made easy for the new generals, who were the old generals over again. German grown-up children, who for two hundred years had been accustomed to play at soldiers in peace time, laughed merrily when Father Christmas handed them their presents. Reading that a brigade had a new commander who had gained distinction during the Wahehe rising in West Africa, they felt that this was the very man needed for high command in Germany. The old insignia of rank, which in November 1918 had, by common consent, been removed from the officers' shoulders, were inconspicuously replaced in January, 1919. In this same month, when a volunteer corps marched once more through the streets of the capital for the first time since the war and the establishment of the Republic, there was to be read in one of the newspapers: "Again this measured tread! Virile discipline, German austerity, a genuinely martial demeanor! How splendid the men looked in their perfect order, their brilliant discipline. Fine figures of men, these volunteer jägers. They were greeted with universal acclamations!"

Among the commanders and organizers of the Reichswehr, von Seeckt was the most interesting personality. Highly cultured, although he was a Prussian general; on bad terms with Ludendorff and Hindenburg, who had been his rivals at the outset of the war—he was fifty-two years of age when the German collapse aroused doubts in his mind as to the soundness of the traditional system, and perhaps brought him new light and a readiness to make innovations. Be this as it may, in reconstructing the officers' corps, he manned it exclusively with those who had been on the general staff during the war, ignoring the officers who had served at the front. The latter, he said, had lost the true military spirit by being four years under fire. That spirit was peculiar to men who knew nothing of the trenches! When, on the day of the Kapp Putsch, the minister for defense asked him to fire on the rebels, he and four other officers of high rank refused, and only a bourgeois general complied. When subsequently, during the inflation period, Bavaria wished to secede from the Reich, which was in greater danger than it had been immediately after the war, Seeckt seemed obviously the man for the dictator's job, and, being in the president's confidence, he was given full power. Yet he hesitated, and showed Fabian trends.

But neither he, nor the minister for defense Gessler (whose name was appropriate), nor yet Groener, the gentlemanly South German, was the real ruler. Behind them, in one of the little rooms of the Ministry for Defense, sat a youthful officer who for a decade was to decide the most important questions concerning Germany's fate. He was shrewd enough to persuade the socialists, at a decisive moment, that they would do well not to appoint one of their number to the post of minister for defense, since abstention in this matter would leave them free to criticize. The man I speak of was Major von Schleicher, whose fortunes and intrigues were subsequently to have a fateful influence.

VI

Hindenburg wrote his memoirs—*Aus meinem Leben.* In a palatial villa presented him by the town, he lived alone with his wife; and, immediately after his second retirement, sought this literary method of escape from tedium. His daughters were married; his son was a captain in the Reichswehr. Committees, festivals, and speeches bored the field marshal; and, as he says, whenever he went out with his wife, it always seemed to produce an obstruction to the traffic. When we contemplate his rooms, we think of Bismarck, who was similarly installed, and who made mock of General Roon's elegantly furnished house, saying, "Only those who know nothing about eating are so splendidly equipped." Amid numerous tokens of esteem, there stood a huge globe, which had been given the field marshal by the court generals in commemoration of the World War. Apropos of this globe, Hindenburg made a memorable utterance. A year after the battle of Tannenberg, while he and his painter-in-ordinary were looking at the map together, Hindenburg said to the artist, "You remember the victory of the Poles at Tannenberg five centuries ago? I can cover with my finger nail the battlefield where the Teutonic knights were defeated. But the battlefields on which I fought are too large for me to cover with my hand."—"When saying these words," adds the painter, "the field marshal seemed deeply moved."

Thus the long-lasting legend which remained at work during the years after the war, and the seductions of fame, had led him astray although he was so very old a man. It was plain that he regarded the Balkans, Asia Minor, all the theaters of the war, as his own battlefields, since the troops fighting in them had, formally, been under his orders. Well, after his painful experiences, we need not grudge him the illusions he cherished.

What were left for him now but the company of his wife, and the sport of shooting, to which everyone with game preserves invited him? Inevitably the Republic was an irritation to him; and he certainly never dreamed, from mere pride, of collaborating with it. That is why he took no action when the honor of the Republic was at stake. When Erzberger in his desperate struggle referred to Hindenburg's grateful handshake after the signing of the armistice, Hindenburg publicly declared that he had thanked Erzberger, but had never pressed Erzberger's hand. Again, when Ebert was fighting for his honor, Hindenburg was silent. A few weeks later, when Ebert was dead, Hindenburg declared, "Ebert never ceased trying to serve the German people faithfully, and the German nation will always recognize the fact gratefully." If Hindenburg had said as much of the socialist president under whom he had served three months earlier, while Ebert was yet alive, he might have saved Ebert's honor, and even Ebert's life.

However, objectivity is a democratic virtue, and Hindenburg had to defend himself in another quarter. From Doorn, the emperor had disseminated his own peculiar version of his flight. This conflicted with other stories of the affair. Those who had been present at Spa on November 9 had published a report which was distasteful to His Majesty. William's aim was to depict himself as a man who had been sent across the frontier forcibly and against his will. The emperor threatened to publish documents confirming this impression—letters written by sometime courtiers. Thereupon Hindenburg, asked by a third party to give his version of the matter, wrote a letter which opens as follows:

"Your Serene Highness and Most Mighty Emperor! Most Gracious Emperor, King, and Lord! I myself am responsible for Your Majesty's resolve to go abroad on that unhappy November 9." But the field marshal continues: "It is incorrect to say that, overnight, I urged your immediate departure, as has recently and publicly been declared against my will. I have no doubt whatever that Your Majesty would not have gone away had not Your Majesty believed that, in my position as Chief of General Staff I had regarded this step as in Your Majesty's interest and in that of the fatherland. But in the minutes . . . it is recorded that I did not learn of Your Majesty's departure until after it had taken place." The letter concludes with the assurance "that all my life I have been and shall remain indomitably loyal to my Imperial and Royal Master."

This remarkable epistle was not answered by the emperor until two months had elapsed. Then the answer was official and for immediate publication, His Majesty doubtless wishing to indicate displeasure by the delay. William said he was glad that the matter had now been cleared up. He had long been waiting for the persons concerned to declare before the whole world "that the decision for my departure was forced upon me by my responsible political advisers in defiance of my own inward conviction. I am grateful to you that you have at length taken this step, which is equally necessary for the maintenance of undeniable historical truth, for the repute of my house, and for my personal honor. . . .   In the belief that you were loyally fulfilling a difficult duty, you gave your emperor and king the advice which you thought it necessary to give as the outcome of your view of the situation. Whether that view was correct cannot be decided until light has been thrown upon all the facts of those unhappy days."

This acrimonious correspondence discloses how the relationship between the two men had been perpetually clouded by their reciprocal mistrust.   But the vassal comes out of the matter a great deal better than the king!   The vassal accepts full responsibility, instead of telling William most emphatically that a man worthy of the name, and still more a king worthy of the name, had to decide such a question for himself.   But Hindenburg will not admit that he urged William to go; and his venturing to point this out, while trying to save both the King's face and his own in a complicated conditional sentence, is the utmost to which the cadet who is still loyal to his monarch can bring himself. William, on the other hand, does not merely emphasize Hindenburg's responsibility, but declares Hindenburg's advice to have been mistaken.   Thus, as William sees the matter, the emperor fled from his country only because Hindenburg was moved by unjustified alarms.

Hindenburg wrote his memoirs, or had them written for him.   His book, so the preface assures us, was not intended either to justify his own cause or to accuse others.   Nevertheless, he does both, as do most autobiographers.   Had he written it himself, the man's essential simplicity would have given it more value as an indication of his character. But inasmuch as he commissioned General von Mertz to pen the reminiscences upon the basis of his own word-of-mouth account, and then corrected and signed (as he did with many of Ludendorff's memorials, though without openly admitting the fact), he was applying to authorship his theory of military command—for has he not told us that the commander "must only lay down the broad lines, leaving details to his subordinates"?

He must surely have approved the bald and cold style of the book, for otherwise he would not have published it as his own. Nevertheless, a comparison with his letters shows that it is quite in keeping with his true style. After the battle of Königgratz, where as a lieutenant he was wounded, he wrote to his parents: "I fell unconscious, and my people thronged round me, believing me dead." But in *Aus meinem Leben* we read, "I felt a proud man and gave a sigh of relief when, bleeding from a slight wound in the head, I stood among the guns I had captured." He also roped the family in as collaborators. Had not his younger brother in a fine book already described him for the German people as long ago as 1915? "The gardener, who must then have been about eighty years of age," wrote Bernhard von Hindenburg, with reference to his brother's youth, "told him that he [the gardener] had served a fortnight as drummer boy under Frederick the Great. Thus to the youngster there came a last gleam of sunshine from that glorious past." Four years later, Hindenburg wrote, or had written for him: "I clearly recall an aged gardener, who had served for a fortnight under Frederick the Great. Thus, so to

22

say, there fell across my childhood a last sunbeam
from that glorious Frederician past."

Since Hindenburg had so precise a mind and loved
to think in figures, a few statistics about his autobiography will be in keeping. He shows amazing brevity
in dealing with his developmental period, devoting no
more than twenty pages to the first forty years, and no
more than four pages to the eight years he spent on
the General Staff. Schlieffen is mentioned once only,
quite casually; Bismarck no more than six times, almost as casually. Three lines are devoted to the visits
of the most famous aviators and submarine-boat commanders. Among the persons referred to are twenty-
six princes—no men of learning or artists with the
exception of two names in one line. All the other
persons of the drama are generals; ninety-seven of
these names are those of nobles, while only six officers
of bourgeois descent get a mention. The other bourgeois referred to in the book are enemy commanders
and statesmen.

Kings, on the other hand, occupy a disproportionate
space. Old Emperor William's habit of repeatedly
asking a question and as repeatedly forgetting the
answer is described as follows: "I was rendered happy
by my War Lord's inquiry under what circumstances
I had earned the Order with the Swords. In later
years . . . my emperor and king, when I had to
report myself to him on the occasion of transference
or promotion, often asked me the same question. Invariably I was thrilled, inspired with pride, and delighted, as at first." If he goes out shooting during
the war, we are told: "The climax is the thanks I owe
to His Majesty for the grace of being able to bring

down a particularly fine elk in the royal game preserves." When the crown prince visits him, he splurges
thus: "On the way thither, His Imperial and Royal
Highness the German Crown Prince joined us, and
honored us at Montmédy by parading a Storm Company on the platform. This reception was thoroughly
in keeping with the chivalrous temperament of that
exalted Prince, whom I was frequently to meet again."

Had the emperor had something more to say about
peace? We are told, "I was witness of the profound
sentiment of duty towards God and man with which
my All-Highest War Lord was animated with regard
to the solution of this peace move." When the
emperor congratulates him on his seventieth birthday:
"His Majesty, my Emperor, King, and Master, did
me the high honor of being the first to congratulate
me personally in my home (G. H. Q.). For me this
was the supreme consecration of the day." Once, by
a mishap, a German airplane dropped a bomb into
G. H. Q. Next day, in the garden, the emperor showed
the field marshal the shell splinters. Hindenburg
concludes his report of the incident with the moving
words, "We, likewise, then, have been in the shadow
of danger."

The colleague who "devils" for Hindenburg reserves his most unctuous phrases for the chief military
collaborator. Always considerate, he touches very
lightly upon Ludendorff's nervous crisis during the
battle of Tannenberg. Immediately after the acceptance of Ludendorff's resignation and the departure of
the chief of staff we read: "Next day I entered what
had been our joint office. I felt as if I had returned to
the deserted dwelling from the burial of an exceptionally

dear friend. Up till now (I am writing in September, 1919) I have not again seen the man who was my loyal assistant and adviser during four years. Thousands of times I have thought of him, and have never ceased to be grateful to him."

Many passages are edited for popular consumption. What need to tell common folk the truth about the dispute with Falkenhayn, which lasted two years? Why should peasants learn that there are sometimes quarrels even in the lord of the manor's palatial dwelling? The ruler must keep his doors shut, lest his vassals should lose respect for him. As regards Falkenhayn, therefore, he knew that a legend had been spun, and, when the emperor sent for himself and Ludendorff to intrust them with the supreme command of the armies in place of Falkenhayn, he was "greatly surprised," but not until he reached Pless did he know why the pair of them had been sent for. Though he had tried to down his rival for a period of eighteen months, and for excellent reasons, a reader of the memoirs might think that Hindenburg had held him in high honor. "The business of taking over from my predecessor was soon completed. As we parted, General von Falkenhayn gave me his hand with the words—'God help you and our fatherland.'" After this operatic touch, Hindenburg continues: "Neither when I took over my new office, nor later, did the emperor tell me the reason for our sudden summons to the new sphere. I never had the inclination, and at this juncture I had no time, to inquire into the matter for purely historical reasons."

Touching things up for popular consumption is not a serious offense so long as the modifications do not

involve blaming anyone. But where responsibility
for blunders is shifted to others' shoulders, Hindenburg's book acquires outstanding political importance.
"My thoughts, my actions, my mistakes, have been
but human," he writes in the preface; though in the
main text there is no word about his own mistakes.
All the mistakes were made by others! With reference
to espionage within the country, he writes: "The
German had not had enough political training to be
able to hold his tongue. He had an itch to express his
thoughts, however devastating the effect might be.
He felt the need to gratify his vanity by proclaiming
his knowledge and his feelings to the wide world. In
our great struggle for national existence, this error
cost us more than any failures on the battlefield."

After leveling this general accusation, Hindenburg
comes to the events that occurred in the autumn of
1918. On September 29, acting in conjunction with
Ludendorff, he had demanded a twenty-four-hour
truce, and had traveled to Berlin in order to compel
Prince Max to send the cablegram. Thus he was the
initiator in this turn of events. The memoirs, however, put a very different gloss on the affair.

"I wanted to be near my emperor in Berlin in case
he should need me these days. I had absolutely no
thought of interfering in political matters. . . . I was
still thoroughly convinced that, notwithstanding the
wastage of our forces, we could keep the enemy from
setting foot on the soil of the fatherland for many
months to come. Could we achieve this, the political
situation was not hopeless. . . . During the night
between the 4th and 5th of October, our peace offer
was sent to the President of the United States. . . .

Thus the final upshot of the struggle could no longer
be altered unless we succeeded in levying the last
reserves of our home forces. A mass levy of the nation
could not have failed to produce an impression upon
the enemy and upon our army. The question was,
however, whether utilizable, vigorous, and self-sacrificing masses were still available. In any case, our
attempt to mobilize such reserves was futile. The
homeland was paralyzed before the army was. In these
circumstances, we could not offer any effective resistance to the continually increasing pressure. Our
government yielded, hoping for moderation and justice.
German soldiers and German statesmen had taken
divergent paths. The gulf between them could not
be bridged."

Surely Hindenburg must have made a mistake in
declaring the Germans to be politically untrained!
Could there be a more elegant way of standing the
truth on its head? In this book intended for the
German people, not a word is said about his having
demanded a truce, about Ludendorff's having in both
their names repudiated the idea of a *levée en masse*,
that he himself, on November 10, had insisted upon
acceptance of the enemy armistice terms with his
hammering words, "nevertheless you must sign," or that
in no document issued over his signature during those
decisive six weeks was there any complaint of the
homeland. But in the aftermath he implies that a
cowardly government and an exhausted people were
to blame for all. To rub in the idea, he opens his
"Farewell" with the words:

"Like Siegfried, laid low by the treacherous spear
of the savage Hagen, our weary front collapsed."

This sentence has been repeated in thousands of
orations, and is graven on millions of German hearts.
Our young folk believe it, for they have heard nothing
else. Our soldiers were glad to hear it, because it
excused a collapse which no army in the circumstances
could have escaped. The civilians at home believed
it, because it did not lay the blame on them for
each of them regarded the others, and especially the
socialists, as the savage Hagen who had treacherously
stabbed the glorious Siegfried.

When the utterance of these words by the German
national hero had sown strife among the Germans,
David (an Aryan) declared in the Reichstag: "Hindenburg has given the weight of his authority to the
stab-in-the-back legend. . . . Nothing could be more
disastrous to the hope of reconciling our internal conflicts than the hurling of this terrible accusation
against our people, against the homeland, which
suffered unspeakably, and which did its utmost to
save us from collapse. . . . The stab in the back was
Hindenburg's telegram demanding an immediate armistice. This was a stab in the back for the troops,
among whom the belief was still general that a victory
could be gained in the field."

In a famous trial, a few years later, the decisive
importance of these words to the Republic was disclosed. The superseded military caste had a phrase
behind which it could conceal its war guilt; the
greatest authority in the country had espoused its
cause. In its official schoolbook[1] the Republic, quoting
Hindenburg, indorsed this stab-in-the-back theory of
the German defeat. The British general to whom the

[1] Quellensammlung, Teubner-Verlag, 1931.

phrase was ascribed has roundly repudiated it. As a matter of fact, Hindenburg did not invent it, but another German general did. Shortly before the emperor's abdication, General von der Schulenburg made the following recommendation, in the forlorn hope of saving the situation:

"Carefully chosen leaders of carefully selected troops should be sent immediately to Verviers, Aix, and Cologne, to restore order there by force of arms. An indispensable requisite is an effective watchword. Among our people the most effective possible watchword would be that with the aid of Jewish war profiteers and shirkers, the navy has stabbed them in the back and has cut supplies off from the army."

After Hindenburg's above-quoted account of the matter had been published, there was an increasingly vociferous chorus of German voices to the effect that victory had been "close at hand," and that only the treachery of the socialists had prevented it. The professor against whom the before-mentioned action was brought had written, "During those very October days, the chances of victory and defeat in the war as a whole hung by a silken thread." At the trial, the following type of evidence was produced as proof of this. In the hospitals the recovering wounded had refused to do the exercises prescribed to promote cure. An invalid officer declared that a tram conductress had been discourteous to him. "The soldiers of other armies have been much more moderate eaters than our German soldiers," said a colonel who had himself, no doubt, throughout the war, taken his meals in the officers' mess. An agitation against the war had been planned and carried out, it was said, by the socialists, who had from the first sabotaged the chances of victory. "We flatly deny that in the autumn of 1918 the High Command's decision to give up the struggle was brought about by the decisive numerical superiority of the enemy. If that had been the case, the collapse would have taken a very different form. The chatter about negotiations, and the whole spirit of the new government which had been at work since July 17, had poisoned the minds of the troops."

The main cause of dissatisfaction at the front was incorporated in a rimed couplet to the effect that had there been equal food and equal pay, the war would have been forgotten many a day! All that the men had really asked, however, was that the officers should not be better fed than the privates. What must the common soldier think when, as late as 1918, the menus at certain messes were still lithographed? The stab in the back, said veteran soldiers at a later date, must have been given with a dagger made out of corkscrews, can openers, and champagne-wire cutters. It is true that soldiers hounded to death in the battles of the last summer of the war called some of the youngsters who were called up to take their places "strike breakers." We know now what they had suffered for years, and what tales were being passed from mouth to mouth! Two men were sent into the trenches, through a barrage, carrying a written message: "Infantry Regiment Kirschbach, 7.10.17. Regimental order. Hindenburg's words of thanks on his seventieth birthday to be cut out of the newspapers and posted in quarters, dugouts, etc." Certainly this order was never issued by Hindenburg; but it was an idiotic order, whoever issued it; and still more idiotic were the soldiers who carried it out instead of trampling the paper in the mud.   When, returning from the front in soiled and ragged attire, they were greeted by dandified staff officers as "pigs from the trenches"; when not one among the thousands upon thousands of reserve officers could rise to a higher position on the staff;   when the callowest junior lieutenants roared abusive orders at the oldest Landsturm man—one can only account for the fact that the army at the front did not start the revolution by remembering that for two centuries it had been subjected to Prussian drill.

One wonders what the field marshal must have thought when he read the testimony of his generals. This referred, not indeed to the personal account of matters given in his memoirs of the year 1919, but to official utterances and doings of the year 1918.   The crown prince extols the fighting spirit of the troops, saying that this did not flag even during the last year of the war, and declares the cause of discontent to have been "the frightful losses of the previous three years, the prospect of further losses, emotional depression, lack of food and fuel, the failure of the submarine campaign."   General von Kuhl, who ardently defended the commanders in the Commission of Inquiry, draws the conclusion that the failure of the last offensive decided the war, but that as late as August, 1918, the troops had fought with the old fire, and adds, in the cold phrasing of a general officer, "The men of the 1899 class had been used up, and the men of the 1900 class were still immature."   The major whom, on October 1, Hindenburg sent to Berlin to tell the deputies the truth, testified, "Our troops have behaved splendidly, and retain their old

heroic ardor!" Major von Hindenburg, the nephew,
concludes his reference to his uncle's accusation of a
stab in the back with the bitter words: "The field
marshal rests assured that a stab in the back was the
cause of the German collapse. Nothing can convince him of the contrary. He cannot see the catastrophic results of Ludendorff's premature offer of an
armistice."

If the field marshal wanted a British testimony, instead of misquoting an English general, he might (later)
have found one in Winston Churchill's book on *The
World Crisis, 1916–1918*. That distinguished member
of the coalition government devotes a fine epilog not
to the German generals, but to the German people.
The field marshal might have quoted the following
passage: "Yet in the sphere of force, human records
contain no manifestation like the eruption of the
German volcano. For four years Germany fought
and defied the five continents of the world by land
and sea and air. The German army upheld her totter-
ing confederates, intervened in every theater with
success, stood everywhere on conquered territory, and
inflicted on their enemies more than twice the blood-
shed they suffered themselves. To break their strength
and science and curb their fury, it was necessary to
bring all the greatest nations of mankind into the
field against them. . . . Surely, Germans, for history
it is enough!"

How would this have been possible without the
millions in the homeland behind the fighting front?
Did the field marshal never see these people with his
own eyes before or after that evening when he ate the
famous soup at Cassel? When he was in the saloon

carriage on his way to Colberg, and subsequently
when he was returning to Hanover, was he never impressed by the wasted faces of the women and children
he must have seen in the streets and on the platforms—
women and children for whom the war had been no
picnic? Thirteen millions of Germans had been under
arms, but the remaining two-and-fifty millions had
been deceived for four years. For four years the
German nation had borne the brunt of this tremendous
war. It was the commanders that lost it.

VII

They seemed determined to refight the battles and
to win a victory in the very midst of the German
people. The memoirs had not yet appeared when, in
November 1919, Hindenburg and Ludendorff were
invited to be present at a great drama which was to
have decisive consequences for Hindenburg's personal
destiny and for the fate of Germany. The Commission of Inquiry appointed by the Reichstag to investi-
gate the catastrophe asked both the commanders to
attend. It was not a tribunal; there was no one to
condemn them, as at those courts-martial which
punished Benedek, Bazaine, and Kuropatkin for lost
wars or battles. The Commission of the Reichstag
was merely to elicit the historical proofs of important
matters. It had, indeed, judicial powers, for it could
subpoena witnesses, examine them under oath, command them or forbid them to speak; and it had fined
Helfferich 300 marks only a few days before for contempt of court. Now Ludendorff declared that he
would only enter the arena jointly with Hindenburg.

If they wanted, they could refuse to appear. What

was to be dreaded from this government of weaklings? Would the authorities send a corporal's guard of Reichswehr men and hale them to the inquiry? Not even in Ludendorff's case would public opinion have tolerated anything of the kind. If they appeared before a commission they despised, they must have had special reasons for doing so. These reasons were soon to be disclosed.

The nationalists did everything they could to convert Hindenburg's reception into a nationalist festival— drawing-room cars, companies of honor, taking-off of hats, two officers of the Reichswehr as personal adjutants, Reichswehr sentries. School children escorted by their teachers paraded before his quarters in Berlin. The Lützow volunteer corps, undisturbed by the police, hoisted an old standard dating from the Wars of Liberation, and marched through the streets, while Hindenburg looked on, bareheaded. Finally, on the morning of the reception, three hundred students arrived in gala dress, surrounded the automobile, and exclaimed, "We will not allow our greatest man to be interrogated by a lot of stupids!"

Helfferich, in front of whose house these episodes took place, since the field marshal was his guest, was one of those weathercock politicians who go to sleep overnight on the left and awake next morning on the right. When the gloomy dream of the war was over, this democrat awoke on the extreme Right, repented of his resistance to the submarine campaign, and, before the Commission of Inquiry, ardently defended everything which he had fiercely attacked three years earlier, before another commission of the Reichstag. Now he had tried to block the appointment of the

Commission of Inquiry. Not having succeeded in
doing this, he joined with some of his friends in preparing a document which they wanted the field marshal
to read aloud. Everything had been arranged with
Ludendorff, so that the utterances of the two commanders should tally. In the villa of that vice chancellor who had been the first during their joint dictatorship to venture opposition, but who had respectfully
given way when they raised their fingers threateningly,
the two commanders met again, a year and a month
since they had last forgathered at their usual hour of
the morning in Ludendorff's room, where the brain of
the German nation was spinning its plans.

Gray November light and a snowstorm; police and
machine guns guarding the Reichstag; cheers for the
occupants of the automobile, and invectives against
the Republic; Helfferich doing his best to keep step
with the field marshal on the way up the grand staircase. In the hall, Ludendorff waiting. In the anteroom,
an ovation. Bethmann-Hollweg, ignored by everyone, watching the acclamations from a sofa, smiling
bitterly. In the hall, reception by the chairman.
Everyone rose; the members of the commission, the
clerks, reporters, the ladies and gentlemen on the
platform, the diplomats of what had been enemy
States, leading painters and actors who wanted to
enjoy the spectacle. First cause of astonishment: the
commanders were in mufti. Men whom everyone had
supposed to be born in uniform had adopted the
pacific costume of the day, and, sacrificing their natural
taste, appeared in black broadcloth without shining
metal buttons. Still, even in mufti, the giant looked
imposing. When he was about to sit down, he found

in his chair a garland of white chrysanthemums, tied with a black-white-red bow, the old imperial colors. Ought the chairman to have removed the ribbons? Certainly not; it was not a flag. And who was the chairman anyway?

He was another uneasy sleeper, but a democrat at heart, or at any rate one not yet awakened from his democratic slumbers, and still lying on the left. For the first time (and for the last) the old potentates are seated before the new ones and are required to give information. There, upon the dais, sits "the people"—or such members of it as have been able to secure cards of admission. Surely the Republic must have chosen its most impassioned and shrewdest citizen to guide the proceedings on this occasion? It has merely chosen the man whose turn it happed to be. He expresses his regret to the field marshal that the latter has had to travel during a spell of such bad weather. Unfortunately General Ludendorff had insisted on his coming.

The field marshal takes the oath. At length the audience will hear his famous bass. Will the sound of it strike the new potentates to earth? What a situation for this Junker of two-and-seventy years of age! For the first time in the last two decades he has to report to someone other than his king. His own view cannot but be that those before whom he is now called to account are those who drove out his king. Will he grind them to powder with his mighty fists? Not a bit of it. Tribunes of the people will listen to the remarks of a veteran officer of the old school. A perfect gentleman. After the field marshal was sworn in, the whole company sat down again. Now Ludendorff enters, and, in biting tones, reads a legal protest in the name of both the commanders, who declare that they might refuse to give evidence, since by giving evidence they expose themselves to the risk of prosecution. Their testimony will be an infringement of the Official Secrets Act. Nevertheless, they have come to make it clear to the German people what really happened. Now the courteous chairman turns to Hindenburg:

"The questions were sent to you, Your Excellency. The first one relates to the submarine campaign."

Hindenburg, also extremely courteous: "Before I answer this question as it is my duty to do, I must beg leave to read a brief explanation of the basis of all our thoughts and actions during the war period, since these reasons formed the motive for everything we did."

Will it be possible to refuse the grim soldier's polite request? "Field marshal," said the chairman, "we had not intended to allow lengthy documents to be read to the Commission, which is only concerned with the eliciting of facts. I do not know how far the exposition which the field marshal wishes to read aloud is concerned with the exposition of facts. For the moment, the Commission wishes to avoid any expression of opinion." Already the chairman has weakened his position. The chairman is a mining expert, civil servant of the old régime, elected by the Commission chosen by the parliamentary deputies of the Republic. Today he, and not the field marshal, represents the German nation. He has sent to the two commanders six questions, precisely worded, as usual among officers and officials. Why does he not insist upon his submarine campaign? Why does he speak in the third person? Must not such a subservient method of address arouse in the field marshal's mind the impression that he himself is here supreme? When he was a lad of ten, a boy-Junker, did not the peasants already address him in the third person, and after them a whole army of common soldiers, orderlies, and officers? Would it ever occur to *him*, in speaking to that poor civilian, to say "the chairman has" instead of simply "you have"? His tone as he answers has already become, by two degrees more, that of the army officer of high rank:

"I purpose only to give historical data; but I regard it as absolutely indispensable that I should read my brief text in order to remind you of them." The implication is, that they must have forgotten everything by now! Besides, he knows perfectly well that the paper he holds in his hand contains something very different from mere data. Now would be the moment for the presiding citizen to inform the subpœnaed Junker that he is not entitled to read his document aloud. But the field marshal has made a strong impression upon Citizen Gothein. Is not the witness the victor of Tannenberg? Is a common citizen to take such a man to task? Hindenburg puts on a great pair of tortoise-shell-framed spectacles, holds up his document, and begins to read in the confident tone of a historian, thus:

"When the High Command was intrusted to our charge, the World War had already been in progress two years. Sustained by the love of our fatherland, we had only one aim, to protect the German empire and the German people from injury, and to work for a good peace. To this end, the will to victory was essential. This was linked with faith in the justice of our

23

cause.   A general who does not intend to fight for the
victory of his country should not feel at liberty to take
over the supreme command unless he has been given
orders to capitulate.   We had received no such instructions.   Indeed, we should have refused to
accept them. . . . Our policy was frustrated! We did
not want war, and yet we began the greatest . . .

The chairman rang his bell. "Hindenburg," so runs
the report, "gave a nervous twitch, looked astonished,
and broke off in the middle of his sentence."   Something almost incredible had happened.   A man, indeed,
a bell, had interrupted Hindenburg!   But a second
unprecedented thing had happened.   Hindenburg was
nervous.   Can we be surprised?   Is such a man as
he, at the age of seventy-two, to allow himself to be
interrupted by a civilian?   Look back into the record
of his life, and you will find that, not only in youth,
but also at forty years of age, he knew how to stand at
attention when an officer of higher rank appeared.
But, since he had never before been called as a witness
in the law courts, he had never been confronted with
a civilian power superior to his own.   This is the first
time in his life when he has been interrupted by a
civilian.   What was Citizen Gothein saying?

"One moment, please!   That is an expression of
opinion, to which, therefore, I must object."   Thus,
with the utmost courtesy, did the chairman explain
the reason for the interruption.   Will Hindenburg grow
violent?   Not yet.   This Junker is a gentleman, although he is a giant.   By a stiff nod, he indicates that
he will comply with the admonition.   What will he
do next?   All look intently at the distinguished
veteran.   He makes a splendid impression.   The

warrior, who has always been at war with the "subtleties of the intellect," finds the right thing to do. He nods dumbly, acknowledging the admonition—and the incident is over. Consequently, looking through his spectacles at the document he is holding in his hand, he goes on reading, with imperturbable tranquillity:

". . . And yet we began the greatest, the most difficult, the most pitiless war known to history." Unhappy president! It is already eleven, and his submarines are drifting away! He sits there, listening anxiously amid the smiles of the audience—for in courts of justice as in the theater, the gallery never applauds right or justice, but always victorious cunning—while the great basso profundo continues:

"I know only one thing with absolute certainty, that the German people did not want the war, that the German emperor did not want it, that the government did not want it, and above all that the General Staff did not want it, for the General Staff knew better than anyone else how terribly difficult would be our position in a war against the Entente." Now he was in full swing; the rebuttal of the accusation was the stepping-stone to the formulation of an accusation of his own. Here it comes! "Nevertheless we could have conducted this incredibly difficult struggle to a favorable end had there been a firm and harmonious coöperation between the fighting front and the noncombatants at home. That, as we saw the matter, was the way in which a victory of the German cause could have been assured. But while in enemy lands all parties worked together as one man, here, in Germany, partisan interests disclosed themselves. . . ."

Bell! But this time he is used to it; this time he

knows that the interruption signifies nothing; he merely breaks off and lifts his eyes. Will the president at length cut him short? Will the field marshal be told that he has not been summoned thither to accuse his German compatriots and the political parties which he detests? Will not the republic at length assert itself against this monarchist, in a pithy, resolute phrase? Nothing of the sort. A courteous voice says:

"Field marshal, that is an expression of opinion [the mining expert's favorite term!], of your private opinion, regarding the people in the interior of Germany, away from the fighting front. The Commission has decided that no such expressions of opinion shall be allowed. I am sorry that I cannot make an exception in the field marshal's case to the decision unanimously and repeatedly arrived at by the members of the Commission. I must therefore request that this passage be left out." Far too many words of humble apology! Surely the witness is justified in sticking to his now well-tried technique, and in continuing to read in his tranquil bass voice:

". . . and these circumstances very soon led to a cleavage and dissipation of the will to victory."

Bell again, that horrid bell! "That, likewise, is an expression of opinion, against which I protest." Disorder among the audience. The chairman admonishes the gallery and the press. "Let me beg . . ." But Hindenburg, having thundered his accusation into the hall, and thence into the world at large, seemed to yield, now speaking extempore: "History will give its final judgment upon that which I am here forbidden to utter." With the word "forbidden" he had completely won the sympathy of the audience, so that he could now proceed without hindrance in his invectives against the noncombatants—

"I wanted vigorous and cheerful collaborators, and found instead shirkers and weaklings."

The mining expert was growing more and more uneasy. Since he did not dare to take decisive measures, he adopted a policy of pin pricks. Since he could not orate, he had recourse to the same foolish phrase, "expression of opinion," which he now used for the fifth time, adding—"against which I must decisively protest."

"The noncombatants in our rear," rejoined the bass of the imperturbable hero, who was now about to deliver his main thrust, "the noncombatants in our rear failed, from this moment, to support us. Anxiety as to whether we could depend upon the noncombatants in our rear never left us. . . . At this time there began a furtive but deliberate undermining of the morale of the navy and the army as the continuation of similar phenomena in peace time. . . . Our brave soldiers, who held aloof from revolutionary contagion, suffered severely from the undutiful behavior of their revolutionary comrades."

Now he has got it off his chest! It was to utter this sentence in this hall that the field marshal had come from Hanover. Summoned to declare why he had decided upon submarine warfare in spite of the effect this was likely to have upon America, and why he had insisted upon an armistice, he had been able, in the innermost cell of the detested Republic, actually in the Reichstag, and before the world assembled, to accuse the party which had created and sustained this Republic. What now? Will the chairman withdraw,

to make up his mind about the witness's behavior?
"Disorder," we read in the report.   Discussion of the
chairman, aside with two deputies.   After this brief
conversation, he turns back to the witness and says:
"Please continue, Field Marshal!"

In exactly the same tone (for what difference can
the civilian's permission now make to him?) Hindenburg finishes his indictment:

"These plans of the army command could no longer
be carried out.   Our repeated demands for stricter
discipline and for new legislation were not complied
with.   Thus the failure of our operations and the consequent collapse became inevitable.   The revolution
was merely the climax. . . .   A British general has
said with good reason that the German army was
stabbed in the back. . . .   There you have the fundamental cause of the tragic upshot of the war as
far as Germany is concerned, after a series of brilliant
and unprecedented successes upon numerous fronts."

To these victorious trumpetings, the chairman had
no answer ready, and therefore cut a poor figure.
Making no attempt to ward off the accusation, he was
content to say: "May I ask you to be good enough to
answer a question, 'Why did you decide to inaugurate
the submarine campaign?' "

Hindenburg: "Because there was no other way of
relieving the pressure upon our western front and of
inducing in our enemies a willingness to make peace.
. . .   There was no other method of ending the war."

When it was Ludendorff's turn to be examined, the
chairman was curter with the man who had only been
an army commander, and was not a popular hero.

Ludendorff's irritable voice rang through the court;

he stormed and raged; there were clashes between him
and the chairman about the famous question of "matters of opinion," Ludendorff shouting, when chidden
on this account, "What is a fact and what is a
matter of opinion? I am giving sworn evidence here!
If you forbid me to say what I want, I cannot answer
to my conscience!" Thereupon the members of the
Commission retired to discuss the question in private,
and the proceedings were interrupted for half an hour.
The onlookers seized the opportunity of leaving their
seats and forming a circle round the two commanders,
who were commanders of the hall of inquiry as they
had been commanders of the army. When the proceedings were resumed, there was a dispute between
Bethmann-Hollweg (who had been called as a witness)
and Count Bernstorff on one side, and the two commanders on the other. Hindenburg declared that the
United States had "from the first been in collusion with
the Entente," and would have come into the war
against Germany in any case. Bernstorff, who had
been ambassador in Washington from 1908 until
America joined the Allies, repudiated the notion.
Ludendorff thumped the table, shouting: "That's
one of the infamous lies spread among the people,
that we have been responsible for everything! On
the contrary, we both of us acted throughout with
absolute loyalty . . . ! Oh, yes, I don't deny for a
moment that Count Bernstorff is a man I cannot
endure. He lied to the chancellor about Wilson.
He was responsible for the vacillation in the matter
of the submarine campaign, for the vacillation which
could not fail in the end to bring America and other
neutrals into the war against us! . . . Count Bernstorff

declares that I did not want peace! [A thump on the table.] I never said any such thing! I insist that the field marshal and my other colleagues shall be asked whether I did not wish peace for the German people! To say such a thing is to mock at the sense of responsibility by which I am animated."

Bernstorff repelled this onslaught with a tranquil mien. Now, however, Hindenburg intervened, saying: "Most explicitly, and with the utmost indignation, I repudiate the charge which has been brought against my collaborator. . . . I doubt if the members of this Commission have a sense of duty towards their country as great as that which has inspired General Ludendorff and myself for years!"

Not even now is there any protest. Not even now does the thunder of another voice answer Hindenburg's. Not even now does the government engineer-chairman espouse the cause of the German nation, or that of the members of the Commission and of the Reichstag, who have all lost sons and brothers in the war. Why not? Because it is two o'clock; everyone is hungry, luncheon is waiting (a hearty luncheon for some, and a meager one for others); and when the modest civilian asks the two commanders whether they will return in the afternoon, they reply that they have another engagement. They never attended any further sittings of the Commission of Inquiry. They drove away, with an escort of police and Reichswehr men, amid the cheers of the populace.

The man who grasped the significance of this scene before it was finished, was an unknown officer who, while it was in progress, addressed the crowd assembled outside the Reichstag, shouting, regardless of the could now proceed without hindrance in his invectives against the noncombatants—

"I wanted vigorous and cheerful collaborators, and found instead shirkers and weaklings."

The mining expert was growing more and more uneasy. Since he did not dare to take decisive measures, he adopted a policy of pin pricks. Since he could not orate, he had recourse to the same foolish phrase, "expression of opinion," which he now used for the fifth time, adding—"against which I must decisively protest."

"The noncombatants in our rear," rejoined the bass of the imperturbable hero, who was now about to deliver his main thrust, "the noncombatants in our rear failed, from this moment, to support us. Anxiety as to whether we could depend upon the noncombatants in our rear never left us. . . . At this time there began a furtive but deliberate undermining of the morale of the navy and the army as the continuation of similar phenomena in peace time. . . . Our brave soldiers, who held aloof from revolutionary contagion, suffered severely from the undutiful behavior of their revolutionary comrades."

Now he has got it off his chest! It was to utter this sentence in this hall that the field marshal had come from Hanover. Summoned to declare why he had decided upon submarine warfare in spite of the effect this was likely to have upon America, and why he had insisted upon an armistice, he had been able, in the innermost cell of the detested Republic, actually in the Reichstag, and before the world assembled, to accuse the party which had created and sustained this Republic. What now? Will the chairman withdraw,

to make up his mind about the witness's behavior?
"Disorder," we read in the report. Discussion of the
chairman, aside with two deputies. After this brief
conversation, he turns back to the witness and says:
"Please continue, Field Marshal!"

In exactly the same tone (for what difference can
the civilian's permission now make to him?) Hindenburg finishes his indictment:

"These plans of the army command could no longer
be carried out. Our repeated demands for stricter
discipline and for new legislation were not complied
with. Thus the failure of our operations and the consequent collapse became inevitable. The revolution
was merely the climax. . . . A British general has
said with good reason that the German army was
stabbed in the back. . . . There you have the fundamental cause of the tragic upshot of the war as
far as Germany is concerned, after a series of brilliant
and unprecedented successes upon numerous fronts."

To these victorious trumpetings, the chairman had
no answer ready, and therefore cut a poor figure.
Making no attempt to ward off the accusation, he was
content to say: "May I ask you to be good enough to
answer a question, 'Why did you decide to inaugurate
the submarine campaign?' "

Hindenburg: "Because there was no other way of
relieving the pressure upon our western front and of
inducing in our enemies a willingness to make peace.
. . . There was no other method of ending the war."

When it was Ludendorff's turn to be examined, the
chairman was curter with the man who had only been
an army commander, and was not a popular hero.

Ludendorff's irritable voice rang through the court;

At the funeral of his wife

police: "This moment is one of historical importance! It is fundamental to the national resistance of our people! The men who protected Germany's honor throughout four long years have just entered that doorway in order to promote the victory of German truth! Hail to them! Our people are awakening! The members of this Commission are really those who betrayed the German people!"

VIII

In the seventy-fifth year of his life, Hindenburg suffered the most cruel blow he had ever experienced. His wife died after their marriage had lasted forty years. The photographers, who since the days of Tannenberg had been more assiduous in their attentions than had pleased him, have preserved an image of him as chief mourner on this occasion—a human document, all the more impressive because the field marshal is in full panoply, much bestarred, surrounded by uniforms and banners, as prescribed by his rank and the custom of his fathers. Among the thousand photographs showing Hindenburg during and after the war, and also in the days of the final disaster, there is not one to be compared with this picture. Heartfelt sorrow! There is nothing to mitigate it, nor to make his aspect symbolical. An old, old man has lost his only friend. The giant looks broken.

With like feelings, a few years later, Ebert's wife stood beside her husband's grave. The biological conditions which, in the case of such unions, make the husband outlive the wife, or the wife the husband, are not wholly determined by the greater exertions of the husband or the greater sacrifices of the wife. Mystical interconnections are also at work, and we cannot decide whether it is more natural that a man should become a widower or that a woman should become a widow. Bismarck once said defiantly: "I should not like to die and leave my wife alone; but neither should I like her to die and leave me alone." His vitality, like Hindenburg's, exceeded the wife's.

Ebert's death in harness brought new confusion into German political life. His appointment as first president of the Republic had been no more than the confirmation of an outstanding position already held. The spectacle of the election which followed his death is significant because now for the first time in their history the Germans were called upon to select as chief one who recommended himself both to their heads and to their hearts. "What will they do?" was the eager question of the onlooking world. Each party presented its own candidate, so that instead of there being a choice between two conspicuous figures, there was a choice from among nine persons, mere politicians, not one of whom was widely known to the people, though among them were a man of learning and a general. Even the man of learning, though distinguished and able enough, had a name known only to the members of his own party and to his South German compatriots. The general was an exception as regards reputation, for the general was Ludendorff.

If one were under the spell of the popular belief according to which the Germans were really still to be regarded as a nation of poets and thinkers, a dozen names might occur to him of persons suitable to become the figurehead of Germany. Not so much as individuals, but as types, I will mention the names of Max

Weber, Simons, Bosch, Eckener—men of learning, discoverers in the practical or theoretical field—suited by
age and versatility, by their knowledge of the structure
of society, and by the liberality of their views, to
occupy the leading place in the German political
organism; safe and moderate, and not likely to be
driven to extreme courses by any alarm; worthy and
solid persons. Not one of those names, nor any of
their kind, was put forward. When, six years earlier,
in the Weimar Assembly, a group of German émigrés
had wired recommending the nomination of Walter
Rathenau as president, the report tells us that the
reading of this proposal was received with "Laughter!"

Only 69 per cent of the Germans took any interest in
this first of their popular elections. The leaders of the
Right and of the Left received eight million and ten
million votes respectively; Ludendorff, no more than
a quarter of a million. During the second ballot, the
Left joined forces with the Center in favor of Marx, the
Centrist leader; and all the parties of the Right were
likewise inclined to concentrate upon their candidate,
a mayor. The men of the Right, however, soon came
to recognize that they had no chance at the polls,
since their nominee was practically unknown. Within
four weeks, a decision must be come to concerning the
representative head of the country for the next seven
years. Everyone was trying to think of a name
which would make a wide appeal, until someone
shouted: "Columbus's egg! Hindenburg!" Such an
idea would have been possible only in a new State, the
internal causes of whose weakness have already been
discussed. The field marshal's brilliant victory over
the Commission of Inquiry seemed to hold out

prospects of success. Since that victory had been possible five years ago, how easy it would be to secure a
majority of votes in his favor. The unknown officer
who at that time had harangued the crowd outside
the Reichstag had been a prophet.

Promptly, however, doubts arose. Would there not
be an inclination to compare Hindenburg with Mac-
Mahon, who, as president of the Third (French) Republic,
had only wished to function as the deposed emperor's
viceroy? What view would be taken abroad? inquired
Stresemann warningly. Should Hindenburg become
president, would not Germany lose moral credit in
foreign lands, and, still worse, lose the power of borrowing hard cash? Hindenburg, however, was approached,
and refused to entertain the idea of standing for the
presidency. Great perplexity on the Right, and a deep
breath of relief on the other side. The Junkers, the
army officers, the great industrialists—all those who
had ruled Germany in the old days, and who, after six
years of republican impoverishment, had made up their
minds to rule Germany once more—got together again,
in order to exert moral pressure on Hindenburg. With
him as figurehead, they thought, they would easily be
able to get their own way; he would look imposing,
and would agree to whatever they wanted. Admiral
Tirpitz, at the outset of the war ten years ago, had
pointed to Hindenburg as born for the chancellorship—he would be the man to persuade the old fellow!
Tirpitz had been the first to grasp the political value
of the legend, writing privately to a friend that,
though he knew practically nothing about Hindenburg,
he was sure Hindenburg would be the best chancellor.
If Hindenburg persisted in his refusal, then Tirpitz

himself would be willing to stand. It was April 6, 1925.
One may suppose that when Tirpitz entered Hindenburg's study, the *Kreuz-Zeitung* was lying on the
table, as it had lain day after day for sixty years. At
the outset of the revolution it had dropped the motto
"Mit Gott, für König und Vaterland," for no one
knew what was going to happen. Still, it had speedily
regained its courage, and for the last six years had
been spitting forth venom against the "Red Jewish
Republic," to indoctrinate its readers, including those
in Hindenburg's house. Now the two old men sat
face to face—Tirpitz, who was seventy-six, and had a
long, white beard; and Hindenburg, who was seventy-
seven, and wore a big, gray mustache. They argued
with one another. Hindenburg's nephew, the major,
would seem to have become acquainted with both
their views at first hand, for he writes:

"The field marshal was clearly of opinion that this
step would involve a breach with his traditions, since,
should he be elected, it would be incumbent upon him
to become the chief and most loyal guardian of the
Weimar constitution. How could he reconcile that
with the oath he had sworn to the emperor? Tirpitz
explained to him that, since he was the darling of the
people, it was his duty to obey the call of the majority.
No doubt it would be a sacrifice, but it was a
sacrifice which Field Marshal Hindenburg must make
to the German people. But," adds the younger
Hindenburg, "the admiral kept to himself the fact
that in many circles, no less solid and no less patriotic,
there would be strong objections to the field marshal's
election as president of the republic. A lot of people
besides Stresemann were afraid that Hindenburg's

election would have an unfortunate effect abroad. They did not believe that the veteran soldier, in view of his education and the traditions which had been operative upon him throughout life, would be able, with the best will in the world, to display sufficient impartiality to overcome the one-sided influence of his closest associates (persons who belonged to the Right), and to devote himself whole-heartedly to the service of the new form of State."

Hindenburg said he must have three days to think things over. What were his reflections?

Hanover, "the dullest town in Germany," had not become livelier since the days of Werther's Lotte or those of the Duke of Cumberland's cream-colored stallions. When, out for his constitutional, the field marshal had taken a look at the winged victory on the Waterloo column in the big drill ground, and at the Guelph charger whose equilibrium is a perpetual mystery; when he had walked down the fine Linden Allée, or, in Döhren Park, had perhaps seen one of the roe deer that graze in freedom on the turf—he might perhaps visit the famous hothouse whose roof had to be raised every five years or so because it sheltered the tallest palms in Europe. Here, too, he could look at the original of the little phœnix palm which had followed him as centerpiece on his table throughout his wanderings in the war. Twice a week, in the gardens of an inn on the shore of the Eilenriede, like all pensioned officers before him, he could sit down to drink his noonday glass of wine.

That was all there was to do, now that his wife was no longer with him to talk over the promotions in that damned Reichswehr, where most of his nephews and the sons of his friends held commissions, or to hear his mingled hopes, fears, and suspicions about the latest news from Doorn, whither their distressful glances were continually turning. The city and the great house wherein he dwelt had lost interest for him now that she with whom he had always lived on such excellent terms had departed. Hindenburg's decision, these days, would probably have been different had it meant leaving a comfortable home with his wife, of whom history has no words of ambition to record.

That was what he had vowed in earlier days when she was still with him. "I love to think how, as soon as the war is over, I shall buy myself a cotton umbrella. As soon as peace is made, I shall ride beside my emperor through the Brandenburg Gate to the palace, to join in the festivities there. Then I shall take a cab to the station, travel back to my dear old wife, and no one will see me again!"

Yes, with the emperor! Colonel Bauer writes: "His attitude towards the emperor was that of one who thought and felt wholly as a soldier, and never transcended that of an officer bound by the military oath. This oath, furthermore, had become a perennial element of his being, rooted in the simple and straightforward, but profoundly devout temperament of the field marshal." This is perfectly true! Did he not avow his faith at the end of his memoirs, writing: "Then, from the tempestuous sea of our national life will once more emerge that rock to which the hope of our fathers clung in days of yore—the German Imperial House!"

What about that oath now? Had not the emperor solemnly freed his officers and officials from their

obligations? Had not thousands sworn loyalty to the
new constitution, while remaining at heart convinced
monarchists? He, he alone, three years after being thus
absolved, had written to the emperor on his own
initiative in the year 1922, saying that he would always
regard himself as inviolably bound to his imperial
master. But what if both obligations could be. combined? Was not his country still the one which had
been and was so dear to his emperor and king? Would
not William himself wish that a man of the good old
stock should rule it, instead of one of those red rascals
who had driven His Majesty out? What if the country
took a higher place than the king, substituted for the
king when the king disappeared, being fixed in perpetuity whereas human beings wander from place to place?

His unhappy fatherland was forsaken? No one but
himself, so Tirpitz had assured him, was so well able
as Hindenburg to guide its destinies with the strong
hand; but he himself, the admiral, if the field marshal
refused, would spring into the breach. Certainly he
was not too old, for during these six tranquil years he
had grown younger rather than older. Had not the
task really been consigned to him? Administrative
work on the grand scale, such as he was accustomed to;
service, as when he had ruled the army, tranquilly
and yet energetically holding people together. Authority—that was what the people needed! Who could
wield so much authority as himself in German-speaking
lands? They had to be kept under command. The
man who commanded them must live in a palace so that
he might inspire his subjects with reverence. He was
familiar with its marble halls. As lieutenant he had
danced there. . . . The headquarters' special train,

which had been at his service for four years, would be
at his service once more, but a finer one still; the gala
evenings of Magdeburg would be renewed but on a
grander scale than ever. He would give a dignified
reception to the white-haired generals who had once
been his rivals. To become sovereign ruler! That
was the highest grade of promotion. Had he not
substantially ruled the country already in the emperor's
name just after William's departure? Was he now to
leave the field open to these poltroons of parliamentarians, to these civilian hares, who interrupted him
with their talk of "matters of opinion," and then
timidly allowed him to say his say after all?

Constitution! The oath he had sworn, he would
keep. Let none believe that an honorable veteran like
himself would play a double game! If his old-time
comrades fancied that he was going to bring back the
emperor, they were mistaken! What need to do that,
anyhow, since power was gradually being resumed by
the hands that had been born to wield it? For there
was nothing in the constitution forbidding him to rule
the land with the aid of his peers. If he rose to power,
he would know how to strengthen his own class without transcending the limits of the constitution. The
German nobles had not been expelled as they had been
from Russia. Titles had not been abolished as they
had been in Austria. In the new State, where all
classes were equal, any gentleman could maintain his
own rights. Could he refuse to give his class the
support to which it was legally entitled? Would he
not become, as it were, commander in chief of the
Reichswehr, thus returning to his accustomed position?
After all, he was as good a man as Tirpitz, and could

24

do anything that Tirpitz could do; besides, Tirpitz was his inferior in rank.

There was no conflict between the two oaths. Render unto Caesar the things which are Caesar's —a profoundly monarchical sentiment, which Hindenburg would always abide by . . . But the old man's energies were his country's, and to reëstablish his country upon a sound foundation was a veteran's duty.

On this occasion, to follow the call of duty meant to overcome one's own inclinations? To a large extent, yes! He would probably have quarrels with this Reichstag, or at least with its ministers. The common people, who, since his early youth, had never been anything for him but persons born to obey, would send delegates to his palace—a peasant, a workman. Perhaps some day a private soldier would come to him as minister of State, or maybe a corporal! It was no small sacrifice he was being called upon to make. If you scrutinize it, the sacrifice was enormous.

Still, Tirpitz was right; one must be willing to make sacrifices! Twice, already, he had tried to retire from public activities but had not been allowed. Service goes on.

IX

The name of Hindenburg appeared before the German elector in letters of flame. He was to choose a chief for himself and his fellows; and, as far as a body could understand, only two requisites were demanded of this chief, who must be a man with a talent for politics and must be a republican. Hindenburg had repudiated both these qualities, declaring himself a monarchist, and a man averse from politics. For that very reason! declared half the Germans. For that very reason? inquired the foreign world. Don't forget that he is the victor of Tannenberg! insisted the Germans. Since, unfortunately, owing to their universal departure, there were no longer any princes before whom they could stand at attention, at any rate they wanted a general in a brilliant uniform whose passing they could greet as they stood on the sidewalk. The Right block therefore found a vigorous catchword for the election by saying: "Hindenburg has made the great sacrifice of becoming candidate for the presidency. We regard it as the obvious duty of all Germans both in town and countryside to devote their utmost energies to securing the return of our Hindenburg." The reasons for his election were thus typically Prussian: the old gentleman must be repaid for the sacrifice he was making, and must therefore be elected. A man in uniform must once more become the figurehead of the realm. By electing him, we make him once more a conqueror although he really was one before. That was how the Germans represented the matter to themselves, fulfilling their secret dreams by electing as president the veteran general, the true-blue, the man of the old nobility, the man with a tender kernel in a rough shell, and one who shunned no sacrifice. Throughout his life, Hindenburg had the good fortune, or the shrewdness, never to find his sense of duty in conflict with his wishes.

With mingled pride and modesty, he spoke only of duty in his appeal to the electors: "My life is open to the world. I believe that in difficult times I did my duty. If duty has now called me, upon the platform of the constitution, regardless of parties or personalities, my origin, and my occupation, to become president of the realm, I will not fail to respond to the call. As a soldier, I invariably considered the nation as a whole and not the parties. Parties are, of course, necessary in a State under parliamentary government; but the head of the State must stand above parties, and must act on behalf of every German irrespective of parties. . . . Just as the first president, when guardian of the constitution, never repudiated his origin from among the social-democratic workers; so, in this case, no one will expect me to repudiate my political convictions. . . . I stretch forth my hand to every German who thinks nationally, who does his best to maintain the dignity of the German name both at home and abroad, and who desires peace among the religions; and I say to him, 'Join with me in helping to bring about the reëstablishment of our fatherland!'"

Since not a single German could fail to understand this patriarchal tone, no one troubled to point out how absurd it was, in one and the same breath, to compare his own record and Ebert's with the spirit of the Republic; and the Catholics and the Jews had received in this appeal and statement of platform a special assurance of consideration.

But he surprised his supporters. They had hoped that they would have nothing more to do than to bring him electoral addresses to sign, while he sat quietly in his big armchair. Instead of that, he hurled himself into the electoral struggle, for, aged though he was, he remained a soldier at heart, and did not wish to be defeated as his sometime assistant Ludendorff had been defeated four weeks earlier.

"When we arrived with our portfolios stuffed full of

papers," relates one of his assistants, "he examined every sentence, every word, and usually simplified the drafts." He was also careful to keep on good terms with the journalists, receiving them in companies or singly. He no longer had a Ludendorff to represent him in these matters as he had had during the war; the victory would be a very personal one; he felt this, and took the field on his own account.

When asked whether he had requested the emperor's permission before standing in the election, he replied: "It is utterly false to say that I did anything of the kind. As regards this matter, I have not got in touch with the House of Hohenzollern." This was the first time that Hindenburg spoke, like one of the Reds, of the "House of Hohenzollern." In his memoirs, he had splashed the royal titles all over the place. He showed quite a humorous vein in his dealings with the press, which is apt to be skeptical: "A veteran like myself is not inclined to use many words. . . . I want to restore peace to Germany. I am not, as my opponents declare, a militarist. I am not a mass murderer, though it is a fact that in war time very little regard can be taken for the personal safety of individuals. Let me repeat, on the other hand, that I am not an old, old man in a wheel chair, as some people try to make out. Not yet; and, by God's will, not for a long time to come!" With these words he won the hearts of something like a hundred journalists, and, through their instrumentality, several millions of readers. To a representative of the Hearst press, he said: "People declare that I am not a professional politician. Everyone knows that contemporary professional politicians are apt to be little suited to become real political leaders. If politics are made too much a matter of business, the politicians concerned lack authority." "How true!" said his German adversaries, when they read these words, which found an echo across the seas. "I was getting into a rut," he said on another occasion. "Now I have been rejuvenated!"

Within a week, by such vigorous words, Hindenburg had made many doubters espouse his cause. He knew well enough, too, although he had often made a mock of pacifism, that it was necessary, at this juncture, to pose more or less as a pacificist. "Anyone who has seen as much of war as I have," he said, "does not want to see another." He added, however: "The German people will rise again, but I shall not be there. My son will take part in the resurrection. . . . God has perhaps preserved me for so long that my son may be enabled to witness what is denied to me. Yes, Germany will rise again!" What, as a veteran soldier, he meant by this "rise again," was disclosed by the words that his son would "take part in" the resurrection! A few years before, he had said to the youths of Hanover: "I shall not be alive then, but from heaven I shall be watching when you young fellows march into Paris!"

For all this, the election showed only a small majority in his favor: Hindenburg received 14.6 million votes as against 13.8 million votes for Marx, the Catholic. He would never have been elected had not the communists, out of hatred for their brethren, split off their two million votes, which were given to a candidate of their own. At this second ballot, three million more Germans voted than on the first occasion. Who were these three millions? Persons with little interest in politics, disgruntled folk, petty bourgeois who rarely left their houses, and had never voted before; impoverished members of the lower middle class, whom the war had robbed of their all. For the first time in their lives did they cast a voting paper into the urn, for their hearts had been touched. "The loyal old man, who fought so long in our behalf, the good field marshal, who has had such grievous personal losses—we must stand by him whatever happens!"

His son, who had been totaling up the results received by wireless, and at first had despaired of success, waked his father in the morning to tell him (such is the painter's report): "Father, you are president of the German realm!"

"Is that so?" replied Hindenburg. "May God give me His blessing in my new position. Well, I think I will turn over and get some more sleep."

At this same hour, some friends came to see Hindenburg's opponent Marx, who said cheerfully: "I went to sleep last night at nine. But just now, when my sister cried as she brought in my coffee, I guessed at once that the election must have gone against me!"

So great was the impetus of the two men who had been picked out as candidates by the German people when, for the first time after a thousand years, it set itself in motion to elect a chief.

On a brilliant May morning, a week later, the new president traveled to Berlin by special train. Things were much as they had been on such journeys in war time, except that the receptions were on a grander scale: companies of honor; chancellor in a swallow-tail coat; little girls with flowers to present and poetical addresses to read; enormous crowds, shouting and cheering. What a pity that, in front of the automobile, the detested colors of the Republic were waving over the radiators! Slowly the car drove through the Tiergarten and approached the Victory Gate. Twice before had Hindenburg, in youth, to the accompaniment of martial music, decorated with orders, and with a smiling countenance, driven along this route among conquerors. Occasionally, at G. H. Q., he had spoken of a third time yet to come. Were not the spirits of the former kings present in the air, when, under the shadow of the great gate, the automobile drove through the central arch usually closed to all but the emperor? Was he the emperor's successor? What a strange fulfilment; but there was one thing lacking! The sword, to whose metallic clanking he had become accustomed throughout his long life, was no longer buckled to his side; and when he raised his fingers to his head in the salute, it was not, as it had been for sixty years past, to touch the brim of a helmet, but that of a tall hat. This seemed a strange way of returning the salutations of the populace. Among the mass of soldiers lining the route, Hindenburg was today the only civilian.

When next day he entered the great hall of the Reichstag, the representatives of the people rose to receive him. Flowers adorned the big room and the presidential dais; from the galleries thousands of eyes looked at him. The place was packed with foreign attachés wearing uniforms which a few years before had been the uniforms of enemies; and with ladies in thin, bright-colored dresses, for it was May. With a firm tread, the giant mounted the steps. Who was waiting there to receive him? A dwarf. A dwarf with a very ordinary face—for that is what Loebe, the president of the Reichstag, looked like beside the mighty form of Hindenburg. What was lying on the desk in front of him? The formal oath in huge letters so that the old gentleman would not need to wear spectacles. But what was that shining from beneath the oath—with what colors was the table decked? It was decked with a black-red-gold cover.

The Junker glared at the colors he had learned to hate in early youth. Black-red-gold had been the flag which had alarmed his father and his mother in the days of the revolution, when, as a little boy, he lay in his cradle. Black-red-gold had been the banner of those German enemies one of whose bullets had wounded his head when, as a lad of eighteen, he had narrowly escaped with his life. Black-red-gold banners were insignia of this Republic, detested by all good Junkers, to whose constitution he was now to swear fealty.

But he stood upright. From the hands of the little workman whom the representatives of the German people had chosen to preside over the Reichstag, the man who had been chosen as chief of the German nation took the formula of the oath. Just sixty years before, he had sworn a long oath of fealty to his king, appealing to Jesus Christ the Redeemer, and solemnly pledging himself for all time to remain the king's vassal. Before he could appear in the Reichstag as president of the German realm that day, he had had to compromise, after his own manner, with that former oath. If he now swore a new oath, he would keep it no less firmly than he had kept the old; such was his fixed determination. The mighty bass thundered through the hall:

"I swear by God the Almighty and All-Knowing to devote my energies to the welfare of the German people, to promote its advantage, to avert from it all harm, to safeguard the constitution and the laws of the realm, to fulfil my duties conscientiously, and to be just to everyone.   So help me, God!"

It is said that his voice trembled a little as he uttered the last words.   It was not without an undercurrent of dismay that the numerous auditors listened to the words of this oath as they fell from the old man's lips.

"Long live the president of the realm," shouted the little proletarian.   The gigantic field marshal looked at Loebe.   Before his eyes were glowing the black-red-gold colors.

BOOK FOUR

BETWEEN THE FLAGS

Man cannot exist without authority, and yet authority brings with it as much error as truth. It perpetuates in the individual what ought to be transient for individuals; it repudiates and dissipates what ought to be firmly retained; and it is the chief reason why mankind does not advance.

—GOETHE

BETWEEN THE FLAGS

I

HINDENBURG had become a monarch. When
Cromwell, long before, rose from the position
of a minor country gentleman to be the commander
of great armies, then becoming Lord Protector, he
surrounded himself with monarchical forms, and was
at one time almost inclined to accept the crown which
was offered him. At first a loyal servant of his king,
he had fought for years against Charles, had conquered the monarch, and, amid much spiritual pertur-
bation, had handed the king over to trial and execution.
When subsequently the Lord Protector grew old in
the king's palace, he was stirred by memories of a
great past.

Although Hindenburg's life had moved in a smaller
orbit than Cromwell's, his assumption of the imperial
rôle was much more paradoxical than Cromwell's
virtual crowning as Lord Protector, for Hindenburg
had never fallen away from William, and still less
handed him over to the executioner. When Hindenburg came to occupy the emperor's place, the emperor
was still living a few miles across the frontier, always
hoping to return; ten years younger than the field
marshal; able to boast of a dozen far more famous
ancestors than Hindenburg could boast of. Yet
Hindenburg had manifestly not now stationed himself
as sentry in front of the royal fortress in order to open
the gates for the king's return. With a contented gesture of power, he had seated himself upon a great throne,

not indeed in the royal castle, but only a few minutes' walk from it in the imperial capital. After a brief interlude, he had assumed the headship of the government to whose establishment the king had had to yield during the last weeks of his reign. The only thing that distinguished Hindenburg and Cromwell from their royal predecessors was a title.

Except for the title, Hindenburg had everything which could inspire reverence in the German people; as Junker, as army officer, and as victor in a great battle, he had what was needed to give him prestige in Germany. In addition, he had the three elements which had formed parts of the legend—his gigantic stature, his advanced age, and his taciturnity. Wherever he appeared, he was the tallest in the company—priceless symbolism for a man whose rank placed him above all others. The keenness of his understanding and the great range of his experience seemed, for the people, to be guaranteed by his white hair and by the chariness of his speech.

Since the legend was already a decade old, and since at the greatly accelerated tempo of modern times a decade now counts for as much as a century counted a while back, its sources were already moss-grown, and it had become venerable. Since Hindenburg himself was ten years older—and a hale man of eighty inspires respect as one who, in the duel with death, has so long maintained the upper hand—everyone was ready to regard him with due reverence.

Nor was he himself any longer in a humorous vein, as he had been for the most part during his "fresh and merry war." There were no longer the lively evenings at the officers' mess; and the field marshal,

who had not escaped the blows of fate, was no longer
in the mood to assume the blunt and cheerful pose of
Blücher. His wife was dead; he had had to leave his
comfortable home for a court; and his son, who had
been wont to come and stay with him when on leave
full of entertaining gossip about garrison life, was now
his working adjutant, and was destined to lead the
father into a maze of interests, struggles, and intrigues.

The men whom he received day after day were new to
Hindenburg. In this capital William II had been wont
to encounter hundreds of persons connected with him
by special ties, were it only of position, of dependence,
or of scandalmongering; here the courtiers and officers,
the men of learning and the great industrialists had
stood at attention before the monarch, an attitude
that could not fail to stimulate his mobile spirit in one
way or another. In this huge realm, through which
its king and emperor had traveled in every direction,
talking at large with all and sundry, so that he knew
his city mayors, his presidents, and his rectors as the
schoolmaster knows the boys of his class—indeed, it
was as such that William regarded them—here now
presided our old titan as a stranger. He knew neither
personalities nor functions; had never studied the
German State or its economic life; and felt himself in
the picture only when he was among those who wore
military uniform.

There he was now, however, figurehead of a realm
which he was expected to represent before the foreign
world. What did the names of the ambassadors
who came to call on him mean when they were
announced? No doubt he knew where Venezuela
was, but since he possessed no gift for languages, had

traveled little outside of Germany, knew nothing
about the economic or political life of the world, he
could only venture to converse with foreign representatives after he had been carefully instructed by
his assistants. Even then he would remain far below
the level attained by William I or Francis Joseph,
who, when they were as old as President Hindenburg,
were able to rely upon a long experience of the world
as a nonagenarian leans on an ivory-handled stick.
When one in so embarrassing a situation is a legitimate
monarch, the fact that he rules by hereditary right
gives him an established position; but even the most
intelligent diplomatists hardly knew what to make of
this president whom the Germans had freely elected
as their ruler. The only thing that carried him through
his difficulties was his imperturbability, intensified now
by the stoicism of age. Otherwise he would have been
filled with alarm, feeling himself a captive in this unfamiliar environment. As things were, however, and as
Hindenburg was, he regarded himself as an officer who
has been transferred to take command of a new garrison
where he has to begin by feeling his way. The chief
trouble was that this garrison was so terrifyingly large!

Still, he seized the reins; and since, his position
being quasi-monarchical, he had to start the conversation and usually to sustain it, he adopted the
expedient of invariably beginning with the question,
"Where did you serve?" That gave him an opening
to go on talking about provinces and persons; and the
fondness people have for discussing joint acquaintances led, in this official atmosphere, to the most
marvelous conversations. Since, even in Prussia,
soldiering is but a casual and occasional part of a

man's life, everyone who came into contact with the head of the State found himself obliged to give account of a period of time in his life in which he had lived abnormally—his war years. While those subjected to this examination could not but wonder at its bluntness, it could not fail to give the old man himself the impression that all Germans were alike, since nearly all of them had served.

Except, of course, the ladies, whom, almost to the last, he received with polished courtesy. The youngest of girls, who was about to make a courtesy, found that the president was kissing her hand, even if she were a socialist woman deputy; and much as men of intelligence were inclined to make fun of old Hindenburg, no woman ever complained of his manners.

Men of note had been among the frequenters of the fine rococo palace. In the 1870's its then owner, a certain Count von Schleinitz, had entertained as members of his circle such men as Wagner and Menzel, Helmholtz and Virchow. New quartets by Brahms had been performed there, and readings of the latest dramas had been given by their authors.

How great a change! The foreign ambassadors, though they held their peace, could not but be astounded, recalling what, in distant universities they had learned about the Germany of Kant and Hegel, and now seeking the shadow of that Germany. What a contrast they saw when they reminded themselves that, in the intellectual void of this palace, they were the guests of the freely elected chief of the Germans. Here they were at the symbolical focus of German life; but what had become of the men, of the works, and of the thoughts for whose sake alone Germany had been

25

accounted one of the premier nations of the world? Did a single word uttered by this chief of all the Germans give any indication that he, or the members of his environment, had, even in youth, or at holiday times, been acquainted with such men as Goethe or Beethoven? Was it possible at his court to meet the discoverers and inventors, the authors and actors, who, after years of outlawry, were beginning to carry the German name as of old, far across the seas, being acclaimed in other lands as "emissaries of the German spirit"? Was there to be seen in these rooms any trace of the refulgence which had outlasted the dreaded empire, had outlasted the militarism which had been detested throughout the world, the arrogance and the defeat of Hohenzollern Germany?

The dulness of the officers' mess, the mental barrenness of Prussian Junkerdom, the absurd and stilted mannerisms of persons who clicked their heels together, who spoke in the grating voices of the members of students' corps, standing stiffly upright as they did so, had become dominant in this palace since it had been degraded from being a center of active mental life to become a meeting place of Junkers returned from active service. The sometime refulgence had dispersed, and nothing was left but a crude imitation. Invention and research, the palladium of the German spirit, were utterly alien to this man who was the chosen head of the German people, and to all his associates. In such matters they had neither part nor lot. Once again the Germans had shown an expectant world that the great distresses through which they had passed had brought them no access of vigor or virtue. Had not destiny operating through defeat taught them the lesson they needed? Had it not shown them that, as members of a great nation, they must at length lay the specter of their longing for an outworn world dominion, cease to idolize their generals, tire of their fondness for standing at attention and instead follow the guiding stars of the philosophers and musicians to whom Goethe had drawn their attention? Had they no desire to hearken to the call which, modified to suit the new times, was sounded by the heroes of invention and discovery, and was embodied in the impulses of chemists and aviators, and in the creations of German artists—who all, immediately after the defeat of one kind of Germany, were pioneers in disclosing to the world a Germany of another kind?

Nor, in this palace, was any trace to be discerned of those impulses which, through Rathenau and Stresemann, had found expression in the political world. An aging general, the descendant of generals and grenadiers, the emblem of the "reasons of State" which were dominant in the eighteenth century and whose dominance still lingered in Prussia, had come to the front here in the heart of twentieth-century Germany. Here he was contemplating the envoys from the outer world as if he had been a shadow personality in a historical film, at a time when other peoples were struggling as to which was the best of two possible ways by which Europe could be made into a commonwealth.

At great receptions, in this historic palace, everything went on as it had done in court days. Ebert had abolished ceremonial, making middle-class manners the rule. He had been extremely thrifty, never allowing champagne to be served. Now the servants had been put back into buckled shoes and smart slippers; an aristocrat acted as master of ceremonies. Diplomatic uniforms, done away with by the Republic, returned as "noblemen's swallowtails." People waited about in muttering semicircles, as in a king's palace, where it always seems as if someone must just have died, until the major-domo knocked on the floor with his gold-headed staff in order to announce the entrance of the president of the realm. In the literal sense of the term, Hindenberg was a great figure, as he entered in evening dress, only the Blücher Star being reminiscent of the good old times of service under the emperor. So greatly concerned was he about his appearance, even when over eighty years of age, that he rejected a portrait as "too old," although it had been painted by a real, live baron, and was an excellent likeness to boot.

Yes, it was service in the grand manner that he was carrying on; and only through the encouragement afforded by this fixed idea could Hindenburg maintain his poise in so remarkable a situation. His exalted sense of his social position gave him self-confidence. His long training as an officer rendered his bearing all that could be desired; thus the only thing that was lacking to the requisites of a monarch was—no, there was nothing lacking.

For now there ensued one of those changes in public sentiment which neither he nor his nationalist electors had foreseen. After Hindenburg had become president, wishes for a monarchist restoration were quickly forgotten. When the saddler had been living in this palace—a little, stocky proletarian with a square-shaped head and simple manners—the differ-

ence from former days was continually in the thoughts
of every old servant of the king, and most living
Germans had been that, so that all cherished ancient
memories of splendor.　Now the emperor's place had
been taken by a man who had much more dignity
than the emperor.　Those who enjoyed ancestor
hunting could follow the Hindenburg family far back
into the twilight of the Middle Ages, as far back
as the Hohenzollern family could be followed—always
being tactful enough not to move away from the
Junker line of the Beneckendorffs to the maternal side
with its grenadiers and joiners.　To German eyes, the
emperor's shadow had seemed to hover behind little
Ebert; but the giant Hindenburg hid the emperor's
shadow.　No one did more to promote the decline of
the monarchical idea in Germany than the king's
most loyal of field marshals.

Beneath his glance, the hearts of the Germans beat
more strongly, for the dignified old gentleman wearing
the Blücher Star on his breast inspired them with renewed devotion.　A ridiculous instance had been the
way in which the Commission of Inquiry had kotowed before the national hero.　Now, in the year
1925, this Commission, after sitting for six years, had
to draft its conclusions regarding responsibility for
Germany's collapse at the end of the war.　It was
rather unfortunate that at this very moment one of the
two culprits should have become president!　Could the
Commission, which decided for the Reichstag, and
therefore for the German people, censure the man who
had been commander in chief in 1917 and 1918 as one
of the two most blameworthy when he was about to
become head of the State?　One of the members of the

Commission, Doctor Bredt, found an appropriate formula: "Hitherto, in the Commission, opinions have been divided; some thinking that Ludendorff was alone to blame, and others that Hindenburg was partly responsible. Now, when Hindenburg has been elected president of the realm, the two parties are deadlocked. . . . I propose that we quietly blue-pencil the whole passage!" That is what happened. After six years' investigation, those whom the German people had appointed to elicit historical truth absolved Hindenburg from responsibility for the disasters of the war, the reason being that in the interim they had elected him president.

In 1924, Ebert, the first president, had been unsuccessful in an action for slander brought against those who had declared he had committed treason in January, 1918! If Hindenburg ever stopped to look at his predecessor's bust in the waiting room, what thoughts must have passed through his mind? Ebert had not been free from a sense of justified pride when he became president, and had filled his high office with skill and dignity. With increased bitterness, however, the ex-saddler had come to recognize how cruel were his old enemies, how jealous his old friends, how nihilistic almost all with whom he came in contact, and how, among his daily associates, there were not as many as three who, like himself, really had the welfare of the Republic at heart. Impartiality was forced on him by his position; and veiled in this impartiality, Ebert, with the nervousness of a new man, had drawn too much into the background, venturing merely to hope that when another president was elected to replace him, he himself might become chancellor of the realm, and at length be able to deliver his mind freely, as he had been accustomed to do during his thirty years as party leader. The highest office in the Republic had brought him no happiness.

Hindenburg had had all the luck. The son of a poor man, for the salary of his father the captain was probably no bigger than had been the wages of Ebert's father, at the age of eighty he had found his way into a palace which, when he had been a slender lieutenant in the guards and awakening to the joys of life, he may perhaps have regarded with some envy as a place which would be his fitting environment. When at length he entered it as master, there was no wonder in his eyes, for such palaces and castles had for centuries been hospitably opened to his ancestors. Ebert was not so well fitted to become an inmate of this palace, which in earlier years he must have regarded with distrust or defiance, because it was a place where, if he entered it, the polished floors would reflect a foot wearing not a patent-leather pump, but the roughly made shoe of a workingman.

The pictures that hung on the walls framing these polished floors had undergone a sudden and spectral change. Whereas above Ebert's desk there had been a portrait of Bebel, an ordinary photograph, there was now a life-size oil painting of old Blücher. From the museum, the new incumbent of the palace had had other pictures brought: *Schwerin's Heroic Death*, *A Vivandière Attached to the Dessau Regiment*, and the *Cavalry Attack at Mars-la-Tour*. He had not hung any pictures relating to the war in which he had played a leading part, preferring war dreams of a romantic past, although nowadays attacks were made with tanks if one had any. A hero's death on the battle-field was very different from Schwerin's, and only the vivandière, though called by another name, continued to bestow her immemorial favors.

The work he had to do was no harder than that of the commander in chief. Instead of signing for an army, he had to sign for a nation. In both cases, a skilled staff had prepared everything for the chief, and, in normal times, his duties were finished when he had spent a couple of hours at his desk. Besides this, he had to receive visitors whose concerns could usually be dealt with in a few words, and to listen to reports when he could play an even more passive part. Now, indeed, Hindenburg read the text of the constitution he had sworn to maintain. The document was printed for him in exceptionally large type, and the two hundred copies of this edition de luxe have become much sought after by bibliophiles. After he had read to the end, the president observed approvingly: "Parts of it seem to me very sensible!" Behind the palace was a fine park where he could stroll unseen attended by his sheep dog; and his only trouble on these occasions was that detestable flag with its black-red-gold colors, which always fluttered over the roof, and which could not fail to catch his eye as he returned to the palace. From time to time he had a review of troops, which came as a real refreshment; and always the field marshal would step up to the fugleman, and would see, with a connois-seur's eye, whether the ranks were well kept. On festive occasions, when the guard of honor stood at attention, the trained eye of the old commissioned officer would look searchingly at the details of collars, buckles, and buttons—his gestures being faithfully reproduced by the inexorable film.

Then there were the newspapers! In the beginning Hindenburg had underlined all passages he could not understand and had made his private secretary explain them to him. Subsequently the latter insisted upon his reading one of the republican journals, and so, at seventy-eight, the old Junker for the first time in his life read the articles in one of these infernal periodicals, but said defiantly to his press chief, "Anyhow, I shall go on reading the *Kreuz-Zeitung* as well." He also read a parochial paper from the Lüneburger Heide, where he had relatives; and would suddenly stop to inquire what on earth the editor of this local rag had meant by his article on America. All this passed his time pleasantly enough. In summer he went to Upper Bavaria, where, until well on into his eightieth year, he continued to hunt chamois. Closer at hand, for sport, was the Schorfheide, near Berlin, where Ebert had sometimes spent his week-ends. Here there were stags and roe deer for the president.

Thus all would have gone well enough had not his new army corps, the German nation, been at odds within itself once more, contrary to all the rules of good discipline. The Germans simply could not make up their minds whether they wanted to be ruled from the right or from the left; and, in times of crisis, his ease and comfort were continually being disturbed by fresh proposals and by conflicting influences, which even aroused pangs of conscience. Then this old man who was a slave to duty was faced by the need for great decisions as he had been in war time; but now without a Ludendorff at his elbow, for during the nine years of his presidency he found no one in whom he could put full trust. During the war, as a general, he was expert enough to know that Ludendorff was much more of an expert than himself. Now, in the political world, he was all at sea amid conflicting currents, because he did not understand the grounds for coming to a decision. Just as everything began late in this life of his—fame and power—so it was not until Hindenburg was eighty that he was called upon to show himself and the world whether the man whose supreme merit had been service was really able to rule, and whether the Junker and field marshal had in him the wherewithal to make a good monarch.

II

The general situation was favorable. Whereas in 1916 he had taken supreme command of an army which was unmistakably defeated, in 1925, when Hindenburg became president, Germany was on the up grade. He had been in retirement during the years that immediately followed the peace, whose difficulties had been initiated by the armistice for which he was responsible. When he now came to the front again, others, with superhuman exertion, had once more set a-going the chariot which he was to drive. Such luck as that may, in itself, be almost regarded as a merit.

Whereas, immediately after the war, Germany had been universally shunned, the genius and the patience of two men, Rathenau and Stresemann, had brought her back into the fold, into the companionship of the nations. Whereas for five years she had been a pariah, cut off from all alliances and even from congresses, she was now about to be admitted to the League of Nations from which, at first, Europe had deliberately excluded her. The days of poverty and inflation were, or seemed to be, over; and the Germans, who had been happy under William because business flourished, were beginning to feel at ease once more, now that money was flowing into the country; for this money, although it did not belong to them, could be used for erecting fine buildings and for promoting new enterprises. Since they were earning money once more, they troubled as little about the Republic as, before the war, they had troubled about the Empire. "The budgetary deficit," writes Major von Hindenburg, the field marshal's nephew, "did not disturb them. . . . The era of building huge sports grounds and stadia had begun. Most people seemed to have forgotten that Germany had lost the war, that the greater part of our substance had been squandered, that ours was an impoverished land which could not afford luxuries."

Then came the British coal strikes of the year 1926, with their favorable repercussions in the coal basins of other lands! Besides, after long years of poverty, one cannot continue indefinitely to pinch and to mourn!

Hindenburg promptly began to interfere in the work of government. Although it was specified in the constitution that he must appoint ministers of State in accordance with the recommendations of the chancellor, who was solely responsible in this matter, he refused to confirm the nomination of Gräfe as a minister, though Gräfe belonged to his own party. He hastened to interfere in questions of national defense. He clung jealously to his right of appointing ambassadors and envoys, choosing them invariably from the circle of his friends and his order. Since the nation as a whole, now as formerly, cared for none of these things, everything at first ran its course quietly. Although he once said tranquilly to a minister of State, "I

don't understand anything about politics," no one
asked why, then, he had been elected president—for
his activities were certainly not confined to those of
the hour or two spent daily in his office.

Towards the ministers of State his attitude was
characteristically monarchical, for he always spoke of
"my chancellor," as a commander in chief says "my
chief of staff." Where the common people were concerned, he showed himself above party, producing his
gun license when he met a gamekeeper on the heath
near Berlin, "for the sake of order, and to show that
I am fully within my rights." Like the good king in
the schoolbooks, he refrained from shooting a stag
that was just over the boundary of the heath, saying,
"As president of the realm it is essential that I should
keep strictly within the law." He now sat to Liebermann for his portrait, although he had refused to do so
during the war; got on well enough with the painter
at the sittings; and, in his conversations on this
occasion, delivered his final judgment upon Goethe,
"Don't try and force Goethe down my throat—a cosmopolitan—and then his perpetual love affairs!"

In this way he had shown the gamekeepeer who was
a man of the people, and the Jewish painter who did
not know how to paint military buttons and decorations rightly, and therewith the great crowd of his
compatriots as well, that he was above party, and was
therefore ruling strictly in accordance with the constitution. Never before in history has any statesman
referred so often to his loyalty to the constitution as
did Hindenburg. If the State was to be a people's
State, he must give the people its rights. Indeed, in the
course of these nine years, he saw no more of the people
than he had seen of them during the four years of the

war; but he was continually harping upon his social sentiments: "Even an ambassador should be a man who is in close touch with the people, and is closely acquainted with its impulses—such a man as a great landlord, a manufacturer on the large scale, or a merchant in a big way of business." For Hindenburg believed that great landlords, great industrialists, and great merchants were really in close touch with the people; and the patriarchal sentiments of a well-disposed Junker, with which he had been inspired in boyhood and which he retained throughout his long life, were now to solve the social struggles of the advancing twentieth century just as in earlier days when he had wished that every workman might have plenty of children and a nice garden.

After all there was not much to be said against a republican form of government. The ministers of State were decent fellows; there were no strikes; the Reichswehr was a disciplined force! About this time a new acclamation was introduced. Though the people might not call out—"Long live the Republic!" they were taught to shout—"Long live the German nation as unified in the German Republic." Such matters could be arranged with a little tact. Still, it was a pity that that damned flag always fluttered before his eyes when he went for a walk in the park, or had to open a poultry show! Consequently, a year after becoming president, he took up this matter which was so great an annoyance to him, writing to his chancellor:

"Nothing could be farther from my mind than to abolish the national colors decreed by the constitution. . . . It is, however, my most heartfelt wish, within a short space of time and in the most constitutional way possible, to achieve a compromise which will be accordant with contemporary Germany and her aims, and will, at the same time, be just to the course of the history of the realm." The Germans, especially those in America, had expressed urgent longings for their old flag. Since, in that part of the world, they enjoyed all the liberties of a long-established Republic, their romantic leanings made them desire that in their dear old homeland across the seas their old flag should wave and their former king should reign. Now Hindenburg hit upon the expedient of commanding that at the embassies and consulates of Germany in lands outside Europe, and at the consulates in European seaports, both flags, the old one and the new, should be hoisted. Thus does a woman of lowly origin who wishes to climb in the social sphere secure her first reception among gentlefolks in the colonies. Then she manages to get an invitation to dinner in the capital, and can flaunt her fine clothes before the eyes of an ambassador.

During this same period, the president had managed to evade the constitution in another quarter. His king was in need of money. Had William II been thrifty for five-and-twenty years, had he been so careful to save the double allowance which had been voted for his grandchildren when he began to reign, that now, though he had spent as little as possible upon war loans and other bourgeois concerns, this infernal Republic should pouch his property? No doubt all that the Hohenzollerns possessed had been taken from the people; and peoples, when their kings have been exiled, are prone to keep a tight grip upon that which monarchs and their fathers have robbed them of. Why, even compatriots who had not scuttled across the frontier, had had their goods confiscated merely because they held other views than those in fashion. Long before Hindenburg became president, these gamblers for millions had gravely discredited the monarchical idea.   The sale of the Kaiser's memoirs to the sometime enemy, and the second marriage, seemed to exclude forever the likelihood of a return (though to-day it may once more have become possible).   At length an agreement had been reached.   Just as it had taken six years to decide the matter of the royal guilt, so it had taken six years to decide about the monies due the king.   The upshot of both trials was that democracy gained a moral victory, but monarchy could reckon up its winnings in hard cash.

When, in a referendum, twelve million Germans now demanded expropriation, the president asked himself whether, as imperial field marshal, he could put up with this, although the constitution forbade his interference.   Talking over the matter with an old friend among the Junkers, a man who had helped to promote Hindenburg's election, and was now devoted to the king's cause, Hindenburg arranged to write a private letter, giving him his personal view, "to assure you that I fully share your concern. . . . I hardly need to dilate to you upon the fact that I, who have spent my life in the service of the king of Prussia and the German emperor, regard this referendum, first of all, as grossly unjust; and, next, that I look upon it as a deplorable breach with German traditional feelings and as a mark of gross ingratitude. . . . It seems to me a serious attack upon the framework of the constitutional State, whose main concern must be respect for law and for legally recognized property.   We should make a great step on the downward path if, as the outcome of the opinion of a passionately excited populace, we should withhold or annul constitutionally owned property. . . . I trust, therefore, that our fellow-citizens will reconsider their decision upon this matter, and will undo the mischief they have done."

This apologia for monarchy signed by the president was posted next day on the hoardings. What could Hindenburg do, when his friends had thus played false? He left the placards where they were. The Germans learned what the highest authority in the land thought of their ungrateful and emotional designs. Had they not been rudely called to heel when they had ventured to take a step or two more in the direction of the land of liberty? What? Are we to leave our sometime king in poverty and distress; our good king who, that day in November, 1918, sacrificed himself to secure a better peace; our good king whose ancestors raised us to greatness as a nation? Although twelve millions had voted for expropriation, this was now repudiated by the majority; and, at the final ballot, the Hohenzollerns, after all that they had received in the year 1919, were granted an additional quarter-million acres of land, numerous palaces and castles, and fifteen million gold marks in cash. The socialists, as supporters of the Republic, were a trifle embarrassed, and abstained from voting in the Reichstag in favor of this reinstatement. As to whether the emperor and king deserved all the wealth he had never earned, they expressed no opinion, remaining unsexed in this question as in so many others.

Hindenburg, like old men in general, valued the past more than the future, especially when the past had

been a glorious one. Where banners and royal property were concerned, he took action; but as regards
the future position of the German realm, he let himself
be guided by his ministers. Was it expedient to make
serious preparations for a war of revenge? Since
Hindenburg had taken the final collapse of Germany
in 1918 so lightly, and since all his life his main longing had been for tranquillity, could it be seriously expected that at eighty he would want to go to war
again? He therefore approved his ministers' pacific
policy, and never interfered in foreign affairs, although,
during these nine years, he was continually meddling
in home politics. Provided no mischief was done to
the persons or symbols of the august age he revered,
so far as he was concerned his ministers could rule as
"good Europeans."

Stresemann's internal conflicts seem to have made
an impression on Hindenburg. In Stresemann, the
old gentleman saw a patriotic German whom the collapse of his country had taught that they must go
slowly, until in the end the intolerable treaty would
prove unworkable. Hindenburg can hardly have
realized that Stresemann was emblematic of those few
Germans who were striving to transform themselves
from resolute Prussians into thoughtful citizens of the
world. To an American he said, "No nation with a
drop of manly blood and honor in its veins will ever
submit its existence and its national honor to arbitra-
tion by other nations." Such were the views, at the
level of William's theses at The Hague Peace Conference of 1907, which prevailed in Hindenburg's palace,
while close at hand Stresemann had to fight against all
the officials of his department, against his own party,

26

and against half of his German compatriots for the
entry of Germany into the League of Nations—far
harder than he had to fight against Briand.

What Stresemann achieved at Locarno a few months
after Hindenburg's election as president was so remarkable that it can only be explained as the fruit of
earlier deeds, in fact those of Rathenau, whose policy
Stresemann himself had opposed for years, but was
now continuing. Here was the first tranquilization of
the nervous and irritable French; here was a consolidation of the idea of international law; here was the first
great relaxation of tension in Europe that had occurred
since the war. When, a year later, Germany entered
the League of Nations, and, in the assembly that represented fifty different countries, a German statesman once more uttered cosmopolitan words; and when
subsequently, at Thoiry, Briand and Stresemann con-
versed with one another as "good Europeans"—the
outstanding intelligences all over the world believed,
for a moment, that a new epoch had dawned. France's
blunder, the Treaty of Versailles, Germany's blunder,
a bitter and revengeful spirit, seemed to be becoming
effaced. Seven years later the world was to learn that
all that had happened at Thoiry was an understanding between two imaginative men, one of whom had
thought that his own cure from megalomania through
severe internal struggles was symbolic of the mentality
of his whole nation, and had succeeded in transferring
this autosuggestion to his French partner, until the
latter, in his turn, came to believe that the metamorphosed Stresemann was Germany.

Hindenburg signed the treaties. His friends, who
had promoted his election that he might prepare for

a war of revenge, were horrified at the proceedings of their nominee. In the League of Nations! Willing to renounce Alsace-Lorraine! Concluding his speech, the German minister who had been corrupted by France actually quoted Goethe before the assembled nations. That was too much! Immediately they resigned from the coalition government, the Junker provinces beside the Elbe and the Oder voted against the laws; and General Litzmann, who sixty years before had been fellow pupil with Hindenburg at the Military Academy, wrote: "We had dreamed that Hindenburg, turning his marvelous popularity to account, would dissolve the Reichstag, and appeal to the nation. Then he would have won an even finer victory than that of Tannenberg!"

Severe blows to be directed against an old man who had passed his whole life in the company of his fellow Junkers, and had never had anything to do with members of other classes! Even Bismarck, who could command much more extensive spiritual resources, would have wavered in such circumstances. When Hindenburg's electors, his friends, and his relatives turned against him a few months after his election as president, he could not, as Bismarck would have done in a similar case, apply for help to the king as his supporter. Now he was to be put to the supreme test: would he stand firm? Could he, in view of his age and his prejudices, reorient himself like Stresemann, the tavern-keeper's son, who was only fifty, and who, like Hindenburg, ten years before had wanted Germany to cling to her conquests?

He would find a means of holding his own stubbornly; he would join forces with the adversaries of those who had elected him. He would take an old man's blunt revenge. He did so twice over, in two different directions.

III

His surroundings and his advisers decided the issue in this matter; in the court atmosphere, it was natural that a camarilla should thrive. The man who, with servile mien, handed him documents day by day for signature, and who actually had himself photographed in this attitude, Meissner by name, a medium-grade official from Alsace, had played the courtier to Ebert when Ebert had been president, and had become accustomed to say what the master would like to hear. He owed his position, which was subsequently to give him decisive influence, to the fact that his predecessor had suffered from insomnia. This predecessor, after a bad night, had never been able to turn up with the documents before eleven o'clock, too late for Ebert, accustomed to get to work early. When Ebert rang, therefore, it was as a rule the second secretary, Meissner, who appeared—Meissner, the belly crawler, a chameleon who always took on the color of his environment. Apart from Hindenburg's fondness for a glass of good beer, Meissner was the only habit which the president took over from his predecessor, for, as he said, "When I was a general, and was transferred from one place to another, I always kept the old adjutants at work."

In addition to Meissner, Hindenburg's only son Oscar, recently promoted colonel, had influence with his father, and, being a man of little intelligence, he was merely the cat's-paw of persons in the background. Still, although this influence was thus more apparent than real, it gave him a sense of importance, and made his head swell, so that he once declared, "Historians shall not say that I have been nothing more than my father's son." This amusing glimpse of the son of a man who himself owed fame to another's achievement, shows how quickly a legend becomes fossilized. Young Hindenburg, who had not even inherited his father's great stature and hard-bitten features, was encouraged by the Hindenburg legend to believe that he was endowed with a genius all his own, but when it came to action was content to play the part of a mere go-between, handing on to his father the views of a third party.

Even this third party was not a man of exceptional intelligence, though he did stand out among the mediocrities of Hindenburg's court. I refer to General von Schleicher, an interesting person who did much to modify German happenings between 1920 and 1932; perhaps it would be better to say to bend them, and ultimately to bend them awry. The amazing principle that the Reichswehr was to be nonpolitical had been persistently applied for fifteen years to its privates and noncommissioned officers, among whom were many thoughtful young fellows. The tradition of the royal lieutenant had led to the belief that no mental development of men of this type was possible even in the new Reichswehr, whereas in reality there was much more thought and discussion in the Reichswehr than generals like to have going on among their soldiers. Generals, furthermore, are as politically minded as men can be, and therefore the generals of the Reichswehr had been prompt to form a political section, of which Major von Schleicher (he was then only a major) was chairman.

General von Seeckt, commander of the Reichswehr, who was likewise a man with strong political views, wanted to drive Schleicher out of this coign of vantage, being moved by a jealousy which was not concerned only with influence upon the rank and file of the Reichswehr, but was intensified by the fact that the two men were rivals for a woman's favor. When Seeckt proved victor in this unquestionably more interesting field, Schleicher's enmity to the general became intensified, and led to Seeckt's fall. (The present recorder is glad to be able, for once, to write about perfectly normal masculine impulses.) Hindenburg had never been able to forgive General Seeckt the latter's victory over the Russians at Gorlice in May—for at that juncture General Falkenhayn had forbidden Hindenburg to fight on his own part of the front, so that now, when Schleicher intrigued to down a successful rival, the president was glad to be freed of the sight of Seeckt's face. A pretext was found in the clamor raised by the Reichstag because a Hohenzollern prince had been allowed to be present at the Reichswehr maneuvers. Hindenburg, although he had himself granted the permission to General Seeckt, now threw him to the wolves.

Now Schleicher was a family friend. As regimental comrade and intimate of Oscar, he had stayed with the Hindenburgs long before the war, when Hindenburg had been in command of the Fourth Army Corps in Magdeburg. Schleicher, therefore, could go in and out of the palace unceremoniously as he pleased, and the friend of his youth was instrumental in conveying his wishes and ideas to the president. Thus Schleicher became a great force as intermediary; and inasmuch as by temperament he was suited for working in that chiaroscuro which used to be regarded as the proper atmosphere of diplomacy, it was thoroughly congenial to him, now that he was relieved from his other duties as an officer, to play a big part in a world of go-betweens where many wished to have a finger in the pie but where he was the real ruler. The others might be in the limelight for all he cared so long as he was stage manager behind the scenes.

But for this job he was really unfitted by two qualities which are inappropriate to the man who wants to rule from offstage: he was sensitive and garrulous. If anyone censured him in a speech, Schleicher would immediately write the offender a letter demanding a withdrawal. He would also light-heartedly talk to all and sundry about schemes which his auditors regarded as definite plans, passing on the information to others. Depraved and weak, faithless and irresolute, his actions were in keeping with the soft sensuality of his aspect. When, at the age of fifty, in the year 1932, he married his early love, a cousin who only procured a divorce for his sake after many years of wooing, this gentler companion exercised a moderating influence in the attempt to free him from connection with everlasting intrigues in which he was hopelessly involved. The gambler's habit had taken too firm a possession of him, and, in the end, he gambled away his head.

Among these three paladins of the old giant, two were always trying to rid themselves of the third, and naturally the son had the best chance of holding his ground. There were rooms giving on the garden, as in *Don Carlos*, where Meissner kept visitors waiting so that Oscar could make his way to them unseen. Letters were carried to and fro by friends, that they might not pass through the hands of inquisitive servants; and, of course, there were luncheons, the chief instruments of modern politicians. Here is an instance. Schleicher was curious to know what Meissner thought of him, and used his friend Moldenhauer to find out. Having invited them both to a luncheon, he left them together for a few moments afterward, by arrangement; and Moldenhauer asked Meissner what he really thought of his host, Schleicher. Meissner said that Schleicher did not run straight. "I asked Meissner, as you wished," wrote Moldenhauer that evening to Schleicher. "This is what he said." Schleicher, his vanity mortified, thereupon sent the letter to Meissner, reproaching the secretary for having said anything so derogatory about him.

It was on the same level that matters of State policy were conducted, since all those concerned identified policy with intrigue. For years Schleicher humbugged Gessler, the minister for defense, about what was spoken of as the Black Reichswehr, saying there was no such body. When, at length, in the Reichstag, Gessler announced in good faith that there was no Black Reichswehr, he made himself ridiculous—but tried to save his face by remarking that, after all, a deceived husband invariably learns in the end about his wife's infidelity.

Among members of the fair sex, Schleicher's rôle was one which might have been taken from a comedy written in the year 1860. He played the part of a daimonic general, declaring: "The red cloak I wear as general, ladies, will some day become an executioner's cloak, when, in the public squares, we come to deal with our enemies!" Yet he could not say whom he meant by these "enemies," for his aim was to be all things to all men, and, especially, to be on friendly terms with the Left. He liked to talk of himself as the "socialist general." For nine years these three men were allowed to follow their own bent in the palace, being treated as pets. With them, however, was always associated a fourth figure, ostensibly more independent, that of the chancellor of the day. Of course there was only one at a time, but there were frequent changes, for in nine years Hindenburg ran through seven chancellors.

When he became president, the times were still favorable for burgomasters. During the war, any burgomaster who had been efficient and thrifty had attracted the attention of the ministers of State, although in peace time they were usually little inclined to let their eyes rest on such minor officials from the provinces. Thus a burgomaster became food minister; and another, Hans Luther, had the luck to stand in Bismarck's shoes. With Hindenburg, who appointed him chancellor, Luther had this in common, that he knew nothing about politics; but he was by no means as willing as Hindenburg to admit the fact. He also resembled Hindenburg in his desire to be "above party," especially above the parties which had elected him, for he said confidentially to every deputy in turn, "You can't imagine how closely my views coincide with those of your party!" If anyone to whom he spoke thus was skeptical, Luther took offense. When he made a joke which was not immediately understood, he would comically draw down the corners of his mouth until his hearers perceived that they were intended to laugh.   After his brief tenure of office, Luther was succeeded by Wilhelm Marx, whom Hindenburg had defeated in the presidential campaign, and who now became chancellor for the second time.

Marx, a Catholic, likewise belonged to that group of German diplomatists who frankly declared that they were nothing of the kind.   Michaelis, it will be remembered, had said he was only a hanger-on in politics.   Baron von Schön, German ambassador in Paris, opens his memoirs with the remarkable statement that his parents had really intended him to adopt an agricultural career.   Marx, on taking office, said: "I should much have preferred a judgeship in Limburg!"   When he had to resign, after the campaign two years later, he said to the leader of the victorious socialists: "I have done pretty well for you.   But for my policy you would not have been successful at the polls!"

Nevertheless this sarcastic little Rhinelander inspired confidence abroad, for he was a straightforward man, scrupulous if severe as a judge, and one who, had he been president, would have worked strictly within constitutional limits, would never have ruled for years without a Reichstag, and therefore would not have ended in chaos.   But he had not won any battles, he was not six feet two inches tall; and therefore it was not he, but Hindenburg, who had become lord of the realm.

Among all who visited the palace, there was only one who wanted nothing for himself, and had some-

Hindenburg and Braun, Socialist President of Prussia, riding through the streets of Coblenz

thing to give, being therefore dreaded. Essentially, he was as powerful as Hindenburg, for Prussia, which comprised two thirds of the Republic, was under his thumb. In the silent struggle which the Junkers now began to organize against socialistic Prussia, and which was not to be decided for another seven years, Otto Braun had a very strong position, though he had been no more than a book printer, and always suspect from the monarchical point of view as to his loyalty. Still, there were three good reasons why he should impress old Hindenburg: he was an East Prussian; he was a sportsman; and he was as tall as Hindenburg himself. Two of these qualities were conspicuous at his first entry; the third was disclosed to his great rival within ten minutes by a shooting anecdote. When, at length, Braun told Hindenburg that he had been born opposite the barracks and had been educated at a school well known to the president, the latter forgave Braun for not having served in the army and for being a Red. Hindenburg was quick to perceive that Braun was something very different from a party man, namely a born ruler, since he was called the tsar of all the Prussias.

Braun was the only man of whom Hindenburg was jealous. "You have everything," said the president of the realm to the Prussian prime minister again and again, "and I have nothing. You have the police, the administration, in your hands, When I want anything, I must apply to you for it. I even have to send pardons to you, for your signature." Thereupon Braun invited the president to shoot in the Prussian forests—and Hindenburg never asked Braun to accompany him. Hindenburg would say to Braun angrily that the position was intolerable: "I am a soldier. I am accustomed to command."

"I, too, would rather command than obey," replied Braun, failing to add that the former was his usual practice.

The ludicrous background for the private conversations between these two ruling antipodes was that Bismarck, the Junker, had in former days wrestled for the hegemony of Prussia over Germany, whereas socialists had resisted this hegemony until they themselves had become the masters of Prussia. Now Hindenburg, to whom, as a Prussian Junker of the old school, Prussia was always more important than Germany, would rather have had Prussia, and Braun would not have been loath to exchange Prussia for Germany.

In this strange interplay of rivalry, Braun's sturdy independence, his East-Prussian accent, and his great stature, inducded Hindenburg—though he had become more wary and mistrustful with age—to overstep the limits of service from time to time, so that he would remark:

"You keep on saying you are afraid of bolshevism. What about Admiral X., or Herr Y. Could not you have a word with them?"

At length one of these Prussian magnates called to see the great enemy, began to talk of revolution and dagger thrusts—and was promptly, though politely, shown the door. When, one day, a Red Week was announced in Berlin, Hindenburg summoned the Prussian premier.

"I am told that you have already chalked crosses on the doors of those who are to be murdered!"

Braun assured him that the demonstration would pass off quietly.

"Then why don't you prohibit the whole affair?"

"Only if you will suppress the Steel Helmets."

"But the Steel Helmets are nationalist and patriotic."

"No less revolutionary than the Reds."

So things were left as they were.

One day the book printer rescued the field marshal from a position of extreme embarrassment. The question had arisen of renewing the Law for the Protection of the Republic, which forbade the return of the emperor. How could the confirmed monarchist bring himself to this? He thought of resigning the presidency. Then he sent for someone to advise him—not his own chancellor, but Braun, the socialist. Braun considered that a presidential election at this juncture might be disastrous. He asked for a glance at the paper, and saw that the old law was merely to be kept in force for a further term. He said:

"You are not permanently forbidding the return of the emperor; there is not a word here to that effect! You are only signing the renewal of a law enacted by your predecessor."

Greatly relieved, the old gentleman glanced thankfully at his Red aide, and signed with an easy conscience.

IV

While the State officials were quarreling in the ministries about precedence and salaries, and, especially, were fighting one another for influence, in the outer world the number of the unemployed was steadily

increasing. The masses of the common folk, for whose
welfare it was alleged that all this was going on, were
more and more seriously affected from the year 1929
onward by the great monetary crisis; for those
who knew so well how to cheapen the production of
goods did not know how to distribute them. It was
not the payment of German reparations to France,
which were repeatedly provided for by American loans,
but the disorder of the currency system throughout
the world, which promoted unemployment in industrial
countries, and, as far as Europe was concerned, to a
more formidable extent in the strongest of these.
Too much leisure, hunger, and consequent nihilism,
drove the unemployed to join the private armies with
which ambitious tribunes of the people were at one
and the same time safeguarding themselves and playing the peacock.

The rulers of Germany were the rulers of a nation
which, though surrounded by armed States, had been
forbidden to bear arms. Could they be expected to
take harsh measures against groups of young fellows
who, in the borderland between sport and military
service, were trying to reorganize the forbidden army?
Some of them were paid for their activities, as soldiers
had been paid from time immemorial; and if they
tumultuously assembled when anyone called them
together, who could expect anything else from immature youths? Inasmuch as the nationalist Right
had formed the first of these private armies, and the
Republic had enrolled its own forces as a protection
against the reactionaries, the two parties were from
the first at odds, and the combativeness of the rivals
naturally led to disorders. When Hindenburg became

president, there were four private armies in Germany, each of them already or soon to become more numerous than his Reichswehr. As he was an honorary member of the Steel Helmets, to the waving of whose banners and the clashing of whose arms as accompaniment he had been elected, of course the forces of the Left, the Reichsbanner, and the Red Front, were uncongenial to him—and his conscience was troubled once more by the question as to how he was to remain "above party" in his dealings with these five armies.

Except for the communist Red Front, all these armed forces had the same ideal: not so much Germany, or revenge, or victory in athletics; it was rather a word. It was a word by which Germans are as readily bewitched as are members of other nations by the word "liberty"; it was the word "legality," to the German imagination supreme. Every one of these private armies, whose forces numbered several millions of hobbledehoys, was inspired by the old folk ideal, each of them wanting to be more legal than the others. True, they murdered one another at large in the streets and squares, in apartment houses and in cellars, and while engaged in these activities might have exchanged rôles while hardly becoming aware of the fact. Their program, however, to which they had sworn beneath their banners and in the presence of their leaders, was in each case insistent upon legality. Although, on the small scale, they were using forcible measures day by day, they repudiated force on the large scale for the conquest of power; and while each of the lesser leaders in the depths of his heart was comparing himself with Mussolini, they were universally

agreed that there was to be no march on Berlin, and
that machine guns must not be used to seize power.
Thus the Right professedly adopted the ballot, the
instrument of the democracy it detested. For the
time being, the members of private armies were content with the pride which every German feels when he
puts on a uniform, for Briand was perfectly right when
he said to Stresemann, "Who can help being pleased
with himself when he puts on a tin hat and fancies
himself a hero?"

Since they all made such asseverations of legality,
the field marshal did not think there was any reason
for regarding these private armies as dangerous to the
country. When he was urged to dissolve them, because they were all illegal, he hesitated to do so; and
no one could very well expect him to take active
measures against these martial youths who reminded
him of his own early ideals. Among all the errors of
his régime, this is the most comprehensible although
it was the most dangerous. His behavior was on the
same footing with the prime cause of the evil, the conquerors' prohibition of German rearmament—natural,
but a blunder. The clash of arms resounded throughout the nine years during which Hindenburg was in
power. The numerous elections in these years,
Hindenburg's own election not excepted, were rendered possibly solely because the meeting halls were
guarded by the candidates' private troops. The
Reichswehr alone remained quasi-invisible; as the
Fifth Army, it was, in a sense, Hindenburg's private
force, and he kept it veiled as jealously as a caliph of
old days had hidden away his women in a harem. In
comparison with the Reichswehr, the other armies

must have appeared much as peace societies or the League of Nations must appear to the Pope, namely as organizations which aim at realizing some of the ideals of the Vatican, but in ways peculiar to themselves, and without the aid of the Holy Father.

The conflict grew fiercer when these leagues for sport and defense, instead of devoting themselves like young fellows in other lands to swimming or to hiking, began to concern themselves mainly with political philosophy. When they paraded with their banners and their music, they did not sing about the sun, the spring, or the love of women, but about the Reds, the Jews, and hatred for the Marxists. Since the clashes between the rival forces became fiercer from year to year, Hindenburg was again and again faced by the question whether he should call upon the Reichswehr to restore order, and temporarily or permanently suppress these private levies. From the roof of his palace and above the radiator of his automobile, the black-red-and-gold flag continued to wave; but the Steel Helmets, of which (as aforesaid) he was an honorary member, hoisted the old German colors, and sang mocking verses about the banner of the Republic. In a program entitled "Message of Hate"—reminding readers of the "ruthless submarine warfare"—the Steel Helmets exclaimed: "We loathe from the depths of our hearts the present political set-up of the State, its form and its content, its origin and its nature."

After such outbursts, Hindenburg summoned representatives of his young comrades. These assured him that there was "no intention of challenging the present republican officials' oath of loyalty." Thereupon the president said he was "glad to hear it"—

27

and everything was in order once more, everything was again perfectly legal. From such quibbles of conscience, such obscure "interpretations," Hindenburg was probably able to gather fresh encouragement whenever he was in doubt. The main thing was that his mother had told him, as the outcome of her experiences after the revolution of 1848, how mental reservations were possible when a flag was forced upon one. Thus he could always come to terms with his own scruples, and probably failed to realize how sultry the atmosphere of his country had become, how false rang the tones of the revolutionists who were marching to the clash of arms and to the strains of their own songs, through the country whose form of government they repudiated even while declaring that, after the British manner, they would reform it with the ballot. The youthful Republic, on which no one professedly wished to lay violent hands, was still in being, hooted at by thousands who went on publicly discussing year after year the best way of violating her in due form of law.

Hitler himself had abandoned the idea of armed revolt, after his unsuccessful attempt at Munich in 1923 had cost him several months' imprisonment in a fortress. The world owes its gratitude to the judge who sentenced him, for in that gloomy cell, as once of old on a byre, the Light was born—the Hitlerite gospel, *My Battle*. Considerable forces gathered round him, because his promises made so wide an appeal and because they were so ambiguous. If, subsequently, he had realized his social program, he would have been a serious rival to the communists—and would probably have done no more than prepare their way to power. For this very reason, the more serious-minded of his followers cut adrift from his movement.

On a memorable occasion, however, one sacred legality came into conflict with another. Three officers of the Ulm Reichswehr had played an active part as Nazis. When they were brought to trial, Hitler was subpoenaed. What were the poor judges to do? They showed that Solomon, though not of "Aryan" descent, must obviously have been reincarnated as a German judge, for they made Hitler swear that he would always abide by the law, and, though they sentenced the officers, it was to an extremely mild punishment, on the ground that the offenders had been animated by the "best possible motives." The minister for defense took another view of officers who engage in political activities, and said: "Soldiers who, before carrying out orders, ask whether these are in conformity with their own political views, are not worth powder and shot. Such notions are but the preliminary stage to mutiny, to the destruction of the Reichswehr. Gloomy indeed for our young defensive force was the day in which some of its officers, in one of the law courts of the realm, gave expression to ideas of that kind."

Thus the highest authorities of the realm were in conflict; and its figurehead, who ought to have been its leader, vacillated, sometimes interpreting matters in the sense of the right, and sometimes coming to decisions that leaned towards the left—so eager was he to avert civil war. Now vengeance was being taken on him for the fallacy which had led him to believe that, although he was a monarchist and inspired with traditional ideas, he could protect the new flag. Now he

began to wander to and fro between the flags, between
the rival political philosophies, between the circles of
society; and, when pressed towards the Left bank, began to look back yearningly towards the Right bank,
away from which he had been thrust.

A speedy development pushed him further yet.
The socialists, as in the critical years 1918 and 1923,
so now in the crisis of 1928, were left at the tiller, having been forced by the creditor States to make new
plans for payment, and were trying to obtain from
Europe a rescue which the Republic at home denied
them. Hindenburg was straightforward with them,
telling them privately that though they had behaved
well during the war, some of them had towards the
end certainly stabbed the army in the back. Müller,
his socialist chancellor, was enthusiastic about him.
Müller, too, was a very tall man, quiet in manner, not
at all proletarian in aspect, and was therefore not uncongenial to the Junker. When the old gentleman,
receiving Frau Loebe, kissed the lady's hand, the press
of the Right wing made fun of him for this preposterous
mark of favor. On such occasions he had a way of
standing beside his secretary of State in front of the
semicircle of ladies and saying in his bass voice: "Now
I am going to flutter from flower to flower like a butter-
fly!" Thereupon he proceeded to suit the action to
the word.

When this "Jewish government"—such was the
name given to the politics of mutual understanding,
although all the German ministers of State were
"Aryans," humiliated itself before the enemy to the
extent of accepting the new scheme of reparations payment called the "Young plan," a hubbub was raised by

those who had been Hindenburg's friends. They demanded a referendum against the acceptance of the "slave treaty"; called everyone who favored the scheme a traitor; and insisted that Hindenburg must be dismissed if he signed. The Steel Helmets led the onslaught upon their honorary member. Stresemann, serious of aspect and an eloquent expositor, had to come to the rescue. Mortally ill though he was, his personal influence was greater than ever. A pledge was given that the Rhine would be freed if the Germans should now promise to pay 122 billions in the course of the next 59 years. "If we can only get hold of the Rhine once more," was every German's unuttered thought, "we shall not have to go on paying for 59 years." On this occasion as so often, the debtor was stronger than all his creditors put together, for two years after the evacuation of the Rhineland, all but three of the 122 billions had been written off, and even these three have never been paid.

The above-quoted reasoning appealed to Hindenburg's simple and straightforward intelligence. He ventured to disregard the clamor of the members of his own class. Having signed the agreement, he publicly announced: "I spent my life in the great school of the fulfilment of duty, that of the old army, where I learned to do my duty to the fatherland regardless of considerations for my own person. . . . Consequently the idea of evading responsibility by a referendum or by retreat could make no headway with me." Although there was more sound than sense in the utterance, it had a great effect upon the common people, who imagined that, reading between the lines, they could detect indications of severe mental conflict on the old man's part, and above all, signs that he was making a great sacrifice in continuing to hold office as president.

Once more Hindenburg was able to enjoy the fruits of others' labors and others' sacrifices, for Stresemann had worn himself out in the struggle. Nine months after his death, the tricolor was lowered in Mainz; the German colors were hoisted on the flagstaffs along the Rhine. The president's visit to the great river was a festal occasion; the bells of Cologne cathedral pealed; banquets and receptions were numerous. But no one shouted a friendly word across the Rhine, although the French could have continued, by the terms of the Treaty of Versailles, to occupy the Rhineland for another five years.

According to a democratic pamphlet issued at the time: "The men whom we have to thank for this day are Walter Rathenau, who paved the way, and Gustav Stresemann, who completed the liberation. Eternal gratitude is due to them for their shrewdness, their clear-sightedness, and their patriotism." Bismarck has told us that it is never wise to count upon popular gratitude. All the same, the populace is wont to speak soft things about its leaders after their death, especially when the death has been sacrificial. On the Rhine, however, three years after this festival, the memorial to Stresemann was removed by Hitler's government, and by this same government, the tomb of the assassins of Rathenau was decked with flowers.

V

For decades the field marshal had continued to dream of Neudeck. He had vivid memories of how, in boyhood, he had first mounted a horse there; how his grandfather, reclining upon the couch in the hall, had told him about the great but wicked Napoleon; how, when he had been a cadet, his grandmother had provided his favorite dishes; how he had been wont to spend his summer holidays there with his wife and to play at campaigning with his children. 'Tis distance lends enchantment to the view, so naturally, as Hindenburg grew older, those distant days seemed more charming to memory. The years of his cadetship and the early months of his marriage, all charming but thoroughly refined; the life of a member of the master class untroubled by servants in uniforms trimmed with gold lace—highly distinguished without the fuss and bother of a court—how remote it all was, yet how near it seemed, close yet legendary!

We can readily understand that the aging titan's heart must have been full of such feelings. Another East-Prussian gentleman, a neighbor at Neudeck, a thoroughly prosaic Junker almost as old as Hindenburg, likewise a conqueror, and no less monarchical in sentiment, seemed likewise to have entertained them. This was Baron von Oldenburg-Januschau, who had an infernally bright thought. Why else had the Junkers elected Hindenburg president than that he should protect the members of his order as his predecessors, the monarchs, had done for centuries? Yet now this fellow, whom they had regarded as their own creature, was advancing with slow and heavy tread along a road that led to everything which endangered them and their property. They were afraid of a so-called "reform" of the East-Elbian estates; for these bolsheviks mocked at the estates as antediluvian, wanting to settle

them with people of their own way of thinking, and to
continue in the open country the intrigues they had
been carrying on for years in the towns. Plans for
agricultural settlements! Partition of the great estates! Those were the lengths to which people could
go who had accepted a slave plan from the league of
the country's enemies. A pretty pass things had come
to when the wife of a Red chancellor could hold out
her hand, a servant maid's hand, to be kissed by the
lord of the German realm!

They had always been an impoverished lot, these
Beneckendorffs, thought Baron Oldenburg-Januschau;
and they would have to get out of their fine palaces
before long if the electors turned against the president, or if, perchance, death should summon him. He
was accustomed to spend his summers among a lot of
old women in Upper Bavaria, listening to an alien
dialect and to alien ideas. Better hale him back to
his native province! Old folks ought to reknit the
ties of their youth. What about presenting him with
the two-for-a-penny piece of property which a childless
she-cousin of Hindenburg's had left behind her in a
bankrupt condition, now to be sold for a song, and
torn up into a dozen strips? Then the East-Prussian
Junkers would have him under their eyes once more;
could awaken in him instincts racy of the soil, instincts
which had animated his landholding forbears; could
make him personally realize how the shoe was pinching
the country squires; and, maybe, persuade young Oscar
Hindenburg that he, and all the rest of them, needed
more money from the funds of the Eastern Aid. Excellent idea! The only question was who was to pay
the piper.

Oldenburg-Januschau made his way to Berlin and then to the Rhine. Welcomed everywhere, because he was not without wit and had a fine palate for Bordeaux, he seized a favorable opportunity for launching his proposal. "Our dear Hindenburg will soon be celebrating his eightieth birthday. Why should we not make him a birthday present of the land of his forefathers?" Within three weeks, the fund had been collected. Hindenburg, the "man without a blade of grass," as the impoverished Junker Caprivi had once described himself, was, at the end of his life, to become a landowner, that he might share the joys of his class, and presumably suffer under a liberal share of its troubles. The coal barons and the iron kings soon found an appropriate formula. Each of them contributed fifty or twenty-five pfennigs per ton of his output; and since, in the end, this was charged to the consumer, the gift of the ancestral property became a sort of national present to the popular hero, and the nation itself never knew where the pinch came.

Since, however, the cunning old fellow thought of everything, it occurred to him that Hindenburg's son would find it a hard job—before long, presumably— to pay the high death duties. There ought to be some way round that. Since Oscar had no private means, he would speedily find himself in difficulties. A good neighbor, and one of the prime movers of the gift, ought really to go out of his way to give him a helping hand. It was therefore decided that on the old man's eightieth birthday they would make the present to the son, who would then be approximately forty-four, so that the ancestry and posterity would be symbolically united by Field Marshal von Hindenburg, the greatest of his name and race. The son, who, though he had been simply brought up, had married a baroness of ancient lineage, would doubtless be well pleased with the gift.

A year later, Hindenburg visited Neudeck as master, or at any rate with the feeling of a master. Everything had turned out as his neighbor von Januschau had planned. True, it had been necessary to tap the pockets of the industrialists a second time, and the seismograph of economic life probably registered this new East-Prussian center of earthquakes by a trifling rise in the prices of coal and iron. The impression made upon old Hindenburg was profound. He had lived eighty years in high honor but with very little money, never having even enough to rent a good shooting, always compelled to live modestly, by no means in the style of his wealthy cousins. In fact, despite his great fame he was scarcely more than a beggar when, as guest, he visited the estates and castles of the great Prussian landowners. Now he had a fine, new, solidly built mansion with twenty-five windows in its frontage, and a big gate flanked right and left by the two cannon he had dreamed of when a cadet; perhaps the very ones he had himself captured sixty-five years earlier at Königgratz!

Of course it was no longer the comfortable little country house of the old days; but then he was no longer the unknown major. He had become a commander of world-wide fame, who had won the battle of Tannenberg and had forced one hundred thousand Russians to surrender.

Now there was a return of the cheerful days of the World War, when evening after evening the members

Reichspresident von Hindenburg, leader and chancellor Hitler, and president of the cabinet council Göring at the great celebration at the Tannenberg Memorial

of his own order had assembled round him as guests. For months in succession, Hindenburg stayed at Schloss Neudeck; the Dohnas—prince and count—the Eulenburgs, the Mirbachs, the Cramons, and a dozen other old gentlemen of title sat over their Burgundy in the handsome new dining room—complaining, one and all, how badly things were going with agriculture in this corner of the world. When the steward came on the first of every month, to show one of his two masters the accounts (which were as incomprehensible to both of them as political statements) the elder would get in a fine rage, and make up his mind that his chancellor must give further help to the farmers—especially to gentlemen farmers on the large scale.

Tannenberg was only two days' march from Neudeck. There, likewise, a new structure had been erected, looking like a fortress though it was only a monument—a gigantic monument in honor of the victory and the dead. When it was unveiled, the veteran field marshal spoke commemorative words, reiterated his assurances that Germany had been innocent of the war. "Pure of heart were we when we went forth to defend our fatherland, and with clean hands did the German army wield the sword."

Nevertheless, the monument was also to serve as a sign of union, so he went on: "May feelings of dissension vanish from the hearts of those who assemble to contemplate this memorial. It is a place where all can join hands in brotherly love, all who are animated by devotion to their country." A few paces from him stood Ludendorff, but the two commanders did not shake hands—a military salute rather divided than joined them. Nothing now prompted Hinden-

burg, chief of the State and of the Reichswehr, to
shake hands in public with this discontented man who
had been his assistant and to whom he owed all his
success. When Ludendorff spoke in his turn, the
field marshal had departed.

VI

From the streets the enmities that divided the German parties made their way into the Reichstag.
Party struggles developed into a will to destroy. Here
were really activities worthy of Herostratus. With
clenched fists, the Reds and the die-hards entered the
hall of parliament in the hope of tearing it down.
From the spring of 1930, Hugenberg, who had become
leader of the German nationalists, would no longer
bow to the will of the majority, wishing to make an
end of parliamentary government. Nevertheless the
crisis could have been overcome. With political wisdom and with patience, and, above all, with the will
to popular government, in Berlin as in other capitals
a solution was possible, if only the State had used its
own forces to deal vigorously with the extremists and
their private armies.

Hindenburg lacked both political wisdom and the
will to popular government; but the third requisite,
patience, was also on the decline. He had a new
chancellor, another Roman Catholic. During his
term as president he had appointed four Catholics and
only two Protestants, although he never really trusted
a Catholic, and in private was wont to ask jokingly
when someone was recommended for the appointment: "Is that another Catholic?"

Brüning, shrewder than Hindenburg's six other

chancellors, better informed, more of a financial expert, thorough, and indefatigable, was a man ready to make sacrifices. He was uplifted by a sense that he had a mission to save his country.

Brüning was a man of sensitive type; an intellectual with thin lips, a slender nose, and eyes that were inconspicuously keen and searching, like those one often sees in a Catholic priest who does not wish it to be known how observant he is; all his features were pallid but clear-cut, showing reserve even in the small size of his spectacles; he was gifted, moreover, with an unusually fine voice, beautiful rather for chamber music than for grand orchestra. In a word, he seemed a man who would have been in place in the Vatican; intense rather than strong; amiable, but cool-headed; and of a metal so finely tempered that one did not wish him to be more ardent. As he was a devout Roman Catholic, the desire for anonymity had become second nature to him, the longing for a position of activity in the wings and not in the center of the stage; studiousness coupled with patience; and, in addition, a mingling of sincerity and suspicion, of tolerance, caution, and cheerful matter-of-factness. In view of his distinguished manners, this might have led him to be regarded as a South German prince who had become, perhaps, a professor of theology, but was, under the rose, the prime minister's confidential adviser.

To these Roman Catholic lineaments were superadded English ones, for he belonged racially, and in large measure also by choice and the impressions of his youth, to the English tribes of the western Germans, so that he grew up devoid of the formalism of the German official and of the hard-bitten logic of the

French politician. He was not a man to trouble so much about the constitution as about its manipulation; a man to fix his attention, not upon the paragraphs of a written document, but upon the changing actualities of the situation. Having spent a dozen years in the whirlpool of party life, he was an adept rather of the older than of the more recent English art of government; of that art which never misses opportunities by clinging too closely to principles; the art of statesmen who give their love to few, but never despise their adversaries. His whole nature, composite of the Roman and the English, of the intellectual and the sensitive, of the doer and the thinker, was unmilitary through and through, inasmuch as God seemed to have created him for higher purposes than those of a warrior.

Still, he was a German, and had to pay the price of holding that unhappy faith in the sword which has wrought mischief in so many valuable Germans: not so much faith in the omnipotence of force, since he was too spiritually minded to make such a mistake; but faith in the romantic sheen and the feudal honor of the man of war—for, after all, the military estate was the highest in the land. When the war broke out, he was thirty; and he went to the front as a volunteer for the very reason that he had never been a soldier, animated by the zeal of the best idealists, who wanted neither position nor decoration, but only the credit of having risked their lives in defense of the fatherland. The fervor which then inspired him did, it is true, obscure his judgment as to responsibility for the war and as to the possibilities of victory, and served to inflame his monarchical sentiments; but it

was significant in other ways. Even today, his political speeches are full of parables drawn from life in
the trenches; and this man of fifty, who has been chief
of a great party, and subsequently a powerful chancellor, speaks with far more enthusiasm of the great
days in the summer of 1918, during which he commanded his machine-gun section, and with this select
troop solved some very difficult problems for the
High Command, than of his victories in the Reichstag
or in the League of Nations, where he was considered
the ablest German statesman after Stresemann.

Experience at the front, besides enlightening him
and shadowing his mind, determined his political
vision. Since his German heart was fired by the glory
of the man at arms, the upshot was that the uniform,
the superior officer, the commander in chief, and the
emperor, became symbolical for him; and his soldierly
feelings were intensified into pride in belonging to the
leading nation of the world, although his admiration
for England and the universal tolerance of the Church
to which he belonged should have warned him against
any such illusions.

We can therefore imagine Brüning's sentiments
when, an inconspicuous lieutenant, twelve years after
the end of the war, he was one day summoned by his
highest superior officer, the field marshal, to accept
the highest trust it was in the latter's power to bestow! Brüning forgot that he was appointed chancellor because he was the omnipotent leader of the
Center Party, and that it was as such that the president of the Republic, in accordance with the terms of
the constitution, was asking him to form a government. What official concern of his were President

Hindenburg's previous doings? Yet we cannot but feel that Brüning overlooked the lack of intelligence and culture in the man before whom he stood, and whom he regarded as superior to himself in achievement and in talent as in stature. He was confronted by the great symbol; the field marshal's baton was grasped invisibly in Hindenburg's right hand; indeed, the president represented for Brüning his royal War Lord. All the chivalrous, all the æsthetic sentiments of a German, admiration for the German pyramid, and pride at being asked to stand just beneath the apex, made him venerate a man who in any case was almost forty years older than himself, and who represented the spirit of the great war—for surely in the huge figure seated at the writing desk, the spirit of the great war had glowed more strongly than in any other human being. Did not thoughts of Bismarck and of William I cross his mind? Yet Brüning failed to perceive that two things were lacking in the comparison: as regards himself, the pride of the dictator; and as regards the other, the good faith of the first William.

It was not ambition that made Brüning accept the chancellorship; not primarily, at any rate. He had acquired fame as a financial expert and had been looked upon as the coming man long before; in 1929, as chief of the Center Party, he had been regarded in parliament as a notable parliamentarian and by the Reichswehr as a notable antiparliamentarian; and this man, a devotee of pyramids, from that of Weimar to the old Bismarckian one, preferring a weak parliament to a strong one, seemed to members of antidemocratic circles, though Brüning was little aware of the fact, to be specially fitted for the chancellorship at that juncture. Although he did not share the arrogance of the generals, still, he was in fundamentals inclined to agree with the views of the chiefs of the military caste; to think that rule should be for the social welfare, indeed, but conservative in character, conducted for the people but as little as possible by the people. Like many experienced parliamentarians of our day, he was weary of committees and of party life in general, and wanted to settle the problems of government single-handed in the grand style; though, not perhaps, as dictator, since he was neither strong enough nor weak enough to be a dictator. The times needed a sort of supreme tribune of the people, a tribune who would be given absolute powers because he did not want them for his own sake but for the sake of all, and understood better than most how to use them; but Brüning could not play such a part.

Hindenburg's peasant cunning scented in Brüning a lance bearer who would relieve him of trouble, would not burden him with responsibility, and would gradually lead back the Junkers to his side—without foolhardy adventures, but with tenacity and self-sacrifice. Indeed, the spirit of sacrifice which flamed up in Brüning flattered Hindenburg's long-standing self-deception, which always made the president believe that in promoting his own advantage he was serving his fatherland; and the reverent glance of this civilian may have been more gratifying to him than the stiff standing at attention of any general whom he might have appointed chancellor. Since Brüning continued too long to regard Hindenburg only as the field marshal, the latter saw in Brüning the people in arms, and thus, by treating each other as symbols, they misconstrued each other.

28

These feelings were manifest in their very first official encounter. Hindenburg, in conversation with his new chancellor, the reserved German of the Center Party, actually wept as he complained of his friends' ingratitude.

"They have all forsaken me," said the president, clasping Brüning's hand in both his own. "Give me your word that, at the end of my life, your party will not leave me in the lurch, as I fear it may do!"

While Hindenburg was making renewed overtures to his friends of the Right, who had first elected him and then abandoned him, and while he hoped that the Center Party would free him from the sinister trammels of the Left, Brüning regarded these maneuvers as premature, and wanted to wait until autumn. Only after long hesitation did he allow himself to be persuaded by two generals to accept the chancellorship, although one of these generals (Schleicher) probably looked on him as no more than a stop-gap. When Brüning now wished to form a cabinet which should be independent of political parties, he won the full confidence of the president, who thereupon began to inaugurate an era of dictatorial rule as during the great days of collaboration with Ludendorff. His new "chief of General Staff" promised to increase the power of the new "Supreme Army Command," and to weaken the Reichstag. He was faced by the same position as had been faced by Ludendorff in 1916—imminent danger which made measures equivalent to a political state of siege necessary and possible, and a Reichstag which was equipped with more extensive constitutional rights than had been the Reichstag of 1916, but really possessing no more power than it had had in war time; and Hindenburg himself represented an emperor who, like the emperor of those days, was a mere figurehead.

For the first time, Hindenburg was content with a chancellor, and perhaps actually began to feel affection for Brüning. Since Brüning made himself independent of the Reichstag, he was responsible only to the field marshal; and since his ministers made themselves independent of their respective parties, they were responsible only to the chancellor. The dissensions of a Reichstag which was rent asunder towards the Right and the Left by the two perpetually growing revolutionary parties on either hand, suited the purposes both of Hindenburg and of Brüning. Since, at times, the old gentleman was troubled by doubts as to whether what was going on was in conformity with the constitution, he would say to Brüning, as he had said previously to Braun: "I have sworn to abide by the constitution. You must help me to keep my oath!" Such, in truth, had always been his attitude, but he had not previously expressed it so frankly. Now, as a monarch, he had sunk to the level of a king who is dependent on his prime minister. Nonetheless he praised his chancellor, and said to various confidants:

"Brüning is my last chancellor! I shall never part with him!"

To emphasize his kindly sentiments towards the chancellor, when Brüning had to make a winter journey to the East, Hindenburg lent him his own fur coat, the tiny chancellor almost disappearing within the voluminous folds of the giant's mantle. As Goliath might have said of David, so, among his intimates, did this giant speak with ingratiating condescension of his shepherd lad, saying: "It is extraordinary how this little Brüning manages to get everything done!"

Thus there was established a relationship resembling that between a feudal chief and a vassal, one in which the vassal was the shrewder of the pair, and remained the leader while the feudal chief was eating or digesting his meals. Brüning, being convinced that Germany needed a military headship, with uniforms and decorations, did his utmost to strengthen the apex of the pyramid, though while doing so he was strengthening a mere semblance. If Bismarck had organized his constitution too much to fit the lines of his own gigantic frame, Brüning, who wanted to revive the Bismarckian constitution, adapted his efforts to a giant's figure which was utterly unsubstantial. One who might have been fitted by talent and by character to become the savior of Germany, was able, by his unselfishness, to strengthen, not the best or mightiest man in the realm, but the symbolical figure of his imagination. Thus the chancellor was able to make of the field marshal and his generals a class that grew more and more powerful, and a class whose traditional custom it was to reward a civilian for such services by breaking faith with him.

VII

As regards matters of detail, Brüning's achievements were remarkable, both in domestic and in foreign policy.

The voice of permanent revolution had been heard in the streets since 1918; but Brüning was the first chancellor who had heard it and had understood its message. Being a man of the utmost personal integrity, and not animated in his financial measures by

any desire for his own advantage, he was able to util-
ize his skill in financial matters, intensified through
ten years' study of the budget, to make serious efforts
at once to dispel the levity that had prevailed. Whereas
the great financiers of recent years had maintained a
false semblance of prosperity, he was able to reduce
the estimates by lowering the salaries of ministers of
State and of deputies as much as possible, and by other
wise economies, from 12 to 7 billions; and whereas
those who had been cut voiced loud complaints, the
socialists acclaimed what was done. His methods
were simple, but perilous; and their application was
only possible for a short spell, by a man whose moral
integrity was above reproach.

Hindenburg, perceiving that it was possible to rule
without the Reichstag, found pleasure in a scheme
which was more congenial to the Junkers and himself
than government by means of coalitions and compromises. Indeed, he had now discovered, in the
black-red-gold constitution, a clause which was very
much after his heart—article 48, which empowered
the president, in times of emergency, to govern temporarily by emergency orders—though, indeed, these
might subsequently be disallowed by the Reichstag.
This article, a stronger weapon in the hands of the
government than the German empire had ever thought
of fashioning, had been enacted in order to avoid
having to declare martial law in times of crisis. It
had been used once only, by Ebert, during the inflation period, to put some check upon the catastrophic
decline in the currency. Plans had been entertained
for a special enactment which should provide safeguards against its misuse; but the socialists, though

they had special reasons for dreading such misuse,
had lacked courage during ten years of power to take
the necessary steps—though the passing of such a
law would have been easy under Ebert's administration. When at length, in the year 1928, a bill for
restricting the use of article 48 was drafted, Hindenburg's advisers recognized the danger, and the president
declared that if the measure was passed he would resign. The giant would not continue to rule unless he
still had a carapace within which to take shelter.
Now that the Reichstag had been rendered powerless,
no one could deprive him of it, and his position was
secure.

Hindenburg and Brüning were determined to make
the fullest possible use of article 48. When the Reichstag refused to admit that there was a state of emergency, they dissolved parliament and issued writs
for new elections. Whether they were within their
constitutional rights in doing so is a moot point. The
elections of September 1930 gave Hitler, who had
hitherto had no more than twelve representatives in
the Reichstag, 107 seats, representing 6,406,397 votes.
But because of its lost homogeneity, because of its
internal decadence, the Reichstag chose to be ruled
by a "nonparliamentary" Brüning rather than by an
"antiparliamentary" Hitler, for it was afraid of Hitler's
shadow. Why, at this juncture, did not Brüning
checkmate the Reichstag?

It is at this point that the drama takes a new turn,
because the chancellor now began to realize that he
was being ensnared, and that he could not count upon
the president's good faith. If, in the beginning of the
year 1931, Brüning had still firmly trusted Hinden-

burg's word, he could have smashed parliament and destroyed the constitutional State. Why he could not venture on this was still a secret hidden away in the depths of his heart. For the moment, he contented himself with dismissing the last democratic ministers —among them ex-chancellor Wirth, though Wirth and Rathenau had been the best statesmen of the German Republic. Thereupon Hindenburg and Brüning began an absolutist rule, with the aid of a few ministerial experts.

Of course there were plenty of persons ready to quiet Hindenburg's and Brüning's consciences by assuring them that everything they did was fully accordant with the constitution. The most grotesque attempts were made to preserve "legality" at all costs. Schleicher, for instance, proposed to "develop" article 48 in the sense of a modification of the constitution. Another of these advisers had the idea of transforming the constitution in the light of "natural law." While the streets were a chaos, devastated by murders and other acts of violence, three eminent jurists, grave of mien, were debating the legal aspects of these infringements of the constitution. Nothing must be done that was not perfectly legal in character. Actually, government was carried on for years in defiance of the first principles of the constitution: namely, the confidence of the Reichstag in the chancellor, and its right to dismiss him as soon as that confidence was forfeited— the sole great acquisition of the Republic. Article 48 had been drafted to deal with cases of extreme and transient emergency, and specified that measures taken to cope with the emergency must be subsequently ratified by the Reichstag; and continued re-

liance upon this article for infringements such as those
of Hindenburg and his chancellor was just about as
justifiable as the act of a householder who, when his
house has been on fire, leaves the firemen's ladders
standing against it for days, weeks, and years, so that
any passer-by can climb in at the upper windows!
Although Bismarck, in the eighteen sixties, had ruled
autocratically, he had never tried to justify himself by
the Jesuitical interpretation of a paragraph, and had
subsequently secured indemnity by two victorious
wars which, like revolutions, seemed to create new
rights.

Hindenburg, pledged to the constitution by the oath
he had sworn in the year 1925, and bound, even against
his own convictions, to accept persons and programs
insisted upon by a majority vote, arrogated to himself
in the year 1930 the unrestricted privilege of forming
governments at his own sweet will and pleasure, calling them "presidial" or "authoritarian" governments,
and making his new ministers solemnly renounce dependence upon the political parties to which they belonged. He could no longer endure that any of these
ministers should tell him that they enjoyed the confidence of their parties, for he said: "You have my
confidence, and that is enough!" With these words
the Wilhelmian State had been reëstablished. Hindenburg was delighted that government was again
being carried out by orders from above. This new
technique, this rhythm of activity, suited his temperament and his habits. After all, it was not without
undergoing modifications that Brüning, the gentle
Catholic, had served as a soldier! Nor had it been a
chance matter that his three predecessors in the

chancellorship had not been soldiers. Now the ruling circle had been narrowed as in an army corps, in which the decisions of no more than four men can settle every question. From the year 1930 onward, people had to report their wishes to State Secretary Meissner, who committed such applications as he disapproved of to the waste-paper basket, and handed on the rest in a portfolio for the president's aye or nay. Hindenburg was now in a similar position to that of Frederick the Great; the monarch had become an autocrat.

Brüning, meanwhile, went on with his work, labors of Hercules such as no German since Ludendorff had performed. The ninety-five emergency orders with which, during two years, he ruled the realm, were all, with one exception, accepted by the Reichstag for the simple reason that, like a French sauce, the German parliament was now composed of such a number of vegetables that people could not distinguish one from another by the taste, and simply had to swallow the whole at a gulp. There were measures brewed out of domestic and foreign political motives; artificial formulas of compromise, whose alluring admixture made them acceptable to all parties—cadences like those which result from the mingling of two orchestral themes, varied according to the taste and skill of the soloist, ultimately to be resolved into their primitive motifs by delighted connoisseurs without anyone's venturing to modify so much as a trill in them. They showed the talent and experience of a maestro who had risen to become the commander of a parliament while lacking the means and even the desire to be a dictator—dictatorship being the last and most dangerous mask of democracy.

Meanwhile the confidence of the outer world in Germany was increasing, because the man who now ruled it as chancellor was not the servant of any economic group, and because his reputation and the tones of his voice showed him to be a gentleman. Here, at length, was a German who did not give the impression of being either boorish or curt, or too amiable, or pompous, or histrionic, or nervous; only of being stable, gentle, and upright. The minor traits of personal disinterestedness which become a man who is at the head of a bankrupt State; the way in which he cut down his own official salary, and made it his practice to use a taxi when paying private visits in order to avoid running up costs by taking out the car which the State put at his disposal; his frugality in the matter of dinner parties and festivals; and also the fact, beyond question, that he was genuinely religious, as shown by his aspect and his habits—made him congenial to foreign ministers of State. When he returned after visiting Paris and London in the summer of 1931 without having been able to raise a loan, he nevertheless brought back with him the invisible and imponderable gift of a confidence which, before him, none but Rathenau and Stresemann had inspired where the new Germany was concerned.

Having a good knowledge of both French and English, and having spent years in the study of the State finances, he was able, in drawing-room carriages, to withstand the onslaughts of Flandin and other statesmen mistrustful of Germany, whatever figures they might produce. Half an hour's talk with business men in London would extract 500 millions for cotton, copper, and other necessaries. The aging Briand, shortly before his death, a man with snowy locks, cordially supported him, and after a dinner party at the Quai d'Orsay, whispered to him: "Now you must win over Herriot; that is your principal task this evening!" When the French statesmen paid a return visit to Berlin, Briand spoke flatteringly about the staging of their reception and about the street decorations, saying: "Et voilà le jeune homme qui apprend son métier de mieux en mieux!"

In the year 1930, to shake off the burden of reparations, Brüning for the first time paid reparations. Since he simultaneously saved five billion on the German budget, although the world crisis was growing worse, the creditors saw that Germany at length wanted to pay, but could not. Speaking generally, the world crisis was most useful to this chancellor, for now the other States began to follow suit in refusing to pay their debts, and they all found the process so agreeable that in the end they were willing to write off the debts of the country that owed them most.

Brüning knew how to derive advantage from extremely dangerous situations; for instance, from Hitler's threatening attitude with his new and huge party and his private army. The chancellor continually animadverted upon the danger that this blustering fellow might establish a dictatorship; and thereby he acquired the "toleration" of the Prussian Cabinet, which had every reason to dread the manifestly armed Hitler more than it dreaded Brüning, who only wore upon his shoulders the invisible cloak of the Reichstag. In such circumstances, while the numbers of the unemployed were increasing by millions, and when the crisis was rising to a climax, to achieve so much was a very great thing. If the "monarch" had remained loyal to him, the vassal could still have done much for Germany.

The chancellor's rapid successes in foreign policy made even his keenest adversaries on the Left regard him with a kindlier eye. Brüning, who had never come in close contact with the people, used his knowledge of the war years, when he had rubbed shoulders with all and sundry in the trenches, with emotional skill; and, lonely man though he was, he thought he knew the minds of the workers, without recognizing the class State with its cruel Prussian injustice. The extent to which he could agree with the socialist leaders does not say so much for him as it says against them; but it also indicates how much both he and they were afraid of Hitler. All the same, he showed himself a skilled statesman by his ability, conservative though he was, to gratify the Left in many instances with his social measures—for, according to Hindenburg's desire, though he was to rule without the parties, he was to rule only with the aid of the Right. "We are playing a game of chess," he once said, "in which one of the players is not allowed to advance his pawns nor to attack his adversary's king."

VIII

Hitler, the unquiet star who was pursuing his own erratic course, was to be attracted into Brüning's orbit —he was, so to say, to become a great planet. Had not the national socialists always experienced a moral failure in their attempts to rule in the various German territories by joining forces with other parties? But what if they were now to try the same game in the Reich? As early as October 1930, and subsequently twice or thrice, the chancellor received the ominous revolutionist into his presence.

With what strange feelings must Hitler have entered the room which, for ten years past, he had dreamed of occupying as master! The chancellery of the realm must have exercised a spell on him, since for a long time whenever he visited Berlin he had put up at the hotel whose windows faced it from across the street. The unduly profound impression which legality has always made upon his fundamentally legitimist nature, made him appear indecisive in his negotiations with the old established powers. His obeisances were too profound, or his aloofness was excessive, as pictures show. Now he found himself facing a man of his own age, whose insight was much too keen to make him regard the clanking gestures of the popular leader as menacing. Brüning proposed to Hitler, since the latter was the only notable rival of Hindenburg in the coming election, although one who had scant prospect of success, that the election should be made needless by the passing of a law which would lengthen the presidential term. As offset for this concession, Hitler should become chancellor.

Had Brüning pricks of conscience when he made this cunning proposal? What was Hitler's pulse rate when he heard it?

Not to become chancellor immediately, went on Brüning, not tomorrow, but in about a year from now. By that time, he himself would have concluded his foreign political negotiations, and would make way for Hitler as his successor. Would not Hitler rise to his feet and eagerly accept such an offer? No, he was uncertain; wanted to think the matter over; went away, and returned next day, again accompanied by Röhm. Having listened to his friends' adjurations, he had come to the conclusion that only a man without hopes could enter into such a pact, which was limited by a dozen provisos and viscissitudes. He would accept, he said, if he were to become chancellor at once; but otherwise he would refuse. He delivered himself of this decision in a torrent of popular oratory, which did not deal with any of the chancellor's concrete arguments, but was accompanied by the songs of the Storm Troops who had been assembled for this purpose beneath the windows.

How could Brüning venture to make such an offer? Was not the man to whom he made it really a communist at heart? Immediately after the great entry into the Reichstag, in October 1930, the Nazis had proposed to confiscate, without indemnification, the property of the princes of the banks and the stock exchange, not that of the Jews alone, and the fortunes made by war profiteers and inflationmongers. Without exception, the great banks were to be nationalized; the salaries of the ministers of State and of the president were to be reduced by half; so were the allowances made to the deputies—alarming proposals, which both socialists and communists were ready to support. What had become of this terrifying notion? Unknown hands had gently guided the frenzied idealist into a different path, and when he came back again, the scheme had been quietly dropped. It has never reappeared. In the chasm where it rests lie the lost victories of a party which had been untrue to itself.

IX

Hindenburg's first presidency was drawing to a close. It had covered seven years which, from the outlook of personal power, he might describe as the seven fat years of his life. This man with the strangest biography known to history had traversed them while entering the ninth decade of his life, not gathering wisdom, not mellowing, but only growing more selfish and rougher. The test of destiny as to whether this man, who had been so excellent a servant, was competent in advanced age to play the part of an efficient ruler, was one he had failed to meet; and the classical notion of the "gerontes" (the elders), who were to rule dispassionately because their white locks made them venerable, had not proved capable of transplantation from the Grecian archipelago to the hyperborean regions. Everyone who occupied a subordinate position towards Hindenburg during these seven years, tells unpleasant things of him today; the president had many million faithful compatriots, but he did not leave behind a single friend.

His autocratic inclinations were ever on the increase. When the arrangements for a day of popular mourning were not to his taste, Hindenburg publicly reprimanded Wirth, the minister for home affairs, as if the unlucky man had been standing in the barracks yard at Carlsruhe and not in the hall of the Reichstag; whereupon Wirth tendered his resignation, but unfortunately let himself be persuaded into withdrawing it. Major Hindenburg, and Oscar von Hindenburg (who had a much coarser tongue than his father), were wont to say in such cases: "This pig, and the

other pigs in the Cabinet, must be cleared out!"
When, in the year 1932, Brüning suggested new boundaries for Prussia, Hindenburg rejoined: "I will never
approve of such a step! It is my determination to
leave the Prussian heritage undiminished to my successor." So completely had he thought himself into
the kingly rôle that he could bring himself to utter
so thoroughly Wilhelmian a sentence—as if he had
any right, in such a matter, to talk of "I," of a "heritage," and of "undiminished territory."

He clung to his position with growing tenacity.
Brüning once proposed that, should Hindenburg be
elected for a second term of office, the monarchy
might be reëstablished by a referendum, without a
coup de main, and, as the chancellor thought, with the
passive consent of the workers—intending, of course,
to appoint as emperor, not William II, but one of the
grandsons. To which the old man brusquely replied:
"I will never become a viceregent, nor tolerate that
any other than the emperor ascend the throne. I am
the emperor's executive officer, and should rather die
than be false to my executorship. Besides, a monarchy
after the English model is not a monarchy at all."
The basic reasons for this remarkable declaration were
perfectly intelligible to the crown prince, who, as he
himself has told us, once said to Brüning: "All that
it means is that the field marshal does not wish to
vacate his throne. He betrayed my father, betrayed
Ludendorff, and will, if anything goes awry, betray
you likewise."

With a second sight unusual among the Hohenzollerns, the sometime crown prince foresaw that
Hindenburg's breaking of that troth of which he was

so fond of talking would never be more cruel than in the case of his favorite chancellor.

While Brüning was accustomed to keep to himself what he had witnessed in the palace, we know of one scene which he passed on to his friends, and which they have with good reason communicated to the world, for no playwright could have invented a more telling outburst.

In one of those extremely rare moments when Hindenburg transgressed the limits of official relationships, on an afternoon in November 1931, the old man, whom memories of November 9 made moody every year at about this season, began to talk of the past. "I will not participate in another electoral campaign," he said to Brüning. "On the hustings, they always dig up the events of November once more. My intentions towards the monarchy were as good as possible. Before now, monarchs have been expelled from their countries, to be recalled by the people when better times came. The front had become untenable, so, as a veteran Prussian officer, I had to do my best to save my king's person."

The promptings of an uneasy conscience which, even during the last years of Hindenburg's life, could not come to rest about this unhappy affair, made themselves heard in these disquieted words, just as they did again and again in his remarks to Braun, Wirth, and Brüning about his oath to the constitution; for the moral problem that troubled the old man, who had broken away too boldly from his past and now shrank from the consequences, was how, when he came to stand before the judgment seat, he would be able to explain away his having taken two such con-

29

flicting oaths, having served under two such different flags.

This time, however, he was not faced by a dumb auditor who, critically or sympathetically, would keep to himself thoughts and philosophical reflections about the mental confusion of a man in his dotage. Before him was the front, the people in arms, and, indeed, one of those who had passionately fought on behalf of his king during the November days thirteen years before. At that time Brüning had been no more than a lieutenant, and Hindenburg had been field marshal; now they were sitting opposite one another as respectively chancellor and president of the realm, and the chancellor was trying to forget, not only his feudal chief's new position, but also his own. While Hindenburg was retrospectively contemplating the scene in that room at Spa which gave on the garden, when he sent his emperor out of the country, the younger man remembered how, at the head of his machine-gun section in Aix station, he had fiercely contended with the war-weary or hostile attitude of a superior officer, who refused him a train and a driver and machine guns, which he wanted to use in Herbesthal to recover that station from mutinous troops. But in the end he had reached Herbesthal, and, during these hours of November 9, midway between Aix and Spa, had kept open the line on the Belgian frontier leading back into Germany, over which the emperor would wish to travel if he returned.

Now the sometime lieutenant went on to recount to his field marshal how, at the head of his company, he had rescued the station from the revolutionists within a few minutes, and, expecting the return of the emperor, had made the route safe for him. But the report sent to the emperor ran contrary to the facts, being to the effect: "Rebel troops, coming from Aix, have just occupied Herbesthal station." Upon receipt of this alarming report, which seemed to cut off the possibility of return to his country, the emperor, after vacillating a while, had finally decided upon making his way into Holland, at a moment when Hindenburg did not yet wish for this retreat. Would not the story move the old man greatly?

Hindenburg sat stonily as he listened, and said, after a while: "It may have been as you say. But the other troops, those in your rear, were no longer to be trusted." Terrible acknowledgment, made in the twilight of this November day to an idealistic servant of the crown! For whereas Hindenburg, who had been in close contact with his sovereign lord and ruler for years, had known William to be faint-hearted, and therefore had not tried to hinder the emperor's flight across the frontier, Brüning perhaps still believed that there had been a disastrous mistake, and may have had it in mind, as an ardent participator in the tragi-comedy, to make a topical application of his anecdote. A false report had been sent concerning the action in which he had so fervently shared, with a result which he, above all, would have hindered if he could. "What," he may have asked himself, "would have happened if I had let affairs run their own course at Herbesthal, so that there would have been no disturbance there, nothing to cause a report to be sent to headquarters? But what then," so his thoughts may have further run, "am I to make of this field marshal, who did not restrain his king from flight?"

It may well be that, during these November hours, the scales fell at length from Brüning's shrewd eyes, and he recognized how shabby a part had been played by the idol whom he was to help to a new lease of power!

Perhaps; but he could not follow the fresh impulse. If he wanted to prevent chaos, he had to stick to his guns, as of old. With the same zeal as in 1918 on behalf of the king, the faithful vassal now devoted himself to the service of his new feudal lord, thrusting himself forward against the multitude of opposing lances. After all, it had been a mere pretense on old Hindenburg's part that he was weary of office and wanted to retire. But why did not this ancient king nod to him, saying: "Son, you may take my spear, for I have done with it"? Why, in his eighty-fifth year, did Hindenburg wish to go on ruling?

He was seven years older than when he had first been candidate for the presidency. At his age that meant that he had grown by seven years more obstinate, more disinclined to change. A man who, at seventy-eight, has accustomed himself to take his constitutional in the afternoon instead of in the morning, will find it hard at eighty-five to return to his former habit. Meanwhile, certainly, he had become lord of the manor and owner of a fine country mansion. But what would life be worth to him in that out-of-the-way place, if he had to spend the whole year there? Would his son return to service in the army, or stay with him? Was he himself to throw down the reins just at this moment, when he was at length in supreme control, and all humiliations with Reichstag and ministers of State were over and done with? Seven

The president and his grandchildren in the garden of the president's palace

years as head of the government had not tired him, but
had refreshed him. If, this time, they should elect
his adversary, so much the better! Then, perhaps, he
would once again give the electors of the Left a surprise! They must not think themselves indispensable!
Was he to make way for this "Bohemian corporal" to
whom he had refused power, and thus, by his own act,
opened the way to power? He was no more inclined
to take such a step than, seven years before, he had
been inclined to make way for Admiral Tirpitz. As
to the election after this one—that was no concern of
his, for God had not vouchsafed more than ninety
years of life to any of his ancestors. This would be
the last act, and he meant to play it to the end.

It need hardly be said that on this occasion, likewise, Hindenburg persuaded himself and tried to persuade others that he was making a sacrifice. When
Braun begged him to remain in office, "for otherwise
Hitler will rise to power," Hindenburg was by no
means difficult to persuade, showing plainly enough
that his class feeling made it easy for him to make a
second "sacrifice." "I must continue to accept full
responsibility for these emergency orders!" he said,
with a sigh. When the campaign opened, far from
playing the enlightened Olympian, he delivered a
fighting speech over the wireless. He was well aware,
he said, that he was charged with playing the dictator:

"Since the proper legislators," he now rejoined,
"since the Reichstag, failed to act, . . . I had to
spring into the breach. I was guided by the sound
military principle that a mistake in the choice of means
matters less than the abandonment of all activity.
. . . Not one of my critics can deny that I am in-

spired with the most ardent love of my country, and
with the strongest possible will that Germany shall
be free. . . . I do not ask a vote from anyone who
is disinclined to vote for me!" Remarkable words
to be uttered into the microphone by a man in his eighty-
fifth year, expounding the simplest motives in the most
hyperbolical terms, and, at the close, referring dis-
dainfully to his adversaries as unteachable.

Since Hindenburg had aroused distrust on both
sides, Brüning was compelled to move cautiously between the parties, and to flutter both flags; in this re-
election he showed more strategical art than his feudal
chief had ever shown in war time. Hindenburg had
not merely, as in the war, shuffled off the work and
the responsibility upon his chief of General Staff; but
even before the battle opened he asked from the latter
a guarantee of victory, and, during the first months of
the year 1932 he pushed his chancellor to almost intolerable limits, so that Brüning had to put aside all
thought of personal dignity if the onset of chaos were
to be avoided. But for the chancellor's efforts on behalf of Hindenburg's reëlection, Hitler would unquestionably have become president, and at that date
it was still possible to hope that such an eventuality
might be averted. Hindenburg was to be elected by a
part of the Right and of the Center; but in any case,
reserve forces from the Left were to be called up.

In this campaign for the consolidation of the traditional powers, it by no means happened that all who
might expect to derive advantage therefrom sprang
forward to support the chancellor. Brüning received
no help either from the president himself, or from the
generals, or from the court. The nobles declared

that "they had had enough of the old traitor," and
wanted a Saxon or Mecklenburg prince as president.
Intrigues were rife between the palace and the Reichswehr, which worked partly against one another, and
partly against Brüning, in a confused interplay of
motives which have now become incomprehensible—
with the result that the chancellor never knew, when
a particular decision had to be made, whether Hindenburg would be influenced by Meissner, by Schleicher,
or by his son Oscar.

While the chancellor was trying to deal with the
matter of taxes upon real property, with the possibility
of a strike, and with the limitation of municipal expenditure, Schleicher was parleying behind his back
with Röhm, and was boasting that he had brought
about this firm attitude on the part of Brüning—for
now he was continually standing in the doorway and
exclaiming: "Herr General, have I your leave to come
in?" When the chancellor was negotiating for a reduction in the price of Bavarian beer, upon which
Hindenburg's election might well turn, or was trying
to determine the reasonable price for lard or red cab-
bage, he would learn that at Neudeck some of the
Junkers had been giving the president false information regarding his plan for the settlement of the eastern
marches, and were inflaming the old man's animus
against "that bolshevik." While the chancellor knew
how to placate the leaders of the Left, who were making their promises of support in the election dependent
upon an increasing wave of popular feeling towards
their direction, or while he was discussing with one
of the foreign powers the preliminaries for a sitting of
the League of Nations, he became aware that he was

being spied upon, with the result that again and again he had to send for technicians from the postal service to see whether and where his private telephone had been tapped, and to have the walls of his office examined for microphones.

Can we not imagine ourselves back in the old Seraglio, where, when foreign ambassadors were visiting the caliph, it was the custom in the divan to let the fountains play more strongly so that the eunuchs of the palace should not be able to eavesdrop upon the conversation? Is not that square outside the great square of Galata, where *personae ingratae* were executed—publicly, then, instead of being "taken for a ride" through the forest surrounding the capital? In the new times and these different latitudes, were there not at work the ancient art of corruption by pelf and place, the old weapons of daggers and pistols, the same eagerness to secure the favor of the aging caliph, who, as caprice dictated, might promote or destroy? Save for a few minor technical differences, all went on at the court of Berlin as it had gone on at the courts of Stamboul and Cairo, except that some of the intriguers displayed a different form of unnaturalness from that of the eunuchs of the East.

What will posterity think of this epoch when it learns that the Corpus Christi procession, in which the chancellor, as a practicing Catholic, participated, was elaborately filmed, so that this kneeling and praying devotee could be exposed in a comic light to the Protestant majority of the population, thus producing the impression that he was something other than an exceedingly active chancellor? What will posterity think when it learns that the highest official of the

German realm, despite every precaution, could have
no guarantee that his telephone was not tapped so
that his conversations over the wire might be continually reported to his enemies—all this being done
with the connivance of officials for whom he was doing
his best?

If he held private converse with certain party
leaders, his adversaries' press would contain a full account of it next day. The existence of secret banking
accounts was discovered, providing inexplicable funds
for persons in high position and their friends; and
these discoveries had to be hushed up, for their disclosure would lead to votes being cast against the
president, though Hindenburg had neither part nor
lot in the matter. When Oscar Hindenburg wanted
Brüning to wink at his illegal acquisition of an estate
adjoining Neudeck, and the chancellor refused the
request, the refusal led to a breach between the two
men; and from this intrigue, in conjunction with half
a dozen others, there resulted a new turn in German
politics which was to lead to the establishment of the
Third Realm.

Can we be surprised that the caliph's caprices made
his grand vizier perpetually afraid of fresh surprises?
Brüning began to ask himself what he was fighting for.
His idol had been shattered. If he stuck to his guns,
bearing these humiliations, it was only because he hoped
to avert the devastation that would follow were he
not steadfast! Now, at length, Brüning knew his enemies. He knew that he was not being mishandled
merely that he might be able to go on fighting on behalf of Hindenburg; but during these last months he
felt it his duty to accept whatever might befall, be-

lieving that he alone was able to ensure the president's reëlection, that he alone had sufficient prestige in foreign affairs to secure the revision of the Treaty of Versailles. What he did not know was how vacillating was the light of the polestar towards which he still steered his course—though he would have known had he been informed about a conversation which took place in December, 1931, between Hindenburg and one of his cronies.

"You are an East Prussian and a Protestant. What do you think of my chancellor?" asked the old man.

The visitor replied that he had the best possible opinion of Brüning.

"Yes," rejoined Hindenburg, "within a few months he will have achieved remarkable successes; he will have freed us from the burden of reparations, secured for us the privilege of re-armament, obtained for Germany equal rights among the nations. But is all this to go down to history as the work of the Roman Catholic leader of the Center Party?"

When, as happened more than once, the chancellor began to feel his position untenable, and tendered his resignation, there ensued a tumult in the palace—for, without Brüning's continued aid they knew that in April they would all have to clear out and make room for Herr Hitler. Thereupon the old gentleman would withdraw the latest clauses he had wished to insert in his electoral address, and would once more begin to talk about his sacrifices for the fatherland.

X

On one occasion, Brüning had a chance of escaping from the snares. When, at the close of the year 1931, a monument to the Prussian soldiers killed in the war was to be unveiled in Unter den Linden, the Prussian prime minister Braun conceived the notion of having the decorations of the veteran Prussian army leaders melted down to make of them a gold and silver garland for these unknown soldiers. The generals were outraged at the thought of the decorations of exalted officers being thus used to celebrate the memory of common soldiers—it seemed to them a typically socialist notion, so that, with two exceptions, they absented themselves from the ceremony. Braun, who had witnessed his own son's death in the field in terrible circumstances, and felt the stress of these memories, spoke in very low tones. Next day the journals of the Right announced that this "November criminal" had had a patriotic speech written out for him and had read it aloud as inaudibly as possible. Since Braun was already near the end of his tether, the accusation depressed him so greatly that he went to Chancellor Brüning and offered to resign, suggesting to Brüning that he should have himself elected as prime minister of Prussia. Such a union of the chancellorship of the realm with the prime-ministership of Prussia, a thoroughly Bismarckian proposition, which would have greatly assisted Brüning in his work of domestic reform and would have relieved him from much of the burden of his personal labors, would also in great measure have made him independent of Hindenburg.

But the old man would not hear of it. The double task, he said, would undermine the chancellor's health! Eight months later, to Hindenburg no less than to Herr von Papen, the latter's strength as well as the strength of the constitution seemed sufficient to en-

dure the union of the two offices. Now Brüning had
to pay for having increased the personal authority of
his field marshal, and for having redoubled Hindenburg's consciousness of power; and we may well suppose that, after dismissal, he reflected on the fate of
Bismarck, who ultimately, in like manner, was ship-
wrecked because he had made an incapable king strong
and had curtailed the power of a previously effective
parliament, with the result that, when the Iron Chancellor fell into disfavor so far as William was concerned,
he could no longer look for support to the Reichstag.

While Brüning, during the most difficult weeks of
his life, was devoting himself to the electoral struggle
on behalf of a chief who, he was aware, had already
forsaken him, he was obliged to keep one ear continually turned towards Paris or London, listening to
discover whether his demands in these quarters would
at length be fulfilled; while he was stampeding from
town to town to speak in huge assembly halls beneath the portrait of his hero and to dilate upon the
loyalty and straightforwardness of a man who was to
betray him on the morrow, it was already common talk
both in the palace and in the street that "the Catholic"
was speedily to be thrown to the wolves. Hindenburg himself, for the first time in his life, became nervous, had fits of panic, and jealously guarded the key
of the left-hand drawer of his writing table, as if this
drawer contained dangerous secrets.

Letters, at this period, were one of the means used
by the Junkers to bring the old gentleman to their
way of thinking—letters calumniating the chancellor,
secretly dispatched by the Pan-German Union and by
the East-Elbian squires. According to Meissner's

account of the matter, there were "clothesbaskets full of them." One of these epistles was specially prized by Hindenburg, who read it aloud to a number of his friends. It professed to come from a certain Serene Highness, and was to the following effect: "Brüning has visited the capital of our hereditary enemy. He received the French in Bismarck's room. He did not succeed in raising a loan. Consequently the price of wood will fall yet further, and we members of the blue-blooded families shall be ruined. For that reason, you must get rid of him." This writer compared Hindenburg to one of the ablest monarchs of old-time Germany.

The chancellor steadily grew in reputation in foreign countries, and the inclination of certain governments to accept his economic schemes was a thing which Protestants could not endure as the achievement of a Catholic, nor yet generals as the achievement of a civilian. At Neudeck, therefore, a number of them went to visit the old gentleman and disclosed to him a plot that was in the wind. "Brüning had planned to divide up the finest estates in East Prussia, to reduce old families to poverty, and, after the bolshevik fashion, to settle unemployed workers on these lands—Catholics to boot! The man who had incited him to this was the renegade Junker, von Schlange." A memorandum relating to the matter, which had never been placed before the Cabinet, was now shown to Hindenburg by the East Prussian Junker, von Sayl. The fire beneath the smoke was that Brüning had actually considered a plan drafted by Schlange for the settlement of Prussian peasants upon certain unproductive lands which were to be paid for at the market price;

but what the Junkers could not forgive the chancellor was that during the last year they had received several millions less from the Eastern Aid than in previous ones. "Brüning must go." He must be used to secure the aid of the despised and detested Left in effecting the president's reëlection; and then he must go.

Were these worthy gentlefolks allowing themselves to be frightened by a potato bogle? Not altogether. In the streets and in the factories millions of young fellows were beating drums, railing, fighting for new forms, throwing at one another's heads ideas and hand grenades, beer pots and problems, in the hope of evolving a new world out of the turmoil. Here at Neudeck, in an out-of-the-way corner of the world, upon a desolate heath, in a new castle which was a mere mimicry of an old one, sat a dozen oldsters, spinning intrigues, painting ghosts on the wall, chattering in outworn phrases about the things of tomorrow; while amid them sat another oldster, equipped with great powers, who could make and break governments as he pleased, obstinate and cunning, allowing himself to be caught in snares by a few conspiratorially minded officers from the capital, involved in a web of folly and lies, believing anything he was told. Was this really the land of thinkers and poets, the land which, called upon for the second time after a thousand years to choose a chief, could hit upon no other man than this one who, waving his hand from one of the windows of his new dwelling house could say: "There lies my battlefield, there lies Tannenberg!"

Everything was at sixes and sevens in this election. The nationalist parties, which seven years earlier had elected him, were now opposed to him; the socialists, his adversaries of those days, were now on his side. Most of the Catholics favored the candidature of the Protestant, whereas millions of North German Protestants were ready to vote for Hitler the Catholic. The *Deutsche Zeitung*, which in the year 1925 had written: "Hindenburg will once more give the German people a form of State which will inspire respect in the foreign world," wrote in the year 1932: "The question at issue is whether internationalist traitors and pacifist swine, with the express approval of Hindenburg, are to bring about the final ruin of Germany;" while the national socialists spoke of Hindenburg as "the candidate of the mutineers and deserters." The electoral struggle, more violent than the one of seven years before, was entirely sustained by Brüning's passionate zeal, for the old gentleman neither made speeches nor traveled, whereas Hitler stormed hither and thither across Germany in railway trains and airplanes. Once more a second ballot was needed, and even in the second Hindenburg obtained no more than 53 per cent of the votes. In the second ballot, the votes for Hitler rose to 36 per cent. It was Brüning who, on the day after the election, lay exhausted on the ground between the rival candidates.

But speedily he leaped to his feet once more. He made a renewed attack on Hitler, since Hitler would not enter into an alliance with him. Four days after the election, Brüning, strengthened by General Groener's aid, suppressed Hitler's Storm Troops. A terrible blow, this, for the demagog, and one which no one previously had dared to deliver! It was carefully explained to the people that private armies must cease to exist. All the Right was on the side of the chancellor, being delighted at Hitler's defeat. Immediately afterwards there were fresh elections in Prussia, as the outcome of which the national socialists emerged strong enough to overthrow the socialist government but not strong enough to rule on their own account, so they decided to leave the outvoted in power. Further elections took place in other German territories, in some of which the votes for Hitler fell as low as 26 per cent. At the same time, there was a resolute revival of the slumbering Reichsbanner, under the new name of the Iron Front, with new badges, and with a new lust for battle. Now Brüning could enjoy the fruits of his victory!

But, in this struggle, he had kept his eyes fixed upon the enemy, for, despite his training in humane letters, he had forgotten Aeschylus's advice to beware of your friends. During these opening months of the year 1932, Brüning had grown too strong for General Schleicher's taste. The suppression of the Storm Troops was effected against Schleicher's will; for the first time in the Cabinet a minister for defense had got the worst of it. Schleicher was not used to such defeats. It is said that he flung out of the room and slammed the door behind him. After his manner, he took his revenge by subterfuges. Now, under his auspices, began the epoch of breaches of faith, which was to last a year, and to lead in the end to his own destruction.

Schleicher's first move was to demand in the Reichstag that the Reichsbanner or Iron Front should likewise be suppressed. This was done to annoy Groener; but when Groener, in a great speech, insisted that the

Reichsbanner was the only civil force that existed for the protection of the Republic, Schleicher took the floor against him, and next day Hindenburg dismissed his well-tried collaborator Groener. It was rank treachery, for Groener had built up Schleicher's position, and had, as he said, loved Schleicher like a son—a statement not likely to be pleasing to an aristocratic officer of the guards when made by one of middle-class origin. But this was no more than the overture. Now Schleicher, having isolated the chancellor, proceeded to mine the ground beneath his feet. He procured from the Supreme Court a decision that the suppression of the Storm Troops had been illegal—while this same Supreme Court did not regard as incriminatory the documents which the Prussian government produced against Hitler.

But what did the reëlected president do? A monarch, when his chancellor had won a great battle for him, would have made this chancellor a count. When Brüning brought him the congratulations of the Cabinet, and, at the same time, since a new government was beginning, announced the formal resignation of all the ministers, Hindenburg had no more to say than: "Of course I expected your resignations. You may make a public statement to the effect that, temporarily, I do not accept them."

Brüning pointed out that next week he was to represent Germany in Geneva, and would not be able to do so after an announcement so worded. Then, inspired with the courage he had shown long before at the fighting front, he added: "Let me implore you not to disappoint the majority of the German people by forming a Cabinet of the Right the day after you

30

have been elected by the Left! If the name of Hindenburg is to maintain its place in history, you will do well to wait a while." The veteran was startled. This was a new tone. The vassal was showing a will of his own. Danger threatened! Ultimately the announcement to the press was worded as follows: "These resignations are not accepted by the president of the realm"—but no one noticed that the stress was laid on the word "these."

When, shortly afterwards, in Geneva, Brüning was received with prolonged acclamations by the representatives of two-and-fifty nations, the old man listening on the wireless was, perhaps, for a moment, perplexed as to his attitude. Brüning secured so favorable a reception because the failure of Hitler's candidature was generally ascribed to the chancellor's electoral campaign, although the increase in the Hitlerian vote was regarded as a warning. This time Brüning must not be allowed to return home with empty hands as he had returned the previous summer. He actually succeeded at Geneva in inducing Britain, America, and Italy to agree to all his demands: canceling of reparations; 300,000 men for the Reichswehr; reduction of the term of service to five years; the levying of a militia; a permit for imports of arms; Germany's right to fortify the frontiers—everything comprised under the empty words "equality of rights." Tardieu alone failed to vote for the proposal. He would not answer the Americans' telephone call, "was ill, would see them next day or the day after." The agreement could not be completed. What had happened?

Round a fireside in Berlin (there still are a few) that evening, the French ambassador had foregathered with General Schleicher and other enemies of Chancellor Brüning and had been made aware that Brüning's fall was imminent.[1] Two telephone messages, between Geneva and Berlin and Geneva and Paris, had obviously sufficed to inspire Tardieu to refrain from joining Britain, America, and Italy in the acceptance of Brüning's demands. During these days, Albert Thomas informed his friends that he knew by what route the French armament industry was financing Hitler's party via Switzerland; he was going back to Paris in order to expose the matter. A week later, on his arrival in Paris, he died. . . .

When Brüning reached home, Papen and Schleicher prevented his being received at Neudeck. Simultaneously one of the foreign ambassadors asked how soon Herr von Papen was to become chancellor. The viceroy of Mecca was in Berlin at the moment. If, by chance, he had overheard the foreign ambassador's question, he might subsequently have told his fellow countrymen that Germany was about to adopt oriental political methods.

When, on May 29, 1932, Brüning was at length summoned to Hindenburg's presence, and complained that a sort of subsidiary government was being established, the old gentleman put on his spectacles and read from a formidable-looking document: "First of all, the government has not been authorized by me to issue any new emergency orders. Secondly, this government has not been granted by me the right of making changes of personnel." When Brüning went on to ask whether Hindenburg wished him to resign, the president replied: "This government must go because

[1] Cf. Wheeler-Bennett, The Disarmament Deadlock, 1934.

it is unpopular. As soon as possible. It is a point of conscience with me to make an end of it. Of course you must remain as minister for foreign affairs."

Thereupon Brüning lost his temper, and said: "I, too, have a conscience. My conscience forbids me, when the State is in the utmost need, to run from one extreme to the other."

When, next morning, at the appointed time, he was making ready to hand in his resignation, one of the foreign ambassadors arrived. Remarking that the urgency of the situation made this independent action requisite the visitor proffered a letter from a colleague announcing that there had been a change in the opinion of some of the French political leaders, who were now prepared to make common cause in the Geneva agreement. The letter concluded with the words: "Persuade the chancellor to return to Geneva as soon as possible, for there is every prospect of his speedy success there." Brüning's complete victory was in sight, but the pity of it was that the chancellor was on the point of resigning!

Besides, his enemies had seen to it that he was not to be allowed time to round off his success. Since everything made its way through the orientally permeable walls, within a few minutes the private visit of the ambassador and what he had said to Brüning had been communicated to the president. At once a telephone message came from the palace to the effect that the chancellor was to have his last audience, not at ten-thirty, but at eleven-fifty-five. At noon a section of marines was to march past in commemoration of the Battle of Jutland. In this way the camarilla protected itself against any weakness on the part of old Hindenburg because of the important news from France, and safeguarded Hindenburg himself from a long and painful scene. When Brüning entered, the president did not utter a single word of thanks, but merely said:

"I must dismiss you for the sake of my name and my honor."

Brüning answered: "I, also, have a name and an honor to defend in history." Silence. Through the open windows came the strains of the approaching band of the marines.

"I should like, all the same, to hook a finger in your belt, so that you could stay on as minister for foreign affairs."

Brüning rejoined: "I am not a Bethmann-Hollweg. If I regard a policy as mistaken, I will have nothing to do with it. I hope your new advisers will not lead you into courses which will involve a breach of the constitution."

The old man drew himself up stiffly. No one had ever ventured to use such words to him. Once more, however, he was rescued by the march past. Someone knocked at the door. The president was summoned to the front staircase.

He stood there as if he were his own ghost, saluting the banner of the war he had lost. Then he turned back into the palace. Unruffled, he sent for his son, and told Oscar to summon Papen, since the sometime chancellor had at length departed.

BOOK FIVE

THE THIRD FLAG

Princes often will mint on copper that's thinly besilvered
  Their so notable phiz: long time the people are fooled.
Humbugs offer as truth what is nothing but falsehood and
  nonsense.
Those who are lacking in wit, value the rubbish as gold.

—Goethe

THE THIRD FLAG

I

ANARCHY WAS raging through the streets of Germany. Four armies, equipped at least with jackknives, daggers, and knuckle dusters, shouted in the squares, rampaged through the towns, beat to quarters all over the country. No one really knew to which of these armies the crowds that thronged the streets were most strongly attached; the populace itself did not know. Long since, the catchwords of the programs, the names of the parties, had lost significance. Voiced by a myriad mouths, they rose into the air and were blown away like street ditties whose origin the very singer can no longer recall. Processions and meetings, leagues and protests, festivals and mourning ceremonies, were as like as two peas, whether they were those of the Red Front or of Hitler. The demonstrators marched to the same rhythm, just as two khaki-clad armies resemble each other, though their respective soldiers are shooting one another at the word of command. Even as during the great war, so now, the leaders, impelled by their own interests, were inciting the masses to a struggle which would have seemed unmeaning had those engaged in it stopped to think what they were about.

That was plainly shown by the desertion of thousands of communists to join Hitler's Storm Troops, and of thousands of men of the Iron Front to join the communists, so that deadly enmity arose between brethren who wished the same thing, but wore different

emblems and obeyed different leaders.   Thus was it in
the year 1932; and thus, in the fight between the
hostile brethren, the Steel Helmets and the Storm
Troops, it would speedily be renewed.   No wonder,
since the same classes were represented in the four
armies, the working class being predominant in all
alike.   Everywhere there were unemployed, adventurers, desperadoes, and gangsters; everywhere there were
idealists and enthusiastic students.   This uprising of
the German youth, whether they joined the Steel
Helmets, supported the Republic, or stooped to the
lure of communism, was nothing more than the mighty
protest of simple-minded young fellows against the
wretchedness of a life which their fathers seemed to
have spoiled for them by an incomprehensible war.
Gregor Strasser put this very clearly when he said
(though speaking only for his own party in words
which applied to all):

"The anticapitalist yearnings which animate our
people do not signify a repudiation of property derived
from labor and from thrift.   They are a protest against
a degenerate economy, and they demand of the State
that it shall break with the demon money, with the
habit of thinking in export statistics and in Reichsbank
discounts, and shall, instead, reëstablish a system that
gave an honest reward for honest work. . . . If, today,
people are no longer able to distribute the wealth of
nature, then the system is erroneous, and must be
changed.   These anticapitalist yearnings indicate the
dawn of a new age: an age in which liberalism will have
been outgrown, in which new thoughts will dominate
economic life, and in which there will be a new attitude
toward the State."

This was two years ago, and this still is today, what makes the masses follow their leaders; and the fog which envelops all who daily listen to and repeat partisan phrases is dispelled by the love of life in the young who desire neither idleness nor conquest, but only to enjoy that share of the good things of life to which their brains and their brawn entitle them. Thus what the Nazi Gregor Strasser said was exactly what the German socialists have long been saying in their May Day celebrations; and the communists, too, say much the same thing. After the war had rent internationalist feelings in sunder, and the quarrel between the western and the eastern workers had confirmed the distinctions of social stratifications, all the socialists left in the world were national socialists, each group of these trying after its own manner to deal with the money power in its own land.

Which of these forms of anticapitalist yearnings would first come to the top in Germany, and which would ultimately make good, depended upon the power of the leaders, and also upon their respective strength or weakness in the fight against money. The Republic had faded away because, being devoid of courage and imagination, it had attempted nothing more than an inglorious liquidation and had made a shameful retreat. The Red Front had dissipated its energies in fighting its own brethren, while it had been as devoid of leadership as of ideas. As far as the Steel Helmets were concerned, the manner of life of the veteran officers was necessarily repugnant to youth.

Hitler's outstanding success was not due to his program, half of which was practically identical with that of the nationalists, and the other half with that

of his socialist rivals; neither did it come from his
very remarkable discovery of the virtues of Jew
baiting. It resulted from the seductions of oratory
and from a generous use of promises. Instead of
trying to console the masses with nothing more than
talk of a war against France in some distant future,
and instead of wailing about the twilight of mankind,
he launched a definite program of "immediate demands." As soon as he was in power, the right to
work would be established by a system of compulsory
civil service which would find jobs, at first for half
a million of the unemployed, and soon for two millions.
The economic incidence of the house-rent tax would
be modified by remitting three fourths of it to everyone who made repairs. "Throughout Germany there
will immediately begin a hammering, a laying of pave-
ments, a painting and plastering, a roofing and cleaning
of houses." After awhile, work was restricted to the
last-named item. All his hearers could understand his
promises; and when he went on to pledge himself to
the introduction of new methods whereby produce
valued at two billions would in future be extracted
from German soil, he kept his own counsel as to the
fact that this annual increase could only be secured
by a preliminary expenditure of ten billions. The
masses believed him, as in *Faust* they had believed
Mephisto's enthusiastic descriptions of the benefits of
inflation when he was recommending it to the emperor.
Hitler had merely to mention that 400,000 new cottages would be built every year, thus providing work
for a million men, and they already fancied themselves
living in them.

Superadded was the effect of the other items of his

vociferous program. Unearned incomes were to be done away with; the trusts were to be nationalized; the workers would share in the profits of enterprise; the land tax would be abolished. "No academicians or other members of the possessing classes will be exempted from their share of hard work, for everyone will have to use pick and shovel." As the Germans are musical folk who would rather sing about a castle in Spain than reckon up its cost, and since their romanticism makes them readier to listen to a Magian than are those who belong to more sober-minded nations, they believed what they wished to believe, especially since they were given such concrete pictures of the good times coming. At least if they were not actually shown the above-mentioned new homes, they could see the painted stage setting, behind which they could picture the cottages in imagination.

Hitler, indeed, having a fine flair for the peculiarities of the German masses, left a great deal to their imagination; and was able, by this Wagnerian technique, to appeal to the feelings of those who were stronger in the heart than in the head. Since, in his speeches, he never counted the cost of any of his schemes, never argued, but was content to call up roseate visions of the future, what he said came as a refreshment to those who, for years past, had continually been disheartened by their leaders' calculations, by interminable columns of figures disclosing to them what they and their grandchildren would have to pay. Yes, Hitler awakened new hopes in a nation which is a bad loser and has never learned anything from its defeats. Pointing with demagogic vigor to the government and not to the war as responsible for the gray years, he showed the people guilty persons at home on whom they could take revenge, whereas vengeance across the frontiers would have been harder to achieve. Not Clemenceau had been the enemy, but Ebert. If the Germans had not begun the war, they would have been attacked by a wicked league of their enemies. They had not lost the war in fair fight, but had been stabbed in the back by some of their more evil-minded compatriots. Was it not natural that young people, whose minds are so open to suggestion, should enthusiastically believe both these assertions, being thus inspired with courage for vengeance abroad, and filled with hatred for those on whom they had to take vengeance at home? One who knew how to talk to them could mislead them easily enough.

Hitler knew how to talk to them. The spoken word, which today—thanks to wireless—has largely replaced the influence of print, has counted for much in this revolution; and when the orator spoke directly to his audience in assembly halls, there were plentiful appeals to eyes as well as to ears. After a decade of colorless discussions, flags began to flutter once more all over Germany. Orders were shouted; bugles were blown, and drums were beaten; and a new pyramid was constructed after the model of the old royal pyramid, one in which every stone could simultaneously bear and press. The whole thing was arranged in accordance with a Wagnerian technique: incessant entries; the unceasing melody of a few persistently reiterated motifs; pure-hearted fools and avaricious demons; dukes with jingling spurs and flashing swords, attended by troops of uniformed vassals; ever-renewed oaths of fidelity and repeated breaches of troth; the mingling of brutality and mysticism; heroism displayed by the petty bourgeois—all Wagner! By transporting the militarist State into the Wagnerian realm, he provided ample opportunities for fulfilling the contrasted dreams of the Germans: obedience and music, discipline and adoration. Thus was transfigured that crepuscular world in which Germans love to combine the victory of the Good with their personal advantage. This is the specifically German form of cant, akin to the British, but with a heroic stage setting instead of an ecclesiastical one—a mixture of Lohengrin with the Three Musketeers.

It was a good thing for Hitler, since someone had to defray the expenses of the great showman, that large-scale industry was affected by his beating of the big drum. Now that, by a quaint detour, the "captains of industry" were beginning to come back to the idea of socialization, they were ready enough to be nationalized, in a gentle and lucrative fashion—after the manner of the great mining combine, the shipping companies, and the banks, which had recently "half in semblance and half thankfully" allowed themselves to be supported by the State, preferring even to be taken over by purchase. Since the Rhenish Siegfrieds foresaw that the twilight of the gods was at hand, it was logical enough that, seeking rescue, they should hire a Wagnerian. They felt, being indeed lords of steel, but by no means men of steel, that all their underground deposits of ore were in danger of being swept away by the great deluge; and, to avert the extremity of disaster, would be glad to take refuge, carrying their check books, upon the last remnant of dry land.

II

Upon this island of rescue flourished the "Herren Club."* A hundred of the lords of creation—or was it three hundred?—smartly tailored gentlemen accustomed to be addressed as "Your Excellency," had got together during the last few years "to build a dam against the Red flood." A bird's-eye view of them might have suggested that they were figures from the decorative embellishments of the old-time Paris opera; but no one got a bird's-eye view of them. Junkers, generals, magnates of heavy industry, the old gods to whom the conduct of the German war, and therefore of the peace as well, had been intrusted, were cudgeling their brains—in the flood-lighted rooms of the clubhouse in the Berlinese Voss-Strasse, at select dinner tables, and after dinner in luxuriously upholstered armchairs. They were trying to solve the problem as to how the raging waters without were to be canalized, used as sources of energy, to irrigate their estates, supply man power to their barracks, and turn the wheels of their factories—in fact, to contribute to the maintenance of the estate to which they were accustomed,

Twelve years before, when the leisurely Republic was appointing commissions with a view to socializing the fundamentals of economic life, the industrialists and the Junkers had been advantaged by the general distress which prevailed during the years immediately after the war. The pleasure of being the king's successors was so small that they were not even inclined to become Herr Krupp's successors. The Junkers, too, had benefited by the disappearance of the burden

---

*Not rendered into English, being the name of an actual club, founded six or seven years ago. "Herr," it must be remembered, means "master" as well as "gentleman."—Translator's note.

of their mortgages during the inflation period; and the generals by the absence of bourgeois competition, since almost everyone was sick of uniforms. Thus all the three main types of gentry profited by Germany's defeat. At the same time, the moderates among the workers were the best safeguards against their Red brethren. Finally, the nationalist armed bands in the streets were useful demonstrators against the bad peace conditions and against those of the workers who had a Red bee in their bonnets.

Hitler's troopers were more dangerous. When the lordly ones contemplated the energetic masks of these armed men from the windows of their clubs or from their limousines, they could never clearly discern whether the Hitlerite forces were to be regarded as predominantly nationalist or socialist—especially seeing that the brown of their uniforms was somewhere between black, yellow, and red, so that it was, like the name of the National Socialist Party, deliberately ambiguous. The more vigorous the measures which the authorities took against them, the more rapidly did their numbers increase; with the result that old hands at the work of government, as the members of the Herren Club were, came to realize that they had better be legalized—all the more since their leader professed himself an enthusiast for legality. But among them there were a good many wild beasts whose behavior could not be counted upon, even though they were penned within a ring fence with the others. It was essential, therefore, to keep them supplied with food lest they should devour their masters.

In the interval between two games of poker, therefore, some of the "Herren" proposed to separate Hitler from his troops, to declare him a gentleman, and to satisfy his appetite by making him a member of an aristocratic government—a course which has been often found in history a successful way of dealing with revolutionaries. But would he be satisfied with that? And if so, what would happen to his troops? The generals, who were being besieged by applicants from their own circles for positions in the growing Reichswehr, hesitated to take on these fellows as well. The Junkers, on the other hand, being especially suspicious of the brown shirts, tried to mobilize the generals against this illegal army, advising the Thyssens and their friends to protest Hitler's drafts, which were increasing no less ominously than did the Reichswehr, though no one knew who was to foot the bill.

Anyhow, all these club calculations were reckonings without the host, for, unless you were positively prepared to make a revolution, you needed, for any form of government, even for a dictatorship, the signature of the only person who, amid the general anarchy, still represented the powers of the State. This signified Hindenburg. Precisely because he had exceeded his powers, precisely because he ruled autocratically in defiance of the constitution and his oath, precisely because the Reichstag had for practical purposes been put out of count as a legal authority, the president of the Reich could not possibly be left out of account as a wielder of power. So the question was mooted whether the Reichstag should not be reinvigorated, that the bold archers might have a second string to their bow. The old man who was the figurehead of the State was indispensable, absolute, and, in addition, incalculable.

All the players, therefore, tried to make sure of the

president's son; and the Herren Club had really been founded to induce him of his own free will to join the born leaders of the nation. Schleicher, who was at one and the same time a friend of Oscar Hindenburg and lord of the Reichswehr, was actually the most powerful factor in the club—and also in the State, in so far as the club could be subjectively identified with the State authority; probably, moreover, Schleicher was the shrewdest among these gentry.

Less intelligent was a certain Herr von Papen, though he was assigned a great rôle in the Herren Club. A man of uncertain age, with the figure of a jockey, light in every sense of the word, and therefore a gentleman rider who was at home in every saddle, a Catholic, but not too devout—Herr von Papen had, through a wealthy marriage, become an influential person in the heavy industry of the Saar district; and the French name of his wife indicated kinship with the Comité des Forges. Thus Papen came to regard himself, in virtue of the internationality of faith and of money, as the heaven-born intermediator between two nations whose armament firms really made more money in peace time even than in war. Being unselfish by nature, he had devoted his services to the cause of promoting good relations between France and Germany; and was one of the gentry who, by their banquets and conferences, had aroused the distrust of the intellectual leaders on both sides of the Rhine.

With a cavalryman's adroitness, and with an equal share of intelligence and fidelity, Papen was a sort of Falkenhayn minus Bülow plus Holstein; but he manifested, in addition, a sort of false uprightness peculiarly his own, since it had not been characteristic of any of

the three others just named.   As such natures thrive
rather upon the soil of old civilizations, in America he
had made himself impossible, not because he spied out
the land during the war—that was his job as attaché
at an embassy—but because he stupidly regarded the
Americans as stupid, the last thing he ought to have
done after his study of the phenomenon of gangsterism.
His schemes for the blowing up of bridges and railways
had been made public by a typical piece of cavalryman's carelessness.   He had left his check book in a
portfolio, with stubs showing the bribes he had paid
out; and this was found, and the publication of the
evidence during the war had brought discredit upon
the name of Germany.   When he returned, he was, for
the good of his soul, sent to join the Turkish forces on
the Jerusalem front, where he left another portfolio
lying about and worked further mischief.   It was
Ludendorff's way to have such soldiers put under lock
and key.   As it was too late for that, Papen secured
election to the Prussian Landtag, where he would have
disappeared from public observation had he not, with
the proceeds of his coal mines, bought *Germania*, the
press organ of the Center, wishing to use it in order to
drag that party to the Right.

In this position of power he made himself odious to
his party.   Since he invariably wished to show the
very latest patriotic complexion, he was a solitary
voter against the Young plan, being first an even more
vigorous adversary of the Republic than Hindenburg.
Soon afterwards, when the socialist government of
Braun was in power, he solicited appointment as
Prussian envoy in Munich.   Braun's answer was to
abolish the post in question, which had probably

lingered on as a vestige of antiquity like the posting of a sentry to keep guard over the first lily of the valley in Empress Catherine's park.

To guide him in intellectual matters, Papen had two friends of very different caliber: Captain Humann, whose gift for intrigue had been fostered at the German embassy in Stamboul when the atmosphere of the old-time seraglio could still be breathed in that city; and Edgar Jung, the philosopher, a muddle-headed idealist who dreamed of a conservative revolution and gave vent in barely intelligible German to his passionate longing for a new Germany. Since neither of them was a Junker, and neither of them sufficiently a political leader to rise to power, one of them inflated Papen's balloon with cunning, and the other with political ideas, in the hope of giving it sufficient buoyancy.

In the chaotic epoch I am now describing, the men of the aforesaid club continued to regard politics as a game of chess, and, when asked what would be the upshot of a move, liked to compare their position to that of a knight or a bishop on the chessboard. Since Papen's skill as horseman was more widely known than the mess he had made of things during the war, the younger Reichswehr officers were inclined to regard him as a diplomatist, while diplomatists fancied him to be a talented officer of the General Staff. In any case, Schleicher, the king maker, had determined to put Papen in one of the seats of the mighty, believing that Papen was stupid enough to keep running in leading strings. Young Hindenburg brought Papen to the President of the Reich.

In folk stories we sometimes read of giants living in caves, who are pleased to have about them small cajoling creatures, all-things-to-all-men, able to jump, run, chatter, and laugh, cheerful and diligent, ever on the go, ready to fetch kindling or stir the soup or to rid the giant of a mischievous kobold. It was in this spirit that Hindenburg found Papen charming. And since Papen had been an officer in the army, and could tell the field marshal an anecdote or two about experiences on distant battlefields; was also wealthy, quite the gentleman, and not (as Brüning had been) a Catholic with burning eyes and a sense of a mission, but so small a fellow that one hardly noticed he was in the room, the old giant did not hesitate to make use of this Ariel to assist him in carrying out his own political designs. Oscar and Schleicher had advised him to the step. Did not Papen promise to bring along the Center, and, in alliance with the centrists, to shake Herr Hitler out of his mystical dreams of leadership into the realities of party life?

Except for Michaelis, no chancellor of the German realm had ever been so completely unknown to the people as Herr von Papen, whose sole acquaintances that mattered were the Americans he had cheated. But never before had any minister of State so clearly recognized the rôle which it was incumbent on him to play, for during the last weeks of the Brüning government Papen had written to a friend in Paris: *"Après Brüning vient le chaos."* Chaos was himself!

Although Hindenburg had ruled unconstitutionally when Brüning was chancellor, Papen was the first man in republican Germany to be appointed to that office without any reference to the Reichstag, as in the days of Emperor William. It was natural, therefore, that Papen, existing only by the grace of the old gentleman,

Hindenburg, October 4, 1915

should appoint as ministers none but persons who would please his patron, members of the Herren Club, gentlemen of family, like General von Schleicher, various feudal barons and counts, and only one bourgeois, a magnate of the strictly loyal dye industry. If, simply as a joke, anyone had troubled to ask on how much parliamentary support this independent Cabinet could reckon, hardly five per cent of the votes would have been forthcoming. The Center, which Papen was to bring along as his first gift, at once showed itself refractory, for its members had been mortified by the contemptuous dismissal of their leader, Brüning, and had been by no means placated by the appointment of Papen, whom they had already expelled.

From June to November, 1932, Papen's cabinet ruled Germany in virtue of article 48; for the old giant had broken this clause out of the constitution to flaunt it in the sun as a precious jewel, while the remainder of the diadem rolled at his feet on the floor of his cave and disappeared into the darkness.

III

The struggle which ensued between populace and Junkers, between the men in the street and the members of the Herren Club, was a drama preceded by a farce whose characters—farce notwithstanding—were to throw tragic shadows upon the drop sheet of history. However easily had run the current of the old autocrat's life since he had discovered the before-mentioned jewel, he had always to reckon with that wretched Prussia; for Prussia was governed by democratic ministers who could continue to hold power although they did not have a majority in the Landtag, because the

brown shirts could not command a majority either.
Behind these formalities of the conduct of business
loomed important questions of power, for the Prussian
police were supposed to be socialistically inclined, or at
least republican in sentiment.   It would appear that
Hindenburg must have made Papen's appointment as
chancellor conditioned upon the cashiering of the
Prussian ministers of State.   Even if confirmatory
evidence of this condition be not yet obtainable, there
can be no doubt that at least the president's signature
was requisite before the action could be taken which
finally butchered the Republic.

If Papen wished to pose as a conqueror with his foot
upon the Prussian dragon, he must be quick about it,
for his great rival without portfolio, Hitler, had long
been ready to slay the monster.   Thanks to the marvelous construction of the Bismarckian realm, which
had been copied in the new constitution, there were in
Berlin two governmental chiefs: a chancellor and
gentleman jockey for the realm; and another ruler for
Prussia, Braun, the socialist premier, who had held his
post for thirteen years.

Braun, however, the only man they were afraid of,
had gone on leave since the overthrow of his government at the April elections, resolved never to return.
After seven years' silent struggle against Hindenburg,
of whose mulish obstinacy the public knew little, and
still knows little today, Braun contemplated with
bitterness the likelihood of similar experiences during
the next presidential term, whose inauguration he had
supported in order to avert a Hitlerite chaos, but
during which he did not wish to continue the struggle,
since there were no men of strong character among

those who immediately surrounded him. A commander rather than a fighter, he withdrew, suffering and dispirited, before the great crash. Among the others, men who for fourteen years had ruled too impartially and justly, not one could be developed at the last decisive hour into a real fighter. We do not know whether any of them foresaw a *coup d'état;* probably they comforted themselves by recalling that Hindenburg had just sworn loyalty to the constitution for a second time, and that he owed his second presidency above all to the parties of the Left, so he would not be likely to attack them in the rear.

Papen counted upon this moral prejudice in the hearts of the Prussians when, at a dinner in the Herren Club (which had now, for practical purposes, usurped the powers of the German Reichstag), in strict confidence, he expounded his plans for the conquest of Prussia. They were plans wherein the comic element was intensified by the fact that victim and executioner were to be in the same place—the Wilhelmstrasse and Unter den Linden in Berlin. Had Hindenburg been won over? Oh, yes, that had been facilitated by a conversation with one of the invariably available jurists, a professor who had convinced the president that everything would be done with strict propriety. True, the old gentleman as late as March had strongly protested against the implication that he wanted to delay the Prussian elections; but now, day after day, he was receiving letters from persons of standing who urged him to sweep away the last vestiges of the Republic whose president he was. Doubtless Hindenburg had forgotten that fifteen years before he had arranged for similar letters to be sent to William, to indoctrinate the emperor with public opinion. For the rest, at this moment the Reich owed Prussia one hundred million marks; and if the Reich did not pay Prussia, Prussia could not pay her officials' salaries. This gave a splendid pull! Now the lordly ones became aware that in internal policy no less than in foreign policy, the debtor is in a much stronger position than the creditor.

General Schleicher foresaw difficulties. What if the lawful rulers of Prussia, who were well acquainted with his socialist leanings, were to urge him to marshal the Reichswehr in their defense? Supposing he were to refuse, the Prussians might have recourse to their own powerful police, might declare a state of siege in Prussia, might call a general strike, mobilize the Iron Front, occupy the wireless stations, arrest Papen. What if they did nothing more than take airplanes to Cologne, establishing themselves in the Zone where no Reichswehr could follow them? The Kapp Putsch, twelve years before, had been frustrated by precisely these means. Nonetheless, after dinner, the Herren Club had made up its mind to take the risk; for over their coffee and liqueurs, the members felt they had surmounted the last difficulties by deciding upon the military occupation of all the airdromes. For executioner, Papen could put his hands upon a burgomaster who, as was now usual in Germany, was prepared for the sake of the fatherland to violate his oath as a Prussian official. Other Berlinese officials who were in the know, were also willing, by maintaining a patriotic silence, to stifle pricks of conscience in favor of reasons of State.

Why was the conquest of Prussia successfully

achieved? The vanquished were fatigued, the victors were fresh and vigorous; the former were democrats, the latter were soldiers; the former were men who went out for a ride every morning, whereas the latter sat in stuffy rooms surrounded by documents. Thus the whole thing went by clockwork. On the appointed July day, Papen informed the Prussian ministers of State that they had been deposed by order of the president of the realm. When Severing, the Prussian minister of the interior, declared he would yield only to force, Papen asked politely at what time the force was to be applied. At the appointed hour, Severing's successor appeared, attended by two policemen. The deposed minister knitted his brows, protested in due form, and quietly walked out of the office which, after his kind, he had successfully administered for ten years. The chief of the Berlin police, whose headquarters were always a menace as the great fortress of the capital, telephoned several times, made a written protest, and then allowed himself to be arrested. An hour afterwards he signed a declaration pledging himself to abstain from any further official proceedings, and was joyfully received the same evening by his family and the newspaper reporters.

However, the dispossessed authorities did not all behave with like equanimity. The chief of police, who had been told the day before what was about to happen, being a philosopher, wrote in his memoirs: "We felt that what must be, must be." He sent back the order of dismissal to have it duly signed and dated, and he records having courteously asked those who brought it back to him to be seated. Severing, on the other hand, seems to have been more nettled, and refused to take the hand which his executioner, with assumed good-humor, stretched out to him.

Hundreds of thousands, nay millions, were disillusioned. While their leaders were quietly allowing themselves to be dismissed, or were yielding to the display of force, the workers were tensely awaiting the summons for a general strike. The constabulary was spoiling for a fight; and the eight Reichswehr soldiers who were sent as a show of force for the removal of the chief of police from the Police Headquarters were pale and nervous, being afraid that the police might shoot them down. Communist leaflets were distributed throughout Berlin. Hundreds of thousands, nay millions, were disillusioned and disheartened; but we can hardly reproach the ministers of State on that account. The situation in 1933 was not like that in 1920, when it had been possible to put an end to the Kapp Putsch by a general strike. The railway employees, the officials of the ports and telegraphs were no longer in a fighting mood; trade unionists in general had no stomach for the fray, since they knew that millions of unemployed were eager to take their places should they down tools, and the tirades of the communists against the socialists by no means served to increase their combativeness, while they believed that the police would turn against them. Besides, there seemed to be a justification for the *coup d'état* in the clash between the laws of the realm and the territorial laws, whereby the police were subordinated to the army; and the way had been prepared for a conflict between the masses and the Reichswehr through the canceling of the suppression of the Storm Troops, and the artificial fostering of disorder.

In view of all these facts the leaders were loath to give a signal which might have led to a blood bath, might have promoted civil war. When, at Christmas, 1918, General Groener had sent a few soldiers to rescue Chancellor Ebert, who was besieged by the radicals, and Ebert begged the general not to fire on the besiegers, Groener replied: "If you say that once more, I shall never trouble to rescue you again!"

Two different worlds! Those of one world wanted power at any cost; those of the other clung to legality and wanted anything rather than that there should be a breach of the peace. In these matters, the fighting men were better pupils of Karl Marx than were the so-called Marxians. It may have redounded to Ebert's honor that he did not wish to take vengeance on his besiegers; but Groener was not best pleased. One who would make such gestures must be a Caesar, and even then he could only venture to make them after great victories. Note that even a Hindu crowd cannot, in the long run, stick to the policy of passive resistance. In this way the leaders of the people not only forfeit their power, but lose their hold on the populace, because they destroy its faith in themselves.

In the same police courtyard where, on November 9, 1918, as previously recorded, a lieutenant had broken his sword because the imperial general ordered him not to fire upon the rioters, now, on July 20, 1932, the officials and constables who thronged the windows shouted: "Liberty forever!" The lieutenant fourteen years earlier, and the constables and officials now, were alike: they appeased their consciences, one by a gesture, and the others by a shout. They wanted to fight for their rights, but refrained because their superior officers did not wish fellow citizens' blood to be shed. The militarist rulers of Germany, on the other hand, had only been momentarily fatigued at the time of their great defeat. They speedily recovered. Democracy, however, fatigued from the start, melted away ineffectually as it had lived, and the only thing left to wonder at was that the masses of the people had still sufficient vim in them to be spoiling for a fight after their anæmic leaders had so tamely submitted.

This inglorious exit of the German Republic did it more harm than any lost battle in the streets of Berlin could have done. The March day of 1848 has never been forgotten, because there was blood-letting on that occasion. A creature which fades out after fourteen years may be lamented, but will never be sung— unless it has been extraordinarily beautiful. The Republic's lack of vitality is explicable because it was procreated in a sleepy condition betwixt exhaustion and fear. If it had been the offspring of battle and sacrifice, of fierceness and passion, the German Republic, had it perished, would have perished in a different way.

What is most tragic in this matter is our recognition that, although the victors greatly excelled the vanquished in verve and imagination, they were animated by ideas about blood and race which belonged to an epoch we have outgrown. It is no more possible to rule enduringly with the will to power but without the finest ideals of one's time, than it is to rule with the aforesaid ideals without the will to power.

IV

In the struggle between the people and the masters, these latter had easily overcome one of their enemies who was outwearied; the other enemy, fresh and vigorous, assembled his forces all the more threateningly in the squares, not allowing himself to be intimidated by eight Reichswehr soldiers, nor yet by eight thousand. Instead of declaring open war against him, therefore, the Herren Club tried to induce the tribune of the people, who was backed up by such formidable armies, to make truce with them. The ideal course would have been to have enticed him into the cabal of the Junkers, entering into alliance with him for their own benefit; much as the Junkers were wont to marry beneath them when the bride was rich, so that her dowry should strengthen their own financial position. Papen's Cabinet, which was supported by only five per cent of the votes, would have acquired by such an alliance, at one stroke, an additional fifty per cent.

As Hitler was crafty enough to resist these allurements, various other plans were discussed in the Herren Club. The first of these was proposed by Schleicher, who had more understanding than his fellows where popular movements were concerned. Because Schleicher was more intelligent than Papen, Hitler could more readily come to terms with the former than with the latter; and was more willing to listen to Schleicher, since, when Brüning was chancellor, Schleicher had resisted the suppression of the Storm Troops. Schleicher, being determined to enter into an alliance with the masses so long as they were not too red, remained throughout the year 1932 in touch with their leaders, treating Hitler much as persons in good society treat a distinguished Jew whose distressing origin can be over-looked because he is a man of might. To his own subordinates the general retailed a few loyalist phrases from Hitler's proclamations; explaining to them, like-wise, that in the war on two fronts Hitler had offered him the help of the Storm Troops for the protection of the eastern marches.

For the rest, Schleicher, being always a schemer, and inquisitive by temperament, liked to glean Nazi gossip in converse with Hitler's understrappers.

Hitler, on his side, had excellent reasons, before the elections in July 1932 (in Prussia, there were to be elections as well as arrests), for remaining on good terms with the Reichswehr. Seeing that, in the civil clashes which were daily becoming more violent, he was gaining more advantage than were his adversaries, it was essential to him that the Reichswehr should remain neutral. If only for that reason, he had for the first time in his life joined forces with the govern-ment. This year he had become strong enough to take such a course. Whereas Brüning had prohibited his private army in April, and wanted to see its leader's head on a golden platter, Papen, in June, had given renewed life to this same army, and was happy to secure from the revolutionary leader a (presumably written) pledge that the latter would tolerate Papen's government. In this matter a personal wish of Hin-denburg's seems to have been decisive, for Hitler, regarding Hindenburg as the source of power, wished to be accommodating to the president. Not that the old gentleman expected that Hitler would desist from his ambitions, but he hoped that Papen, his new confidant, would be able to keep the devil quiet for a time.

When, at this juncture, the Storm Troops appeared freely in the streets once more, no longer hostile to the State, they had acquired a more strictly military aspect.

Hitler conducted his election campaign with his usual skill in these matters, whereas the Cabinet of the Herren Club was unacquainted with the political technique, and the socialists had been disheartened by the collapse of their leaders. At the end of July, therefore, the Nazis won nearly half of all the seats, and, in alliance with the Center, could have decided everything.

Papen, who was fonder of conferences than of elections, since he understood only the language of the Masters (though he understood this in several dialects), proceeded without difficulty to garner the fruits which Brüning's dismissal had snatched from the latter's hands at the eleventh hour. In Lausanne, at the close of conferences which had lasted twelve years, the claim for reparations was dropped, except that it was thought more tactful to agree upon the retention of a liability for three billions. Concerning this the representatives of Germany, an hour after they had solemnly signed a pledge to pay them, confided smilingly to two foreign journalists that the creditors might whistle for their money. Rejuvenated by his success, Herr von Papen forgot that he was now chancellor, and no longer a secret agent trying to bring about the destruction of American bridges.

Meanwhile the field marshal, eighty-five years of age, was on holiday at Neudeck. No one calculated on his speedy death. When people spoke of his age, it was usual to remind the auditors that William I had lived

32

to be six years older.   But Hitler had recognized the symbolism of these vital stages, publicly declaring, "He is eighty-five, I am forty-three—I can wait."   In despondent moments, however, the Leader would say that it was time for him to take over the realm, since he was now more than forty.

In Hindenburg, during this last act, the harsher lineaments of his character had become intensified, just as the furrows had deepened on the old man's face, while the kindlier traits disappeared more and more.   Not one of those who served him at close quarters in the nine years of his presidency had anything good to say of him when he had gone; and Brüning, the last man who really honored him, let fall the following words to some English friends, "The day before he dismissed me, he lied to me three times."   The veneration which the field marshal had formerly inspired gave place in the end to fear; and whereas previously he had aroused confidence, the feelings which animated him and those with whom he worked were now feelings of mutual mistrust.   His antagonism toward those to whom he owed his reëlection ate into him like a canker, for he could not but regard the success that had been due to the assistance of the detested Reds as a source of undesired legitimation of his going over to the Republic.   The circles to which he had belonged, or as he put it, in which he had served until his eightieth year, did not spare him their jibes for having been granted a triumph "by Jews and deserters."   Nevertheless the estate and the fine new country mansion, together with self-interest and class feeling, renewed his ties with those from whom he had sprung.

Even though the acuteness of these conflicts might be blunted by the natural dulness of extreme old age, he could never forget that he was serving under the black-red-gold banner, which, since he was president of the realm, had to wave in the Prussian wind even over his roof at Neudeck. Amid the confusions of this year, when he was continually justifying his dictatorial measures as strictly legal, the question of the significance of his oath of loyalty to the Republic must have been more and more disturbing to the mind of the veteran officer. Although we have no memoirs relating to this period, there are two remarkable indications of what was going on within him—of matters which, according to the present writer's understanding of history, are more important than the figures of ballots or of treaties involving the payment of billions. In the middle of a conversation with Braun, the Prussian premier, the president said:

"I kept my oath to my king. Now I shall keep my oath to the constitution."

We see, then, that Hindenburg clearly separated the two epochs in his mind. Like a careful steward, he had, as it were, two sets of books, and was sedulous to avoid mixing the royal accounts with those of the Republic. With the extinction of the monarchy, his duty to that institution was over, at any rate from the outlook of those who are sticklers for legality and nothing more. It need not trouble his conscience that at Doorn he was regarded as the arch traitor—a position of honor at first reserved for Prince Bülow. In any case, years after having been absolved from his oath, he had voluntarily assured his king of his eternal loyalty. Besides, Hindenburg had not dragged William

down from the throne as Cromwell had dragged
Charles, but had never ceased to insist that he was
monarchical in sentiment.   If he had become president
of a republic which, according to his theory of the
matter, had driven out the king, that concerned the
politics of the interior of Germany, and had nothing
to do with an ex-king living abroad.

What came to trouble Hindenburg at the age of
eighty-five was not so much the contradiction between
the two oaths as the interpretation of the second.   His
having transferred at the age of seventy-eight from
service under the first flag to service under the second
gave him no pricks of conscience.   A return to the
first flag might arouse the unpleasant impression that
he was a backslider—yet he could not but feel how
far he had transcended the limits of the constitution
now that he was ruling like an absolute monarch.
Unquestionably such feelings must have stirred within
him, for one day, when discussing with Wirth certain
matters of State, he rose to his feet suddenly, and,
without transition, said, "Believe me, Sir, I shall keep
my oath to the constitution!"

There stood the old giant, and since the minister was
disinclined to discuss the question with the president
of the realm, he bowed and went away.   The topic was
never reopened between the two.

These abrupt asseverations, made to two serious-
minded men, irrelevant in each case to the remainder
of the conversation, and not evoked by any constitutional crisis, give us a profound insight into the mon-
olog that must have been going on within the old
man, who had sworn loyalty to the second flag with
the firm intention of keeping his oath, and was now

being led into devious paths by the course of public
affairs and by the peculiarities of his own character.
He found a way out of his difficulties as he had found
guidance in early youth, by reiterating the words
"duty" and "service," which, rightly interpreted, can
always grant absolution. "How will posterity judge
me?" he asked a friend one day. "I lost the greatest
war in history. Our people, that appointed me to the
highest post in the realm, I have been unable to help.
Still, what matters most is that one should always have
tried to do one's duty to the best of one's ability."

What did the eyes of this old, old man, eyes that
were sometimes clouded and then for a moment would
become as clear as they had ever been, see when he
contemplated the chaos in the country he had been
called upon to rule? What his gaze first lit upon would
be his son and his grandson. They were unchanged;
the tranquillity of his household was undisturbed.
Then there were the ancient acres which his ancestors
had tilled, but whose cultivation could no longer be
made to pay. Cousins and nephews wrote to announce
that the oats crop was middling good, that the new
artificial manures had had an excellent effect; it would
be a good thing if someone would keep a tighter hand
on the brown shirts—though Hitler himself had the
best intentions. Others wrote saying that without
state aid, farming was no longer a paying proposition.
Those bloated industrialists were getting all the money,
while the country squires were neglected. As he was
reading these laments, Meissner would enter with the
portfolio. Why, it was like the old days in Magdeburg!

But it was a great nuisance when Papen turned up
by airplane to report that during the previous week

civil war had broken out again in various places; that seventeen persons had been killed in the streets of Hamburg; and that there seemed no likelihood of an end to the disorders. Would he not perhaps do well to receive the dangerous tribune once more, just to show Germany why he would have nothing to do with the man?

There can be no doubt that the gentleman jockey never gave the field marshal so much as a hint of half the intrigues that were going on; and, indeed, Papen hardly guessed that there were various intrigues about which he was not fully informed. Hitler, who liked to support himself on a big gun, or at least by leaning against the gunner, had been engaged after his victories at the polls in the beginning of August in dangerous conspiracies with General Schleicher, which only became known to some of the latter's friends after Schleicher's death. Since Hitler was eager to be in the saddle, and used the time-worn argument of the Reichswehr generals that otherwise he could not be responsible for the behavior of his troops, Schleicher seriously debated the plan of making himself chancellor, of taking three Nazis into the Cabinet, of then compelling old Hindenburg to resign, and appointing Hitler president of the realm. In the Herren Club this was called "military dictatorship, mitigated by brown masses." The conversations during which these schemes were laid took place at maneuvers in Fürstenberg; and Hitler, who, as a Wagnerian, contemplated his career in scenes and acts, probably as a trilogy, declared upon the field of maneuvers, "Here, some day, will be erected a tablet recording for posterity the agreement to which Schleicher and Hitler came at this spot!"

Invited a few days later to visit Papen, Hitler received a new offer from the government. Would he like to become vice chancellor? How absurd! So recently Schleicher had held out prospects of his being made president; and here was Papen proposing to hide him away, him, the great tribune of the people, in the interstices of the Cabinet! The indignation among his subordinates waxed even fiercer. Göring spoke of a "trap having been set." A brusque refusal! Oscar Hindenburg, Meissner, and Papen, who had found it difficult to wring this concession from the old gentleman, were annoyed. After such an affront—for both parties felt themselves affronted—a meeting between the two chief actors to secure peace had to be postponed for a while. Hitler made it a condition of the meeting that his chief of staff Röhm must be present. Hindenburg, who had been informed about Röhm's sexual perversion, and was nice in these matters, found it hard to agree. As a soldier, he made merry because Hitler spoke of Röhm as his "chief of staff" whereas there was no "staff," but only a mob of brown shirts without officers.

On August 13, 1932, Hindenburg, at the appointed hour, supporting himself on his stick, placed himself in the middle of the room, surrounded by his son, Papen, Schleicher, and Meissner. Hitler appeared, accompanied by Röhm and Frick. All present were in civilian attire, except Schleicher. Hitler turned round to close the door behind him, but found that this had already been done by a servant. He stumbled over the carpet as he advanced because his head was turned over his shoulder, and made a deep bow. The whole group remained standing, no one being asked to sit down.

In the group of seven men, there was no one as tall as Hindenburg, to whom, on this occasion likewise, the heritage from his ancestor the grenadier gave a dominant position despite his age. Four Junkers on one side, three petty bourgeois on the other, and Meissner to form a transition between the master class and the people. In the contrast between undue slimness and excessive obesity, Papen and Röhm were caricatures of the distinction between the Herren Club and middle-class plumpness, and were thus symbolical. Hindenburg and Hitler, who had studied one another a hundred times in photographic newspaper reproductions and on the wireless, were now meeting in the flesh for the first time.

What they had in common was their profound conviction that might was right, and that Germany, the victim of malicious neighbors, must rearm speedily for a war of revenge. Ignorant of other nations and civilizations, extremely narrow in their outlooks, they manifested their devotion to their own people in distrust of their neighbors, so that, instead of wanting to form ties with them, they were eager to attack them with machine guns, and from the air with high explosives, incendiary bombs, and poison gas. They were also of the same way of thinking in respect of their repudiation of popular government, and of their preference for brawn as against brain. But how greatly the two men differed as regards their conception of the way in which the renewal of Germany would take place, in their dream of the Germany of tomorrow! For, as the tribune of the people entered the palace, he was holding unseen in his right hand the secret key which would open to him the heart of the people, whereas the president with his marshal's baton had become a distant legend.

Here was a man of mighty frame, who for seventy years had been accustomed to wear uniform, confronted by an uneasy fellow who had come to wear uniform only through the chances of the war, and had speedily relinquished it; a man whom nothing fitted, not even the brown shirt which had been his own invention, whereas old Hindenburg had devoted whole days of his life to the important problem of buttons, buckles, and decorations. The man with the biggest mustache in all Germany was confronted by the man with the smallest; a square head by an oval head. A man with no nerves was face to face with one who was a bundle of nerves; a healthy man with a neurasthenic; a good trencherman with a vegetarian; a paterfamilias with a confirmed bachelor.

The man who produced an effect spontaneously and without effort was confronted by the man who was unceasingly trying to produce an effect; the man who did not know the meaning of fear by one who was always in a state of excitement; the man born to command by one who was always eager to command; the man who had grown naturally and easily to his high position by the man who had shot up into the firmament like Jack's beanstalk. A Junker was faced by a petty bourgeois; a Protestant by a Catholic; a Prussian by an Austrian; a man estranged from the people by a man who had sprung from the people; a man of race and blood, who believed in classes, by a man of class who believed in race; a rationalist by a mystic; a man born to high position by an upstart; a man who was silent by a man who was loquacious; one who was fundamentally indifferent by one who was fundamentally ambitious.

Thus a gulf yawned between them, a gulf which nothing could bridge. In every one of his traits, the young man was distasteful to the old; in every one of his traits, the old man was an offense to the young. The field marshal contemplated a civilian who was in a state of extreme tension; the tribune of the people, on the other hand, contemplated a gigantic Roland, a monument, perhaps a demon.

The impression now derived from personal observation must have intensified the field marshal's dislike for the tribune of the people, for otherwise Hindenburg would never have treated Hitler like a schoolboy:

"I have sent for you to ask you whether you will collaborate with Chancellor von Papen as his subordinate."

"I have already stated my conditions to the chancellor."

"You insist, therefore, on holding the premier position?"

"I want some such position as Mussolini holds in Italy."

"I cannot square that with my conscience." Pause. "For the future I should advise you to show chivalry in political struggles."

According to the reports of the others who were present, these were the essentials of the interview, though wrapped in a few conversational flourishes. No one sat down. All was over after six or eight minutes.

Wishing to show Germany and the world at large his contempt for the Leader, Hindenburg in official utterances expressed his regret "that Herr Hitler was

unable in accordance with statements made by him
before the elections to support a government which
would have the confidence of the president of the
realm.   The president cannot conscientiously, and
with due regard to his responsibility toward the fatherland, appoint Herr Hitler chancellor and intrust him
with the guidance of German destinies."   Thus Hindenburg had publicly declared that the Leader was
untrustworthy, and after the interview Hitler was
poorer than he had been before.

V

Mortified by the upshot, Hitler pondered vengeance.
He had an army under his command larger than
Hindenburg's Reichswehr; his prestige was as great
as his adversary's.   He could, therefore, though no
more than a private individual, venture a campaign
against the president of the realm.   Since, throughout
this year, there were repeated elections, he always had
a platform from which to go on singing the same tune.
Here is an extract from Hitler's manifesto to his party.
The style, this time, is modeled on Lassalle's:

"Every one of you animated with the desire to
struggle on behalf of the honor and the freedom of the
nation will understand why I refused to enter this
government.   Maybe the justice of Herr von Papen
will in the end sentence thousands of national socialists
to death!   Now I know your sanguinary dispassionate-
ness, Herr von Papen!   I would not join you in your
work as executioner of those who are fighting for
national liberty!   Thanks to the nationalist uprising,
we shall make an end of this system no less surely than
we shall make an end of Marxism despite the present

attempt to save it!" When during these days five
assassins in this party were condemned to death
because they had—literally—cut a communist to
pieces, Hitler wired to them: "Comrades, I am with
you! It is our duty to continue the struggle against
the government under which this has been possible!"

During weeks of negotiation with the Center and
with Brüning, Hitler, in the autumn of 1932, remaining
always in touch with Schleicher, was doing his utmost
to strengthen his position as against Hindenburg.
There was talk of deposition of the president, a step
which the Reichstag could have submitted to the
people by referendum; but the notion was ultimately
shelved, not because the Center had any great reverence for Hindenburg, but because it was afraid of
Hindenburg's successor, who could not have been anyone but Hitler. Papen, attacked on all sides, even by
his protector Schleicher, clung all the more firmly to
Hindenburg's son, and was easily able to secure an
undated order for the dissolution of the Reichstag—
the famous "Red Portfolio," with which William had
come to the aid of his chancellor during times of difficulty. Had not all the Reichstags of this Republic
been dissolved? Well, the order of dissolution would
be kept ready.

Two hundred thirty national socialists entering the
Reichstag in September were legally able to appoint
one of themselves, Göring, president of the assembly.
Thereupon Göring, in alliance with his deadly enemies
the communists, ·immediately decided to depose the
Papen government by a joint decision of the radicals.
A very useful thing, a legal constitution! It can be
used to overthrow a government! In like manner

there are marriages which are more romantic than any liaison. Will Papen now open the Red Portfolio, and use the document it contains in order to anticipate and prevent his downfall? He is accustomed to the Herren Club; but here he has to do with a sort of Men's Club, whose manners and customs are unfamiliar to the chancellor. Thus it comes to pass that he leaves his portfolio at home, and it is not available when he wants to read the order aloud to the Reichstag. But Göring, who has hitherto been more of an aviator that a parliamentarian, is likewise in a tight place; and thus one of the amateurs institutes a pause in favor of the other.

Hitler, not being a deputy, was awaiting his friends in the mansion of the president of the Reichstag. They hurried across, certainly not by the famous underground passage, to ask the Leader's instructions. Simultaneously Papen departed at top speed in his automobile to the chancellery, in search of the Red Portfolio. When he got back and the sitting had been resumed, he requested the floor, intending to tell the Reichstag that it had been dissolved. But Göring was deaf to this request, for a vote was in progress; so poor Papen's only resource was to lay the document on the table in front of the president of the Reichstag and quit the hall with the other members of the government. Thereupon Göring had the government dismissed by the vote of a Reichstag which in fact was already dissolved.

By such puppet-show maneuvers, the principles of popular government were being brought into discredit, because the two parties which were at odds both wished to remain legal while simultaneously preparing for revolution from beneath and revolution from above.

The scenes in which the forgotten Red Portfolio and the president of the superseded Reichstag played their respective parts were symbolic of the fact that nothing but obsolete forms prevailed in a realm where everyone had long since grown accustomed to thinking in terms of hand grenades and magazine pistols.

During these months, however, Hitler's power had been likewise undermined. For a time the public was waiting eagerly to see whether the star performer would succeed in making his masterly leap—higher, higher, now he will manage it! If such an attempt is muffed, the ungrateful spectators turn their backs on him and go elsewhere to watch another artist. After November 1932, the Germans were stampeding away from Hitler. The elections necessitated by the above-mentioned dissolution showed a remarkable decline in the votes for Hitler, from 14 to 11.7 millions. The number of Nazis in the new Reichstag was only 197, whereas it had been 230 in the last; but the communists, this time, had 100 representatives. In the territorial elections of the next few weeks, there was likewise a rapid decline, the votes for Hitler falling to little more than half of what they had been. The new commander, then, was not unconquerable! A wave of astonishment swept across the country. The rival faction, that of Hugenberg's German nationalists, grew stronger; and the Herren Club drew a breath of relief.

The reason was shortage of funds. Since Hitler won adherents among the masses mainly by appeals to their eyes and their ears, very little by touching their hearts, and not at all by influencing their brains, they wearied of him when there were fewer bands and processions, not so many flags and firework displays, a decline in propaganda by song and cinema. From September to January, Doctor Goebbels's diary refers again and again to the perilous state of the party funds. "Propaganda impossible through lack of money." In December, he speaks of a "desperate situation"; "gloomy Christmas days"; and records that the dispirited Leader had said: "If the party breaks up, I shall end matters as far as I am concerned within three minutes with my own pistol."

For, at this juncture, Hitler's position was further endangered by the falling away of his friend Gregor Strasser, who was in the act of joining forces with Schleicher, and for that reason, although not a party chief, had been received by Hindenburg. Schleicher, who continued to dream of armed forces plus workers, was more inclined now to negotiate with the clear-headed Strasser than with Hitler; but he was also in treaty with the leader of the German trade-unions. He hoped to reduce these two socialists to a common denominator, and, simultaneously with Strasser's aid, to win over a big fraction of Hitler's party. *Divide et impera!*

What had now become of Hitler's confident mood of the previous summer? By circuitous paths he made fresh approaches to Hindenburg, to whom he sent a memorial concerning Germany's War of Liberation under Hindenburg's command, thoughts about a new "offensive campaign in the West" through southern Limburg—but at the same time, wishing to make headway with the field marshal as a landowner, laying before him new plans for freeing the East Prussian estates from mortgages, for this, said Hitler, would make the region more efficient should war break out.

The palace became a nest of complicated intrigues. Meissner and Schleicher, Oscar Hindenburg and Papen, Hitler's envoys and the Junkers of the Neudeck region, priests and generals, walked softly across the polished flooring of the rococo halls as in an old-time drama of intrigue—everyone being mistrustful of all the rest. What they wanted was to get the old man's signature to one document or another during some lively moment when he had been roused by campaigning memories. It was plain to everyone that he had long since ceased to be an alert ruler, and the whole band of suitors were in search of the documents with whose aid alone "legal" government was possible. Under the Prussian monarchy, lady favorites and court tricksters had played a great part; during the brief episode of democracy, party alliances, concessions, and compromises had been rife. Now a climax was reached. Everyone was trying to work upon or to placate the suspicions of the senile field marshal, whose intelligence was no longer brisk enough to enable him to form a sound judgment of the value of the influences that were brought to bear upon him, and of the genuineness of the news that was poured into his ears.

If, amid these obscurities and complications, Schleicher was able to bring about Papen's downfall, this was possible only through the latter's coöperation, for Papen wished to return to power after a few days of crisis, when he hoped to enjoy renewed confidence. Besides, Hindenburg stood by him, since, in daily intercourse, Papen was more congenial to him than anyone else. When, in November, the persistent crisis was intensified by Papen's temporary withdrawal, Hindenburg had to interview the new popular hero a second time, for Hitler's supporters made up the strongest single party, and no one was to be allowed to say that, in the palace, the bible of the constitution was not kept on the domestic altar.

Once more all turned to the Weimar constitution as to Holy Writ; once more everyone tried, each after his own manner, to translate this sacred book into his own comfortable vernacular. Whereas, in the previous summer, Hindenburg had kept the powerful Hitler standing, now, reasonably enough, since Hitler was weaker, the president asked his visitor to be seated, and the two were closeted together for an hour. At length Hindenburg asked Hitler, in due constitutional form, to set up a parliamentary Cabinet which must be supported by a majority in the Reichstag.

This was a cunning proposal, made because the task was impossible. Hitler, having propounded his questions in writing, then sent in a lengthy memorial to show why it was impracticable to discharge the president's commission. Under the ægis of constitutional law, and correct in his personal attitude, he must arouse the sympathy of everyone who read this document attentively, whereas the polished floor of Hindenburg's palatial room obviously reflected nothing but cunning and intrigue. Since no majority in the Reichstag was obtainable, Hitler advised his own appointment as chancellor, in an authoritarian position like that which had been held by Papen.

"You know," rejoined Hindenburg in writing, "that I am in favor of the notion of a presidial Cabinet—headed, not by a party leader, but by a man above party and one in whom I can repose especial confidence. You, however, have explained to me that you are only

33

prepared to become the head of a Cabinet over which you will preside as party leader. If I agree to this, I must insist that such a Cabinet shall be able to command a majority in the Reichstag." To conclude, having thus checkmated Hitler, he goes on: "The president of the realm cannot but be afraid that this will lead to a partisan dictatorship with all its consequences, such as an extraordinary intensification of the internal clashes among the German people, which the president, in view of his oath and the admonitions of his conscience, cannot make himself responsible for."

To such a politely muted wrestle had the struggle between the Junkers and the people been reduced; thus it was carried on between the field marshal's palace and the tribune's residence, while the streets were rendered noisy by demonstrating crowds. Hitler's advantage in this and every other tussle was that he alone was able to change the scene at will, appearing whenever he liked either in the streets or in halls of public assembly, where, with his oratorical arts, he could produce far greater effects than could any of the Jesuits of the palace. Really, in the palace, no one was troubling about majorities, oaths, or conscience. All they wanted was to rid themselves of this dangerous seducer— though, of course, without hurting a hair of his head. If he was ready to play second fiddle, the place was open to him. According to Hindenburg's tradition, the first violin must be a Junker; and Junkers, persons belonging to old families, must continue, as in the past, to occupy the highest positions in the General Staff and in the civil service.

First, however, during this polite duel between the gentleman jockey and the Leader of the people, a third person emerged victorious, naturally a general. During Papen's regime, Schleicher had so successfully occupied the key positions, that the Reichswehr and the police, the industrialists, and even some of the great agriculturists, espoused his cause with the president. Unwillingly had Hindenburg dismissed his favorite chancellor, allowing Papen to go only as it were on furlough, and giving him a photograph with the subscription, "I had a comrade!" Never before had Hindenburg done such a thing; and one may well doubt whether Papen had ever received a similar memento.

In this emergency, Schleicher was somewhat alarmed, after so many years in which he had been the real power behind the throne, at being practically forced by Hindenburg to become chancellor. Hindenburg was out of humor with him, ascribing to Schleicher's intrigues his own temporary separation from Papen. "Someone must at length talk to the people in plain German!" said the president. "A general must be chancellor of the realm!" Then, somewhat dolorously, he added: "They have taken my Papen away from me." When, at the last moment, Schleicher ventured the objection that the foreign powers would grow uneasy if a German general became chancellor, the old gentleman lost his temper, and said, "Anyhow, I am a general, and surely the foreign world regards me with respect!"

In a situation which grew more perplexing day by day, it is manifest that Hindenburg came to rely upon a general because no other course was open to him. Why not bring back William II? According to one plan, the ex-emperor was to be received by the

Reichswehr close to the Dutch frontier, and to be brought home in triumph. According to another, a German cruiser would be sent to take him aboard at a Dutch seaside resort, so that he would be restored to the throne by the navy, which, according to the current version, had been responsible for his dethronement. Conversations between the crown prince and General Schleicher led to widespread disquiet—not because there was any unwillingness to have the Hohenzollern ruler back, but because not one of the loyalist parties wished the other to enjoy the kudos of the restoration. Papen and some more of the Junkers had been talking for years of the possibility of a restoration. What did not become generally known was that, as late as August 1933, at a speech in Sigmaringen, made to about fifty persons especially invited, he declared that Hitler himself wanted a Hohenzollern restoration.

Another scheme of the Herren Club was to make the crown prince chancellor and Hitler president of Prussia; a third plan was, following the example of the sometime Crown Council, to establish a "Presidential Council" which would have only a consultative voice, the actual decisions being left to the president of the realm. At the same time, proclamations made by officers' associations insisted that only such parties should be elected as desired a monarchical restoration. Thus muddle-headed were the vacillations of the German leaders and parties at the close of the year 1932—a fact which makes it easier to understand how, at last in a moment of panic, private circumstances decided the issue.

The internal causes of this vacillation are discoverable in the insincerity with which all the factions, while wanting to make a revolution, and, by means of a *coup d'état* to establish a dictatorship, wished to do so without transcending the bounds of legality. Once more the complicated intrigues proved that the will of the Germans to order is stronger than their will to freedom; and that even gangsters, in so desperate an epoch when civil war was being carried on among four armies, believed—or rather the leaders of these gangsters and armies believed—that the worthy and kindly Germans would never forgive a *coup de main*. At the same time, each of them, when on the lookout for something that would sanction the seizure of power and make it ostensibly legal, looked, not to productive ideas, but to the irrelevant suggestions of the street or of title or of oratory or of the club.

Schleicher continued to play about with the constitution, threatening Hitler with a dissolution of the Reichstag, which to this assembly, in the days of its decadence, could not but seem dangerous, but which Schleicher himself wished to avoid because he was afraid of the steadily growing power of the Left. While he called the political parties to order, and made a feint of returning to parliamentary government, he was repeatedly admonished by the parties to safeguard the constitution, while Hindenburg was taking one authoritarian step after another. It was as if people had ceased to use a sitting room, but suddenly, when they fell out, unlocked the door in order to go for one another with the legs of the rickety chairs and tables. When, now, the infirm old Reichstag was actually reopened, its venerable president brandished the leg of a chair in order—to everyone's astonishment—to hurl it at Hindenburg. This was General Litzmann, a man who belonged to Hindenburg's generation, and who, being a Nazi, wanted to turn his brief moment of power to account. Thereupon a second general, likewise able to claim reverence on account of his extreme age, ventured, under cover of the powerful party, to proclaim his views to the world.

"They were unwilling to put power into our Leader's hands, and therefore imposed on him unacceptable conditions. The president of the realm, who gave full confidence to such men as Müller, Brüning, and Papen, refused it to one whom millions regard as the greatest and the best in contemporary Germany. . . . I trust that Hindenburg may not be accursed for having driven the German people to despair and handed them over to the clutches of bolshevism when the savior stood ready to hand!" Next day, when the Hindenburg press reminded the speaker of the claims of comradeship, the elderly general wrote:

"Sixty years ago I was at the Military Academy with Herr von Hindenburg. Thirty years ago, we stood side by side as commanders in the Fourteenth Army Corps. In the World War I was, for years, one of his subordinates. During all this time, however, Herr von Hindenburg never showed any comradeship towards me." This was Hitler's revenge for the defamatory way in which Hindenburg had referred to him in the above-quoted official utterance.

Schleicher, the new chancellor, had so much confidence in his long-standing friendship with the house of Hindenburg that, on taking office, he did not even trouble to make sure of his position against a hostile Reichstag by providing himself with the notorious weapon of the Red Portfolio. Since, as a quasi-socialist general, there loomed before his eyes the possibility of a "government of soldiers and trade unions"—that is to say a sort of glorified Workers' and Soldiers' Council under the leadership of the Herren Club—he had been negotiating with the Left, regardless of Reichstag and party. He had revived Brüning's plan of land settlement in East Prussia, had offered Strasser the post of Prussian premier, and had made all these things acceptable to the old gentleman by telling him that they were likely to lead to the break-up of the biggest of the parties and the downfall of its Shock Troops. When Strasser went to see Hindenburg once more, he wished to learn the president's attitude towards Hitler. Before he accepted the premiership (the interview took place in the presence of Schleicher and Meissner, who reported the incident) Hindenburg replied that nothing would ever induce him "to put the government of Germany in the hands of such a man." Strasser's report to the Leader increased the mortification of a political adventurer who is both techy and spoiled, with the result that Strasser, obeying Hitler's instructions, refused General Schleicher's offer, resigned his high offices in the party, and, while remaining an ordinary member thereof, resumed his work in a chemical factory.

VI

In this situation, at the New Year of 1933, the conduct of the two chief actors, Hindenburg and Hitler, becomes comprehensible only to one who scrutinizes the financial basis of their respective political existences. Though neither of them wanted money for personal reasons, both had good grounds to dread the disclosure of the financial situation of their parties. In both cases the sum at issue amounted to many millions; in both cases, moral consequences in the political world were at stake.

Hitler's case was the simpler. While the faithful were beginning to fall away, creditors were becoming troublesome. The press published the letters of various district leaders whose drafts for considerable sums had not been honored. The newspapers declared that the Nazi factions had not even given the customary Christmas boxes to the attendants in the Prussian Landtag, and in Germany anyone who runs counter to Christmas sentiment incurs a grave risk. Everywhere the men of the Shock Troops rattled collecting boxes and refused to flock to the assembly halls because these were no longer heated; and later the *Angriff*, writing retrospectively about these winter months, declared that many friends of the movement had advised in despair that the leaders should content themselves with a few ministerial posts instead of starving the party by insisting on impossible demands. The sums involved amounted to twelve millions, needed to defray debts, and the uncounted millions that would be needed during the year 1933.

One reason for this scarcity of funds was the falling off in the Hitlerian vote, and the consequent disinclination of the industrialists to go on paying the piper; the other reason was that Strasser and his socialist friends had come to the front, persons who took the radical section of Hitler's program in earnest, and were eager to collaborate with the quasi-socialist general and chancellor. The view of the great entrepreneurs was that if Hitler did not rise to power, he would be

unable to pay the debts of his party; still less would
he be able, as chief minister of the State, to make the
latter buy the famous "blocks of shares," and thus
set heavy industry on its feet once more—this being,
in our days, the dream of all the wealthy. If Hitler
were to escape from his embarrassments, he must take
a decisive stride to the right, for that alone could solve
the problem of finance and the problem of power.

The other group, that which centered round Hindenburg, had been accustomed for a century to look to the
State for monetary aid. The East-Elbian Junkers had
originally discovered a patriotic pretext. It was their
mission "to check the advance of the Poles," and
without State subventions, since it did not pay them
to till their lands, they could not maintain the Prussian
spirit in that region. The Republic had provided
funds only to a few of them while taking over some of
the land. Neudeck had been one of those estates which
the Prussian government had refused to trouble itself
about, since it seemed absolutely worthless. In
accordance with the new fashion after the war, instead
of appeals to stay the advance of the Poles there had
been talk of helping "the poor peasants" with the
fund which had been called the "Eastern Aid"—but
no one knew how much out of the millions voted for
"the poor peasants" had found its way into the
pockets of the Junkers. A bank established in the
year 1924 to carry out the Dawes plan, had of late
devoted itself to the financing of the very Junkers
who, in their grief for the fatherland, had rejected
this same plan.

Apart from the Junkers, however, no one had any
precise information about these matters until the

Center and the socialists appointed a commission in the Reichstag for the study of this interesting Eastern Aid. Then it was divulged that for 12,000 peasant farms, comprising 230,000 hectares, the sum of 69 million marks had been disbursed by the State; and for 722 big farms belonging to Junkers, comprising 340,000 hectares, 60 million marks. Herr von Olden-burg-Januschau, Hindenburg's friend and neighbor, had seized the opportunity, at the time when the gift of Neudeck to the president had been made, of grab-bing a strip of land hard by; and he had received 621,000 marks for the financing of his three estates. With these public funds, he had bought himself a fourth estate, and had then put in a claim for further assistance to help him cultivate the whole. A certain Herr von Zitzewitz had also purchased a new estate out of moneys thus acquired. A Herr von Quast, who had gambled away his property, nevertheless secured an allowance of a quarter of a million on the ground that the land had belonged to his family for several centuries. One landowner used money obtained from the Eastern Aid to set up a racing stable; Emperor William's second wife also applied for relief. Another Junker, whose estate had been financed four times over, arranged, when he became bankrupt for the fifth time, that his ten-year-old daughter should buy the land for a song, his creditors being thus defrauded. A certain Silesian count, having obtained a grant, went with the cash to Monte Carlo, lost the lot at roulette, and came home to put in a fresh claim for assistance.

A great stir was made by the publication of figures and names, which leaked out through the indiscretions of the members of the Commission. The minister for food and agriculture, a Junker, of course, tried to check this leakage of information by reminding those who had blabbed that they were liable to penalties under the Official Secrets Act. But the warning came too late, and scandalmongering speedily became a political weapon—not so much in the hands of the people against the master class, but the other way about, for General Schleicher threatened his adversary Hugenberg with the publication of compromising data. In the then state of public feeling, which was strongly adverse to the Junkers, an exhaustive inquiry after the American model in cases of corruption would have led to trouble for the Junkers such as they had not known for a couple of centuries. The Hindenburgs, whose property had been acquired by a gift, and who, in December 1932 had received a sum of 450,000 marks privately collected to help them finance it, had had nothing to do with the Eastern Aid, so that all they had to dread was what might happen to their friends and the members of their order in the event of a prosecution. Still, Schleicher drew Oscar von Hindenburg's attention to the fact that, in the event of public discussion of such matters in the Reichstag, the socialists might raise the question of the inheritance taxes on Neudeck.

But before anything could be done to avert trouble, one of the Centrist deputies brought up for discussion in the Commission the results of a preliminary survey, which showed that 70 per cent of all the funds of the Eastern Aid had been paid over to the Junkers instead of to the peasants, that today, as formerly, 13,000 families were supported by the taxes levied from 62 millions of Germans—thus arousing widespread anger, especially among the Nazis. These latter were in a cleft stick, for their peasant supporters urged that an end should be put to such corruption, whereas their Junker hangers-on wanted matters to be hushed up. The consequence was that, in the Commission of Inquiry, von Sybel, the national socialist, defended the Junkers, whereas Reinhard, the secretary of State, promised to put in evidence against them. The idea was to give them a scare, but not to attack them seriously, since the Nazis posed as a party representing the interests of rich and poor alike—the implication being that Dives and Lazarus could rest cosily side by side in Abraham's bosom.

Oscar von Hindenburg, who wanted to avoid a scandal, fell away from his long-standing friendship with Schleicher, and joined forces with Papen, who promised help if he should be restored to power.

In January 1933, these financial scandals had a marked repercussion in the political world. Perhaps events would have taken a very different course had it not occurred to an architect that the president's palace in Berlin was in need of renovation. Hindenburg, being therefore compelled to remove for a few months to the neighboring imperial chancellery as it had formerly been, became house mate there of his comrade Papen, who had not vacated the chancellery, since Schleicher, the new chancellor, did not wish to live there. These two men, who in turn made one another chancellor and then deposed one another, actually determined history by their respective attitudes towards this matter of a change of residence. Now Papen, probably acting on a hint from Hindenburg, was able to go on living in the chancellery, in daily converse with the president, strolling to and fro with him in the garden, and, as of old, putting whatever gloss he pleased on the progress of public affairs—just as he had done in the days of his chancellorship. Thus, in these morning hours, from the day when Schleicher assumed office, Papen was paving the way for a crisis in Schleicher's affairs.

When Schleicher noticed that Papen was working against him underground, remembering that he was a soldier, he made up his mind to put up a fight. If, with his big bodyguard of Reichswehr generals, he could press the gentleman jockey to the wall, he would be in a strong position, for Hitler, his second rival, was *persona ingrata* to the president. But Schleicher was loose-tongued, and this led to his downfall. Why, in December, was he so indiscreet as to tell one of the socialist leaders, that is to say a member of the hostile camp, that Oscar Hindenburg had asked for promotion to the rank of general, which he (Schleicher) had refused on the ground that there were many senior staff officers with higher claims to promotion? Why did he blab to some of the Junkers that he proposed, in accordance with the scheme of Schlange-Schöningen, to partition barren estates in East Prussia? Why did he pass on Hindenburg's private remarks about Hitler to Strasser?

On the other hand old Januschau, his adversary, knew how to act without chattering. For the winter, when Hindenburg no longer stayed at Neudeck, but went on shooting in the Schorfheide near Berlin, his neighbor from Neudeck had purchased an estate adjoining the heath, and had placed his carriage at the president's disposal. Now, toward Christmas, he sent to all the officers who had landed .interests a memorial describing the "agrarian bolshevism" of their chief, General von Schleicher.   He induced the Land League to issue a manifesto "against the spoliation of agriculture in favor of the monetary interests of internationally minded export industry."   When Hindenburg received the governing committee of this Land League, two Junkers of his acquaintance who had a friendly talk with them, and gave a great banquet at which Chancellor Schleicher was the guest of honor, in order to show how hard up they were.   But the morning number of their newspaper had contained a frontal editorial attack on Schleicher!   Learning this, Schleicher and his generals quitted the festive board.

A few days later, on January 20, 1933, the quarrel between Schleicher and Hindenburg became acute.   The old gentleman spoke about attacks upon persons "whose historical services to the fatherland" were indisputable.   No lord of the manor who retained a spark of honor or the least remnant of a sense of duty would put up with the threatened withdrawal of the Eastern Aid.   "What do you think of doing against these criminal bolsheviks?"

Schleicher was confronted with an old, old man of eighty-five whose acquaintance he had first made when Hindenburg had been a man in the middle sixties, never distinguished for his intelligence, but always decently behaved, and accustomed, with a certain pride, to talk about the impoverishment of his house.   Now he saw this same man in a furious temper, repeating the nonsense he had read in a Junkers' newspaper, waving his stick threateningly, and anxious, above all, to stifle adverse voices in the

Reichstag. It had come to a breach between them, after thirty years of personal friendship and seven years of close political association. The breach had become inevitable seven weeks before, when Schleicher had accepted the chancellorship under the patronage of his former protector. Schleicher knew that his position was lost, and yet he would not yield. Perhaps at this moment he was mentally reviving those plans which had been mooted in the autumn for the deposition of Hindenburg.

"Any attack on the Commission," he rejoined, "will be an attack on the constitution. I cannot be a party to such machinations."

"Machinations?" growled the old man. "The columns of the newspapers are stuffed with lies! It is the duty of the State"—Hindenburg was repeating what he had read in the papers—"to reëstablish large-scale agriculture, which those Marxians have ruined! Without it, how shall we able to feed ourselves in the next war? Will you do what I want, and break up that wretched Commission?"

Schleicher refused.

The old gentleman hooked his finger in his interlocutor's swordbelt: "You have heard my orders. I expect my chancellor to obey them!"

These may have sounded like a spectral echo, from the walls of the same room in the same chancellery, of the words which, on a certain March day in 1890, young Emperor William had uttered to old Bismarck the day before "dropping the pilot."

When, next day, Chancellor Schleicher asked the president whether he still enjoyed the latter's confidence, Hindenburg demanded the declaration of a state of emergency. Schleicher explained that scandal could be averted for another three months by dissolving the Reichstag, and asked for the Red Portfolio. Meissner, and doubtless Oscar Hindenburg as well, had foreseen this move. Acting on their advice, Hindenburg refused to sign the desired order for the dissolution of the Reichstag. Schleicher said he was perfectly willing to resign, but that he would certainly make public the reasons for his dismissal. Hindenburg, whose feeling was that he and his chancellor were only two officers of higher and lower rank, would have had anyone else arrested for such words. He did not venture to go to such lengths with Schleicher. Besides, he had another arrow for his bow.

VII

Herr von Papen was a wealthy man. He was troubled neither by death duties, nor by landed estates on which agriculture could not be made to pay even with the aid of State subsidies, nor yet by having to discharge notes of hand signed in order to defray the expenses of election campaigns. His estate contained rich deposits of coal and iron, and thousands of horny hands were at work by day and by night extracting these mineral resources. Was not he fortunate? Of high rank, educated at the best schools, put beyond the possibility of want by having married money, so powerful that in the political parties and the clubs he could continually widen his already great influence and find opportunities for concealing his political blunders, he had attained the highest office in the realm without having done anything to merit it, protected by the favor of the aged national hero, who had given him a hint that he would be restored to power. The only thing that he lacked was close touch with the people, which, in this disastrous epoch, had become an unfortunate necessity.

It was essential to woo the favor of the man in the street, instead of keeping the beggar at a distance! Especially was it requisite to win over the new tribune of the people. Well, what matter? The man was no gentleman, of course, such were Papen's contemptuous thoughts, but he had decent table manners, was well informed though only self-taught, one who could be safely asked to take a countess in to dinner. Besides, he had quite the aspect of a genius, with his untidy hair and his dark eyes. So long as he could be kept from making a platform speech in the drawing room, he pleased people in his cordial and essentially modest way. Now, when he was on the down grade, besieged by his "bolshevik" comrade Strasser, abandoned by his wealthy patrons, menaced by Schleicher who was moving towards the Left—now was the moment to seek alliance with him. The money of Papen and his friends was the very thing that Hitler needed; the popular favor which was Hitler's almost exclusive prerogative was what Papen lacked. A conversation, no more than an hour of private talk, and everything could be regained!

"It seems possible," writes Goebbels, in his diary under date of December 29, "that the Leader will have an interview with Papen a few days hence. That opens a new chance." This is the first cheerful note after weeks of complaints about shortage of funds and the consequent decline in the movement. When Hitler and Papen met on January 5, 1933, at the house

34

of Schroeder, the Rhenish banker, it was not difficult for Papen to make headway with Hitler. After the conversation, Goebbels wrote, and even had printed, the following sentences: "If this coup comes off, we shall almost have power in our hands. Should fresh difficulties arise, they will not be financial ones."

Hitler, habitually irresolute, vacillated to begin with in this case as well. His attention was concentrated upon an election in an out-of-the-way corner of Germany, a constituency in Lippe, where he had set his heart on gaining a victory. He neglected the great financiers to speak to meetings of two hundred persons in villages. If only he could get better results at the polls! He was acting in the spirit of an operatic tenor, who will rather forgo the opportunity of signing an important contract than allow his understudy to take his place for one evening.

When, a few days later in the Herren Club, Schleicher asked von Papen whether he and Hitler had had a pleasant conversation, Papen denied having met the Leader. With a smile, Schleicher took out of his pocket a photograph of the two men meeting in Cologne. Confidence for confidence! Hindenburg, too, was at first so much annoyed by what Papen had done, that at the festival of the Kyffhaüser League, he gave his former favorite the cut direct. Papen swallowed the snub, for a gentleman must not be too fastidious. He knew that even men as big as Hindenburg would soon be glad to ask his good offices. He had been spinning the web of a great intrigue; that was why he looked so cheery. He had given Hitler the records of the Eastern Aid for the latter to use against the Junkers and in the campaign against Schleicher and Hindenburg.

That is what matters had come to. When the old man's annoyance with Schleicher had risen to fierce anger because Schleicher would not stop this troublesome inquiry, Papen must have given Oscar Hindenburg a hint of what Hitler would now be able to do—raise a scandal if he liked, or hush up the whole business if Hindenburg and Co. would make it worth his while. Hitler, feeling himself in a strong position, made his newspapers attack the government; Hugenberg did the same thing. There was a press campaign of all against all; for all were awaiting that sitting of the Reichstag in which the "bolshevik proposal" to modify the Eastern Aid would come up for discussion. Would Schleicher dissolve the Reichstag before matters came to that pass? Would he have the Red Portfolio to use on that occasion? There was a turmoil of opinions in the Reichstag, in the editorial offices, and even in the palace. Oscar Hindenburg regarded Papen as the possible savior.

On January 27, 1933, Papen told the president that Hitler would clear out the Reichstag and would make an end of the Eastern Aid Commission, being ready to form a Cabinet of "National Concentration" if he were appointed chancellor. When Hindenburg objected, Papen explained that it would be easy to keep a tight rein on Hitler. If he, Papen, were at hand, he could edit Hitler's proposals. The Reichswehr and the Foreign Office, which were dear to the old gentleman, would remain his private preserves. Thyssen and his friends were the paymasters of Hitler's movement, and those who paid the piper could call the tune. There were to be only three Nazis in the Cabinet, the other members could be appointed by Hindenburg.

When Hindenburg dismissed Chancellor Schleicher, on January 28, he was inwardly much perturbed, feeling that he was behaving badly to an old friend of the family. In these circumstances, when Schleicher raised objections and uttered warnings, the president replied in the classical utterance: "Well, just let's see now which way (with God's help) the cat will jump!" The sentence, repeated by the retiring chancellor an hour later—it is one which Schleicher was not imaginative enough to invent—is Hindenburg all over. Besides, when he spoke, the president had not yet made up his mind. Hitler to become chancellor— the very man he had refused to appoint, and whom he had told others nothing would induce him to appoint? The possible candidates were seated restlessly in their respective headquarters, for no one knew what would be decided from moment to moment in the palace. They were all powerless in face of the old man, save for him who was master of the heavy artillery.

When Schleicher returned to his office after receiving his dismissal, he sent for the representatives of the Catholic and socialist trade unions with whom he had been parleying of late weeks. Would they call a general strike, with the support of the Reichswehr? Some were willing; others said they must think matters over. Consultations with General von Bredow and others. The generals who were in the know were willing to join in a small, legal *coup de main*. The day after tomorrow, on Monday, January 30, the Potsdam garrison, or at any rate part of it, should march into Berlin through the Brandenburg Gate. State of siege, general strike, Papen and Hitler under preventive arrest, Hindenburg to be faced by accomplished facts and to be told that the critical situation had made prompt action essential. Bredow to Potsdam for an interview. The generals were sanguine. All of them were sick to death of intrigues of the presidential palace, and were eager for action. Next day the military dictatorship would have been set up. In the hands of the socialist general, order would perhaps have been restored after the anarchy of the last few weeks. On February 2, General von Bredow admitted that these plans had been set afoot, by naïvely remarking to a political friend that he could not understand why he had been dismissed, for "nothing more than a state of siege" had been decided on!

But General von Schleicher talked instead of acting. One of the initiates, perhaps three or four, wired to an English newspaper the news of the Putsch planned by General Schleicher and had it telephoned back to them, in order to communicate it to the palace. Another possibility is that Bredow's ravings in the style of the "mad Junker" had disclosed as fixed plans of Schleicher's what were no more than cloudy schemes; and that the previous evening, in his cups, Bredow had blabbed more than he had intended. Anyhow, by Sunday the plan was known to the two Hindenburgs.

Nothing more was needed to make the field marshal's wrath boil over! He, supreme commander of the armed forces of the realm, was to be coerced by his own generals! There were a number of reasons to strengthen his determination. The world of the Junkers, of the titled landowners, had to be saved from destruction; discipline had to be maintained in the army. Next day was Oscar's fiftieth birthday. Was a family festival to be transformed into a dynastic crisis?

On Sunday, January 29, 1933, Hitler, summoned by Papen, turned up as savior of the situation. On Monday Hindenburg appointed as chancellor the very man whom he had twice refused to appoint in days when the Leader had been more powerful than he was now. No doubt Hitler had to take office as member of a coalition, a scheme he had previously rejected; for, though two of his associates were Nazis, he was compelled to accept his enemy Hugenberg, a baron, a count, and Herr von Papen, as members of his cabinet. Two of the elect, who had failed to turn up on Sunday night at the riding school and gymnasium where the cabinet was being huddled together (a center of force and beauty, and of delight in men and horses), were given the surprise of their lives next morning. Count Schwerin, summoned to be sworn in as a member of the new Cabinet, inquired on the phone who, then, was to be chancellor. History does not relate whether he tumbled back into his bed or fell flat on the floor on hearing the name of Hitler. Seldte could not be wakened, for he had been having a night out. In default, a hurried decision was reached to replace him by another Steel Helmet leader, Seldte's rival and enemy Düsterberg—seeing that the essential matter was to appease Hindenburg by convincing him that the Steel Helmets had been won over. Düsterberg arrived in a frock coat, and sat down in the anteroom. Hindenburg was expected at eleven for the swearing in of the new ministers of State. Five minutes before the hour, Seldte, having slept off his carouse, put in an appearance in the nick of time. Düsterberg had to surrender his portfolio, a new commission of appointment having been hastily typed for

The president greets Hitler

Seldte.   Thus Düsterberg lost his job, and later narrowly missed losing his life—and the world lost the
crowning joke of having a man with a Jewish grandfather as a member of Hitler's first Cabinet.

What a change had been brought about by Papen's
intervention!   The Leader of the people had saved the
Junkers!   At noon on January 30, when the refer-
endary was about to begin his report upon the first
of the twenty volumes of the documents of the Eastern
Aid, the news of the dissolution of the Reichstag
literally took the words out of his mouth.   Everyone
went home; and not a soul, since then, has seen any
of the documents in question.

"Awakening Germany" was created on January
30 out of the absurdities of the Eastern Aid with its
squandered millions, and the needs of a political party
which had outrun the constable, out of the conflicting
intrigues of the Junkers, and out of the menace of a
military Putsch.

In the evening, at one of the windows of the old
chancellery, stood the field marshal, grave of mien,
saluting the thousands of torch bearers who streamed
along below.   Close at hand, at one of the windows of
the new chancellery, stood Adolf Hitler, also saluting
and smiling.   The president saluted in military fashion,
as a Prussian officer; the new chancellor saluted in
Roman fashion, as disciple of a greater man than himself.   The old man felt that he had been saved from
a twofold danger; the younger man, that he had
suddenly been granted multifarious powers which for
years he had dreamed of wielding.   The old man felt
safe, believing that he had tied the hands of the
revolutionist by surrounding him with persons sworn

to abide by legal methods. The other was a tribune of the people, inhaling with deep breaths the acclamations of the multitude from whom he had sprung, and feeling confident that victory awaited him.

VIII

In the torchlight procession of the first evening, which he contemplated with such serious eyes, the field marshal saw the beginning of an endless movement which would traverse all Germany, singing and shouting, acclaiming and storming, rejuvenating and destroying with elemental force. Week after week, the daily work of these millions seemed at a standstill; the great festival of joy and vengeance held the whole population in thrall. The self-confidence which the tribune restored to the Germans found vent in acts of mad terrorism; and the wrath with which they flung themselves upon the old-time potentates sometimes took the form of splendid enthusiasm. A whole nation which fancied that the gates of paradise had at length been opened to it, turned for a moment before entering, to hurl itself upon those who had hitherto barred the way, and, in the voluptuousness of the struggle that went on outside the gates, no one stopped to notice that the "paradise" within was nothing more than the old, wintry garden.

This was the work of one single man, who, from his magician's cell, discharged words, words, words which, intensified a millionfold by the sorcerers' apparatus of the day, deafened the ears of a people intensely longing for new formulas. With an inspired imagination, he launched upon the populace a rain of fire balls, a cannonade of curses, an unceasing flutter of flags, crying to them with the strength of an indefatigable automaton, "Yesterday you were freed," again and again, until at last they came to believe it. So great was the enthusiasm of these first weeks, that nobody stopped to inquire whether there was any content within the forms. No one noticed that all the hubbub was raised by the festival of victory of a party which, after a decade of struggle, had at length achieved the conquest of power. For this was nowise the festival of victory of a nation. No one asked how strong the enemy might be, or whether he still had strength at all. No one asked what actual pledges were being made and how they were to be kept; who were being crushed beneath the wheels of this victorious chariot, and whether those thus crushed had deserved their fate. The vigor of the onslaught on the populace, who were to be won over to the new flag, was so overwhelming that all succumbed before an unprecedented blast of verbiage.

"It often happens," wrote Abbé Galiani, "that the thought which wins the victory is sheer folly; but as soon as the folly has found expression, imperceptibly reason, practical purposes, and the interests of individuals, are incorporated in it, organize it, make it viable— and the folly forthwith becomes an institution."

With amazement the field marshal, slow by nature, and rendered cautious by age, looked on while a torrent of ordinances was being launched, so that morning after morning he had to sign a dozen decrees which in earlier years could only have been issued after long struggles with the parties, and which, even under the three authoritarian chancellors, would have needed lengthy discussion. It was as in battle when the metallic hammer of command crushes everything that stands in the way, when no time is left for doubt, when no subordinate is allowed to answer back, and when all obey because one thinks for all. These things, bewildering though they were, were very much to his taste; and so was the warrior mood displayed in a hundred manifestos, and by the people he saw in the streets. Perhaps this frenzy of the German people was the beginning of the great vengeance for the defeat of fourteen years ago; perhaps he was to be granted the privilege of seeing that vengeance! Yes, there was a spirit of renewed youth in his people, and some of it found a way even into his tired heart and aged blood vessels.

Did it not bring a gleam to the giant's elderly eyes when, after a few days, he saw the black-red-white banner fluttering once more—the colors to which his heart had always remained true. Was it not only yesterday that they had waved before him, at parades and maneuvers, and at length over bloodstained battle-fields? But those days in which he had sworn fealty to the black-red-gold banner seemed a hundred years back, a gloomy dream, a melancholy interlude. They had been God's punishment because the nation had lost faith in victory. If only the emperor were to return, things would be as of old, and a man could sleep peacefully.

But side by side with the old flag of war and peace, the field marshal caught glimpses of a new, a third banner. More than glimpses, for there were hundreds and thousands of them. Crude they were in design. In the middle of a square of red bunting was a white circle, and in this circle an enigmatic emblem which

was certainly not an eagle. That was the emblem of
the party. Well, let them hoist it, although it seemed
foreign, intrusive, boastfully troubling the repose of
the old German colors.

Here was a new decree on his table awaiting signature; a decree which gave this strange flag a legal
position beside the others. Was he to approve it?
Had he not just appointed a Cabinet in which the
party leader was only first among equals, surrounded
by others to whom the new flag made no appeal?
If the emblem of this party was to be hoisted over the
government offices beside the old insignia of German
glory, the return of the old banner had been falsified,
and, instead of the old Germany which he had believed
to be restored, there was a new Germany, alien to him!
Must he not exert his prerogative and repudiate it?
Where were his advisers?

Astounded and inert, they were standing at the
windows, listening to the wireless, reading the newspapers, looking at the illustrations, and watching what
went on outside. His old friends and his new ministers
shook their heads when they called on him; even the
skilful Papen had lost his tongue. The Herren Club
was silent; the Junkers were silent; the Steel Helmets
were silent. All of them, as if under a spell, contemplated the grotesque evolution of this party in
which the populace was solemnly and revengefully at
work, at the beck and call of the invisible Leader.
The only one who hardly ever came to see the field
marshal, and then but for a moment, was his new
chancellor, though the man was daily present unseen,
in a concatenation of decrees and manifestos.

Before long his son's and his friends' astonishment

was transformed into alarm. The commander of the Steel Helmets, who was one of the members of the Cabinet, reported the first clashes among the allied private armies. Papen reported the first molestations of the Catholic unions. When, in the end of February, 1933, the Reichstag was burned, the ministers came to Hindenburg, closed the gates of the palace, and reported the evil tidings. A week later, the opinions of all the world were laid before him, speaking with one voice. The field marshal was alarmed to know what sort of people he had put in power in his own country. Had he perhaps acted too hastily on that day of panic? Had the safeguards he had insisted on been consumed in the fires of a will to power which overtopped the pinnacles of the Reichstag? Ought he to have paid more heed to the inner voice which, throughout these years, had warned him against this tribune of the people, and by which he had been confidently guided as late as November? Still, one hope was left. Everything would quiet down after the elections!

Hardly were they over, than a great victory stimulated the leaders of the national socialists to extinguish all other parties and to establish themselves as the State. They now held the instruments of power in their hands, and since henceforward their pecuniary resources were limitless, no others than they could achieve anything among the people. The brightest light shone where the strongest currents were at work.

Once more, however, the field marshal was recalled to memory, for it seemed to have been almost forgotten that he was still, after all, president of the realm. It is possible that he remembered at this juncture, with

mingled alarm and disillusion, the impetus with which
he and Ludendorff had been able to push the emperor
into the background until the two of them had become
the effective rulers of the empire, merely preserving
outward forms of respect towards their supreme
War Lord—as now the Nazis did in the case of the
president?

At a State festival organized one day in early spring
at Potsdam, chosen by the young party in symbolical
repudiation of the spirit of Weimar, the field marshal
was seated on a sort of throne set up in the middle
of the ancient church. He was in uniform, wearing
all his decorations, and holding his field marshal's
baton in his right hand. Having read a few sentences
aloud, he made way for his new chancellor to speak.
When the latter had announced his program, the
strains of the organ rang through the church. Then
the veteran rose and walked alone to the tomb of the
soldier kings, while the assembled deputies watched in
silence from the gallery. How cleverly had the effect
upon the old man's mind been foreseen! Nearly
seventy years before, when he was a young lieutenant
in the guards, he had led his company to the mausoleum
of Frederick the Great before setting forth on his first
campaign. From this cold sarcophagus rose, so it
seemed to him, the ghostly forms of those monarchs
whose legend throughout life had filled him with pride
in his fatherland. Was not he their descendant, who
had, a minute or two before, come down from the
throne in order to utter a prayer among his predecessors? The ring of illusion was complete.

When the ceremony was over and he came out of the
church to be welcomed by the cheers of the multitude,

his chancellor seemed to vanish.   Gigantic, grizzled, helmeted and bestarred, looking like a knight from earlier centuries, he stood there with deep-set eyes, bluish-white complexion, and vacant gaze, hand on sword hilt, a monumental figure from the distant days of chivalry.   On his left, wearing a cutaway coat and a tall hat, stood a man in early middle age, looking like one of the train of those waiting for instructions. That was the impression aroused by the tribune of the people when he was not using the weapon of his oratory.

Two days later the bill was presented.   The Reichstag, which had become practically nothing more than a docile party congress, had surrendered all power to the Cabinet, which, in its turn, was nothing more than the chorus that echoed the words of the soloist.   In three lines, the powers of the German realm were formally assigned to eight ministers of State, and for practical purposes to one.   Hindenburg read: "1: The laws of the realm can . . . also be enacted by the government of the realm.   The laws enacted by the government of the realm are not bound by the limitations of the constitution in so far as they do not concern the institutions of the Reichstag and the Reichsrat.   2: The rights of the president of the realm are unimpaired."   This was termed the Authorization Law.   It was to run for four years, by which time Hindenburg, if he survived so long, would be ninety.   He was to sign a document which would make him a prisoner of the chancellor whose hands he had so carefully endeavored to tie. Where, now, were his advisers, who, in that disastrous day of universal panic barely two months before, had talked of the silken or leathern snares with which the quarry could be bound?   In embarrassment they stood around him, and could do nothing to save him from binding himself in iron chains.

Now he faced up to the realities of the situation. The dream of power was over!

Supreme command, which had been his during a great part of the war, and the absolutist position which he had carried from his army days and maintained for three dictatorial years of peace in this palace, had fallen into the hands of another, or rather had been put into those other hands by his own! Of what use to him was the old flag when this third, queer, and unfamiliar bunting fascinated everyone because a new wind machine kept it continually waving? Who was he—Hindenburg? Why did he continue to live in this moldy old palace when the commandership had been usurped by a man who lived hard by, and who daily sent him a bundle of documents that he might sign his honored name beneath a hundred laws which he and the rest of the world disliked?

As if in answer to these questions, there came with irresistible impetus the abundance of deeds and misdeeds which the new commanding officer ordered. The first against whom the Nazis turned, because these victims were the weakest and therefore the easiest to crush, were the Jews. As recently as the previous August, when some of them came to Hindenburg complaining of the outrages of the Nazis, he had pledged his word to safeguard them, because he "disapproved of any attempt to infringe the constitutionally guaranteed political and religious rights of Jewish members of the German nation." He was familiar with the statistics which showed that of 600,000 German Jews, 100,000 had taken part in the war, and 12,000 had been killed. His intimate friends, the Cramons, Silesian Junkers, had a son and a daughter who had married Hebrews. His own aunt, his father's sister Fräulein von Beneckendorff-Hindenburg, had married the Jewish medical councilor, Dr. Cohen van Baren; and after her premature death, her younger sister had married the brother-in-law. It was in this Jewish house in Posen that Hindenburg's father had made acquaintance with his mother. Neither in war nor in peace had any member of the house of Hindenburg been known to say a word unfriendly to the Jews.

Now he had either to subscribe to that pogrom of the Aryans against the Jews whose echo throughout the world was bringing discredit upon the German name—or if he did not subscribe to it, at least look on supinely. Furthermore, after having for eight years maintained peace among the priests, he must countenance an attack on the Catholics such as had never happened under Bismarck's rule—although Hindenburg himself was partly of Catholic descent. He knew, too, how the world had been outraged by the cruelty of re-awakened Germany, which was penning from eighty to a hundred thousand men in places unfitted to house cattle, because they were out of sympathy with the administration, or because (retrospectively) it had been established, they had been antimilitarists. He was informed, moreover, how his chancellor was sacrificing the Polish Corridor, for which both as military commander and as statesman he had so long battled. He learned that the world, which, during his presidency, had resumed intercourse with Germany, was again refusing the new government goods, orders, and credit. Every week fresh abominations occurred. There he must sit silent, a man full of age and honor, president of the realm, while the mercenaries of his chancellor fought with the Steel Helmets to which he himself belonged; disarmed them, plundered them, and made mock of them.

He sat paralyzed, as the two ideals of his life, God and the king, were hacked to pieces before his very eyes. A year after he had appointed Hitler chancellor, the Leader launched an attack against the kings of the past, had all the schoolbooks revised, poured abuse on the Hohenzollerns, and spoke of the "few pages" on which some worthy deeds of the former kings of Prussia were inscribed. From the mouths of his oldest comrades he learned how, on the emperor's birthday, a number of officers who were celebrating the occasion had been dispersed. It was monstrous! Was that why he had solemnly marched through the church to the tomb of the Hohenzollerns before the assembled populace? That impressive ceremony, the throne and the organ playing, had only been a last mockery at their Authorization Law, which was really a law to deprive him of authority, and had been passed to make a prisoner of the last of the royalists.

What tradition would this wild rabble fail to sweep away with their irreverent hands? Even God no longer pleased them; Jesus was to be done away with, or at least transformed into a Nordic deity. When, in his despondent mood, the old man tried to learn the truth by reading his chancellor's papers, and studying the speeches of accredited professors, he learned that the Old Testament was "a book full of stories about pimps and cattle drivers"; that the crucifix was to be done away with, and a hero-like Christ to be

35

introduced. He read the cries of distress wrung from dismissed and imprisoned clergymen whose only crime had been that they clung to the Old Testament.

What, to conclude, must he think of the means that were being used to tranquilize *him*? The very premier, Langenau, who had taken the estate adjoining Neudeck from Prussian State dominions—an estate which Hindenburg had doubtless looked at longingly both in youth and in old age—in order to present it to him, had demanded, when making this gift, immediate promotion to the rank of general of infantry. The field marshal, whose thoughts ran in terms of seniority, for the first time in his life had to approve the impossible, to allow an ordinary captain to jump five grades at once, and had at the same time to send him a word of commendation!

Once only did the old man venture to revolt against this slavery. When his foreign minister complained that Hitler's ambassadors were acting on their own initiative, the president sent for the chancellor, expounded the situation, and concluded with the surprising threat:

"Don't you believe that I will sign whatever you like! At any moment I can resign!"

With this cunning turn of phrase, which menaced the chancellor, not with dismissal, but with the disappearance of his prop, Hindenburg's peasant ancestors surged up from the past, for it was in these times of faction and folk struggle that the field marshal may really have begun to remember them.

IX

In the summer of 1934, Hindenburg had retired to Neudeck, where it was easier—unseen by the potentate of the capital—to keep himself informed as to the truth through the instrumentality of Papen, the Junkers, and some of the generals; and to discuss with them what rival system might be set up against the present one should a favorable opportunity arise. He had been more or less reconciled with Schleicher. Being rash and garrulous, Schleicher, who associated with conservatives hostile to the government, had let his tongue wag too freely concerning his hopes for the speedy collapse of the present system. Indeed, he talked of these hopes to anyone who would listen, and his hearers repeated his words. Papen, who was in the Cabinet, had also kept up relationships with Neudeck, though more cautiously, and only in so far as no obstacles were interposed.

The field marshal was so greatly attached to Papen that it was to the latter and not to Oscar that, in the spring—probably in May—he confided his will, which subsequently, though an amazingly long time after his death, became known to a smiling posterity. In this document he specified his wish to be buried according to Christian ritual in Neudeck cemetery, without adulatory speeches, in a grave covered by a plain block of stone on which nothing but his name should be inscribed. He had no idea how soon his dead body was to become a public show, and then, in the chancellor's funeral oration, was to be committed to the pagan Valhalla! Despite the infirmities of old age, in the early summer of 1934 this man of eighty-six continued to believe that a turn of events was possible. He discussed with Papen the terms of a speech in which the latter was to repudiate the "totalitarian State," and was to demand the reëstablishment of a constitutional State, so that Germany could again become a member of the society of nations. Hardly had the speech, touched up by Papen's friend Jung, been delivered in Marburg—this was the first counter attack of the defeated Junkers—than it was prohibited. Hitler came to Neudeck and complained to the president, who, it would seem, did not send the chancellor away with a rough answer. This happened on June 23, 1934. So much alarm was aroused among the malcontents that Papen was afraid to visit Neudeck, and Hindenburg no longer received his correspondence, for Meissner, always determined to be in with the dominant power, wanted to stand well with the mighty chancellor, and intercepted letters in whatever way he thought would be best pleasing to Hitler. Hitler, with a typically Austrian locution, said to Papen after this speech: "That was a breach of faith on your part. For the rest, I am ninety-five per cent of your way of thinking."

A week later, Hitler decided to have all his adversaries, past, present, and future, murdered by his henchmen in one night and the early hours of the morning. There was no communist rising to invoke as a pretext this time. The slaughtered were mostly his own followers, who were said to have conspired against him.

No one has ever learned what was Hindenburg's horror when, on July 1, 1934, he heard about the murders. It is possible that they disturbed him very little. What did it matter that the tribune of the people had proscribed Röhm, Hitler's oldest friend and chieftain? Had not the Leader already had Jews and communists butchered? But this time the proscription list included a number of Junkers and generals, few of whom were Nazis. These were names and families with which Hindenburg had been allied for eighty years. Among the victims was a General von Bredow, a Baron von Falkenhausen, a Baron von Wechmar, a von Hohberg, a von Heydebreck, a von Detten, a von Beulwitz, a von Krumhaar, a Baron von Meden, a General von Lossow; and there were many others whose deaths were only disclosed later, so that Hindenburg perhaps never heard of them. One cannot doubt that it was with some agitation that Oscar told his father about the assassination of General von Schleicher. These revelations had on Hindenburg the effect which the news of the revolution had on William II. Like the emperor on November 9, Hindenburg, on July 1, was completely at a loss. Terrible was the collapse of an old, old man, equipped with all the emblems of power, a thorough gentleman and a valiant soldier who had no means of avenging his own friends and the members of his own order. When he asked how it had all happened, his son told him that most of them had been dragged off to the Military Academy in Berlin, and shot there. From the shades of distant youth rose memories of that courtyard in which the field marshal had begun his blameless military career. Now he could see it only as a place of execution of butcheries ordered by a vengeful tyrant, and effected without warning, without judgment, and without sentence.

Hindenburg was informed that the wife of a high

official, who anxiously inquired why her husband was so late in coming home, was given by the porter a number for which she was to ask on the following Friday. When she did so, she was handed a box bearing this number, a box which contained her husband's ashes. The president had to learn how his friend Papen had only been saved at the last moment by the intervention of a private in the Reichswehr, after his chief permanent official had been shot in the anteroom; and in their dwellings the same fate had befallen three more of Papen's collaborators, one of them Jung, the dithyrambic idealist.

He was informed how Schleicher, who so recently had been chancellor of the German realm, had sat among friends the evening before in his villa near Berlin, had clinked glasses with them, and had said: "Who knows what tomorrow will bring forth?" The next afternoon six S.S. men[1] had arrived, had rushed past the old housekeeper, had asked her master what his name was, and shot him at his writing table, and immediately after him his wife, standing aghast at her husband's murder. All this had happened because one of the lords of Germany wished to avenge himself on his opponents; because each of the leaders wished to rid himself of his private adversaries; and because Hitler, in particular, wished to pay off old scores on von Kahr, minister of State, a man of seventy-three, who a decade before had forsaken the Leader during the Munich Putsch. The leaders of the people had slaughtered the nobles, just as in Russia the communists had slaughtered the nobles—the communists,

[1] "Schutzstaffels," Storm Guards, another section of Hitler's "Troops," to be distinguished from the S. A., or Storm Troops.—TRANSLATOR'S NOTE.

to fight whom the Nazis had ostensibly come into power.

Still, there was no time to spare for mourning. Service goes on. Already, in his flunkey attitude, Meissner was standing beside Hindenburg's desk, and laying on it a document for the president to sign. It was a telegram. A wire of congratulation to the chancellor, drafted by the latter. It ran:

"Neudeck, July 2, 1934. From the reports submitted to me I learn that, by your resolute intervention and by the bold way in which you have risked your own person, you have nipped treasonable intrigues in the bud, and have thus saved the German people from a grave peril. For this I express to you my most heartfelt thanks and my most sincere recognition. With warmest greetings. . . ."

There sits the broken giant, a beaten man, who for the last time has to sign his name to a monstrous falsehood. He had carried on the great war in accordance with Prussian rules to the best of his ability and had been defeated. The dictatorship which his wartime assistant had forced upon him had led to the prolongation of the war. The powers of government which he had intensified into a dictatorship had been snatched from him. He had solemnly refused to hand over the chancellorship to one particular party; and yet, in his name, one party and one only now ruled. He had abandoned the old flag, had sworn fealty to the new one, but had revived the old one; and although he would not tolerate the third flag above his own house, it now waved above millions of German homes.

On this spot of earth he had grown up. Here he had been happy. Here service and family life, duty and

idyllic calm had been the foundations of his career—
here, where his forefathers, faithful to God and loyal
to the king, had breathed out their lives. Now the
Germans had betrayed God and the king. Here, under
his consulship—*Te consule*—they had deposed both the
one and the other. Why, on that day of panic, had he
believed his son and his advisers? Why, when he was
still in the fulness of his powers, had he not stood firm
as aforetime? How did his neighbors' agricultural
difficulties concern him, when his honor was at stake
and the welfare of his country? What did he want
with this mansion? It had brought him nothing but
disaster, dread, and mistaken decisions.

Over there, behind that wood, was Tannenberg.
That was where he had fought his great battle and had
won fame. Thenceforward they had made a god of
him—his German fellow countrymen—though he had
never wanted to be idolized. The war and the victory,
trust, negotiations, and peace, they had laid upon his
knees, for him to decide. That was how he had
been led astray. He could not give more than he
possessed. How glad he had been to return home,
expecting to enjoy a tranquil old age in his wife's
company! Had she not died before him, he would
never have allowed himself to be seduced from his
domestic comforts to live in that palace haunted by
evil spirits, amid a maelstrom of figures and interests,
of avarice and jealousies—continually being asked to
decide things beyond the scope of his understanding!

Now he sat alone in the big country mansion. Only
the two cannon in front of the gate reminded him of
his happier days; they and the globe which showed
his battlefields. He could no longer cover these

battlefields with his hand, for they comprised all Germany. But neither globe nor cannon gave him, field marshal and president of the German realm, power to crush this piece of paper in his soldierly grip—this piece of paper in which, behaving like a timid schoolboy, he was to express his heartfelt thanks to the murderer of his friends. Did the emperor have like feelings, years and years ago, when the instrument of abdication was laid before him, and William signed it without a word?

Amazed at the prolonged hesitation, but silent, the secretary continued to stand beside the writing desk, awaiting the signature of the All Highest. In the tremulous handwriting of a very old man, the beaten giant subscribed the world-famous name to the document. Meissner put it into his portfolio, bowed, and departed. The old man was left alone, and groping for a last support. What had all this meant? Service goes on.

Four weeks later he was dead.

WORKS BY THE SAME AUTHOR

•

GIFTS OF LIFE: A RETROSPECT

ON MEDITERRANEAN SHORES

GENIUS AND CHARACTER

TALKS WITH MUSSOLINI

TALKS WITH MASARYK

SCHLIEMANN OF TROY

TOM AND SYLVESTER

HISTORICAL DRAMAS

THE SON OF MAN

MICHELANGELO

WILLIAM II

JULY, 1914

NAPOLEON

BISMARCK

LINCOLN

DIANA

GLOSSARY

Aisne, a small river in the northern part of France, flowing from a point near Verdun westward into the Oise near Compiègne, about 40 miles from Paris.

Aix (Ger. *Aachen*), city (pop. 155,816) in Prussia, near the Belgian boundary and Liége: short for *Aix-la-Chapelle*.

Alsace (Ger. *Elsass*), ancient German province, awarded to France following the Thirty Years' War, in 1648, except the ten largest cities; which, however, were seized by Louis XIV in 1681; ceded to Germany in 1871 as part of Alsace-Lorraine, and again to France in 1918. Principal city, Strassburg.

Amiens, city (pop. 91,576 of France, on Somme River, 75 miles N of Paris, occupied by Germans in September, 1914, but retaken by French.

Article 48. An article of the Weimar constitution, in part as follows:

If public safety and order . . . is materially disturbed or endangered, the National President may take the necessary measures to restore public safety and order, and, if necessary, to intervene by force of arms. To this end he may temporarily suspend, in whole or in part, the fundamental rights established [in the articles which guarantee personal liberty, inviolability of the home and of private communication, as by letter, freedom of speech and the press, private property, and the right to form religious and other associations and to meet in peaceable assembly].

The National President must immediately inform the National Assembly of all measures adopted by authority of [the above provision]. These measures shall be revoked at the demand of the National Assembly.

Ballin, Albert (1857–1918), a German shipowner, director of the Hamburg-America line, who committed suicide during the War.

Bavaria, a political division of the German Reich, the largest except Prussia, before 1918 one of the four kingdoms among the 26 independent States which formed the Reich.

Bazaine, Achille François, French marshal in the Franco-Prussian War, whose army was bottled up in Metz as a result of the battle of Gravelotte (1870), and surrendered to the Germans. He was later accused of incompetence and of treasonous negotiations with the Germans.

Bebel, August (1840–1913), leader of the Social Democratic party in Germany for nearly 50 years, a friend of Liebknecht.

Benedek, Ludwig, Austrian general in the Seven Weeks' War of 1866, compelled against his judgment to fight the Prussians, and defeated by them at Königgratz. He was suspended from his command.

Bernhardi, Friedrich von, German soldier and writer.

Bernstorff, Johann Heinrich von (1862–   ), German diplomat, ambassador at Washington 1908–1917.

Bethmann-Hollweg, Theobald von (1856–1921), German chancellor 1909–17.

Beuthen, a city (pop. 62,643) at the extreme S E limit of Silesia, in Germany.

Bialovich (*Byelovitsa*), a great forest (area 376 sq. m.) near Grodno, E S E of Königsberg, in Poland near the Lithuanian boundary.

Bismarck-Schönhausen, Otto Leopold, Prince von (1815–98), German chancellor 1862–1890: called *Iron Chancellor*.

Black Eagle, Order of the, the most distinguished order of the former kingdom of Prussia, founded 1701, conferring nobility upon the recipient.

Blücher, Gebhard Leberecht von (1742–1819), Prussian field marshal, defeated Napoleon at Leipzig 1813, took Paris 1814, and upon Napoleon's return, assisted Wellington to defeat him decisively at Waterloo 1815.

(535)

Bosch, Karl (1874–), German chemist and industrialist.

Boyen, Hermann von (1771–1848), German field marshal; introduced universal military service in Prussia.

Braun, Otto (1872–), Social Democrat, originally a printer; prime minister of Prussia 1920–32.

Bredt, Viktor (1879–), German politician and economist, member of the Prussian diet and the Reichstag.

Brest-Litovsk, a city (pop. 29,100) and fortress, formerly in Russia, now in Poland, 120 miles E of Warsaw: scene of negotiations between Germany and Russia early in 1918, and of a treaty by which Russia, under compulsion, ceded large territories to Germany, signed March 8, 1918.

Briand, Aristide (1862–1932), French liberal statesman, premier; negotiated Locarno pact 1925; received Nobel peace prize.

Briey, town (pop. 2,894) of France, 15 miles N W of Metz.

Brüning, Dr. Heinrich, German statesman, Catholic; chancellor 1930–32.

Bülow, Bernhard, Prince von (1849–1929), German diplomat, chancellor 1900–09; succeeded by Bethmann-Hollweg.

Cambrai, city (pop. 26,047) of northern France, 25 miles from Belgium.

Cannae, an ancient town in the lower part of Italy, near the Adriatic coast, where Hannibal inflicted a crushing defeat upon the Romans in 216 B. C. In modern times Schlieffen has referred to Hannibal's enveloping tactics, and Hindenburg used them at Tannenberg.

Capelle, Eduard von (1855–), German admiral; instituted the ruthless submarine policy 1917.

Caprivi, Count Georg Leo von (1831–1899), German soldier and statesman; succeeded Bismarck as German chancellor, 1890–1894.

Catherine (1684?–1727), empress of Russia.

Chemin des Dames, a ridge north of the Aisne River in France, a few miles E of Soisson and N W of Rheims.

Clemenceau, Georges Eugène Benjamin (1841–1921), French journalist and statesman: the dominant figure at the peace negotiations.

C. O., commanding officer.

Coblenz, city (pop. 58,322) of Germany, at junction of the Moselle and the Rhine: seat of the G. H. Q. during much of the World War.

Colberg, city (pop. 30,276) of Pomerania, Prussia, on the Baltic Sea.

Comité des Forges, an industrial union, or association of manufacturers, in the munitions industry of France.

Commission of Inquiry, a commission appointed by the Reichstag in November, 1919, to establish certain data with regard to the conduct of the war.

Compiègne, town (pop. 14,460) of northern France, near confluence of Oise and Aisne rivers, 50 miles N N E of Paris: near scene of meeting between Foch and Erzberger in November, 1918, to discuss terms of armistice.

Conrad von Hötzendorf, Franz (1852–1925), Austrian field marshal in command of Austrian forces during the first three years of the World War.

Corfu (ancient *Corcyra*), island in the Mediterranean, close to the west coast of Greece and Albania, where the Kaiser had a villa.

Courland, a coastal district of Latvia, just south of the Gulf of Riga.

Crown Prince, the eldest son of Emperor William of Germany.

Cumberland, Duke of, an English title borne by various Germans, last by Ernst August, whose father, George V, was king of Hanover.

Czernin, Ottokar, Count (1872–), Hungarian statesman, minister of foreign affairs in negotiating the treaty of Brest-Litovsk.

Dehmel, Richard (1863–1920), German author and poet.

Delbrück, Hans (1848–1929), German historian, professor of modern history in the University of Berlin.

Dobrudja, a region of southeastern Rumania (pop. 700,000); annexed in 1918 by Central Powers and restored to Rumania by Treaty of Neuilly, 1919.

Doorn, village in Holland, 12 miles S E of Utrecht.

Drews, Bill (1870–   ), Prussian minister and university professor.

Düppel, village in northern Schleswig, now in Danish territory. There was fighting here in 1848 and 1849, and again in 1864.

Düsseldorf, city (pop. 429,516), in Rhenish Prussia, Germany, 24 miles N W of Cologne: a great commercial and manufacturing center.

Eastern Aid (German *Osthilfe*), financial assistance from public money rendered to the large landowners of East Prussia, since their estates were so barren, or the operation of them so inefficient, that they were not self-supporting: a source of a national scandal which came to a head in 1932.

Eastern estates, large landed estates in East Prussia. Many of them were the feudal gifts of the rulers of Brandenburg-Prussia to their subjects for military services, but could not be used economically for agriculture.

Ebert, Friedrich (1871–1925), German saddler, socialist, first president of the German Republic: died in office, succeeded by Hindenburg.

Eckener, Hugo (1888–   ) ,German aëronautic expert, head of Zeppelin Co.

Elbe, a river of Germany, west of Berlin, flowing N W into the North Sea.

Engels, Friedrich (1820–1895), German socialist, collaborator of Karl Marx.

Erzberger, Matthias (1875–1921), a German political expert, prominent for his participation in the armistice and peace negotiations; chancellor of the Exchequer in the Bauer government which signed the peace; shot by emissaries of one of the Bavarian secret societies.

Falkenhayn, Erich von (1861–1922), Prussian general; Prussian war minister 1913–15, succeeding von Moltke as commander in chief on November 3, 1914, and succeeded by Hindenburg on August 29, 1916.

Flanders, two Belgian provinces: East Flanders and West Flanders, comprising the western part of Belgium, between France and the Channel.

Foch, Ferdinand (1851–1929), a French marshal who checked the German invasion in 1914 at the Marne; was relieved of command after the Somme, but was recalled and made chief of the Allied forces in 1918; negotiated the armistice in November, 1918.

Fourteen Points, the aims of the United States in entering the war, as announced by President Wilson on January 8, 1918, and, with additions made in subsequent addresses, used as the basis of the armistice offer of the Germans, and acknowledged by the Allies as such. The most important of the Fourteen Points, many of which were ignored by the Allies in forming the Treaty of Versailles, provided for the following:

Open covenants between the nations, openly arrived at.

Complete freedom of the seas. [Upon this item of the armistice terms Great Britain reserved the right of putting her own construction.]

The removal, so far as possible, of all economic barriers and the establishment of an equality of trade conditions among all the signing nations.

Adequate guarantees given and taken that national armaments will be reduced to the lowest point consistent with domestic safety.

The evacuation and restoration of all invaded territory, and compensation for damage done to civilian population.

"The righting of the wrong done to France by Prussia in 1871 in the matter of Alsace-Lorraine."

Further, in the address before Congress: "There shall be no annexations, no contributions, no punitive damages. . . . Self-determination is not a mere phrase." In an address delivered in New York: "All international agreements and treaties of every kind must be made known in their entirety to the rest of the world."

François, Hermann von (1856–   ), German general and military writer.

Frederick I (1657–1713), first king of Brandenburg-Prussia 1701–13: succeeded by Frederick William I.

Frederick II (the Great) (1712–1786), king of Brandenburg-Prussia, a military genius who, after the Seven Years' War, made Prussia one of the great powers: succeeded by his nephew, Frederick William II.

Frederick III (1831–1888), king of Brandenburg-Prussia and German emperor March 9–June 15, 1888, son of William I: succeeded by his son William II.

Frederick William I (1688–1740), king of Brandenburg-Prussia, father of Frederick the Great: one of Prussia's greatest administrators.

Frederick William II (1744–1797), king of Brandenburg-Prussia 1786–97, nephew and successor of Frederick II (the Great): succeeded by Frederick William III.

Frederick William III (1770–1840), king of Brandenburg-Prussia 1797–1840, succeeding Frederick William II: succeeded by Frederick William IV.

Frederick William IV (1795–1861), king of Brandenburg-Prussia 1840–1861, who was succeeded by his brother William I, the first German emperor.

Frick, Wilhelm, minister of the interior for the Reich in Hitler's cabinet.

Galata, the mercantile and shipping quarter of Istanbul (Constantinople).

Galiani, Fernando (1728–87), Italian statesman and art critic.

Galicia, a former crownland of Austria, now forming the southern strip of Poland, including Cracow, Przemysl, and Lemberg.

Gallwitz, Max von (1852–   ), German general, fought at the Masurian Lakes and elsewhere on the Eastern and Western Fronts.

Germany, in early times, the German-speaking States of Europe, often including Austria; from 1871 to 1918, applied to the German Empire, a federation composed of the following 26 States:

    The four kingdoms of Prussia (which in 1871 included the twelve provinces of East Prussia, West Prussia, Pomerania, Posen, Brandenburg, Saxony, Silesia, Hannover, Schleswig-Holstein, Westphalia, Hesse-Nassau, and Rhine Province), Bavaria, Würtemberg, and Saxony;

    The six grand duchies of Baden, Hesse, Mecklenburg-Schwerin, Saxony, Mecklenburg-Strelitz, and Oldenburg;

    The five duchies of Brunswick, Saxe-Meiningen, Saxe-Altenburg, Saxe-Coburg-Gotha, and Anhalt;

    The seven principalities of Schwarzburg-Sondershausen, Schwarzburg-Rudolstadt, Waldeck, Reuss of the Older Line, Reuss of the Younger Line, Schaumburg-Lippe, and Lippe;

    The three free cities of Lübeck, Bremen, and Hamburg;

    The imperial province of Alsace-Lorraine.

Gessler, Otto (1875–   ), Bavarian statesman, minister for defense in the Republic; built up the standing army.

G. H. Q., general headquarters: at Berlin in peace time, at Coblenz through much of the World War.

Gleiwitz, city (pop. 81,552) of Upper Silesia, 35 miles from S E corner: railroad junction and industrial and mining center.

Gneisenau, August, Count Neidhardt von (1760–1831), Prussian field marshal, fought for England in the American Revolution 1782–83, and in the wars against Napoleon 1806–1815.

Goltz, Colmar, Baron von der (1838–1916), Prussian general, later field marshal, with extensive military experience, including service in Turkey.

Göring, Hermann, German national socialist, minister of aviation and president of the Reichstag in the Republic under Hitler.

Gorlice, city (pop. 5,111) in Galicia, Poland, 60 miles E S E of Cracow.

Gothein, Georg (1857–   ), German politician and mining engineer.

Grodno (*Gardinas*), city (pop. 61,600) and fortress on the boundary of Poland (formerly in Lithuania), 150 miles S E of Königsberg: railway center.

Groener, Wilhelm (1867–   ), German general and statesman, chief of transportation on the General Staff during the World War.

Haase, Hugo (1863–1919), German lawyer and politician of the Left wing of the Social Democratic party, of Jewish origin: assassinated.

Haber, Fritz (1868–   ), German chemist, inventor of poison gas.

Haig, Douglas, Earl (1861–1928), British field marshal in command of the British expeditionary forces in France during the World War.

Hardenberg, Karl August von (1750–1822), Prussian statesman.
Hartung, Fritz (1883–   ), German professor of history.
Hauptmann, Gerhart (1862–   ), German dramatic poet.
Helfferich, Karl (1872–1924), German statesman.
Helmholtz, Hermann von (1821–94), German scientist.
Herostratus, a Greek who fired the Temple of Diana at Ephesus, 356 B. C.
Herren Club, a club of Junkers and industrialists in Berlin. See page 464, *note.*
Herriot, Edouard (1872–   ), French politician and premier.
Hertling, Georg, Count von (1843–1919), German statesman, succeeding
  Michaelis as chancellor, 1917–18.
Herwegh, Georg (1817–75), German poet of freedom.
Heydebrandt und der Lasa, Ernst von (1850–1924), German politician,
  Junker, defender of Junker privileges in Prussia.
Hindenburg, Bernhard von, brother of the field marshal.
Hindenburg, Gert von, Major, nephew of the field marshal.
Hindenburg, Oscar von, son of the field marshal.
Hintze, Paul von (1864–   ), German politician, succeeding Kühlmann as
  vice chancellor.
Hitler, Adolph (1889–   ), an Austrian, later German, citizen, politician,
  leader of the National Socialist party since 1920; chancellor since 1933.
Hodler, Ferdinand (1853–1918), Swiss allegorical and historical painter.
Hoffman, Max (1869–1927), German general, was present at Tannenberg,
  followed Ludendorff as chief of staff of the Eastern Front, conducted
  negotiations at Brest-Litovsk, but in 1918 condemned Polish annexations.
Hohenzollern, 1, a principality in southern Germany, the earliest feudal possession of the Hohenzollern family, held since the eleventh century: capital,
  Sigmaringen; **2,** a family or dynasty, originally counts, then burggraves,
  electors, kings, and finally (until 1919) emperor-kings, who acquired additional territory in Brandenburg, Prussia, and along the Rhine and elsewhere; of latter decades thought of primarily as sovereigns of Prussia.
Holstein, Friedrich August von (1837–1909), Prussian diplomat, collaborator
  of Bismarck; after his dismissal leader in matters of foreign policy.
Holtzendorff, Henning von (1853–1919), German admiral who urged ruthless
  submarine warfare.
Hötzendorf, see **Conrad von Hötzendorf.**
House, Edward Mandell (1858–   ), American diplomat, personal repre-
  sentative of President Wilson.
Hugenberg, Alfred (1865–   ), Prussian statesman, leader of the Nationalist
  party in the Reichstag, and member of Hitler's first cabinet.
Hutten, Ulrich von (1488–1523), German humanist, vigorous defender of
  Luther and the Reformation, ally of Franz von Lickingen.
Imperial Provinces, Alsace and Lorraine: so called because recovered from
  France in 1870–71 by joint action of the German States which later federated
  into the German Empire.
Iron Chancellor, see Bismarck.
Iron Front, or *Reichsbanner,* a republican organization founded in 1924,
  supporting the Weimar constitution.
Jutland, the peninsula constituting the western part of the kingdom of Den-
  mark. The battle of Jutland was an indecisive naval battle in the North
  Sea May 31, 1916, which, however, left the British fleet in control of the seas.
Kahr, Gustav von (1862–   ), Bavarian statesman and minister.
Kapp, Wolfgang (1868–1922), German politician born in New York. March
  13, 1920, he occupied government buildings in Berlin at head of a Right
  Putsch with Lüttwitz, which was defeated by a general strike on March 17.
  Kapp escaped to Sweden.
Königgratz (*Hradec Králové*), town (pop. 13,115) of Bohemia, Czecho-
  slovakia, 65 miles E of Prague: famous for the battle there (also called battle
  of Sadowa) in the Austro-Prussian War of 1866.

Königsberg, city (pop. 279,926), on the Baltic, capital of East Prussia, 397 miles N E of Berlin: an important naval and military fortress.

Kovno, town (pop. 92,446) of Lithuania, fortified by the Russians, but captured by the Germans in 1918. Now called *Kaunas.*

Kuhl, Hermann von (1856–   ), Prussian general during the World War.

Kühlmann, Richard von (1873–   ), German diplomatist and vice chancellor; appointed German representative to Brest-Litovsk negotiations; also negotiated Peace of Bucharest with Rumania.

Kuropatkin, Alexei Nikolaievich (1848–1921), Russian general; fought in war against Turkey, 1877–78, and in World War.

Landsturm, the forces available as a last line of defense in case the forces already fighting in the army are not sufficient to repel invasion or meet some grave national emergency; all men between seventeen and forty-five not already in service: usually those between forty and forty-five.

Landtag, formerly, in Prussia and other States of the German Empire, the legislative branch of the government.

Landwehr, in the imperial German army, a part of the home reserves. Those who have passed through two or three years of the universal military service and four years of service as army reserves are members of the Landwehr; subject to the first call from twenty-eight to thirty-three years of age, to second call from thirty-three to forty. After that, up to forty-five, they are members of the Landsturm.

Lassalle, Ferdinand (1825–64), German author and socialist, one of the founders of the Social Democratic party in Germany.

Lenin, Nikolai Vladimir Ulyanoff (1870–1924), Russian socialist and founder of the Russian Socialist Soviet Republic.

Lersner, Kurt von (1883–   ), German diplomat, in the German foreign office during the war; chairman of the German delegation at Versailles.

Levée en masse, a levy in mass; a calling out of all reserves up to the extreme age limit.

Lichnowsky, Karl Max, Prince (1860–1928), German diplomatist, ambassador at London in 1914; was accused of incompetence, fled to Switzerland.

Liebknecht, Karl (1871–1919), son of the following, German socialist, member of Reichstag, where he opposed war credits during the war; imprisoned 1916–18; founded Spartacus Union of Left-wing socialists, led insurrection of Spartacists in Berlin 1918, was killed January 15, 1919.

Liebknecht, Wilhelm (1826–1900), German socialist, founder of Socialist party in Germany, edited *Vorwärts.*

Liége, city (pop. 169,566) of Belgium, near German boundary, site of first battle of World War, 1914.

Limburg, a province of Holland, and an adjoining province of Belgium, where the boundary between them joins the Prussian boundary, just west of Düsseldorf and Cologne.

Lithuania, a republic on the Baltic Sea, between East Prussia and Latvia.

L. H. Q., little headquarters.

Litzmann, Karl (1850–   ), Prussian general on the Eastern Front.

Lloyd George, David (1863–   ), British statesman, prime minister during the World War.

Loebe, Paul (1875–   ), German writer and politician, of Social Democratic party, long president of the Reichstag.

Longwy, fortified town (pop. 9,033) of northeastern France, 90 miles N N W of Nancy: noted for iron and steel works.

Ludendorff, Erich (1865–   ), German general; when Hindenburg became commander in chief of the armies in the field, Ludendorff became his chief of staff, being relieved by Groener October 26, 1918. At the close of the war he fled to Sweden, returned in 1919 and took part in the Kapp Putsch and Hitler's beer-hall Putsch. He is rated a military genius.

Lusitania, British passenger steamer, sunk by German torpedo 1917.

Luther, Hans (1879–   ), German statesman, minister of finance to the Republic, chancellor (1925–26), and ambassador to Washington.

Lützow, Ludwig Adolph Wilhelm, Baron von (1782–1834), founded a volunteer corps in 1813, mostly of students, to fight in the Wars of Liberation.

Luxemburg grand duchy in between Germany, Belgium, and France.

Lys, river flowing from northern France, through Armentières, near Lille, into Belgium, meeting the Scheldt at Ghent.

MacDonald, James Ramsay (1866–   ), British labor leader, first labor premier 1924, labor and coalition premier since 1929.

Macedonia, an ancient kingdom of Europe, just north of the Ægean Sea, now the northeastern part of Greece and the southern part of Bulgaria.

MacMahon, Count de (1808–93), marshal and president of France.

Magdeburg, city (pop. 293,959) of Prussia, 80 miles W S W of Berlin.

Marienburg, town in East Prussia (pop. 21,000), about 30 miles S E of Danzig and 50 miles N W of Tannenberg.

Marne, river of northern France, flowing into the Seine just east of Paris.

Marteau, Henri (1874–   ), French violinist and composer.

Marx, Karl Heinrich (1818–83), German socialist, editor, and writer, founder of Socialism: driven out of Paris 1845, collaborated with Engels in Brussels, returned 1848 to Germany, then went to London, where he collaborated with Liebknecht, published the first volume of *Kapital* in 1867, the second in 1885, the third in 1894; died in London.

Marx, Wilhelm (1863–   ), German socialist statesman, active in the Reichstag and in the national assembly at Weimar; chancellor 1924–25, also 1926–28 under Hindenburg; chief rival of Hindenburg in 1925 for president.

Masurian Lakes, in East Prussia, about 75 miles S E of Königsberg.

Max, Prince (*Maximilian Alexander Friedrich Wilhelm*) of Baden (1867–   ), heir to the grand ducal throne of Baden until the revolution of 1919; succeeded Hertling as, chancellor October 3, 1918, when the Kaiser abdicated.

Meissner, Otto (1880–   ), German politician, secretary to both Ebert and Hindenburg.

Menzel, Adolf von (1815–1905), German engraver and painter.

Mertz, General von, ghost writer for Hindenburg's *Aus meinem Leben*.

Metz, city (pop. 69,624) and former fortress of Lorraine, now in France, 40 miles S of Luxemburg, 80 miles N E of Strassburg.

Michaelis, Georg (1857–   ), German statesman, chancellor for a few months in 1917, between Bethmann-Hollweg and Hertling.

Moldenhauer, Paul (1876–   ), German politician, professor of insurance, member of the Prussian diet and the Reichstag; a friend of Schleicher.

Moltke, Helmuth Carl Bernhard, Count von (1800–91), German field marshal, directed wars of 1866 and 1870.

Moltke, Helmuth Johannes Ludwig von (1848–1916), nephew of preceding, Prussian chief of staff just before the war, modified Schlieffen's plan (see *Schlieffen*) by strengthening Alsace and Lorraine, and assuming the offensive against Russia, thus weakening the German attack at the Marne; was succeeded by Falkenhayn September 14, 1914.

Moscow, city (pop. 2,025,947), 400 miles S E of Petrograd, 700 miles N E of Warsaw: now capital of Russian Socialist Federal Soviet Republic.

Müller, Hermann (1876–   ), called Müller-Franken because there are two other prominent Hermann Müllers, German politician of the Social Democratic party, chancellor March–June, 1920, under Ebert and 1928–30 under Hindenburg.

Mussolini, Benito (1883–   ), Italian premier and soldier, founder of the Italian Fascisti.

Napoleon Bonaparte (1769–1821), a Corsican-French soldier and conqueror, emperor of France 1804–14, and March–June, 1815: finally defeated at Waterloo in 1815 by the English under Wellington and the Prussians under Blücher.

Nazi, a contraction of German *National* in the name of the German National Socialist Workers party, founded by Hitler in 1920; now the sole party, coextensive with the State, in Germany.

N. C. O., noncommissioned officer.

Neudeck, the ancestral family estate of the Beneckendorff-Hindenburgs, near the town of Greystadt, in East Prussia, 30 miles S S E of Marienburg, 60 miles S S E of Danzig.

Nikolsburg, a town (pop. 7,699) of Czechoslovakia, near the Austrian boundary, 45 miles N of Vienna, where Bismarck negotiated a truce in the war between Prussia and Austria in 1866.

Noske, Gustav (1868–   ), German politician of the Social Democratic party, first minister of defense under the Republic.

November criminals, in the political cant of the national socialists, those who sued for peace in November, 1918, and thus "betrayed" an army which was unbeaten in the field: used in general of socialists, Jews, liberals, etc.

Oder, 1, a large river of Germany, between the Vistula and the Elbe, east of Berlin, flowing N into the Baltic Sea; **2,** a river in southern Germany, flowing westward into the Rhine at Mainz.

Oldenburg-Januschau, Elard von, Nazi member of the Reichstag, a Junker neighbor of Hindenburg.

Osthilfe, see **Eastern Aid.**

Pan-Germanism, an imperialistic movement in Germany which took shape before the World War, aiming to create a confederation, under German dominance, of all the central European States, including Germany, Austria, Holland, Belgium, Lorraine, Switzerland, the upper part of Italy, part of the Balkan peninsula, and Russian Poland.

Papen, Franz von, German soldier and politician, military attaché to the German embassy at Washington, recalled by request because of alleged misuse of diplomatic privileges; a friend of Hindenburg, succeeding Brüning as chancellor June 1, 1932; succeeded by Schleicher December 2, 1932.

Paris, city (pop. 2,871,429), capital of France, on the Seine, 90 miles from the ocean: captured by the Germans in the Franco-Prussian War of 1870–71.

Payer, Friedrich von, vice chancellor in Prince Max's government, 1918, and a leader in the Democratic party.

Peipus, Lake, a large lake lying between northwest Russia and Estonia, just south of the Gulf of Finland.

Pepin, king of the Franks from 752 to 758.

Piave, a river in Italy, at the head of the Adriatic Sea, where the Italians defeated the Austrians in October, 1918.

Poland, an independent republic, formally constituted on March 21, 1921, out of territories that had for the most part constituted the former kingdom of Poland, but had been included since 1815 in Prussia, Austria, and Russia.

Polish Corridor, northern part of Pomorze province, Poland, between Pomerania and East Prussia, to Danzig and the Baltic.

Posen [*Poznan*], city (pop. 184,756), capital of the province of Posen, in Poland, 150 miles E of Berlin.

Pour le Mérite, an order established by Frederick the Great in 1740, originally a military order, later enlarged to include nonmilitary persons.

Prittwitz und Gaffron, Friedrich Wilhelm von (1884–   ), German diplomatist, ambassador at Washington in 1928.

Putsch, a political insurrection or unsuccessful revolution on a small scale.

Rathenau, Walter (1867–1922), German statesman and industrialist, in cabinet of Chancellor Wirth; on the Peace Treaty conference; assassinated.

Reichsbanner, see **Iron Front.**

Reichswehr, the standing army and navy of the German Republic.

Rennenkampf, Paul (1854–1918), Russian general; suspected of treachery in battle of Tannenberg; dismissed from service; killed by Bolsheviks.

Rheims, city (pop. 97,825), of northeastern France, 98 miles E N E of Paris;

suffered severely during the World War; the cathedral has been restored.

Riga, seaport (pop. 285,000) of Latvia, at the southern extremity of the Gulf of Riga; occupied by German troops, 1917 to 1919.

Röhm, Ernst, a friend of Hitler, accused of conspiracy and killed in the Blood Bath of June 1934.

Roi Soleil, Le, King Louis XIV of France: so called because he adopted the sun as his emblem.

Roon, Albrecht Theodor Emil, Count von (1803–1879), Prussian general, field marshal; succeeded Bismarck as president of the Prussian ministry.

Rumania, a kingdom of southeastern Europe, between Bulgaria and Poland.

Rupprecht (Rupert) (1869–   ), crown prince of Bavaria; commander of Sixth German Army; made field marshal.

Russian revolution, March 11, 1917.

S. A., abbreviation for German **Sturm-Abteilung,** "storm-troop division," the uniformed fighting organization of the Nazis. The S. A. wears brown uniforms. It was suppressed by Brüning, but later reinstated.

Saar basin, the lower corner of the German Rhine province, between the Palatinate, Lorraine, and Luxemburg, a district about 35 miles in diameter noteworthy for the coal mines and iron and glass industries which center in Saarbrücken (pop. 125,141): detached from Germany by the Treaty of Versailles and governed by the League of Nations until 1935, when after a plebiscite it was returned to Germany.

Saint Privat, village (pop. 1,041) in Lorraine, 8 miles W N W of Metz, 6 miles N of Gravelotte. In the famous battle of Gravelotte in the Franco-Prussian War (1870), the action centered about Gravelotte, Saint Privat, and Amanweiler; it resulted in the defeat of the French under Bazaine.

Saint Quentin, city (pop. 49,683) of France, on the Somme River, 80 miles N E of Paris: the center of heavy fighting 1914–16; destroyed 1917.

Saint Stephen's, a cathedral at Vienna, regarded as one of the finest Gothic cathedrals in the world, with a tower 450 feet high.

Samsonoff, Alexander (1859–1914), Russian general, fought in the war with Japan 1904–05; advised that his army was not ready to advance into East Prussia in 1914, and when he was ordered to attack contrary to his better judgment, was defeated at the battle of Tannenberg and committed suicide.

Scheer, Reinhard (1863–1928), German admiral, collaborator with Tirpitz, in command of the German fleet at the battle of Jutland.

Scheidemann, Philipp (1863–   ), German journalist and politician, leader of the majority socialists during the World War, associate of Erzberger in presenting the resolution in the Reichstag in 1917 which demanded "peace without annexation or indemnities," a member of Prince Max's cabinet in October, 1918. He opposed the Treaty of Versailles and resigned when the Weimar assembly voted to accept it.

Schleicher, Kurt von (1882–1934), German soldier and politician; succeeded Papen as chancellor December 2, 1932, and was succeeded by Hitler January 30, 1933; killed during the Blood Bath in June 1934.

Schlieffen, Alfred, Count von (1833–1913), Prussian soldier and strategist, served in 1866 and 1870–71, chief of the General Staff of the army 1891–1907, succeeding Moltke. He faced the problem of the war on two fronts which Germany would presumably have to wage, emphasizing the necessity of not only defeating but destroying the enemy, and hence of throwing the greatest strength into the right wing of the Western Front, leaving Alsace-Lorraine and the entire Eastern Front on a bare defensive basis until the western wing of the Western Front could encircle the French eastern wing, pivoting about Metz, and destroy it by attacking it front and back. His plan was the only one which could give swift victory (and only swiftness could bring victory at all) to the Germans; but it was disastrously diluted by the desire for conquest in the East.

Schlange-Schöningen, Hans (1886–), Prussian soldier and economist.

Schön, Wilhelm, Baron von (1851–), German diplomatist, ambassador at Paris 1910–14.

Schorfheide, a section of open country near Joachimsthal, a town (pop. 2,078) and resort 35 miles N N E of Berlin, where there is a hunting lodge called *Hubertusstock*, built in 1849.

Schücking, Walther (1875–), German jurist, member of the Weimar assembly and of the Reichstag, active in affairs of the World Court.

Schulenburg, Count von der (1865–), German general and politician.

Schwerin, Ludwig, Count von, minister of finance in Hitler's first cabinet.

Schwertfeger, Bernhard (1868–), German historian and professor of military science, disputed Germany's sole war guilt.

Seeckt, Hans von (1866–), German general, organized the standing army, but refused to fire on the insurrectionists of the Kapp Putsch in 1919.

Seldte, Franz (1882–), German soldier and politician, founder of the Stahlhelm, 1918; minister of labor in Hitler's first cabinet, 1933.

Severing, Wilhelm Karl (1875–), German socialist statesman, originally a metal worker, member of the Reichstag, Prussian minister of the interior when Papen took over the Prussian government, July 20, 1932.

Sickingen, Franz von (1481–1523), German knight, a vigorous defender of the Reformation and ally of Ulrich von Hutten.

Sigmaringen, a city (pop. 5,299) and district in the principality of Hohenzollern, on the Danube, in southern Germany.

Simons, Walther (1861–), German jurist and diplomatist, commissioner of the peace delegation at Versailles, 1919, who, however, refused to sign the treaty; director of the policies of German industry 1919–20; president of the supreme court 1929.

Solf, Wilhelm (1862–), German statesman, active in colonial affairs, minister for foreign affairs at the outbreak of the war, secretary of state 1918, ambassador at Tokyo 1921–28.

Somme, department in northeastern France; principal town, Amiens; also, a river, 147 miles long, flowing W from St. Quentin to the English Channel: the site of the Franco-British offensive in 1916: important in relieving the German pressure on Verdun.

Spa, city (pop. 28,000, of which 20,000 are visitors) and health resort in the province of Liége, Belgium, 20 miles S E of the city of Liége, near the German boundary, occupied by the Germans 1914–18. A council of war was held here August 14, 1918, at which the military authorities assured the emperor there was still hope. At another council here, November 8, 1918, it was decided that William II should abdicate, but not the Hohenzollerns; and from here William fled, November 9, to Holland.

Spa conference, held July 5–16, 1920, at which representatives of the German and Allied governments met to discuss the execution of the disarmament clauses and the coal-delivery clauses of the Treaty of Versailles.

Spartacists, a radical group within the Socialist party, formed under the leadership of Karl Liebknecht and Rosa Luxemburg. The name is derived from a set of political writings by Karl Liebknecht called *Spartakusbriefe* (Spartacus letters), in allusion to Spartacus, a Thracian prisoner of war who led a revolt of Roman slaves 73–71 B. C., but was defeated and crucified.

Spree, a river that flows N W through Berlin, uniting at Spandow, 10 miles from Berlin, with the Havel, which flows into the Elbe.

S. S., abbreviation for German *Schutzstaffel,* "guard in military formation," a select body of members of the fighting organization of the Nazis. The S. S. wears black uniforms.

Stahlhelm (German=steel helmet), an organization of German soldiers, somewhat resembling the American Legion, who had seen service at the front; founded 1918 by Franz Seldte.

Steel Helmets, see **Stahlhelm.**

Stein, Hermann von (1854–1927), Prussian general, chief of staff at the outbreak of the war.

Stinnes, Hugo (1870–1924), German industrialist and financier.

Storm Troops, see **S. A.**

Strassburg, a city (pop. 164,136) near the left bank of the Rhine, in Alsace, 50 miles N of Basel: anciently a German city, seized by Louis XIV of France in 1681, recovered, with Alsace and Lorraine, in the Franco-Prussian War of 1870–71, given again to France in 1918.

Stresemann, Gustav (1878–1929), German industrialist and liberal statesman, member of the Reichstag 1907–12 and 1914–18; a leader in forming the Social Democratic party; chancellor under Ebert 1923–24, afterwards foreign minister; active at Locarno 1926, and at discussions of the Young plan 1929; recipient of the Nobel peace prize in 1926.

Stürmer, Boris Vladimirovich (1849–1917), Russian politician of German birth, premier of Russia 1916, then minister for foreign affairs.

Sussex, a French channel steamer, torpedoed by the Germans March 24, 1916. Since an American was drowned, Germany offered indemnity, but was obliged by President Wilson to restrict submarine activity after May 10.

Tannenberg, village in East Prussia (pop. 725), about 80 miles S E of Danzig and 85 miles S W of Königsberg: too small to be marked on ordinary maps. Near this point the Poles and Lithuanians defeated the Germans in 1410, and the Germans, under Hindenburg and Ludendorff, defeated the Russians in August, 1914. The great monument to the battle of Tannenberg is erected at Hohenstein, about 10 miles N of Tannenberg.

Tardieu, André (1876–   ), French statesman and premier.

Thirty Years' War, a terrible and exhausting war (1618–48) fought mostly in Germany, mainly between Catholic and Protestant sympathizers.

Thoiry, village (pop. 1,013) in eastern France, a few miles from Geneva, where Briand and Stresemann met to discuss withdrawal of the French from the Rhine provinces, the Saar plebiscite, etc., on September 17, 1926.

Thomas, Albert (1878–1932), French politician and historian, socialist deputy, minister of munitions, director of the International Labor Office in the League of Nations.

Thyssen (pron. tissen), August (1842–1926), German industrialist, founder of Thyssen u. Co., a great iron and steel business in the Ruhr, and of related businesses which form one of the great centers of power and influence in German heavy industry.

Tirpitz, Alfred von (1849–   ), German admiral, built up the fleet, urged vigorous use of the navy during the war, in opposition to Bethmann-Hollweg, was relieved 1916; founded the Vaterlands–Partei with Kapp in 1917, joined the Nazis and became member of the Reichstag 1924–28.

Trotsky, Leon (real name *Leiba Bronstein:* 1877–   ), Russian politician and author; exiled to Siberia 1928; escaped to London 1902, where he collaborated with Lenin in publishing *Iskra* (Spark); returned to Russia 1905, was exiled again but escaped to Vienna; opposed the war, was exiled from France and Spain to America, returned to Russia after the revolution 1917, became people's commissar in the Soviet government; opposed Lenin; was expelled from Communist party in 1927.

Ukraine, a socialist soviet republic, about the size of Germany or France, just N of the Black Sea: a part of the USFSR.

Valentini, president of Crown Civil Cabinet, a confidential adviser of William II.

Vaterlands-Partei, an organization founded by Kapp and Tirpitz during the World War, for the purpose of strengthening the 'will to victory of the Germans: dissolved after 1918.

Verdun, town (pop. 12,651), in northeastern France on the Moselle (Meuse) River; it was the greatest center of resistance to German advances 1914–18, being nearly encircled by German forces, but never occupied.

Versailles, Treaty of, the treaty of peace between Germany and the Allied Powers signed June 28, 1919, and ratified January 10, 1920.

Verviers, town (pop. 41,663), in the province of Liége, Belgium.

Vilna, town (pop. 128,900) of Poland, capital of the province of Vilna, 180 miles E of Königsberg.

Virchow, Rudolf (1821–1902), German pathologist and politician.

Vistula, a river rising in Czechoslovakia, running through Poland, along the frontier of East Prussia, and emerging in the Free City of Danzig.

Vogel, Hugo (1855–   ), painter and professor of art, adopted by Hindendorff as his personal painter: author of *Als ich Hindenburg malte.*

Wagner, Wilhelm Richard (1813–1883), German dramatic composer, poet, and essayist, born at Leipzig.

Wahehe, one of the tribes of Tanganyika Territory, in East Central Africa.

Waldeck, a principality in the German empire, dependency of Prussia, about 25 miles W of Cassel, area about 433 sq. m., pop. 55,816.

Waldersee, Alfred, Count (1832–1904), Prussian general and field marshal, who, though enjoying the favor of William II, subjected his military theories to searching criticism.

War of Liberation, the war waged by Germany and allied nations in 1813–14 to throw off the yoke of Napoleon I.

Warburg, Max (1867–   ), German banker.

Waterloo, village (pop. 5,033), in Belgium, 12 miles S of Brussels: French forces under Napoleon were defeated June, 1815, by English, Dutch, and Germans under Wellington and Blücher.

Weber, Max (1864–1920), German economist and sociologist.

Weimar, city (pop. 46,003), of the new German republic of Thuringia: scene of the national assembly, 1919, at which the constitution of the German Republic was adopted.

Wels, Otto (1873–   ), German politician, party secretary and later leader of the social democrats.

White Book, a set of state papers issued by a government.

Wildenbruch, Ernst von (1845–1909), German poet and dramatist, with strong nationalist sympathies, but without chauvinism.

Wilson, Thomas Woodrow (1856–1924), president of the United States 1913–1921.

Wirth, Karl Joseph (1879–   ), German statesman, a member of the Reichstag in 1914; in 1920 succeeded Erzberger as Reichsminister of Finance; chancellor from 1921–22.

Wrangel, Friedrich Heinrich Ernst, Count von (1784–1877), Prussian general field marshal.

Young plan, a plan in effect September, 1929, to succeed the Dawes plan, proposed by a committee under the leadership of Owen D. Young, for the payment of German reparations to the Allies. It fixed the total amount of reparations at about eight billions, provided for the payment of annuities for fifty-nine years and for their allocation, and relieved Germany from foreign financial oversight.

Ypres, town (pop. 14,845), in West Flanders, Belgium, 35 miles S of Ostend; from 1914–18 it was the center of a salient of the British armies, and was reduced to ruins; it has been largely rebuilt.

Zabern (French *Saverne*), a town (pop. 6,954) in Alsace, 20 miles N E of Strassburg.

Zurich, city (pop. 217,750), capital of Zurich Canton, Switzerland; it is a meeting place of international trade, and the banking and intellectual center of Switzerland.

INDEX